Fundamentals of Accounting

10e | Course 2

Claudia Bienias Gilbertson, CPA
Retired
North Hennepin Community College
Brooklyn Park, Minnesota

Mark W. Lehman, CPA, CFE
Associate Professor Emeritus
Richard C. Adkerson School of Accountancy
Mississippi State University
Starkville, Mississippi

Debra Harmon Gentene, NBCT
Business Teacher
Mason High School
Mason, Ohio

SOUTH-WESTERN
CENGAGE Learning

Australia • Brazil • Japan • Korea • Mexico • Singapore • Spain • United Kingdom • United States

SOUTH-WESTERN
CENGAGE Learning

**Fundamentals of Accounting, Course 2,
Tenth Edition**

Claudia Bienias Gilbertson, CPA
Mark W. Lehman, CPA, CFE
Debra Harmon Gentene, NBCT

Executive Vice President, Learning Operations and
Development: Sean Wakely

Senior Vice President, LRS/Acquisitions & Solutions
Planning: Jack W. Calhoun

Vice President/Editor-in-Chief: Karen Schmohe

Publisher: Mike Schenk

Editorial Assistant: Tristann Jones

Development Editor: Diane Bowdler

Senior Brand Manager: Robin LeFevre

Senior Market Development Manager: Mark Linton

Content Project Manager: Jana Lewis

Production Manager: Sharon Smith

Consulting Editors: Bill Lee, Bob First

Manager of Technology, Editorial: Matthew McKinney

Senior Website Project Manager: Ed Stubenrauch

Media Editor: Lysa Kosins

Manufacturing Planner: Kevin Kluck

Production Service: LEAP/Cenveo

Rights Acquisition Specialist Image/Text: Deanna Ettinger

Senior Art Directors: Tippy McIntosh/ Michelle Kunkler

Photo Researcher: Darren Wright

Internal Designer: Ke Design

Cover Designer: Ke Design

Cover Image: © Christopher Futcher/iStockphoto.com

For product information and technology assistance, contact us at
Cengage Learning Customer & Sales Support, 1-800-354-9706

For permission to use material from this text or product,
submit all requests online at **www.cengage.com/permissions**
Further permissions questions can be emailed to
permissionrequest@cengage.com

ISBN-13: 978-1-111-58118-3
ISBN-10: 1-111-58118-5

South-Western
5191 Natorp Boulevard
Mason, OH 45040
USA

Microsoft Office Excel is a registered
trademark of Microsoft Corporation.

Intuit and QuickBooks are registered
trademarks of Intuit, Inc.

Sage Peachtree is a registered
trademark of Sage Software, Inc.

Cengage Learning products are represented in Canada by
Nelson Education, Ltd.

For your course and learning solutions, visit **www.cengage.com/school**
Visit our company website at **www.cengage.com**

The Career Clusters icons are being used with permission of
the States' Career Clusters Initiative, 2010,
www.careerclusters.org

**All illustrations, tables, and graphs are © Cengage Learning.

Printed in the United States of America
1 2 3 4 5 6 7 17 16 15 14 13

Fundamentals of
Accounting

10e Course 2

Contents

Part 3

Accounting
for a Merchandising Business Organized as a Corporation—Adjustments and Valuation

Part 4

Additional
Accounting Procedures

Transform Your Accounting Course with Fundamentals of Accounting,
from the leader in accounting education for 100+ years.

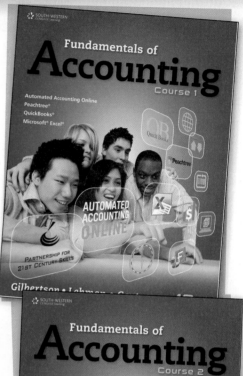

Input from educators, accounting professionals, content experts, and accounting students has shaped the 10th Edition of Fundamentals of Accounting. New critical-thinking activities, real-world applications, and enhanced online learning solutions—including Online Working Papers and Automated Accounting Online computerized accounting software—help you transform your accounting course.

▶ **Proven pedagogy** using a **renowned instructional design** supports teaching the mechanics of accounting and measuring learning outcomes in the 10th Edition.

▶ **Greater emphasis on conceptual understanding and financial statement analysis** encourages students to apply accounting concepts to real-world situations and develop higher-level thinking skills to make informed business decisions.

▶ **Critical thinking and technology use**, as defined by the Partnership for 21st Century Skills, have been expanded throughout with these new features to give students real-world practice and help them master valuable skills:

Forensic Accounting   *Think Like an Accountant*
Financial Literacy   *Why Accounting?*

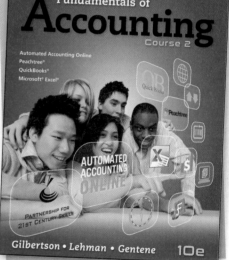

▶ **Commercial technology** is integrated throughout the text to equip students to work with Microsoft Excel®, Peachtree®, QuickBooks®, and Automated Accounting Online. Students are given step-by-step instructions and the flexibility to use a variety of popular commercial software.

▶ **Unparalleled teaching tools and assessment resources**—in addition to exclusive CourseCare instructor training support—help ensure your success.

CourseCare

The Fundamentals of Accounting program provides students with a complete learning system designed to keep students on track and helps you measure outcomes.

The **organization** ensures clear student understanding. Students start with a service business organized as a proprietorship and merchandising businesses organized as corporations before concluding with special topics, partnerships, and the recording of international sales and electronic transactions.

The **step-by-step instructional approach** clearly reinforces text concepts, while the consistent use of T accounts increases student comprehension of journalizing transactions.

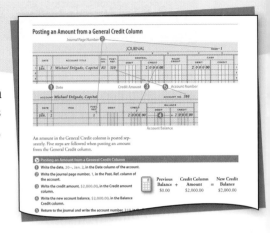

NEW! **Learning Objectives** connect the chapter coverage from beginning to end. Learning objectives are identified at point of introduction and in the end-of-chapter problems, making it easier for students to stay on track. By paying attention to the Learning Objectives, students can focus on what is important and you can better measure outcomes.

> " The tagging of the Learning Objectives is such an easy and effective way for students to look back at a particular objective when they are working problems instead of having to flip through pages randomly until they find what they are looking for. "
>
> Rosemary Hemsell,
> Grapevine High School,
> Grapevine, TX

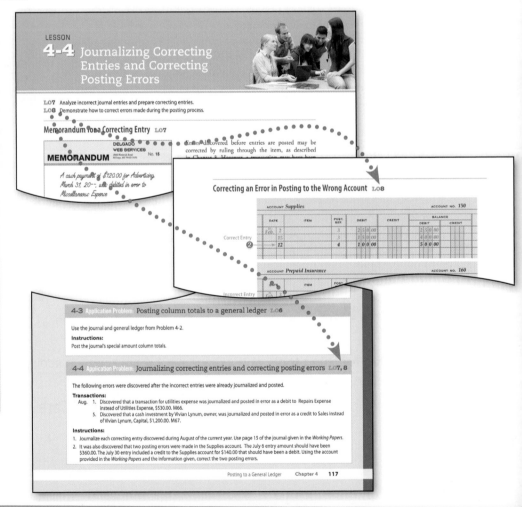

Measurable Outcomes

The **lesson structure** consists of three to five lessons per chapter and corresponding assessment activities. Each end-of-lesson section includes a **Work Together** problem and an **On Your Own** assignment. The Work Together problem allows you to demonstrate the new accounting concept to your class. Students can then check their understanding by completing the On Your Own assignment.

The **end-of-chapter material** includes short application problems to ensure students' understanding before they tackle the longer mastery and challenge problems.

> " *I like how the problems address objectives separately, then together in the Mastery problem, and at another level with the Challenge problem.* "
>
> Rosemary Hemsell,
> Grapevine High School,
> Grapevine, TX

End of Lesson Review

LO4 Describe accounting procedures used in ordering merchandise.

LO5 Discuss the purpose of a special journal.

LO6 Journalize purchases of merchandise on account using a purchases journal.

Terms Review

inventory
merchandise inventory
perpetual inventory
periodic inventory
physical inventory
cost of merchandise
requisition
purchase order
special journal
purchase on account
purchases journal
special amount column
purchase invoice
terms of sale
due date

Audit your understanding

1. What is the difference between a periodic inventory system and a perpetual inventory system?
2. When the perpetual inventory system is used, in what account are purchases recorded? In what account are purchases recorded when the periodic inventory system is used?
3. Identify the four special journals typically used by a business.
4. How are special amount columns used in a journal?
5. Why are there two account titles in the amount column of the purchases journal?
6. What is the advantage of having special amount columns in a journal?
7. What information is contained on a purchase invoice?

Work together 9-2

Journalizing purchases using a purchases journal

The purchases journal for Golden Fabrics is given in the *Working Papers*. Your instructor will guide you through the following examples. Save your work to complete Work Together 9-3.

Using October of the current year, journalize these transactions on page 10 of the purchases journal. Purchase invoices are abbreviated as P.

Transactions:

Oct. 2. Purchased merchandise on account from Pacific Supply, $3,252.00. P162.

7. Purchased merchandise on account from Coastal Company, $532.00. P163.

11. Purchased merchandise on account from Yeatman Designs, $866.00. P164.

On your own 9-2

Journalizing purchases using a purchases journal

The purchases journal for Copperland Company is given in the *Working Papers*. Work this problem independently. Save your work to complete On Your Own 9-3.

Using November of the current year, journalize these transactions on page 11 of the purchases journal. Purchase invoices are abbreviated as P.

Transactions:

Nov. 5. Purchased merchandise on account from McKell Supply, Inc., $2,548.25. P244.

10. Purchased merchandise on account from Tresler Corporation, $1,525.00. P245.

17. Purchased merchandise on account from Lawes Imports, $2,643.50. P246.

©CANDICE CUSACK, ISTOCK

Problem Solving Creativity

Greater emphasis on conceptual understanding and financial statement analysis
has been incorporated into the 10th Edition, making it easier to balance coverage of accounting mechanics with how accounting information is used to make business decisions.

CRITICAL THINKING ACTIVITIES

are infused throughout the text to provide more opportunities for higher-level thinking and analysis, preparing students for college and career readiness.

NEW! 21ST CENTURY SKILLS

included in the end-of-chapter material, provides activities that cultivate mastery of essential skills such as problem solving, communication, and technology use as defined by the Partnership for 21st Century Learning. Acquisition of the knowledge and skills taught in this feature will prepare students to compete in a workplace that demands creativity and innovation.

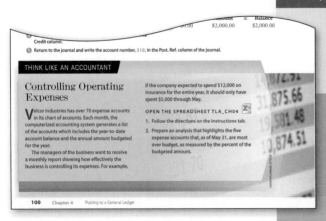

NEW! THINK LIKE AN ACCOUNTANT

presents challenging problems that correspond to higher-level thinking skills based on the criteria established in Bloom's Taxonomy.

Excel templates are provided for students to use as an analysis tool to compare and contrast employer benefit plans and analyze how their decisions affect the company's bottom line.

Communication
Information Literacy

NEW!
FINANCIAL LITERACY

guides students in the exploration of both business finance issues and critical personal finance topics through engaging activities that provide opportunities for students to apply valued skills such as problem solving, critical thinking, and technology use as defined by the Partnership for 21st Century Skills.

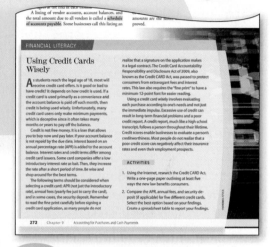

NEW!
GLOBAL AWARENESS

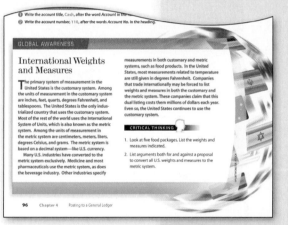

presents the role of accounting in a global environment and the cultural implications that occur as a result of the trans-migratory nature of the marketplace. It reflects current trends, concerns, and issues in global business, and cultural diversity in the workplace. Cultural topics will address both international and domestic issues.

NEW!
ETHICS IN ACTION

responds to the increasing importance of ethics and personal character in accounting today. These ethical dilemmas assist students with decision-making and critical-thinking skills and challenge students' personal character development.

> *"The use of Excel in this feature is an extremely important skill. Many of my high school students who come back to visit while they are in college have said they wish they would have used Excel more in class, because it is something they are doing a lot of in college business courses."*
>
> Kevin Willson, York Suburban School District, York, PA

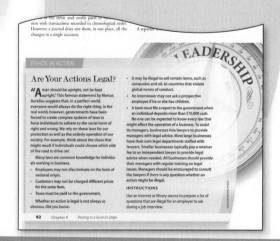

Forensic Accounting presents criminal investigations involving fraud, providing students the opportunity to apply what they're learning in class to a real-world scenario. Students will examine the fraud scenarios using Excel® to analyze the data and continue the investigation.

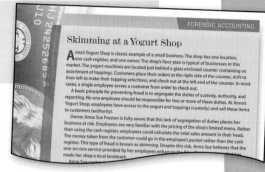

Why Accounting? provides examples of how accounting skills are applicable in a variety of business situations. Tied to the National Career Clusters, this feature illustrates how accounting knowledge transfers into the workplace and validates accounting's importance in the marketplace.

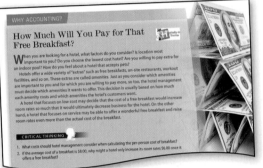

Careers in Accounting, designed to encourage students to think about their future in accounting, features a broad range of careers in the accounting field and promotes accounting as a profession through one-on-one interviews with various accounting professionals.

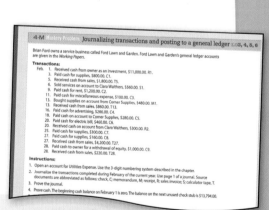

Accounting in the Real World: Fascinating chapter openers spotlight actual businesses that interest students, such as TOMs Shoes, iTunes, McDonald's, and Google, with intriguing questions that connect chapter topics to what's driving business decisions in today's organizations.

Commercial technology, integrated into the end of each chapter, equips students to work with **Microsoft Excel®, Peachtree®, QuickBooks®,** and **Automated Accounting Online** with step-by-step instructions and the flexibility to use multiple versions of software.

Accounting Practices to Life

Bring Accounting Practices to Life with
Relevant Simulations

Manual and automated simulations for each cycle give your students hands-on, real-world experience in accounting practice. Automated simulations are completed using Automated Accounting Online, powered by CengageNOW.

❯ First Year

Simulation 1: Red Carpet Events

Students encounter accounting principles and practical applications as they experience the challenges of operating an event-planning service business organized as a proprietorship. Students complete the simulation after Chapter 8. *Completion time 4-8 hours.*

Simulation 2: Authentic Threads

Students bring fashion trends into the world of accounting while they practice accounting applications in this dynamic merchandising business organized as a corporation. Students complete the simulation after Chapter 17. *Completion time 10-17 hours.*

Simulation 3: Digital Diversions

Students go digital in this engaging simulation with the latest retail software, cell phones, video cameras, music, and more in this merchandising business organized as a corporation. Students complete the simulation after Chapter 22. *Completion time 10-15 hours.*

Online Working Papers

The market's first **Online Working Papers**, *powered by Aplia*, feature automatic grading for instructors and immediate feedback for students. C21 Accounting Online Working Papers mirror the print working papers and tests including online journals, ledgers, worksheets, financial statements, and other forms students use to complete their textbook problems and tests.

▶ Mirror the Print Working Papers
▶ Immediate Feedback for Students
▶ Automatically Graded Assignments for Instructors
▶ Chapter tests included

Students who stay engaged with material put more effort into the course. Century 21 Online Working Papers give **students instant feedback**, making sure they are learning from each question while gaining a better understanding of accounting basics.

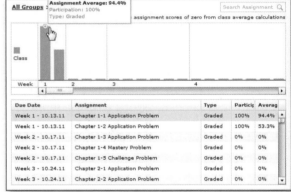

NEW TO ONLINE WORKING PAPERS FOR 10E

▶ Enhanced student feedback will provide students with additional instruction beyond right and wrong answers

▶ Algorithmic problems will provide students with additional opportunities to practice

▶ Device independent, the new online working papers will work on PCs, MACs, iPads, and other devices

The Online Working Papers **automatically grade assignments**, relieving instructors of the burden of grading homework by hand. As students complete the assignments, the instructor receives a complete assessment of their work and comprehension levels, while their grades are instantly recorded in the instructor's online grade book.

The Online Working Papers keep instructors informed about student participation, progress, and performance through real-time graphical reports. Instructors can easily download, save, manipulate, print, and import student grades into their current grading program.

What Users are Saying!

▶ **73%** say that **student performance has improved** in their class since using the Online Working Papers!

▶ **82%** report that their students are **more engaged** in the Accounting course.

▶ **75%** say their ability to **monitor student progress** has improved.

▶ **57%** say that after using Online Working Papers, their students are **more likely to enroll in further study in accounting** and/or other business education courses.

Visit **www.cengage.com/school/accounting** for a demo!

Accounting Digital Solutions

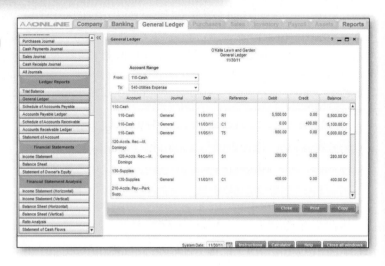

NEW! **Automated Accounting Online** is the next generation of the Automated Accounting software program that has successfully introduced students to computerized accounting for many years. Automated Accounting Online provides the functionality of commercial software incorporated with educational features that make teaching and learning computerized accounting easy. The completely redesigned interface is even more realistic and similar to what users see in commercial software programs such as Peachtree® and QuickBooks®.

Automated Accounting Online:

▶ Is integrated into every chapter of Fundamentals of Accounting

▶ Provides immediate feedback for students

▶ Allows automatic grading for instructors

▶ Is compatible with PCs and MACs

▶ Is available anywhere with Internet connection

For a demo, visit **www.cengage.com/school/accounting**

Student Companion Website extends the learning experience well beyond the book with instructional games, study tools, chapter outlines, math worksheets, and data files.
www.c21accounting.com

Getting ready to start your class?
Need help getting started?

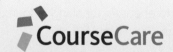

Available exclusively from Cengage Learning, **CourseCare** is a revolutionary program designed to provide you with an unparalleled user experience with your Cengage Learning Digital Solution.

▶ 24/7 on-demand training resources
▶ Regularly scheduled professional training
▶ Dedicated Digital Solutions Coordinator

Please contact the CourseCare team at schoolscoursecare@cengage.com.

To learn more about the live and recorded training sessions available, please visit www.cengage.com/school/coursecare.

Transform Your Teaching Experience
with **tools to make your job easier**

Automatic grading with Online Working Papers and Automated Accounting Online, designed to minimize your time grading, while maximizing your impact within the classroom. Immediate feedback for students and automatic grading for you will save you time and give you an instant sense of each student's comprehension. Grades are automatically entered in an instructor's online gradebook.

Wraparound Instructor's Edition features reduced student pages with comprehensive instructor support, including:

▶ An updated instructional design framework

▶ Common Core call outs

▶ Essential questions

▶ Tips for differentiated instruction

▶ Teaching ideas to increase student engagement

▶ An overview of each accounting part

▶ Resource Integration Guide

▶ Check figures

Written by accounting instructors, for accounting instructors.

Instructor's Resource Kit includes comprehensive teaching resources all in one place, including:

▶ Working Paper and Recycling Problem solutions (textbook problems)

▶ Chapter and Part Tests and solutions

▶ Simulation keys

Instructor's Resource CD places all key instructor resources at your fingertips in this all-in-one convenient tool that includes:

▶ Lesson plans and PowerPoint® presentations

▶ Chapter and Part Tests

▶ Solutions to Working Papers, Tests, Audit tests, Peachtree®, QuickBooks®, Simulations

▶ Crossword puzzles and solutions

▶ Competitive event prep for BPA and FBLA

▶ Correlation to the NBEA standards

▶ Transparency masters (Solutions, Ruling, Full Color Illustrations)

▶ Interactive spreadsheets

▶ Block scheduling correlation with Fundamentals of Accounting

Instructor Companion Site offers password-protected instructor resources including solutions, lesson plans, PowerPoint Presentations, and simulation keys.

Assessment Resources

▶ **ExamView® computerized test bank** allows you to easily create custom tests within minutes. Simply edit, add, delete, or rearrange questions with this easy-to-use software.

▶ **Chapter and Part Test Masters**
Two separate test masters for every chapter and part include problems and objective questions.

▶ **Instructor's Edition Chapter and Part Tests**
Provide solutions for convenient grading.

21st Century Skills

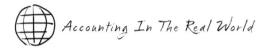 *Accounting In The Real World*

Careers In Accounting

ETHICS IN ACTION

EXPLORE ACCOUNTING

FINANCIAL LITERACY

FORENSIC ACCOUNTING

GLOBAL AWARENESS

THINK LIKE AN ACCOUNTANT

WHY ACCOUNTING?

Reviewers

Cindy Anderson
Business and Computer Teacher
Wyndmere Public School
Wyndmere, North Dakota

Carolyn Holt Balis
Business Educator
Parma City School District
Parma, Ohio

Doris Curry
Business Teacher
Alief Kerr High School
Houston, Texas

Dan Doseck
Business Instructor
Alexander High School
Albany, Ohio

Fahryka P. Elliott
Business Education Teacher
Henrico High School
Henrico, Virginia

Kathryn L. Focht CPA
Educator
Wilson High School
West Lawn, Pennsylvania

Kathleen O'Connor Ford
Business Teacher
Rochester Adams High School
Rochester Hills, Michigan

Mike Hackman
Business and Accounting Teacher
Columbus North High School
Columbus, Indiana

Kathleen Harenza
Business Education Teacher
Mukwonago High chool
Mukwonago, Wisconsin

Rosemary Hemsell
CTE Teacher
Grapevine High School
Grapevine, Texas

Dana R. Hurda
Business and Accounting Instructor
Evansville High School
Evansville, Wisconsin

Joseph Kramer
Business and Information Technology
    Teacher
Seton-La Salle Catholic High School
Pittsburgh, Pennsylvania

Alvin R. Kroon
Teacher
Kamiak High School
Mukilteo, Washington

Cheryl L. Linthicum CPA, PhD
Accounting Professor
University of Texas
San Antonio, Texas

Claire Martin
Business Educator
Sully Buttes High School
Onida, South Dakota

Jane Melroy
Business Teacher
Skyline High School
Pratt, Kansas

James P. O'Connell
Business and Technology Teacher
Bishop Canevin High School
Pittsburgh, Pennsylvania

Rose Pettit
Business Education Teacher
Hopkins High School
Minnetonka, Minnesota

Matthew H. Pohlman
Business Instructor
CAL Community School District
Latimer, Iowa

Sherilyn Reynolds
Business Teacher
Sam Rayburn High School
Pasadena, Texas

Martha Scarberry
Vice Principal
B. Michael Caudill Middle School
Richmond, Kentucky

Lisa Slattery
Accounting Teacher
Spring Woods High School
Houston, Texas

Alice Smith
Business Teacher
Lafayette Central Catholic Jr./Sr. High
    School
Lafayette, Indiana

Jeynelle M. Strickland
Teacher and Chairperson
Savannah Christian Preparatory
    School
Savannah, Georgia

Eileen Wascisin
Business Teacher
Lynden High School
Lynden, Washington

Kevin W. Willson
Business Education Department
    Chairperson
York Suburban School District
York, Pennsylvania

Part

3 Accounting

for a Merchandising Business Organized as a Corporation—Adjustments and Valuation

©OLGALIS, ISTOCK

SUN TREASURES, INC.

Sun Treasures, Inc., the business described in Part 3, is a retail merchandising business organized as a corporation. Sun Treasures purchases and sells a wide variety of souvenirs. It rents free-standing buildings near east Florida beaches.

The corporation was originally organized and owned by Nathan Morgan. Over time, he sold common stock to family members and gave stock to his children. Several years ago, the company sold common stock to the public. The Morgan family still owns over 50% of the outstanding shares. The Morgan family holds five of the seven positions on the corporation's board of directors.

The board has adopted a ten-year plan to expand its business to the Florida west coast. The strategy includes opening new retail stores and a distribution center in central Florida.

Chart of Accounts
SUN TREASURES, INC.

GENERAL LEDGER

Balance Sheet Accounts

(1000) ASSETS
- 1100 Current Assets
- 1110 Cash
- 1120 Petty Cash
- 1130 Accounts Receivable
- 1135 Allowance for Uncollectible Accounts
- 1140 Notes Receivable
- 1145 Interest Receivable
- 1150 Merchandise Inventory
- 1160 Supplies—Office
- 1170 Supplies—Store
- 1180 Prepaid Insurance
- 1200 Plant Assets
- 1210 Office Equipment
- 1215 Accumulated Depreciation—Office Equipment
- 1220 Store Equipment
- 1225 Accumulated Depreciation—Store Equipment

(2000) LIABILITIES
- 2100 Current Liabilities
- 2110 Accounts Payable
- 2120 Sales Tax Payable
- 2130 Notes Payable
- 2140 Interest Payable
- 2145 Line of Credit
- 2147 Unearned Rent Income
- 2150 Employee Income Tax Payable
- 2155 Social Security Tax Payable
- 2160 Medicare Tax Payable
- 2165 Medical Insurance Payable
- 2170 Retirement Benefits Payable
- 2175 Unemployment Tax Payable—State
- 2180 Unemployment Tax Payable—Federal
- 2185 Federal Income Tax Payable
- 2200 Long-term Liabilities
- 2210 Long-term Notes Payable
- 2220 Bonds Payable

(3000) STOCKHOLDERS' EQUITY
- 3110 Capital Stock—Common
- 3120 Paid-in Capital in Excess of Par—Common
- 3130 Capital Stock—Preferred
- 3210 Retained Earnings
- 3220 Dividends
- 3230 Income Summary

Income Statement Accounts

(4000) OPERATING REVENUE
- 4110 Sales
- 4120 Sales Discount
- 4130 Sales Returns and Allowances

(5000) COST OF GOODS SOLD
- 5110 Purchases
- 5120 Purchases Discount
- 5130 Purchases Returns and Allowances

(6000) OPERATING EXPENSES
- 6105 Advertising Expense
- 6110 Cash Short and Over
- 6115 Credit Card Fee Expense
- 6120 Depreciation Expense— Office Equipment
- 6125 Depreciation Expense— Store Equipment
- 6130 Insurance Expense
- 6135 Miscellaneous Expense
- 6140 Payroll Taxes Expense
- 6145 Rent Expense
- 6150 Salary Expense
- 6155 Supplies Expense—Office
- 6160 Supplies Expense—Store
- 6165 Uncollectible Accounts Expense
- 6170 Utilities Expense
- 6200 Income Tax Expense
- 6205 Federal Income Tax Expense

(7000) OTHER REVENUE
- 7105 Gain on Plant Assets
- 7107 Rent Income
- 7110 Interest Income

(8000) OTHER EXPENSES
- 8105 Interest Expense
- 8110 Loss on Plant Assets

The chart of accounts for Sun Treasures, Inc., is illustrated here for ready reference as you study Part 3 of this textbook.

Chapter 18

Acquiring Capital for Growth and Development

LEARNING OBJECTIVES

After studying Chapter 18, in addition to defining key terms, you will be able to:

LO1 Identify available sources of debt financing.

LO2 Journalize transactions related to short-term debt financing.

LO3 Identify the components of a loan application.

LO4 Journalize transactions related to long-term financing.

LO5 Journalize transactions related to equity financing.

LO6 Identify factors influencing financing decisions.

LO7 Analyze the impact of financial leverage.

©DANIEL KOUREY, ISTOCK/©JIM PRUITT, ISTOCK

EDHAR/SHUTTERSTOCK.COM

Accounting In The Real World

DreamWorks Animation SKG

He's crude, loud, and green. Yet the lovable ogre, Shrek, has taken his place among widely recognized animated characters. The creative minds at DreamWorks Animation SKG (DreamWorks) have entertained both young and old with over 20 animated feature films, including *Madagascar*, *Bee Movie*, and *Kung Fu Panda*.

DreamWorks was once a division of Old DreamWorks Studios. The studios were created in 1994 through a partnership of Steven Spielberg, Jeffrey Katzenberg, and David Geffen. In 2004, the animation division was spun off to form a new company, DreamWorks Animation SKG, with Katzenberg serving as its chief executive officer. The new corporation raised additional capital by issuing common stock on the New York Stock Exchange. Its Class A stock trades under the stock symbol DWA and has over 70 million shares outstanding. The stock now trades on the NASDAQ exchange.

A second class of common stock, Class B, is owned entirely by Katzenberg and Geffen. Class B stock has different voting rights than the Class A stock available to independent investors. Each share of Class A stock has a single vote. Each share of Class B stock has 15 votes. Class B stock represents 13% of DreamWorks' total stockholders' equity and 69% of its voting rights. As a result, Katzenberg and Geffen can control all issues brought to a vote by the stockholders.

DreamWorks' capital structure is not uncommon. Individuals who start a business often maintain control of the corporation after stock is sold to the public.

Potential investors should understand the capital structure of a corporation before investing in its common stock.

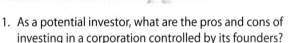

CRITICAL THINKING

1. As a potential investor, what are the pros and cons of investing in a corporation controlled by its founders?

2. Suppose the corporation you created intends to issue stock to the public. Why would you want to maintain control?

Source: DreamWorks Animation SKG, Form 10-K, 2010.

Key Terms

- revenue expenditure
- debt financing
- line of credit
- prime interest rate
- interest expense
- non-operating expenses
- capital expenditures
- collateral
- bond
- bond issue
- stated interest rate
- equity financing
- par value
- issue date
- preferred stock
- cost of capital
- financial leverage

18-1 Short-Term Debt Financing

LO1 Identify available sources of debt financing.
LO2 Journalize transactions related to short-term debt financing.

Short-Term Debt Financing Options **LO1**

Every business needs cash to pay its operating expenses. Purchasing inventory and paying the payroll are examples of daily activities that require a business to earn revenue. The payment of an operating expense necessary to earn revenue is called a **revenue expenditure**. Over an extended period of time, a business must generate enough cash from sales to pay these expenses. However, from time to time, a business may find itself short of cash. When this happens, the business may need to borrow money for a short period of time.

Many business events and decisions make it necessary for a business to borrow money. For example, a garden center has its peak season in the spring. Extra cash may be required to purchase an adequate supply of merchandise to meet customer needs. Additional employees are usually hired to service a larger number of customers, so extra cash may be needed for higher payroll expenses.

A business might experience an emergency. For example, a storm can damage plant assets and destroy merchandise inventory. The business must quickly pay for repairs and restock its merchandise inventory to avoid lost sales.

Obtaining capital by borrowing money for a period of time is called **debt financing**. There are several ways for a business to borrow money from a bank or other financial institution. A bank loan agreement that provides immediate short-term access to cash is called a **line of credit**, or *credit line*. There are different kinds of credit lines. The loan agreement sets the maximum amount that can be borrowed and the repayment terms. It will also set the interest rate and the length of time the agreement will be in effect. The business can draw any amount it needs within the terms of the loan agreement.

The interest rate charged on a line of credit can change based on market interest rates. The interest rate charged to a bank's most creditworthy customers is called the **prime interest rate**. Interest rates are often based on the prime interest rate. For example, a line of credit may have an interest rate of 2% over the prime interest rate. This rate would be stated as *prime plus 2%*.

A business needing to borrow money might elect to sign a promissory note, which it would record as a note payable. The note would state the principal, interest rate, and repayment terms. Unlike a line of credit, a note is signed for a specific number of months and the interest rate is fixed for the term of the note.

ETHICS IN ACTION

The Newspaper Test

A code of conduct should provide employees with a guide for making an ethical decision. The ethical model presented in Chapter 2 provides employees with a structured method of evaluating all the implications of an action. Yet, even with these aids, employees can still find it difficult to make a decision.

Some companies provide their employees with a simple set of questions. One popular question is: "Would I be comfortable if my actions were reported in the newspaper?" If employees are uncomfortable with their actions becoming public knowledge, chances are their actions are unethical. At the very least, employees should know that, if they are in doubt about an ethical question, they should consult their company's ethics officer or legal department.

INSTRUCTIONS

Use the Internet to access the code of conduct for Lockheed Martin Corporation, Yahoo! Inc., and Royal Dutch Shell plc. Prepare a list of questions that could help you determine if an action is ethical.

Drawing on a Line of Credit LO2

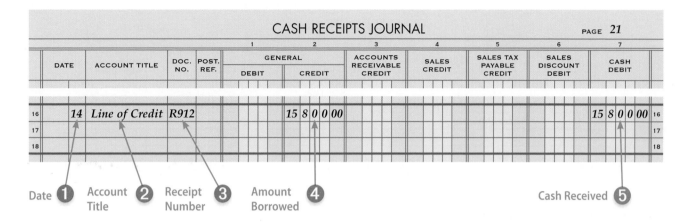

					GENERAL		ACCOUNTS RECEIVABLE CREDIT	SALES CREDIT	SALES TAX PAYABLE CREDIT	SALES DISCOUNT DEBIT	CASH DEBIT	
	DATE	ACCOUNT TITLE	DOC. NO.	POST. REF.	DEBIT	CREDIT						
16	14	Line of Credit	R912			15 8 0 0 00					15 8 0 0 00	16
17												17
18												18

Date ①   Account Title ②   Receipt Number ③   Amount Borrowed ④   Cash Received ⑤

Line of Credit

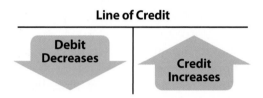

Debit Decreases   Credit Increases

Sun Treasures has arranged a line of credit with First National Bank that provides the company with immediate access to a maximum of $50,000.00. Sun Treasures can transfer money from its line of credit to its checking account using an Internet site or by calling a bank loan officer. Sun Treasures pays an annual interest rate of prime plus 2.5% on its daily outstanding balance. The line of credit requires Sun Treasures to pay monthly interest and at least 10% of its outstanding balance at the end of every month.

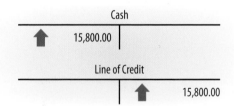

Cash

15,800.00

Line of Credit

15,800.00

Sun Treasures draws on its line of credit to prepare for its peak selling season. The company regularly maintains an inventory of about $150,000.00. However, prior to its peak selling season, the company increases its inventory to over $200,000.00. Sun Treasures plans to repay the borrowed funds as it collects cash from the sale of this extra inventory.

> **November 14.** Drew $15,800.00 on its line of credit. Receipt No. 912.

A receipt is prepared to document the amount of funds drawn on the credit line. [CONCEPT: Objective Evidence]

Journalizing the Receipt of Cash from a Line of Credit

① Write the date, **14**, in the Date column.

② Write the account name, **Line of Credit**, in the Account Title column.

③ Write the cash receipt number, **R912**, in the Doc. No. column.

④ Write the total amount borrowed, **$15,800.00**, in the General Credit column.

⑤ Write the cash deposited, **$15,800.00**, in the Cash Debit column.

Note to Student:

The journals and ledgers illustrated in Parts 1 and 2 of this textbook included detailed steps for recording the date, source document, and other information about the transactions. Because you now know these standard steps, future illustrations will focus on the account titles and amounts of the transactions.

Signing a Promissory Note for an Extension of Time

	DATE	ACCOUNT TITLE	DOC. NO.	POST. REF.	DEBIT	CREDIT	
23	30	Accounts Payable/Hass, Inc.	M142	/	4 2 0 0 00		23
24		Notes Payable				4 2 0 0 00	24
25							25

GENERAL JOURNAL   PAGE 9

① Debit Accounts Payable and Vendor's Account   ② Credit Notes Payable

A business that is unable to pay its account when due might ask the vendor for an extension of time. The vendor may ask the business to sign a promissory note. The note does not pay the amount owed to the vendor. However, the form of the liability is changed from an account payable to a note payable. When this entry is posted, the balance of the Accounts Payable account for Hass, Inc., will be zero. One liability, Accounts Payable, is replaced by another liability, Notes Payable.

GENERAL LEDGER

Accounts Payable

⬇ 4,200.00 |

Notes Payable

| ⬆ 4,200.00

ACCOUNTS PAYABLE LEDGER

Hass, Inc.

⬇ 4,200.00 | Bal.   4,200.00

> **September 30.** Sun Treasures signed a 60-day, 12% note to Hass, Inc., for an extension of time on its account payable, $4,200.00. Memorandum No. 142.

The interest rate on promissory notes signed with a vendor may be rather high. A business should avoid signing a note for an extension of time. Instead, the business should consider borrowing funds against a line of credit or obtaining a loan from its bank.

> **Journalizing Signing a Promissory Note for an Extension of Time**
>
> ① Record a debit, $4,200.00, to Accounts Payable/Hass, Inc., in the general journal.
>
> ② Record a credit, $4,200.00, to Notes Payable.

remember

For transactions to Accounts Payable or Accounts Receivable, draw a diagonal in the Post. Ref. column. The line allows for the posting of the transaction to the general ledger and subsidiary ledger account.

Paying Principal and Interest on a Promissory Note

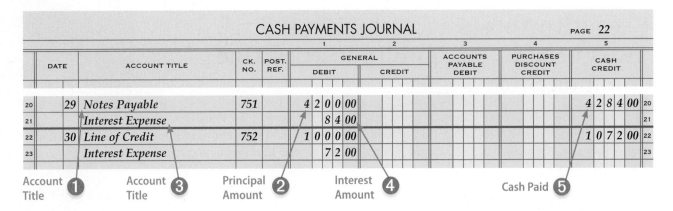

					GENERAL		ACCOUNTS PAYABLE	PURCHASES DISCOUNT	CASH	
	DATE	ACCOUNT TITLE	CK. NO.	POST. REF.	DEBIT	CREDIT	DEBIT	CREDIT	CREDIT	
20	29	Notes Payable	751		4 2 0 0 00				4 2 8 4 00	20
21		Interest Expense			8 4 00					21
22	30	Line of Credit	752		1 0 0 0 00				1 0 7 2 00	22
23		Interest Expense			7 2 00					23

Account Title **1** Account Title **3** Principal Amount **2** Interest Amount **4** Cash Paid **5**

When a promissory note reaches its maturity date, the maker of the note pays the maturity value to the payee. Interest incurred on borrowed funds is called **interest expense**. The interest incurred on a note is debited to an expense account titled Interest Expense.

Interest Expense

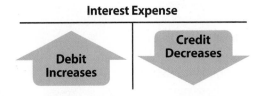

Expenses that are not related to a business's normal operations are called **non-operating expenses**. Interest expense is a financing expense rather than an operating expense. Non-operating expense accounts such as

Interest Expense are listed in a section of the chart of accounts titled Other Expenses.

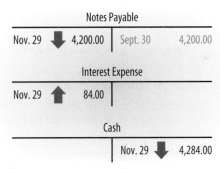

Sun Treasures paid the 60-day note it signed on September 30.

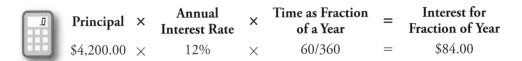

$$\text{Principal} \times \text{Annual Interest Rate} \times \text{Time as Fraction of a Year} = \text{Interest for Fraction of Year}$$

$$\$4{,}200.00 \times 12\% \times 60/360 = \$84.00$$

> **November 29.** Paid cash for the maturity value of the August 30 note: principal, $4,200.00, plus interest, $84.00; total, $4,284.00. Check No. 751.

Sun Treasures also makes monthly interest payments on its line of credit. On November 30, Sun Treasures paid $1,000.00 on its outstanding balance plus $72.00 of interest. This transaction is also recorded in the cash payments journal. The debit reduces the balance of Line of Credit and increases Interest Expense.

> **Journalizing the Payment of Principal and Interest on a Promissory Note**
>
> **1** Write the account name, Notes Payable, in the Account Title column.
>
> **2** Write the note's principal amount, $4,200.00, in the General Debit column.
>
> **3** Write the account title, Interest Expense, in the Account Title column on the next line.
>
> **4** Write the interest expense amount, $84.00, in the General Debit column.
>
> **5** Write the amount of cash paid, $4,284.00, in the Cash Credit column on the first line of the entry.

Executive Abuses at Adelphia and Tyco—Two Corporations, Two Industries, One Common Story

At its peak, Adelphia Communication Corporation was one of the largest cable television providers in the United States. Adelphia was founded in 1952 by John Rigas and headquartered in Pennsylvania. Adelphia's stock was traded on NASDAQ. In 2003, its revenues exceeded $3.6 billion.

Tyco International was a diversified business that specialized in security, fire protection, and flow control equipment. Tyco was founded in 1960 and headquartered in New York. Its stock traded on the New York Stock Exchange (NYSE). In 2007, its revenues exceeded $17 billion.

What could these corporations possibly have in common? Each chief executive officer was charged and convicted of using corporation funds to support a lavish personal lifestyle.

John Rigas and two of his sons were accused of spending $100 million of Adelphia funds on personal assets and expenses. For example, Rigas used $26 million to purchase land surrounding his estate to ensure that his view would not be obstructed. They spent $12.8 million to construct a golf course on land they controlled. They had sole use of several luxurious condominiums and private jets. At the age of 80, John Rigas was sentenced to 15 years in prison.

Dennis Kozlowski became the chief executive officer of Tyco in 1992. In 2002, it was learned that he illegally avoided $1 million of New York sales taxes on the purchase of paintings for his apartment. That accusation prompted an investigation which revealed that Kozlowski had used $600 million of Tyco funds on personal assets and expenses. Some of those purchases included a $30 million Fifth Avenue apartment, a $29 million vacation home, and a $5 million diamond ring. Tyco even paid for half of his wife's $2 million birthday party featuring entertainment by Jimmy Buffett. Kozlowski was sentenced to a minimum of eight years and four months in prison.

In each case, the abuse of corporate funds was the tip of the iceberg. Adelphia used fraudulent accounting entries to hide over $3 billion in loans to the Rigas family. Tyco used questionable methods in accounting for its acquisition of over 1,000 companies. Both Adelphia and Tyco were forced to restate some prior-year financial statements.

There the similarities end. Adelphia declared bankruptcy in 2002 and soon went out of business. Its assets were sold to Time Warner and Comcast. In contrast, Tyco survived its scandal and continues to be a profitable business.

ACTIVITY

PlyCorp Industries has hired you to search for any signs of fraudulent accounting entries. One of your standard tests is to search for entries contrary to the normal balance of income statement accounts.

INSTRUCTIONS

Open the spreadsheet FA_CH18 and complete the steps on the Instructions tab.

Sources: http://en.wikipedia.org; Cecil W. Jackson, *Business Fairy Tales* (Thomson, 2006); Jerry W. Markham and M. E. Sharpe, *A Financial History of Modern U.S. Corporate Scandals* (Armonk, New York and London, England, 2006).

©BURWELL AND BURWELL PHOTOGRAPHY, ISTOCK

End of Lesson Review

LO1 Identify available sources of debt financing.

LO2 Journalize transactions related to short-term debt financing.

Terms Review

revenue expenditure

debt financing

line of credit

prime interest rate

interest expense

non-operating expenses

Audit your understanding

1. What information is specified in the loan agreement for a line of credit?

2. On a line of credit, how would an interest rate of 3% over the prime rate be stated?

3. Is interest expense an operating or a non-operating expense?

4. Where is interest expense listed in a chart of accounts?

Work together 18-1

Journalizing entries for short-term debt

The journals for Klein, Inc., are given in the *Working Papers*. Your instructor will guide you through the following examples.

Using the current year, journalize the following transactions on page 5 of a cash receipts journal, page 8 of a cash payments journal, and page 4 of a general journal. Source documents are abbreviated as: check, C; receipt, R; memorandum, M.

Transactions:

Mar. 3. Drew $6,500.00 on its line of credit. R146.

26. Signed a 90-day, 10% note to MVT Supply for an extension of time on its account payable, $2,400.00. M92.

June 24. Paid cash for the maturity value of the March 26 note: principal, $2,400.00, plus interest. C362.

30. Paid cash for the monthly payment on its line of credit: principal, $1,500.00, plus interest, $64.20. C369.

On your own 18-1

Journalizing entries for short-term debt

The journals for Placid Stores are given in the *Working Papers*. Work this problem independently.

Using the current year, journalize the following transactions on page 7 of a cash receipts journal, page10 of a cash payments journal, and page 5 of a general journal. Source documents are abbreviated as: check, C; receipt, R; memorandum, M.

Transactions:

Apr. 16. Drew $2,250.00 on its line of credit. R206.

May 28. Signed a 60-day, 12% note to Gates Supply for an extension of time on its account payable, $3,660.00. M85.

July 27. Paid cash for the maturity value of the May 28 note: principal, $3,660.00, plus interest. C421.

31. Paid cash for the monthly payment on its line of credit: principal, $800.00, plus interest, $24.10. C426.

LESSON
18-2 Long-Term Debt Financing

LO3 Identify the components of a loan application.
LO4 Journalize transactions related to long-term financing.

Applying for a Business Loan LO3

As a business expands, it must purchase more equipment and other plant assets. The assets or other financial resources available to a business are called capital. Purchases of plant assets used in the operation of a business are called **capital expenditures**. These plant assets will be used for many years to support the operations of the business.

Corporations often require large amounts of capital to finance capital expenditures. A business can obtain this capital from both internal and external sources. The portion of net income not paid as a dividend is an internal source of capital. But internal capital may not be adequate. Thus, a corporation must acquire additional capital from external sources. These might include borrowing money or selling stock.

Banks are a convenient source of external capital. The first step in obtaining a loan is completing the bank's loan application. The application collects basic information about the business and its primary owners. Before approving the loan, the bank must be confident that the business is capable of repaying the funds. The business must convince the bank to approve the loan. Thus, the business should submit a business plan describing how the borrowed funds will be used and how they will be repaid.

THINK LIKE AN ACCOUNTANT

Authorizing a Dividend

At each November meeting, the board of directors of Natchez Finance Corporation reviews the company's financial performance. The information is used to determine the dividend per share for the next four quarters. For the past 24 years, the board has authorized an increase in the quarterly dividend.

Board members are aware that many stockholders are retirees who rely on the income provided by the quarterly dividend. However, the corporation cannot afford to pay out all of its earnings in dividends. The business must retain some of its earnings to finance future growth.

The board considers two financial ratios in making its decision:

Payout Ratio: The board attempts to pay out between 60%–70% of its earnings. The board believes stockholders deserve to receive a dividend of at least 60% of company earnings. However, the board needs to retain at least 30% of company earnings to finance future growth.

Dividend Yield: The board wants the financial markets to view the corporation's stock as

an *income stock* that yields at least a 5.0% dividend.

During 20X4, Natchez Finance Corporation was negatively impacted by a severe economic downturn. To obtain the funds needed to operate, the corporation was forced to issue more stock than usual. Further complicating the situation was a decline in the market price of the common stock. Although the board believes the economy is recovering, it is seeking your recommendation on the amount of the dividend for the next year.

OPEN THE SPREADSHEET TLA_CH18

The worksheet contains the relevant data for 20X1–20X4. Analyze the data to suggest an amount for the new quarterly dividend. Answer the following questions:

1. How often has the corporation achieved the payout ratio target?
2. How often has the corporation achieved the dividend yield target?
3. What dividend per share do you recommend? Support your answer.

©DAN BACHMAN, ISTOCK

With each loan, the bank takes a risk that the borrower will not repay it. Banks only earn money if borrowers repay borrowed funds with interest. Banks will often require a business to pledge certain assets to secure a loan. Assets pledged to a creditor to guarantee repayment of a loan are called **collateral**. If the borrower is unable to repay the loan, the creditor can take the collateral and sell it to pay off the debt.

Sun Treasures has a goal of opening two new stores on the west Florida coast. It estimates it will need $400,000.00 to fund the expansion. Of this amount, $300,000.00 must come from external sources. A summary of the primary sections of Sun Treasures' business plan follows. Each section addresses common questions that will be asked by the bank's loan officers.

Section Title	Questions of Interest to Bank Officers	Summary of Sun Treasures' Business Plan
Use of funds	What portion of the funds will be used for revenue expenditures and capital expenditures?	Sun Treasures expects to use $150,000.00 for equipment at each location. Another $50,000.00 per store will be used to purchase inventory.
Business experience	What experience do the primary owners and managers have in the industry? Do the decision makers understand how to operate the business? Can they anticipate problems and react to ensure success?	Sun Treasures has been in this business for 15 years. The primary owner and chief operating officer have a combined 40 years of experience in the industry. The manager of the west coast stores has been in a management position with Sun Treasures for nine years.
Market demand	Is there a proven consumer demand for the product or service? What competition does the business face?	Sun Treasures contracted Delson Marketing to perform a market survey. The survey indicated that opportunities exist for souvenir stores in Venice and Fort Myers Beach.
Financial projections	When will the project become profitable? What assumptions is the business using to make its projections?	The new locations are expected to lose $50,000.00 over the first 18 months of operation. A loss is common while new stores develop a loyal customer base. This loss will be funded with profits from the existing stores. Based on a conservative 6% per year growth in sales, the new stores will be able to repay the loan in five years.
Collateral	What assets will be offered as collateral that could be claimed if the business is unable to pay the loan? How easy will it be to resell those assets?	All store equipment from the existing and new stores will be offered as collateral. This equipment will be purchased from vendors that also actively repurchase equipment.
Capital profile	What is the business risking in the project? Does the business have an adequate stake in the project to ensure management is motivated to succeed?	Sun Treasures plans to issue common and preferred stock to fund at least 10% of the project.

 Other financial institutions include insurance companies, investment firms, and mutual funds.

Signing a Long-Term Note Payable LO4

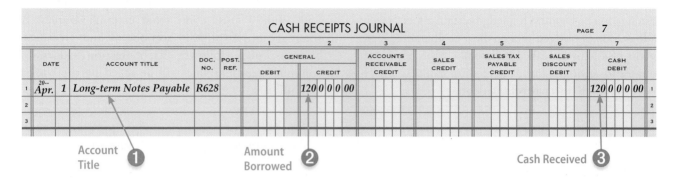

	DATE	ACCOUNT TITLE	DOC. NO.	POST. REF.	GENERAL DEBIT	GENERAL CREDIT	ACCOUNTS RECEIVABLE CREDIT	SALES CREDIT	SALES TAX PAYABLE CREDIT	SALES DISCOUNT DEBIT	CASH DEBIT	
1	20-- Apr. 1	Long-term Notes Payable	R628			120 0 0 0 00					120 0 0 0 00	1
2												2
3												3

CASH RECEIPTS JOURNAL PAGE 7

Account Title ①   Amount Borrowed ②   Cash Received ③

Long-term Notes Payable

Debit Decreases	Credit Increases

A note payable is signed as evidence of the debt when receiving a bank loan. Notes payable signed to fund revenue expenditures usually have terms of 12 months or less. However, long-term notes are common when the borrowed funds are used to purchase plant assets. That's because plant assets are useable as collateral for the notes that are issued to fund them. When a note payable is signed for a period greater than one year, it is usually recorded to an account titled **Long-term Notes Payable**.

In response to Sun Treasures' loan application, the bank agreed to provide only a portion of the funds needed to open the new stores. After Sun Treasures signs the note, the bank deposits the principal amount of the note in Sun Treasures' checking account.

> April 1. Signed a 5-year, 8.0% note for $120,000.00. Receipt No. 628.

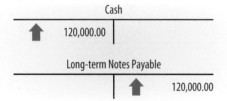

Cash	
▲ 120,000.00	

Long-term Notes Payable	
	▲ 120,000.00

A receipt is prepared as evidence of the deposit of the principal amount in Sun Treasures' bank account. [CONCEPT: Objective Evidence] No entry is made for interest until a later date when interest is paid.

> **Journalizing the Signing of a Long-term Note Payable**
>
> ① Write the account name, Long-term Notes Payable, in the Account Title column.
>
> ② Write the total amount borrowed, $120,000.00, in the General Credit column.
>
> ③ Write the cash received, $120,000.00, in the Cash Debit column.

Making a Monthly Payment on a Long-Term Note Payable

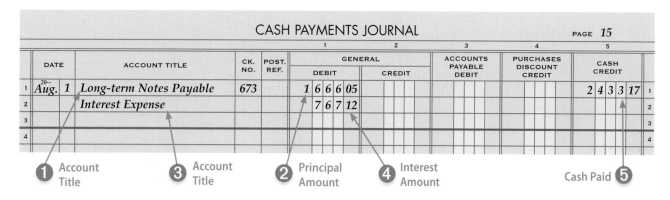

DATE	ACCOUNT TITLE	CK. NO.	POST. REF.	GENERAL DEBIT	GENERAL CREDIT	ACCOUNTS PAYABLE DEBIT	PURCHASES DISCOUNT CREDIT	CASH CREDIT	
1	20-- Aug. 1	Long-term Notes Payable	673	1 6 6 6 05					2 4 3 3 17	1
2		Interest Expense		7 6 7 12						2
3										3
4										4

① Account Title   **③** Account Title   **②** Principal Amount   **④** Interest Amount   Cash Paid **⑤**

Amount Borrowed			$120,000.00		
Term of Note (Months)			60		
Annual Interest Rate			8%		
Monthly Payment			$2,433.17		

Payment Number	Payable 1st day of	Beginning Balance	Interest	Principal	Ending Balance
1	May	$120,000.00	$800.00	$1,633.17	$118,366.83
2	June	$118,366.83	$789.11	$1,644.06	$116,722.77
3	July	$116,722.77	$778.15	$1,655.02	$115,067.75
4	August	$115,067.75	$767.12	$1,666.05	$113,401.70
5	September	$113,401.70	$756.01	$1,677.16	$111,724.54
6	October	$111,724.54	$744.83	$1,688.34	$110,036.20
7	November	$110,036.20	$733.57	$1,699.60	$108,336.60
8	December	$108,336.60	$722.24	$1,710.93	$106,625.67

Sun Treasures' note agreement requires that it make a payment on the first of every month. Upon signing the note, the bank provided Sun Treasures with a schedule of monthly payments.

August 1. Paid cash for monthly loan payment, $1,666.05, interest, $767.12; total, $2,433.17. Check No. 673.

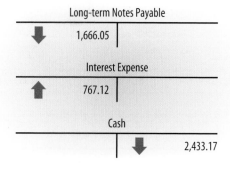

Sun Treasures is required to pay $2,433.17 each month. A portion of the payment is interest on the

outstanding balance of the loan. The remaining amount reduces the outstanding loan principal. The interest and principal portions of the August payment are highlighted in the payment schedule. The monthly payment will enable Sun Treasures to fully repay the loan by the end of the five years (60 months).

Journalizing the Monthly Payment on a Long-term Note Payable

① Write the account name, Long-term Notes Payable, in the Account Title column.

② Write the principal portion of the August payment, $1,666.05, in the General Debit column.

③ Write the account title, Interest Expense, in the Account Title column on the next line.

④ Write the interest portion of the August payment, $767.12, in the General Debit column.

⑤ Write the amount of cash paid, $2,433.17, in the Cash Credit column on the first line of the entry.

Issuing Bonds

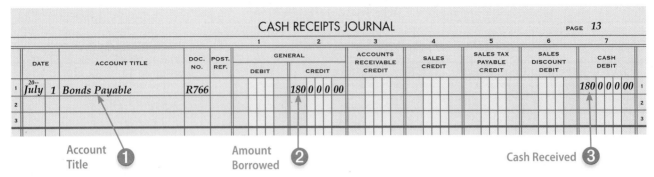

Large loans can be difficult to obtain from a single bank. An alternative to borrowing money from a bank is to borrow money from individual investors. A long-term promise to pay a specified amount on a specified date and to pay interest at stated intervals is called a **bond**. Like notes payable, bonds are written promises to pay. Bonds generally have extended terms such as 5, 10, or 20 years. Also, bonds payable tend to be issued for larger amounts than notes payable.

Bonds Payable

Debit Decreases	Credit Increases

All bonds representing the total amount of a loan are called a **bond issue**. A corporation usually sells an entire bond issue to a securities dealer who sells individual bonds to individual investors. The process of selling bonds is commonly referred to as *issuing bonds*.

Each bond states the face value, interest rate, and due date. The face value is the amount to be repaid at the end of the bond term. The interest rate used to calculate periodic interest payments on a bond is called the **stated interest rate**. The face value is multiplied by the stated interest rate to calculate periodic interest payments to investors. Many bonds pay interest semiannually.

July 1. Issued 20-year, 6.5%, $5,000.00 bonds, $180,000.00. Receipt No. 766.

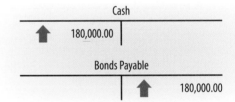

Journalizing the Issuance of Bonds Payable

1. Write the account name, Bonds Payable, in the Account Title column.
2. Write the bonds' total face value, $180,000.00, in the General Credit column.
3. Write the amount of cash received, $180,000.00, in the Cash Debit column.

Paying Interest on Bonds

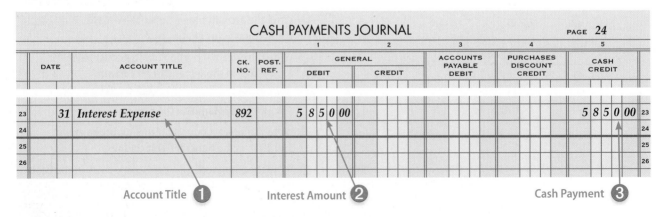

Similar to stock, bonds are securities that can be bought and sold. Sales between investors have no impact on the corporation. However, the corporation does need to maintain current records of who owns each bond in order to make proper interest payments. Corporations issue one check for the amount of interest to be paid, usually to an agent such as a bank. The agent then handles the details of sending interest checks to individual bondholders.

Sun Treasures' bonds require that interest be paid semiannually on June 30 and December 31. Interest on the bond is calculated as the face value multiplied by the stated interest rate.

	Face Value	×	Stated Interest Rate	×	Time as Fraction of a Year	=	Interest Payment
	$180,000.00	×	6.5%	×	180/360	=	$5,850.00

December 31. Paid cash for semiannual interest on bonds, $5,850.00. Check No. 892.

Interest Expense
⬆ 5,850.00

Cash
⬇ 5,850.00

Sun Treasures writes a single check to its agent who then writes individual checks to the bondholders. The investors who own the bonds on the payment date receive the interest payments. Thus, an investor who purchases a bond from another investor on December 29 would receive a check for $162.50 ($5,000.00 × 6.5% × 180/360 = $162.50 per bond).

Journalizing the Payment of Interest on Bonds Payable

1 Write the account name, Interest Expense, in the Account Title column.

2 Write the interest expense amount, $5,850.00, in the General Debit column.

3 Write the amount of cash paid, $5,850.00, in the Cash Credit column.

WHY ACCOUNTING?

Costs Determine Pricing

Have you ever thought that the price you paid for a product was too high? Did you think about all the costs that went into making the product available to you? Manufacturers and retailers must charge enough to cover all their costs plus make a reasonable profit.

You can probably imagine most of the retailer's costs, but consider the manufacturer's costs. Calculating the manufacturing cost is not as easy as it may seem. Take a bicycle for example. Besides the actual materials used in the bike, there are many other costs that must be included such as:

- Machines used, as well as the parts and supplies required to maintain the machines.
- Labor, including factory supervisors.
- Utilities for the factory.

- Labor and supplies to keep the factory clean.
- Employee benefits, vacations, and training.

The price charged for the bike must also include all the administrative costs of the company and produce a profit for the company's stockholders. It is the job of the company's accountants to make sure all of these costs are identified and measured accurately. If any costs are missed, the company will make less profit on each bicycle it sells. If enough costs are missed, the company might actually lose money on every bike it sells. The field of accounting that identifies and measures costs is called cost accounting.

CRITICAL THINKING

Select a product of your choice and make a list of all the costs that went into the making of the product. Be prepared to defend your list in class.

End of Lesson Review

LO3 Identify the components of a loan application.

LO4 Journalize transactions related to long-term financing.

Terms Review

capital expenditures

collateral

bond

bond issue

stated interest rate

Audit your understanding

1. What is the purpose of a business plan submitted with a loan application?

2. What can happen to collateral if a borrower is unable to repay a bank loan?

3. Identify the primary sections of a business plan.

4. Investor A sells a bond to investor B just days before the interest payment is made. Which investor receives the interest payment?

5. What are two common differences between notes payable and bonds?

Work together 18-2

Journalizing entries for long-term debt

The journals and a loan payment schedule for Lambers Stores are given in the *Working Papers*. Your instructor will guide you through the following examples.

Using the current year, journalize the following transactions on page 6 of a cash receipts journal and page12 of a cash payments journal. Refer to the loan payment schedule when journalizing the December 1 transaction. Source documents are abbreviated as: check, C; receipt, R.

Transactions:

June   1. Signed a five-year, 9.0% note, $25,000.00. R337.

July   1. Issued 20-year, 6%, $5,000.00 bonds, $200,000.00. R345.

Dec.   1. Paid cash for the December payment on the June 1 note payable, $518.96. C842.

      31. Paid cash for the semiannual interest on bonds. C861.

On your own 18-2

Journalizing entries for long-term debt

The journals and a loan payment schedule for Belmar Co. are given in the *Working Papers*. Work this problem independently.

Using the current year, journalize the following transactions on page 8 of a cash receipts journal and page 15 of a cash payments journal. Refer to the loan payment schedule when journalizing the November 1 transaction. Source documents are abbreviated as: check, C; receipt, R.

Transactions:

July   1. Issued 20-year, 5.5%, $10,000.00 bonds, $300,000.00. R621.

      1. Signed a four-year, 7.5% note, $32,000.00. R622.

Nov.   1. Paid cash for the November payment on the August 1 note payable, $773.72. C902.

Dec. 31. Paid cash for the semiannual interest on bonds. C928.

LESSON
18-3 Capital Stock

LO5 Journalize transactions related to equity financing.

Issuing Capital Stock LO5

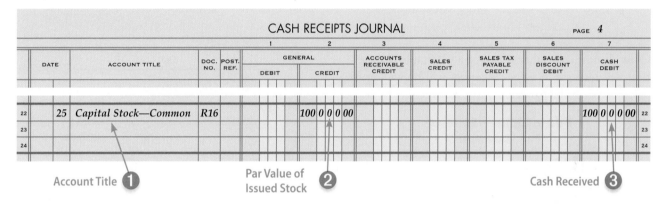

	DATE	ACCOUNT TITLE	DOC. NO.	POST. REF.	GENERAL DEBIT	GENERAL CREDIT	ACCOUNTS RECEIVABLE CREDIT	SALES CREDIT	SALES TAX PAYABLE CREDIT	SALES DISCOUNT DEBIT	CASH DEBIT	
22	25	Capital Stock—Common	R16			100 0 0 0 00					100 0 0 0 00	22
23												23
24												24

CASH RECEIPTS JOURNAL — PAGE 4

Account Title **1**   Par Value of Issued Stock **2**   Cash Received **3**

A corporation may elect to raise capital by selling stock. Obtaining capital by issuing stock in a corporation is called **equity financing**. Selling stock increases the stockholders' equity in the business.

Capital Stock—Common

Debit Decreases

Credit Increases

An advantage of selling stock is that the capital becomes a part of a corporation's permanent capital. Permanent capital does not have to be returned to stockholders as long as the business continues to operate. Another advantage is that dividends do not have to be paid to stockholders unless the earnings are sufficient to warrant such payments. A disadvantage of selling more stock is that the ownership is spread over more shares and more owners.

Shares of stock are often assigned a value. A value assigned to a share of stock is called the **par value**. The par value has nothing to do with the market value of the stock. State laws use the par value to determine the minimum amount of equity that must be retained in the corporation.

Several years ago, Sun Treasures issued stock to raise the capital required to open its first store.

> February 25. Sold 10,000 shares of $10.00 par value common stock at par value, $100,000.00. Receipt No. 16.

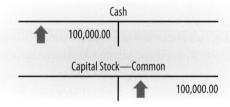

Cash

100,000.00

Capital Stock—Common

100,000.00

The date on which a business issues a note, bond, or stock is called the **issue date**. The issue date is required to determine the proper payments of interest or dividends.

Journalizing the Sale of Common Stock at Par Value

1 Write the account name, Capital Stock—Common, in the Account Title column.

2 Write the stocks' total par value, $100,000.00, in the General Credit column.

3 Write the amount of cash received, $100,000.00, in the Cash Debit column.

Issuing Stock in Excess of Par Value

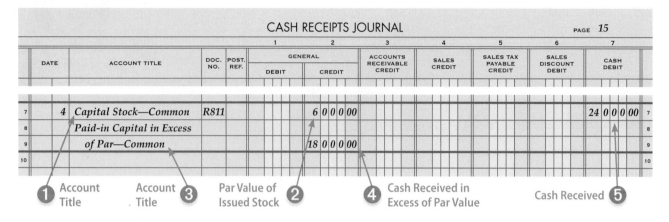

CASH RECEIPTS JOURNAL   PAGE 15

| | | | | | GENERAL | | ACCOUNTS RECEIVABLE CREDIT | SALES CREDIT | SALES TAX PAYABLE CREDIT | SALES DISCOUNT DEBIT | CASH DEBIT | |
| | | | | | 1 | 2 | 3 | 4 | 5 | 6 | 7 | |
	DATE	ACCOUNT TITLE	DOC. NO.	POST. REF.	DEBIT	CREDIT						
7	4	Capital Stock—Common	R811			6 0 0 0 00					24 0 0 0 00	7
8		Paid-in Capital in Excess										8
9		of Par—Common				18 0 0 0 00						9
10												10

① Account Title   **③** Account Title   **②** Par Value of Issued Stock   **④** Cash Received in Excess of Par Value   **⑤** Cash Received

Over time, the common stock of a profitable corporation will increase in value. Investors will be willing to pay more than the par value of the stock.

Paid-in Capital in Excess of Par—Common

Debit Decreases	Credit Increases

The par value of the issued stock is recorded in Capital Stock—Common. Any additional amount received is recorded to Paid-in Capital in Excess of Par—Common. The account is an equity account and appears on the statement of stockholders' equity under common stock.

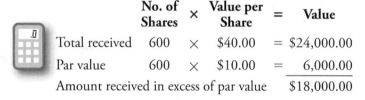

August 4. Sold 600 shares of $10.00 par value common stock at $40.00 per share, ~~$40,000.00~~. Receipt No. 811.

24,000.00

The amount credited to Capital Stock—Common is always the par value multiplied by the number of shares issued. The issue price of the stock does not have any impact on this amount. The balance of Capital Stock—Common is useful to satisfy information required by certain state laws and taxing authorities.

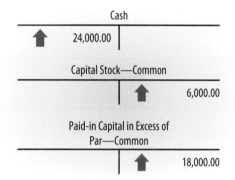

Cash

24,000.00

Capital Stock—Common

6,000.00

Paid-in Capital in Excess of Par—Common

18,000.00

> **Journalizing the Issuance of Stock in Excess of Par Value**
>
> **①** Write the account name, Capital Stock—Common, in the Account Title column.
>
> **②** Write the total par value amount, $6,000.00, in the General Credit column.
>
> **③** Write the account title, Paid-in Capital in Excess of Par—Common, in the Account Title column on the next two lines.
>
> **④** Write the difference between the total par value and the cash received, $18,000.00, in the General Credit column.
>
> **⑤** Write the total cash received, $24,000.00, in the Cash Debit column.

	No. of Shares	×	Value per Share	=	Value
Total received	600	×	$40.00	=	$24,000.00
Par value	600	×	$10.00	=	6,000.00
Amount received in excess of par value					$18,000.00

Issuing Preferred Stock at Par Value

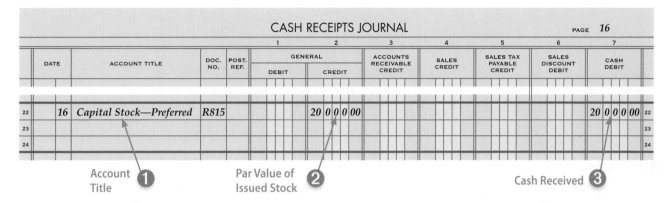

					GENERAL		ACCOUNTS RECEIVABLE CREDIT	SALES CREDIT	SALES TAX PAYABLE CREDIT	SALES DISCOUNT DEBIT	CASH DEBIT	
CASH RECEIPTS JOURNAL PAGE 16					1	2	3	4	5	6	7	
	DATE	ACCOUNT TITLE	DOC. NO.	POST. REF.	DEBIT	CREDIT						
22	16	Capital Stock—Preferred	R815			20 00 0 00					20 00 0 00	22
23												23
24												24

Account Title ❶   Par Value of Issued Stock ❷   Cash Received ❸

Some investors are uncomfortable with the risks of owning common stock, especially if dividends have not been paid consistently. To attract these investors, some corporations offer a different class of stock in addition to their common shares. **Preferred stock** is a class of stock that gives preferred shareholders preference over common shareholders in dividends along with other rights. Preferred stock is typically described by referring to the stock's dividend rate and par value. Sun Treasures plans to issue 6%, $50.00 par value preferred stock.

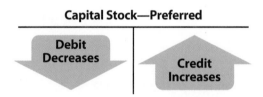

Capital Stock—Preferred

Debit Decreases	Credit Increases

August 16. Issued 400 shares of 6%, $50.00 par value preferred stock at par value, $20,000.00. Receipt No. 815.

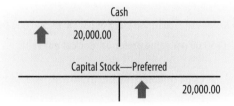

Cash	
20,000.00	

Capital Stock—Preferred	
	20,000.00

Corporations are not required to pay dividends on stock, whether common or preferred. However, when dividends are paid, all the dividends owed the preferred stockholders must be paid first. Preferred stock dividends are determined by the par value and the stated interest rate. Sun Treasures' annual preferred dividend is $3.00 (6% × $50.00) per share. Thus, Sun Treasures is expected to pay annual total dividends of $1,200.00 ($3.00 × 400 shares) to preferred stockholders. Any additional dividends declared are paid to common stockholders.

Preferred stockholders can have other preferences over common stockholders. Unpaid dividends may accumulate from one year to another. These dividends must be paid before common stockholders receive any dividends. If the corporation is dissolved, preferred stockholders receive cash for their stock before any cash is distributed to common stockholders. However, preferred stockholders do not have the same voting rights as common stockholders.

Journalizing the Sale of Preferred Stock at Par Value

❶ Write the account name, Capital Stock—Preferred, in the Account Title column.

❷ Write the total par value amount, $20,000.00, in the General Credit column.

❸ Write the total cash received, $20,000.00, in the Cash Debit column.

End of Lesson Review

LO5 Journalize transactions related to equity financing.

Terms Review

equity financing

par value

issue date

preferred stock

Audit your understanding

1. Is a corporation required to issue dividends? Explain.

2. How is preferred stock typically described?

3. In what order is cash paid to preferred and common stockholders if a corporation is dissolved?

4. What is the most common reason that investors purchase preferred stock?

Work together 18-3

Journalizing the sale of common and preferred stock

A cash receipts journal for Center Fashion is given in the *Working Papers*. Your instructor will guide you through the following examples.

Using the current year, journalize the following transactions on page 6 of a cash receipts journal. Source documents are abbreviated as: receipt, R.

Transactions:

June 1. Sold 6,000 shares of $10.00 par value common stock at par value, $60,000.00. R258.

9. Sold 2,000 shares of $10.00 par value common stock at $10.50 per share, $21,000.00. R267.

22. Issued 500 shares of 5%, $60.00 par value preferred stock at par value, $30,000.00. R289.

30. Issued 500 shares of $10.00 par value common stock at $11.25 per share. R301.

On your own 18-3

Journalizing the sale of common and preferred stock

A cash receipts journal for Main Station is given in the *Working Papers*. Work this problem independently.

Using the current year, journalize the following transactions on page 8 of a cash receipts journal. Source documents are abbreviated as: receipt, R.

Transactions:

Aug. 3. Sold 40,000 shares of $1.00 par value common stock at par value, $40,000.00. R311.

14. Issued 2,000 shares of 6%, $50.00 par value preferred stock at par value, $100,000.00. R325.

21. Sold 8,000 shares of $1.00 par value common stock at $1.40 per share, $11,200.00. R330.

29. Issued 6,000 shares of $1.00 par value common stock at $1.60 per share. R338.

LESSON
18-4 Acquiring Additional Capital

LO6 Identify factors influencing financing decisions.

LO7 Analyze the impact of financial leverage.

Making Financing Decisions LO6

Most businesses need additional capital to finance a major expansion or the purchase of expensive plant assets such as buildings and machinery. How a business elects to obtain funds for expansion or development will impact its earnings. Each method has a different impact on earnings. Borrowing money increases interest expense. Issuing stock may result in dividend payments.

The ratio of interest and dividend payments to the proceeds from debt and capital financing is called the cost of capital. A business should only raise capital if the projected increase in earnings exceeds the cost of capital. A business that elects to raise capital has several options: a line of credit, notes payable, bonds, common stock, and preferred stock. Each option can have positive and negative effects on a business and its owners. The following factors should be considered in deciding how a business should raise capital.

Interest Rate. A business seeks to minimize its interest expense. The interest rate of a loan or bond is dependent on several factors. Short-term interest rates are usually less than long-term interest rates. Interest rates can change from events in the regional or global economy. Creditors demand higher interest rates if they loan money to a business with a less than perfect credit history.

Impact on Earnings. Interest on debt financing is an expense that reduces net income before federal income taxes. But interest payments also reduce federal income taxes. For a company with a marginal tax rate of 25%, a $1,000.00 interest payment reduces its federal income taxes by $250.00. Thus, the net cash outlay is only $750.00. In contrast, dividends are not an expense and do not reduce federal income taxes. The primary benefit of dividends is that the payments are made to the stockholders rather than creditors and bondholders.

Repayment Terms. A business must decide how quickly it wants to repay borrowed funds. Debt financing is often extended for a term similar to the useful life of the assets purchased. Funds used to purchase extra merchandise for a busy season should be repaid quickly. Funds used to purchase plant assets are often repaid over several years. Bonds usually provide the longest repayment terms. In contrast, equity financing is typically never repaid.

Ownership Control. The existing owners of a business maintain full control of a business when expansion is achieved with debt financing. If funding is obtained through equity financing, a proportional share in the control of the business goes with each new share of stock. This spreading of the control over the business is known as *dilution of control.*

Debt Ratio. A business may not have total control over which financing method it selects. Creditors may be unwilling to lend money to a business with a high debt ratio. Such a business is perceived to be a high credit risk. The business may have no choice but to issue additional stock. In contrast, lenders are more willing to lend money to a business with a low debt ratio. Creditors perceive such a business to be a low credit risk.

AQUACOLOR/ISTOCKPHOTO.COM

India—An Expanding Market

A company that wants to expand into a foreign market should consider India. With 1.16 billion people and 240 million households, India is the fourth largest economy in the world. It is also a nation with a young population. The average age of an Indian citizen is 25.3 (compared to 36.7 in the United States). India is known for its competitive education system and large pool of highly skilled workers.

Like any nation, India has unique political and cultural practices. It is very important to be aware of these practices in order to have a successful business relationship. India is a culturally diverse country. Four factors affect the difficulty of doing business there: regionalism, religion, language, and caste. The first three factors are closely related. India is made up of several states. These states (or regions) vary greatly in religious beliefs and language. For example, Hindi is the official language of India, but states within India have their own official languages—21 in all. English is considered an associate language and is used in most business dealings.

Historically, India's social structure involved a caste system—class distinctions based on the occupation and ethnicity of the family into which a person is born. Although this system has been officially dismantled, there are still many signs of it in Indian culture. Organizations have a hierarchy which is strictly followed. A simple task can take hours because a worker at the right level must complete it. This hierarchy determines each individual's role and status. Most decisions are made by the owner of a business rather than someone in a lower-level position.

Relationships are critical in business practices. Business decisions are not based solely on financial facts and figures. A person hoping to do business with an Indian firm must be patient and allow a relationship to develop. In negotiations, being forceful might be misinterpreted as a sign of disrespect.

Many foreign businesspeople find it extremely helpful to follow two strategies when beginning an expansion into India:

1. Work at a local level rather than marketing to the entire country.

2. Form a partnership with an Indian businessperson or company instead of operating individually. A local partner can provide priceless information on local customs and practices.

CRITICAL THINKING

Although a handshake is usually required when meeting someone in India, Namaste is also practiced. Use the Internet to research the word "Namaste" and the gesture that accompanies the greeting. In a written report, explain the meaning of the word and the gesture.

Sources: www.buyusa.gov/india; www.export.gov/india; Doing Business in India, Ernst & Young, India; and www.kwintessential.co.uk.

©FONTMONSTER, ISTOCK

Financial Leverage LO7

Suppose a business wants to purchase $50,000.00 of equipment. The equipment will enable the business to serve more customers and earn more income. The company only has $10,000.00 it can afford to invest in the equipment. Should the company borrow the $40,000.00 needed to complete the purchase? If so, how should the company raise the necessary cash?

The ability of a business to use borrowed funds to increase its earnings is called **financial leverage**. For financial leverage to be a benefit, the borrowed funds must be invested in the business and increase income by more than the interest paid. The following table presents three possible outcomes of borrowing $40,000.00 at 8.0%.

	Outcome			
	8.0%	10.0%	12.0%	6.0%
Operating income	$ 4,000.00	$ 5,000.00	$ 6,000.00	$ 3,000.00
Interest expense	3,200.00	3,200.00	3,200.00	3,200.00
Net income (loss) before federal income tax	$ 800.00	$ 1,800.00	$ 2,800.00	$ (200.00)
Federal income tax (25%)	200.00	450.00	700.00	(50.00)
Net income after federal income tax	$ 600.00	$ 1,350.00	$ 2,100.00	$ (150.00)
Investment	10,000.00	10,000.00	10,000.00	10,000.00
Return on investment	6.0%	13.5%	21.0%	–1.5%

In the first column, the business earns an annual operating income of $4,000.00, a return of 8.0% on its $50,000.00 purchase of equipment. After interest expense and federal income taxes, the business earns an additional $600.00. However, the business only invested $10,000.00 of internal capital. Thus, the business earns 6.0% ($600.00 ÷ $10,000.00) on its investment.

What if the company can earn $5,000.00 in operating income, a return of 10.0% on the $50,000.00 purchased equipment? The second column shows the power of financial leverage. The return on the company's investment jumps to 13.5%. The interest expense is unchanged. Thus, the $1,000.00 of additional operating income belongs to the business. Earning a 12.0% return on the purchased equipment, as shown in the third column, results in the business earning 21.0% on its investment.

It might appear that a business should always borrow money when it needs additional capital. That is not the case. Borrowing money can be risky. The fourth column shows how financial leverage can be harmful. What if an economic decline causes the company to earn only $3,000.00, or 6.0% on the purchased equipment? Interest must be paid regardless of the income earned with the borrowed funds. As a result, the business loses $150.00, a negative return of 1.5% on its investment.

A business can have too much debt. A business having a high level of debt is perceived to be a credit risk. Creditors and investors may be unwilling to loan money or invest in the business. A business having a high level of debt is said to be *highly leveraged* or possibly *over-leveraged*.

©ORANGE LINE MEDIA/FOTOLIA.COM

Selecting Financing Methods

A business needing to raise additional capital has many decisions to make. Does it use debt financing, equity financing, or a combination of both? What form of debt financing should be used? Should equity financing involve common or preferred stock? The best choice will be unique for each business.

A business wants to take advantage of financial leverage. At the same time, a business cannot risk having too much debt. It is very hard to determine the exact amount of capital that should be raised by debt versus equity financing.

Several years after opening its west coast stores, Sun Treasures is ready to expand again. Sun Treasures needs to raise $340,000.00 of capital to finance a third store and a distribution center. The company will need $250,000.00 to purchase equipment and $60,000.00 to purchase inventory. The remaining $30,000.00 will be required to pay expenses prior to opening.

The board of directors used the following schedule to guide its decision-making. Using current balances of the liability and equity accounts, the schedule enabled the board to examine the new balances after financing decisions were made.

	Current	Debt Financing	Equity Financing	New Balances
Financial statement balances				
Line of credit	$ 14,200.00	$ 18,000.00		$ 32,200.00
Notes payable	50,000.00	160,000.00		210,000.00
Bonds payable	100,000.00			100,000.00
Other liabilities	16,800.00			16,800.00
Total liabilities	$181,000.00			$359,000.00
Stockholders' equity	190,000.00		$162,000.00	352,000.00
Total liabilities and stockholders' equity	$371,000.00			$711,000.00
New capital financing		$178,000.00	$162,000.00	$340,000.00
Other information				
Debt ratio	48.8%			50.5%
Shares owned by majority owners	48,000		1,000	49,000
Total shares outstanding	90,000		3,500	93,500
Percent of shares owned by majority owners	53.3%			52.4%

The board decided to take the following actions to finance the expansion of the business:

1. Draw $18,000.00 on its $50,000.00 line of credit. This debt financing source has the lowest interest rate, 6.0%, of the three debt financing options. The new balance of $32,200.00 will preserve the board's target emergency balance of approximately $15,000.00.
2. Sign a $160,000.00, 7.5% note payable on the equipment. The interest rate on this debt is higher than the interest rate of the bonds. Sun Treasures projects that company earnings will enable the loan to be repaid within four to six years. The board elected to pay a slightly higher interest rate for a few years rather than be obligated to pay interest on additional 6.5% bonds for 20 years.
3. Sell 4,500 shares of common stock at the current market price of $36.00 per share. The stock will

generate the remaining $162,000.00 of financing needed to fund the expansion ($178,000.00 + $162,000.00 = $340,000.00).

The debt financing alone would raise the company's debt ratio to 65.4%. This ratio exceeds the board's maximum benchmark of 60.0%. Thus, equity financing is required to raise the additional funds and bring the debt ratio down.

The total number of shares outstanding will increase to 94,500 (90,000 + 4,500). To hold onto a majority of the outstanding shares, the founding family has elected to purchase 1,000 shares. The family will then own 52.4% of the outstanding shares. A family united in its decisions can guarantee its control over the corporation by owning a majority of the common stock.

After the equity financing, the debt ratio of 50.5% will be within the benchmark range of 40.0% and 60.0%.

End of Lesson Review

LO6 Identify factors influencing financing decisions.

LO7 Analyze the impact of financial leverage.

Terms Review

cost of capital

financial leverage

Audit your understanding

1. Identify five options available to a business to raise capital.

2. Identify five factors that a business should consider in deciding how to raise capital.

3. What is necessary for financial leverage to increase earnings?

4. How might individuals describe a business having a high level of debt?

5. What might force a corporation to issue additional stock?

Work together 18-4

Analyzing the impact of financial leverage

A form is given in the *Working Papers*. Your instructor will guide you through the following example.

1. KMT Stores is considering a renovation of its store. The project will cost $100,000.00. The company can issue 7%, $5,000.00 bonds to finance 90% of the project. The remaining capital will come from internal sources. The renovation should enable the business to serve more customers. Complete the form to evaluate the effect of financial leverage on the proposed renovation. Evaluate the earnings potential of the project assuming that operating income will increase by 6%, 7%, or 8% of the project cost.

2. Under what conditions should KMT Stores renovate the store?

On your own 18-4

Analyzing the impact of financial leverage

A form is given in the *Working Papers*. Work this problem independently.

1. Daniel Electric is planning to open a distribution center. The center will cost $500,000.00. The company can finance 96% of the project with 8.2%, $10,000.00 bonds. The remaining capital will come from internal sources. Complete the form to evaluate the effect of financial leverage on the proposed center. Evaluate the earnings potential of the project assuming that operating income will increase by 7.6%, 7.8%, or 8.0% of the center cost.

2. Under what conditions should Daniel Electric open the distribution center?

©CANDICE CUSACK, ISTOCK

A Look at Accounting Software
Accounting for Credit Card Payments in the Banking Module

In this chapter, you learned several different ways that businesses can raise capital for growth and development. But notes payable, credit lines, bond issues, and stock issues don't provide the cash a business needs for its daily operations.

Just like consumers, businesses use credit cards to finance some of their day-to-day expenses.

Unlike the usual expenditures for inventory and supplies, credit card charges tend to be small and occur in large numbers. These are tedious to account for manually, but technology simplifies the process significantly.

Using the Internet, a business can link directly to its bank's accounting system. Credit card charges can be downloaded from the bank directly into the business's accounting system, where each charge can easily be posted to the proper account.

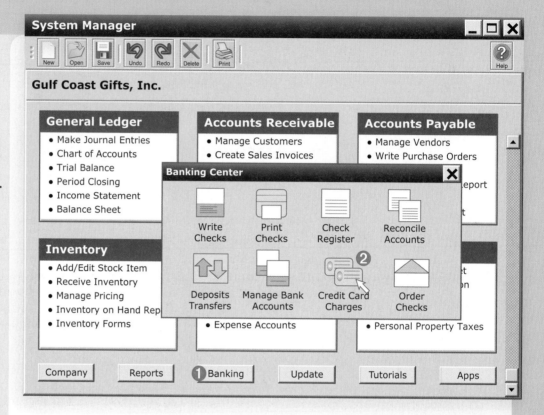

① The user clicks on the Banking button to open the Banking Center navigation pane.

② The user clicks on the Credit Card Charges icon to open the Credit Card Charges window.

③ From the drop-down list, the user selects a credit card account. Many businesses have more than one credit card account.

④ The user clicks on the Download button and the current charges are listed in the frame below. The Internet connection data were entered when the American Express—First American Bank account was set up. The system makes that connection and does the download automatically.

⑤ The current charges are displayed the same as they would appear on a credit card account statement. Gulf Coast Gifts, Inc., has provided three employees with cards on this account. The Card column identifies the employee who made each charge.

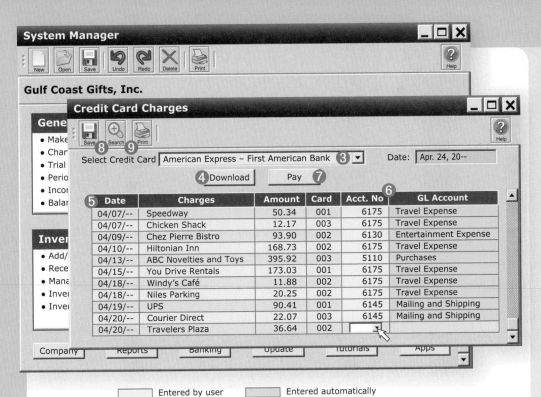

6 The Acct. No. and GL Account columns are empty until the user begins to assign account numbers to the charges. As account numbers are assigned, the system automatically displays the GL account titles.

7 At any time the user chooses, he or she can access the Credit Card Charges window, select a credit card account, and click the Pay button. That opens a new dialog box in which the user will designate the bank account the funds are to be paid from and the amount of the payment. The funds are automatically drawn from the business's checking account and paid on the credit card account. The system automatically credits the Cash account and debits the American Express—First American Bank account.

8 When the user has finished assigning the charges to the proper accounts, he or she clicks Save to post the charges. The next time charges are downloaded, only charges not posted will appear in the window.

9 Clicking on Search opens a search box allowing the user to quickly find and review any individual charge that has been posted. Clicking Print gives the user a choice of reports, including a report of the charges that have been posted.

Chapter Summary

At some point, every business needs to raise capital. A business might need extra cash to prepare for its prime selling season. An unexpected event, such as a storm, may cause a business to need extra cash for repairs. Businesses also need capital to fund expansion plans.

A business can raise capital through internal or external sources. The portion of net income not paid as a dividend is an internal source of capital. This source is rarely adequate to fund major expansion plans. In these cases, a business must raise capital from external sources. External sources include debt and equity financing.

Several types of debt financing are available. A line of credit is a flexible, short-term bank loan. A note payable is a bank loan for a stated amount, period, and interest rate. Notes can be signed for several months or several years. The term of the note determines whether the transaction is recorded to Notes Payable, a current liability, or Long-term Notes Payable, a long-term liability. Bonds are long-term promises to pay that are sold to investors. Bonds are often issued for 5, 10, and 20 years.

A business can raise equity financing by selling common or preferred stock. Common stockholders have voting rights and the right to the earnings of the business. A business can, but is not required to, pay dividends on its common stock. Preferred stockholders expect to earn a stated dividend rate along with other preferred rights. Preferred stockholders, though, do not have voting rights. Shares of both common and preferred stock are often assigned a par value. The par value has nothing to do with the market value of the stock. The amount of a stock sale above the par value is credited to an account titled Paid-in Capital in Excess of Par.

How a business raises needed capital is a complex decision. A business wants to reduce its obligation to pay interest to external sources. Each type of debt financing has different repayment terms. In contrast, equity financing does not have to be repaid. But equity financing may reduce the amount of control held by current stockholders by giving a share of the control to new stockholders.

The financial leverage of using debt financing can be a powerful tool to increase earnings. Whichever way a business elects to fund its operations, it must take care not to become over leveraged.

EXPLORE ACCOUNTING

Corporate Reporting with EDGAR

Public mistrust stemming from the 1929 stock market crash threatened the ability of corporations to obtain equity financing. In response, Congress created the Securities and Exchange Commission (SEC) in 1933 to restore public confidence in the financial markets. Corporations offering stock and bonds for sale to the public must register these securities with the SEC. Each quarter, corporations must submit financial reports containing their financial statements. The most common SEC reports include the Form 10-Q quarterly report and the Form 10-K annual report. Corporations also commonly file a Form 8-K to report significant events, such as a change in auditor, corporate mergers, and changes in the board of directors. Corporations have only four days after such an event to file Form 8-K.

The SEC has the authority to establish the accounting principles that must be used in preparing financial reports. However, the SEC has permitted the accounting profession to develop generally accepted accounting principles (GAAP). The SEC does require additional information not normally found in financial statements prepared in accordance with GAAP. For example, a corporation must describe its business and list the members of its board of directors.

Investors can obtain access to the SEC reports from many sources. Most corporations post these reports on their websites. Key search words such as *investor relations* or *corporate governance* are useful in searching for the reports. The SEC also posts reports to its Electronic Data Gathering, Analysis, and Retrieval (EDGAR) system at http://www.sec.gov/edgar.shtml. An investor can enter a company name or stock symbol to access the reports.

INSTRUCTIONS

Use EDGAR or a corporate website to access the latest Form 10-K for a corporation of your choice. Prepare a list of the topics discussed in the Item 2—Properties section of the report.

Source: www.sec.gov.

Apply Your Understanding

INSTRUCTIONS: Download problem instructions for Excel, QuickBooks, and Peachtree from the textbook companion website at www.C21accounting.com.

18-1 Application Problem: Journalizing entries for short-term debt LO2

The journals for Gift Shack are given in the *Working Papers*.

Instructions:

Using the current year, journalize the following transactions on page 9 of a cash receipts journal, page 14 of a cash payments journal, and page 8 of a general journal. Source documents are abbreviated as: check, C; receipt, R; memorandum, M.

Transactions:

Aug. 29. Signed a 90-day, 15% note to Mann Co. for an extension of time on its account payable, $2,950.00. M153.

Sept. 24. Drew $12,900.00 on its line of credit. R337.

Nov. 27. Paid cash for the maturity value of the August 29 note: principal, $2,950.00, plus interest. C669.

30. Paid cash for the monthly payment on its line of credit: principal, $2,400.00, plus interest, $108.90. C674.

18-2 Application Problem: Journalizing entries for long-term debt LO4

AAONLiNE

1. Go to www.cengage.com/login
2. Click on **AA Online** to access.
3. Go to the online assignment and follow the instructions.

The journals and a loan payment schedule for PAL Industries are given in the *Working Papers*.

Instructions:

Using the current year, journalize the following transactions on page 7 of a cash receipts journal and page 14 of a cash payments journal. Refer to the loan payment schedule when journalizing the December 1 transaction. Source documents are abbreviated as: check, C; receipt, R.

Transactions:

Apr. 1. Signed a six-year, 7% note, $16,000.00. R552.

July 1. Issued 20-year, 5%, $5,000.00 bonds, $250,000.00. R606.

Dec. 1. Paid cash for the December payment on the April 1 note payable, $272.78. C968.

31. Paid cash for the semiannual interest on bonds. C997.

18-3 Application Problem: Journalizing the sale of common and preferred stock LO5

 Peachtree

1. Journalize and post transactions related to the sale of common and preferred stock to the general journal.
2. Print the general journal and the trial balance.

QB Quick Books

1. Journalize and post transactions related to the sale of common and preferred stock to the journal.
2. Print the journal and the trial balance.

A cash receipts journal for Southern Supply is given in the *Working Papers*.

Instructions:

Using the current year, journalize the following transactions on page 9 of a cash receipts journal. Source documents are abbreviated as: receipt, R.

Transactions:

Sept. 2. Sold 350 shares of 7.5%, $100.00 par value preferred stock at par value. R525.

8. Issued 20,000 shares of $1.00 par value common stock at par value. R531.

10. Issued 4,000 shares of $1.00 par value common stock at $1.30 per share. R533.

21. Sold 250 shares of 7.5%, $100.00 par value preferred stock at par value. R543.

28. Sold 6,000 shares of $1.00 par value common stock at $1.40 per share. R549.

18-4 Application Problem: Analyzing the impact of financial leverage LO7

A form is given in the *Working Papers*.

Instructions:

1. UpTown Café wants to begin providing live music in its dining area. The plan will require the company to invest $30,000.00 in sound equipment. The vendor maintains that other restaurants have increased their annual operating income by 8.5% to 9.5% of the cost of the equipment. The vendor has offered to finance $28,000.00 of the purchase with a 9% note. The remaining capital will come from internal sources. Complete the form to evaluate the effect of financial leverage on the proposed center. Evaluate the earnings potential of the project assuming that operating income will increase by 8.5%, 9.0%, or 9.5% of the equipment cost.

2. Assume the company is successful in increasing its operating income by 9.5% of the sound equipment cost. Explain the impact of financial leverage on the return on UpTown Café's investment.

18-M Mastery Problem: Journalizing transactions related to debt and equity financing LO2, 4, 5

The journals for Teller Tires are given in the *Working Papers*.

Instructions:

Using the current year, journalize the following transactions on page 7 of a cash receipts journal, page 12 of a cash payments journal, and page 7 of a general journal. Refer to the loan payment schedule when journalizing the December 1 transaction. Source documents are abbreviated as: check, C; receipt, R; memorandum, M.

Transactions:

July 1. Issued twenty-five 20-year, 6%, $10,000.00 bonds. R359.
3. Signed a 180-day, 12% note to PTS Corp. for an extension of time on its account payable, $3,200.00. M98.
8. Issued 8,000 shares of $25.00 par value common stock at par value. R362.
12. Sold 500 shares of 6.5%, $50.00 par value preferred stock at par value. R370.
18. Drew $24,800.00 on its line of credit. R376.
23. Issued 6,000 shares of $25.00 par value common stock at $28.00 per share. R385.
31. Signed a five-year, 8% note, $45,000.00. R392.
Dec. 1. Paid cash for the December payment on the July 31 note payable, $912.44. C745.
2. Paid cash for the monthly payment on its line of credit: principal, $3,000.00, plus interest, $128.95. C746.
30. Paid cash for the maturity value of the July 3 note to PTS Corp., $3,200.00, plus interest. C762.
31. Paid cash for the semiannual interest on bonds. C763.

AAONLINE

1. Go to www.cengage.com/login
2. Click on **AA Online** to access.
3. Go to the online assignment and follow the instructions.

Peachtree

1. Journalize and post the July transactions to the general journal.
2. Journalize and post the December transactions in the Write Checks window.
3. Print the general journal, cash disbursements journal, and trial balance.

 QuickBooks

1. Journalize and post the July transactions to the journal.
2. Journalize and post the December transactions in the Write Checks window.
3. Print the journal, check detail, and trial balance.

X

1. Journalize and post the July transactions to the journal.
2. Journalize and post the December transactions to the cash payments journal.
3. Print the general journal and cash payments journal.

18-C Challenge Problem: Selecting financing methods LO7

Windsong Corporation needs to obtain $500,000.00 of financing for a distribution center. Using the form provided in the *Working Papers*, develop a financing plan to fund the project.

Instructions:

1. Use the following information to determine an appropriate amount of debt and equity funding.

   a. Current liability and equity account balances are presented on the form.

   b. The project involves the opening of a distribution center. The funds will be used to purchase $380,000.00 of equipment and $70,000.00 of additional merchandise inventory. The remaining funds will cover pre-opening expenses.

   c. The company has a $25,000.00 line of credit with a 6.5% interest rate.

   d. A bank is willing to loan up to $250,000.00 at 8% for up to ten years.

   e. The company can issue up to $200,000.00 of 7%, 20-year $5,000.00 bonds.

   f. The Windsong family currently owns 8,000 of the 12,000 outstanding shares. The Windsong family wishes to keep control of a majority of the outstanding common stock.

   g. The company can sell up to 20,000 of its $10.00 par value common stock to independent investors for $15.00 per share.

   h. The board has a target debt ratio benchmark of 30% to 50%.

   i. Windsong projects that it will earn 12% on its investment in the project.

2. What number of shares of common stock should be purchased by the Windsong family to maintain voting control?

1. Use the worksheet to develop a financing plan to fund the distribution center project.
2. Select an appropriate mixture of debt versus equity financing.
3. Print the worksheet.

Heavenly Deals

Theme: Financial, Economic, Business, and Entrepreneurial Literacy

Skills: Critical Thinking and Problem Solving, Communication and Collaboration

PARTNERSHIP FOR
21ST CENTURY SKILLS

Many great business ideas never become reality because entrepreneurs are unable to raise the capital to get started. The types of financing that businesses normally use to raise capital are seldom available for high-risk ventures. Many of those ideas are simply left behind.

The business of raising capital is rarely considered a heavenly undertaking—unless an angel is providing the financing. The term *angel* originally came from Broadway in the 1900s. It described a wealthy individual who provided money for theatrical productions. Today, an *angel investor* is usually a successful businessperson who wants to invest in startup companies with the potential to produce huge returns on their investments. Angel investors seek startups that would be too risky for banks; and they often contribute expertise and experience in addition to capital.

Many angel investors choose to invest for reasons that go beyond a monetary return. They may choose to invest close to home in an effort to help their local community with technological or environmental advancements, or to help create jobs. It is difficult to account for the number of angel investors. Some studies indicate there may be over 12,000 of them. The angel investor might be a name you recognize, like Jeff Bezos, founder of Amazon. He was an angel investor for both Google and Twitter. Or, PayPal's cofounder, Peter Thiel, who helped Facebook get its start. There might be an angel investor in your own community willing to invest in your idea!

APPLICATION

1. You have created a more efficient solar panel, and you have identified potential customers who have said they would be willing to purchase a large number of panels. Unfortunately, you do not have the production capacity to manufacture the panels, which will cost $10,000,000.00. Compose a persuasive letter to a potential angel investor. Describe your business idea and state the amount of capital needed. Be sure to list at least three reasons why this would be a worthwhile investment.

2. Together with a classmate, brainstorm at least five characteristics of an angel investor who might be interested in investing in your Online Homework Tutoring business.

Analyzing Nike's financial statements

Investors use a ratio known as the *dividend yield* when making investment decisions. The dividend yield is calculated as follows: Dividend Yield = Dividend per Share ÷ Market Price per Share.

Companies with large dividend yields (greater than 3%) are typically considered to be *income stocks*, meaning that investors own the stock primarily to earn the dividend. In contrast, companies with no dividend or small dividend yields (less than 2%) are often referred to as *growth stocks*, meaning that investors are counting on the market value of the stock to increase over time.

INSTRUCTIONS

Use Nike's Selected Financial Data on page B-3 in Appendix B to answer the following questions.

1. For each year, calculate Nike's dividend yield using the high price of common stock. Calculate percents to one decimal place.

2. Would you classify Nike as an income or growth stock?

Chapter 19

Accounting for Plant Assets, Depreciation, and Intangible Assets

LEARNING OBJECTIVES

After studying Chapter 19, in addition to defining key terms, you will be able to:

LO1 Record the buying of a plant asset.

LO2 Analyze the cost of individual assets bought as a bundle.

LO3 Calculate and record the payment of property tax.

LO4 Calculate depreciation expense.

LO5 Calculate depreciation for a partial year.

LO6 Calculate accumulated depreciation and book value.

LO7 Prepare plant asset records.

LO8 Journalize annual depreciation expense.

LO9 Record the sale of a plant asset for book value.

LO10 Record the sale of a plant asset for more/less than book value.

LO11 Calculate depreciation using the double declining-balance method.

LO12 Record the buying of an intangible asset.

LO13 Calculate and record amortization expense.

©DANIEL KOUREY, ISTOCK/©JIM PRUITT, ISTOCK

DIGITAL VISION/GETTY IMAGES

Accounting In The Real World
Cinemark Holdings, Inc.

At a movie theater, the experience begins when you walk through the door and smell the popcorn. These days, it is about more than just the movie. How you feel about the experience is a combination of many items, including seating, theater size, audio system, and visual impact.

Cinemark Holdings, Inc., of Plano, Texas, is in the process of improving your experience. Cinemark's circuit is the third largest in the United States. It has 292 theaters and 3,816 screens in 39 states. Cinemark also has 139 theaters and 1,125 screens in 13 countries in Latin America. It is opening more screens and plans to continue doing so in the future. Cinemark features stadium seating in 86% of its first-run theaters.

Besides opening new theaters, Cinemark is making a huge investment in state-of-the-art equipment in many of its current theaters. It has developed a large-screen digital format which it calls XD Extreme Digital Cinema. XD theaters include wall-to-wall and ceiling-to-floor screens and wrap-around sound. Cinemark feels that all of these investments will add to the total experience of each customer.

Cinemark also offers Summer Movie Clubhouse Fun Film for Kids. Available at over 150 locations, this is a ten-week series of G- or PG-rated movies. The best part of this series is the price—$1 per person per show. A series punch card is available for $5 and is good for all ten movies. The Cinemark website states that "The Summer Movie Clubhouse offers an affordable way to beat the summer heat and enjoy some great family films. Our customers look forward to this successful program every year."

The large investment in equipment and special programming seem to be paying off. During a recent year, Cinemark ranked either 1 or 2 in box office revenues in 25 of its top 30 markets.

Cinemark estimates that its furniture and equipment will last for five to 15 years. In compliance with GAAP, Cinemark depreciates the costs of the furniture and equipment over their estimated useful lives. Thus, a portion of each item of furniture and equipment is recorded as an expense every period until only the salvage value remains.

CRITICAL THINKING

1. The digital projection equipment may last longer than Cinemark's estimated useful life. Why do you think Cinemark estimates a shorter useful life for its equipment?

2. What is the effect on the income statement of estimating a useful life of ten years rather than 15 years for projection equipment?

Key Terms

- return on investment
- real property
- personal property
- assessed value

- plant asset record
- gain
- gain on plant assets
- loss

- loss on plant assets
- accelerated depreciation
- declining-balance method of depreciation

- double declining-balance method of depreciation
- intangible asset
- amortization

19-1 Buying Plant Assets and Paying Property Taxes

LO1 Record the buying of a plant asset.
LO2 Analyze the cost of individual assets bought as a bundle.
LO3 Calculate and record the payment of property tax.

Plant Assets

Physical assets that will be used for a number of years in the operation of a business are known as *plant assets*. A business may have several types of plant assets, including equipment, buildings, and land. Businesses often subdivide plant assets into more focused categories and create an account for each category. For example, a company may divide its equipment into office, store, warehouse, and transportation equipment.

Sun Treasures, Inc., owns its equipment but rents the building and the land where the business is located. Therefore, Sun Treasures only has accounts for equipment. To provide more detailed financial information, Sun Treasures records its equipment in two different equipment accounts—**Office Equipment** and **Store Equipment**. [CONCEPT: Adequate Disclosure]

Sun Treasures is going to be investing in plant assets as it opens new stores. When a company buys a plant asset, it expects that the asset will help the company earn revenue. Since companies have limited resources to invest in plant assets, managers must often decide between investment opportunities. Accounting data can be used to predict the efficiency of an investment. The ratio of the money earned on an investment relative to the amount of the investment is called **return on investment**, or *ROI*. The more efficient the investment, the higher its ROI. These predictions will help company managers decide which assets to buy.

Most plant assets are useful for only a limited period of time. Over time, most equipment wears out and can no longer perform its functions. Other equipment, such as computers, becomes technologically outdated. Regardless of the reason, the cost of a plant asset should be depreciated over its useful life. Each plant asset account should have a related accumulated depreciation account—a contra asset account—to accumulate the annual depreciation expense of the plant assets in the account.

ETHICS IN ACTION

Lifelong Learning

When you are ill, you expect your doctor to know the latest methods and medicines to restore your health. Businesses should expect nothing less from their accountants. Therefore, accountants must constantly improve their knowledge and skills to provide their clients, employees, and the public with the highest level of professional service.

The code of conduct for every major accounting organization includes some reference to lifelong learning. Most organizations require their members to continue their education throughout their careers. For example, certified public accountants must complete a minimum number of continuing education hours every year. This education may be in the form of self-study courses, college courses, seminars, and conferences.

INSTRUCTIONS

Access the codes of conduct from the American Institute of Certified Public Accountants (AICPA), the Institute of Internal Auditors (IIA), the Institute of Management Accountants (IMA), and the Association of Certified Fraud Examiners (ACFE). Identify what each code states about lifelong learning.

©LUCA DI FILIPPO, ISTOCK

Recording the Buying of a Plant Asset LO1

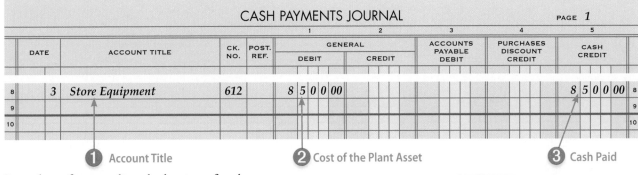

	DATE	ACCOUNT TITLE	CK. NO.	POST. REF.	GENERAL		ACCOUNTS PAYABLE DEBIT	PURCHASES DISCOUNT CREDIT	CASH CREDIT	
					DEBIT	CREDIT				
8	3	Store Equipment	612		8 5 0 0 00				8 5 0 0 00	8
9										9
10										10

1 Account Title   **2** Cost of the Plant Asset   **3** Cash Paid

Procedures for recording the buying of a plant asset are similar to procedures for recording the buying of current assets such as supplies. The amount paid for a plant asset is debited to a plant asset account with a title such as Store Equipment. Regardless of their actual value, plant assets are always recorded at their original cost. [CONCEPT: Historical Cost]

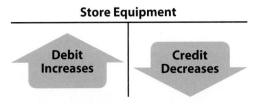

January 3, 20X1. Paid cash for a shelving unit, $8,500.00. Check No. 612.

Journalizing the Buying of a Plant Asset

1 Write the plant asset account, Store Equipment, in the Account Title column of the cash payments journal.

2 Enter the cost of the plant asset, $8,500.00, in the General Debit column.

3 Enter the same amount, $8,500.00, in the Cash Credit column.

Recording the Buying of a Group of Assets LO2

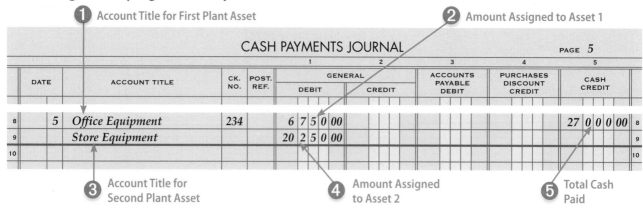

1 Account Title for First Plant Asset

2 Amount Assigned to Asset 1

3 Account Title for Second Plant Asset

4 Amount Assigned to Asset 2

5 Total Cash Paid

A company may buy several assets as a group with a single discounted price for all the assets. That often happens when a vendor offers a bundled price to encourage the sale of more items. Even though one price is paid for all the assets, each asset must be assigned (or allocated) a price. The cost allocated to each asset is debited to that plant asset account. [CONCEPT: Historical Cost] This allocation must be done so that each plant asset can be depreciated individually.

Dufore Company buys a copy machine (office equipment) and a display case (store equipment) for a total cost of $27,000.00. The copy machine has an estimated value of $7,500.00. The display case has an estimated value of $22,500.00.

The first step is to calculate the total estimated value of all the assets bought:

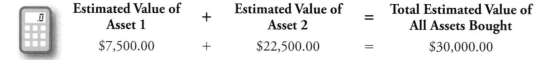

Estimated Value of Asset 1	+	Estimated Value of Asset 2	=	Total Estimated Value of All Assets Bought
$7,500.00	+	$22,500.00	=	$30,000.00

The cost assigned to the copy machine (Asset 1) is calculated as follows:

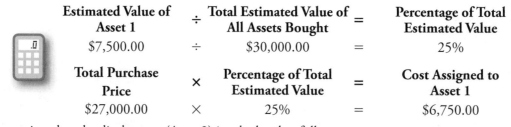

Estimated Value of Asset 1	÷	Total Estimated Value of All Assets Bought	=	Percentage of Total Estimated Value
$7,500.00	÷	$30,000.00	=	25%

Total Purchase Price	×	Percentage of Total Estimated Value	=	Cost Assigned to Asset 1
$27,000.00	×	25%	=	$6,750.00

The cost assigned to the display case (Asset 2) is calculated as follows:

Estimated Value of Asset 2	÷	Total Estimated Value of All Assets Bought	=	Percentage of Total Estimated Value
$22,500.00	÷	$30,000.00	=	75%

Total Purchase Price	×	Percentage of Total Estimated Value	=	Cost Assigned to Asset 1
$27,000.00	×	75%	=	$20,250.00

March 5, 20X1. Dufore Company bought a copy machine and a display case for $27,000.00. Check No. 234.

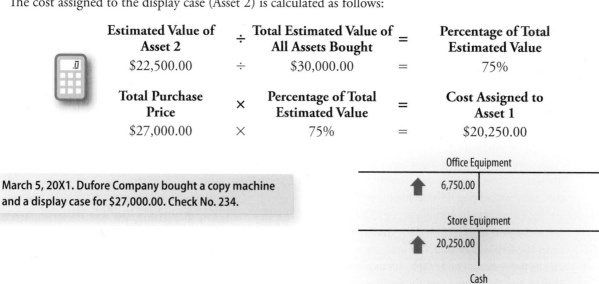

Office Equipment

6,750.00

Store Equipment

20,250.00

Cash

27,000.00

① Write the title of the first plant asset account, Office Equipment, in the Account Title column of the cash payments journal.

② Enter the cost assigned to the copy machine, $6,750.00, in the General Debit column.

③ Write the title of the second plant asset account, Store Equipment, in the Account Title column on the next line of the cash payments journal.

④ Enter the cost assigned to the display unit, $20,250.00, in the General Debit column on the same line.

⑤ Enter the total cash paid, $27,000.00, in the Cash Credit column.

Calculating and Paying Property Tax LO3

						1		2		3	4	5	
	DATE	ACCOUNT TITLE	CK. NO.	POST. REF.	GENERAL				ACCOUNTS PAYABLE DEBIT	PURCHASES DISCOUNT CREDIT	CASH CREDIT		
					DEBIT		CREDIT						
14	15	*Property Tax Expense*	551		1 0 4 0 00							1 0 4 0 00	14
15													15
16													16

CASH PAYMENTS JOURNAL — PAGE 3

① Account Title   ② Amount of Tax   ③ Cash Paid

For tax purposes, state and federal governments define two kinds of property—real and personal. Land and anything attached to the land is called **real property**. Real property is sometimes referred to as *real estate*. All property not classified as real property is called **personal property**. For tax purposes, these definitions apply whether the property is owned by a business or an individual.

Most governmental units with taxing power impose taxes based on the value of real property. Real property taxes are assessed on buildings and land. Some governmental units also tax personal property such as cars, boats, trailers, and airplanes.

The value of an asset determined by tax authorities for the purpose of calculating taxes is called the **assessed value**. Assessed value is usually based on the judgment of officials referred to as *assessors*. Assessors are elected by citizens or are specially trained employees of a local (usually county) government.

A tax rate is used to calculate property tax. The tax rate is multiplied by an asset's assessed value, not the value recorded on a business's records.

Brighton Bikes, Inc., owns real property that has been assessed for a total of $80,000.00. The city tax rate is 1.3%.

The assessed value of an asset may not be the same as the value on the business's or individual's records. The assessed value is assigned to an asset for tax purposes only. Often, the assessed value is only a part of the true value of the asset.

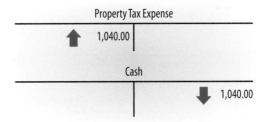

Property Tax Expense
↑ 1,040.00

Cash
↓ 1,040.00

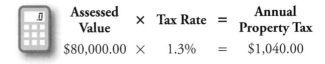

Assessed Value	×	Tax Rate	=	Annual Property Tax
$80,000.00	×	1.3%	=	$1,040.00

February 15, 20X1. Brighton Bikes, Inc., paid cash for property tax, $1,040.00. Check No. 551.

Payment of property taxes is necessary for a firm to continue in business. Therefore, Brighton Bikes classifies property tax as an operating expense.

◆ Journalizing Paying Property Tax

① Write the title of the account, Property Tax Expense, in the Account Title column of the cash payments journal.

② Enter the amount of the property tax, $1,040.00, in the General Debit column.

③ Enter the same amount, $1,040.00, in the Cash Credit column.

End of Lesson Review

Terms Review

return on investment

real property

personal property

assessed value

Audit your understanding

1. Which accounts are affected, and how, when cash is paid for office equipment?
2. Why must a cost be allocated to each asset bought in a group?
3. What items are included in real property?

Work together 19-1

Journalizing buying plant assets and paying property tax

The cash payments journal for O'Donnel Copy Center is given in the *Working Papers*. Your instructor will guide you through the following examples.

Journalize the following transactions completed during the current year. Use page 1 of a cash payments journal. The abbreviation for a check is C.

Transactions:

Jan. 3. Paid cash for a copy machine for use in the store, $800.00. C241.

5. Paid cash for an office chair, $500.00. C244.

Feb. 26. Paid property taxes on real property with an assessed value of $200,000.00. The tax rate in the city where the property is located is 2.0% of assessed value. C268.

July 2. Paid cash for a filing cabinet (office equipment) and a paper cutter (store equipment), $600.00. The filing cabinet has an estimated value of $300.00, and the paper cutter has an estimated value of $450.00. C331.

On your own 19-1

Journalizing buying plant assets and paying property tax

The cash payments journal for Foreman Floor Center is given in the *Working Papers*. Work this problem independently.

Journalize the following transactions completed during the current year. Use page 3 of a cash payments journal. The abbreviation for a check is C.

Transactions:

Feb. 2. Paid cash for a computer for use in the office, $1,200.00. C335.

5. Paid cash for a carpet stretcher, $600.00. C340.

Mar. 24. Paid property taxes on real property with an assessed value of $84,000.00. The tax rate in the city where the property is located is 3.5% of assessed value. C371.

28. Paid cash for a desk (office equipment) and a display case (store equipment), $2,100.00. The desk has an estimated value of $600.00, and the display case has an estimated value of $1,800.00. C380.

©CANDICE CUSACK, ISTOCK

19-2 Calculating Depreciation Expense

LO4 Calculate depreciation expense.
LO5 Calculate depreciation for a partial year.
LO6 Calculate accumulated depreciation and book value.

Calculating Straight-Line Depreciation LO4

Original Cost	−	Estimated Salvage Value	=	Estimated Total Depreciation Expense	
$8,500.00	−	$500.00	=	$8,000.00 ←	**1** Calculate Total Depreciation Expense

Estimated Total Depreciation Expense	÷	Years of Estimated Useful Life	=	Annual Depreciation Expense	
$8,000.00	÷	4	=	$2,000.00 ←	**2** Calculate Annual Depreciation Expense

Plant assets are expected to be used in the business for many years. GAAP requires that the cost of a plant asset be expensed over the plant asset's useful life. [CONCEPT: Matching Expenses with Revenue] The annual expense is recorded in **Depreciation Expense** and the contra asset account **Accumulated Depreciation**.

Several methods for calculating depreciation expense are available. The easiest and most widely used method is known as the *straight-line method of depreciation*. This method requires the business to know the cost of the plant asset and to estimate two amounts:

1. The amount the business expects to receive when a plant asset is disposed of, known as the *estimated salvage value*. The salvage value of an asset can be zero if the company plans to discard it when it is no longer useful.
2. The number of years a plant asset is expected to contribute to the earnings of a business, known as the *estimated useful life*.

The straight-line method of depreciation charges an equal amount of depreciation expense in each full year in which the asset is used. Other methods of depreciation will be explained later in this chapter.

On January 3, 20X1, Sun Treasures bought a shelving unit for $8,500.00 with an estimated salvage value of $500.00 and an estimated useful life of four years.

Calculating Annual Depreciation Expense

1. Subtract the asset's estimated salvage value from the asset's original cost. This difference is the estimated total depreciation expense for the asset's entire useful life.

2. Divide the estimated total depreciation expense by the years of estimated useful life. The result is the annual depreciation expense.

fyi The estimated useful life should be based on prior experience with similar assets and on available guidelines. Trade associations frequently publish guidelines for specialized plant assets. The Internal Revenue Service also publishes depreciation guidelines for plant assets.

Careers In Accounting

Casey Hepburn
AUDITOR

NEUSTOCKIMAGES/ISTOCKPHOTO.COM

Casey Hepburn, CPA, is an auditor for a major public accounting firm. He works with a variety of clients ranging from small companies to huge multinational corporations. It is an auditor's responsibility to determine if a client's financial statements have been prepared and reported in compliance with generally accepted accounting principles (GAAP). If the client is a large firm, Mr. Hepburn will work with a team of accountants to perform the audit.

When auditing a company's accounts and transactions, the team cannot possibly look at all transactions to see if they are recorded correctly. Instead, the team uses a technique called *sampling*. In sampling, only selected transactions are verified. If those transactions were recorded according to GAAP, the team makes the assumption that all similar transactions have also been recorded correctly. In order to do a thorough job, the audit team must have access to all necessary company records. The audit team follows established standard procedures to ensure that their audits are done correctly.

As a requirement of the Sarbanes-Oxley Act of 2002, the audit team must also review the client's internal control system as it relates to financial reporting. The audit team must point out any weaknesses it finds in the internal control system.

At the conclusion of the audit, the auditor issues an *opinion*. The opinion is directed to the client's board of directors and shareholders. Without this opinion, the shareholders would have no assurance that the financial statements were prepared in compliance with GAAP.

As an auditor, Mr. Hepburn must be objective. This means that he must be independent of his client. An auditor must not have any personal stake in the client's financial position, whether good or bad. The audit team usually reports to an audit committee, which is a subcommittee of the board of directors. It is essential that the auditor have unrestricted access to the audit committee without needing permission from the board.

Salary Range: Salaries vary depending on company size, job responsibilities, and experience. The average entry-level salary is $44,000 to $55,000. The average salary for a senior audit manager is $96,000 to $141,500, plus bonuses.

Qualifications: Minimum education for an auditor is a bachelor's degree in accounting and a CPA certificate. A master's degree is often preferred. Most employers also require past experience in the field of accounting. Many auditors have some education in law, forensics, finance, math, and economics.

Effective communication skills are essential for an auditor. Auditors interact with the client's employees, managers, customers, vendors, bankers, and directors. They often must explain accounting standards and clarify expectations. The preparation of written reports is also required.

To perform well in their positions, auditors must be able to gather, organize, and process information; solve problems; understand the consequence of errors; and keep up to date with technology. They must be able to plan and direct projects, deal with high-stress situations, maintain confidentiality, and prioritize tasks. An auditor must also be ethical, reliable, and responsible.

Occupational Outlook: The growth for auditor positions is projected to be faster than average (20% or higher) for the period from 2008 to 2018.

Sources: www.investopedia.com, www.online.onetcenter.org, and www.roberthalffinance.com/SalaryCenter.

ACTIVITY

Look for a job opening in auditing. Write a paragraph about the position, including educational requirements and salary range.

©MILENNY, ISTOCK

Calculating Depreciation Expense for Part of a Year   LO5

Annual Depreciation Expense	÷	Months in a Year	=	Monthly Depreciation Expense	
$900.00	÷	12	=	$75.00	← ❶ Calculate Monthy Depreciation Expense

Monthly Depreciation Expense	×	Number of Months Asset Is Used	=	Partial Year's Depreciation Expense	
$75.00	×	4	=	$300.00	← ❷ Calculate Partial Year's Depreciation Expense

A month is the smallest unit of time used to calculate depreciation. A plant asset may be placed in service at a date other than the first day of a fiscal period. In such cases, a business may elect to calculate depreciation expense to the nearest first of a month. A partial year's depreciation may also be recorded in the year the plant asset is sold or disposed of.

Sun Treasures bought an office computer on September 3, 20X1. The annual straight-line depreciation expense is $900.00. The depreciation expense is $300.00 for the remaining four months of the year in which Sun Treasures used the computer.

⬎ Calculating Partial Year's Depreciation Expense

❶ Divide the annual depreciation expense by 12, the number of months in a year. The result is the monthly depreciation expense.

❷ Multiply the monthly depreciation expense by the number of months the plant asset is used in a year. The result is the partial year's depreciation expense.

The three years' depreciation expense is illustrated below. In the first year, a partial year's depreciation is recorded: September 3, 20X1, to December 31, 20X1— four months. If the asset had been bought September 16 or later, only three months' depreciation would be expensed because the date would be closer to October 1 than September 1. In the next two years, a full year's depreciation, $900.00, would be expensed each year. In 20X4, the original three-year useful life ends August 31, so eight months' depreciation would be recorded.

Office computer: $3,000.00
Estimated salvage value: $300.00
Useful life: 3 years
Annual depreciation ($3,000.00 − $300.00) ÷ 3 = $900.00 per year
Monthly depreciation: $900.00 ÷ 12 = $75 per month

20X1 Sept. 3	20X1 Dec. 31	20X2 Dec. 31	20X3 Dec. 31	20X4 Aug. 31
	4 months $75 × 4 = $300.00	1 year $900.00	1 year $900.00	8 months $75 × 8 = $600.00

Calculating Accumulated Depreciation and Book Value LO6

Plant asset:	*Office Computer*	Original cost:	$3,000.00
Depreciation method:	*Straight-line*	Estimated salvage value:	$300.00
		Estimated useful life:	3 years
		Date bought:	*September 3, 20X1*

Year	Beginning Book Value	Annual Depreciation	Accumulated Depreciation	Ending Book Value
20X1	$3,000.00	$300.00	$ 300.00	$2,700.00
20X2	2,700.00	900.00	1,200.00	1,800.00
20X3	1,800.00	900.00	2,100.00	900.00
20X4	900.00	600.00	2,700.00	300.00

CALCULATING ACCUMULATED DEPRECIATION

Depreciation is not recorded as a reduction of the plant asset account. Instead, the depreciation expense for each year of a plant asset's useful life is recorded in an accumulated depreciation account. The accumulated depreciation for a plant asset in the current year is calculated by adding the depreciation expense for the current year to the prior year's accumulated depreciation.

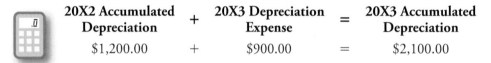

	20X2 Accumulated Depreciation	+	20X3 Depreciation Expense	=	20X3 Accumulated Depreciation
	$1,200.00	+	$900.00	=	$2,100.00

CALCULATING BOOK VALUE

The original cost of a plant asset minus accumulated depreciation is known as the *book value of a plant asset*. The book value is calculated by subtracting the accumulated depreciation from the original cost of the plant asset. The ending book value, at the end of the fiscal year, is the beginning book value for the next year. Plant assets may continue to be used after their estimated useful lives have ended; however, no additional depreciation is recorded.

The book value can also be calculated by subtracting the year's depreciation from that year's beginning book value. Either method of calculating a book value is acceptable because both methods calculate the same amount.

	Original Cost	−	Accumulated Depreciation	=	Ending Book Value
	$3,000.00	−	$2,700.00	=	$300.00

End of Lesson Review

LO4 Calculate depreciation expense.

LO5 Calculate depreciation for a partial year.

LO6 Calculate accumulated depreciation and book value.

Audit your understanding

1. Which accounting concept is being applied when depreciation expense is recorded for plant assets?

2. What three amounts are used to calculate a plant asset's annual depreciation expense using the straight-line method of depreciation?

Work together 19-2

Calculating depreciation

Forms are given in the *Working Papers*. Your instructor will guide you through the following example.

Brookdale Banners bought the following assets during 20X1. Brookdale uses the straight-line depreciation method. Calculate beginning book value, annual depreciation, accumulated depreciation, and ending book value for each asset for each year of estimated useful life. If the asset was not bought at the beginning of 20X1, calculate the depreciation expense for the part of 20X1 in which the company owned the asset. Save your work to complete Work Together 19-3.

> Transactions:
>
> Jan. 4. Bought a display case costing $4,040.00; estimated salvage value, $200.00; estimated useful life, 8 years.
>
> Sept. 20. Bought a work station, $4,800.00; estimated salvage value, $0.00; estimated useful life, 5 years.

On your own 19-2

Calculating depreciation

Forms are given in the *Working Papers*. Work this problem independently.

Royal Repair Co. bought the following assets during 20X1. Royal uses the straight-line depreciation method. Calculate beginning book value, annual depreciation, accumulated depreciation, and ending book value for each asset for each year of estimated useful life. If the asset was not bought at the beginning of 20X1, calculate the depreciation expense for the part of 20X1 in which the company owned the asset. Save your work to complete On Your Own 19-3.

> Transactions:
>
> Jan. 5. Bought a stitching machine costing $2,500.00; estimated salvage value, $340.00; estimated useful life, 6 years.
>
> June 13. Bought a notebook computer, $2,070.00; estimated salvage value, $150.00; estimated useful life, 4 years.

19-3 Journalizing Depreciation Expense

LO7 Prepare plant asset records.

LO8 Journalize annual depreciation expense.

Preparing Plant Asset Records LO7

PLANT ASSET RECORD No. __62__   General Ledger Account No. ____1120____

Description ___*Shelving Unit*___   General Ledger Account ___*Store Equipment*___

Date Bought ___*January 2, 20X1*___   Serial Number _____   Original Cost ____$8,500.00____   ❶

Estimated Useful Life ___*4 years*___   Estimated Salvage Value ___*$500.00*___   Depreciation Method ___*Straight-line*___

Disposed of: Discarded _____   Sold _____   Traded _____   ❷

Date _____   Disposal Amount _____

Year	Annual Depreciation Expense	Accumulated Depreciation	Ending Book Value	
20X1	$2,000.00	$2,000.00	$6,500.00	
20X2	2,000.00	4,000.00	4,500.00	❸
20X3	2,000.00	6,000.00	2,500.00	
20X4	2,000.00	8,000.00	500.00	

Continue record on back of card

Accountants keep a separate record for each plant asset. An accounting form on which a business records information about each plant asset is called a **plant asset record**.

Plant asset records may vary in arrangement for different businesses, but most records contain similar information. Sun Treasures' plant asset record has three sections. Section 1 is prepared when a plant asset is bought. Section 2 provides space for recording the disposition of the plant asset. When the asset is disposed of, this information will be filled in. Section 3 provides space for recording annual depreciation expense and the changing book value of the asset each year it is used.

At the end of each fiscal period, Sun Treasures brings each plant asset record up to date by recording three amounts: (1) annual depreciation expense, (2) accumulated depreciation, and (3) ending book value.

The amount recorded in the Annual Depreciation Expense column is the amount calculated for each year. These amounts may be different if the asset is bought or sold at a time other than near the fiscal year beginning or end.

For any plant asset, accumulated depreciation for the first year is the annual depreciation expense for the first year. For each year thereafter, accumulated depreciation for any plant asset is the depreciation expense that has accumulated over all prior years added to that year's annual depreciation expense.

The ending book value for any given year is the original cost less that year's accumulated depreciation.

PHOTODISC/GETTY IMAGES

Preparing a Plant Asset Record

1. Write the information in Section 1 when the plant asset is bought.

2. Do not write in Section 2 until the asset is disposed of.

3. Each year the asset is owned, record the year's annual depreciation expense in Section 3. Calculate and record accumulated depreciation and ending book value.

THINK LIKE AN ACCOUNTANT

Applying International Accounting Standards

Accountants using GAAP commonly assign a useful life of 25 or 30 years to a building. The cost of a building includes everything needed to occupy a building, including its foundation, electrical wiring, plumbing, light fixtures, and carpet. All of these costs are combined and depreciated as one asset having one cost, one salvage value, and one useful life.

Does every part of the building depreciate over the same number of years? The answer is no. A foundation can last a lifetime, depending on how it is constructed. In contrast, carpet usually becomes worn or goes out of style as early as five to seven years.

International financial reporting standards (IFRS, pronounced i'fers) take a different approach to depreciating a building. IFRS require that a building be divided into its component parts. Each component is depreciated over its expected useful life. Thus, the foundation may be depreciated over 30 or more years. In contrast, the carpet may be depreciated over a shorter period, such as seven years.

Most of today's computerized accounting systems are designed to apply GAAP depreciation methods. A company having purchased a building would have recorded the entire cost as a single asset in its accounting system. Until accounting systems are modified to comply with IFRS rules, accountants must use other computer technologies to generate the required information.

OPEN THE SPREADSHEET TLA_CH19
Follow the steps on the Instructions tab.

Bryan Creek Stores has completed a project to divide the costs of its existing plant assets. Each plant asset is assigned a number in the format XXXX-YY. The XXXX is the plant asset number in its existing accounting system. The YY is a code for each component part, such as foundation and carpet. Use the worksheet to complete a table of plant asset information supporting amounts in IFRS financial statements.

Journalizing Annual Depreciation Expense LO8

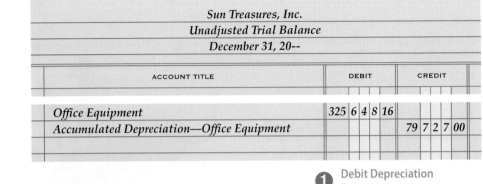

Sun Treasures, Inc. Unadjusted Trial Balance December 31, 20--		
ACCOUNT TITLE	**DEBIT**	**CREDIT**
Office Equipment	325 6 4 8 16	
Accumulated Depreciation—Office Equipment		79 7 2 7 00

1 Debit Depreciation Expense

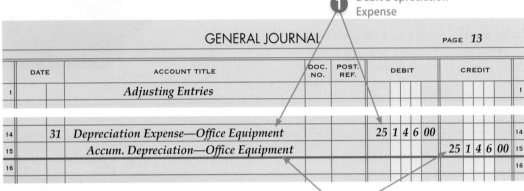

GENERAL JOURNAL						PAGE 13
DATE	ACCOUNT TITLE	DOC. NO.	POST. REF.	DEBIT	CREDIT	
	Adjusting Entries					1
31	Depreciation Expense—Office Equipment			25 1 4 6 00		14
	Accum. Depreciation—Office Equipment				25 1 4 6 00	15
						16

2 Credit Accumulated Depreciation

At the end of the fiscal year, Sun Treasures calculates the depreciation expense for each plant asset. The depreciation expense for each asset is recorded on its plant asset record. Next, the total depreciation expense is calculated for all plant assets recorded in the same plant asset account.

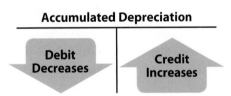

Accumulated Depreciation

Debit Decreases	Credit Increases

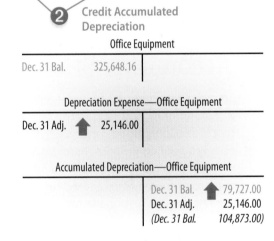

Office Equipment

Dec. 31 Bal.   325,648.16

Depreciation Expense—Office Equipment

Dec. 31 Adj. ⬆   25,146.00

Accumulated Depreciation—Office Equipment

Dec. 31 Bal. ⬆ 79,727.00
Dec. 31 Adj.   25,146.00
(Dec. 31 Bal.   104,873.00)

Sun Treasures determined that total depreciation expense for store equipment is $25,146.00. Using this information, an adjusting entry is then recorded in a general journal.

It is important to retain original cost information for plant assets. Rather than credit depreciation to a plant asset account, depreciation is recorded to the asset's accumulated depreciation contra account. At any time, the book value of a plant asset can be calculated by subtracting its accumulated depreciation from the plant asset account.

⮊ Journalizing Annual Depreciation Expense

1 Debit Depreciation Expense—Office Equipment for the amount of depreciation expense, **$25,146.00**.

2 Credit Accum. Depreciation—Office Equipment for the same amount, **$25,146.00**.

End of Lesson Review

LO7 Prepare plant asset records.

LO8 Journalize annual depreciation expense.

Term Review

plant asset record

Audit your understanding

1. How is accumulated depreciation recorded so as to retain the original cost information for plant assets?
2. How does an adjusting entry for depreciation expense change the balance of the asset account?

Work together 19-3

Journalizing depreciation

Use the depreciation calculations from Work Together 19-2. Additional forms are given in the *Working Papers*. Your instructor will guide you through the following examples.

1. Complete each plant asset record for the years 20X1 through 20X3. Use the following additional information:

Description	General Ledger Account	Date Bought	Plant Asset No.	Serial No.
Display Case	1220—Store Equipment	Jan. 4	105	374-02
Work Station	1210—Office Equipment	Sept. 20	106	X56Y17

2. On December 31, 20X3, Brookdale Banners determined that total depreciation expense for office equipment for the year was $13,125.00. Record the adjusting entry on page 23 of a general journal. Save your work to complete Work Together 19-4.

On your own 19-3

Journalizing depreciation

Use the depreciation calculations from On Your Own 19-2. Additional forms are given in the *Working Papers*. Work this problem independently.

1. Complete each plant asset record from the years 20X1 through 20X3. Use the following additional information:

Description	General Ledger Account	Date Bought	Plant Asset No.	Serial No.
Stitching Machine	1220—Store Equipment	Jan. 5	276	GH-422-J
Notebook Computer	1210—Office Equipment	June 13	277	81763273

2. On December 31, 20X3, Royal Repair Co. determined that total depreciation expense for store equipment for the year was $15,775.00. Record the adjusting entry on page 20 of a general journal. Save your work to complete On Your Own 19-4.

LO9 Record the sale of a plant asset for book value.

LO10 Record the sale of a plant asset for more/less than book value.

Selling a Plant Asset for Book Value LO9

					GENERAL		ACCOUNTS RECEIVABLE CREDIT	SALES CREDIT	SALES TAX PAYABLE CREDIT	SALES DISCOUNT DEBIT	CASH DEBIT	
	DATE	ACCOUNT TITLE	DOC. NO.	POST. REF.	DEBIT	CREDIT						
4	2	Accum. Depr.—Store Equip.	R543		8 0 0 0 00						5 0 0 00	4
5		Store Equipment				8 5 0 0 00						5

CASH RECEIPTS JOURNAL PAGE **1**

① Remove the original cost of the plant asset and its related accumulated depreciation. Record the cash received.

② Complete Section 2 of the plant asset record.

Disposed of:	Discarded _____	Sold ✓	Traded _____
Date	*January 2, 20X5*	Disposal Amount	*$500.00*

When a plant asset is no longer useful to a business, the asset may be disposed of. The old plant asset may be sold, traded for a new asset, or discarded.

When a plant asset is disposed of, a journal entry is recorded that achieves the following:
1. Removes the original cost of the plant asset and its related accumulated depreciation.
2. Recognizes any cash or other asset received for the old plant asset.
3. Recognizes any gain or loss on the disposal.

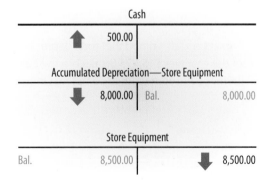

January 2, 20X5. Received cash from sale of shelving unit, $500.00: original cost, $8,500.00; total accumulated depreciation through December 31, 20X4, $8,000.00. Receipt No. 543.

Cash received		$500.00
Less: Book value of asset sold:		
Cost	$8,500.00	
Accumulated depreciation	8,000.00	500.00
Gain (loss) on sale of plant asset		$ 0.00

The amount of gain or loss, if any, is calculated by subtracting the book value from the cash received. The display case was sold for its book value. Therefore, no gain or loss exists.

> **⊗ Recording Sale of a Plant Asset for Book Value**
>
> **①** Record an entry in the cash receipts journal to remove the original cost, **$8,500.00**, from **Store Equipment** and **$8,000.00** from **Accum. Depr.—Store Equip.** Record the cash received from the sale, **$500.00**, as a debit to Cash.
>
> **②** Check the type of disposal, Sold, and write the date, **January 2, 20X5**, and disposal amount, **$500.00**, in Section 2 of the plant asset record.

Recording Depreciation Expense on Disposal of an Asset

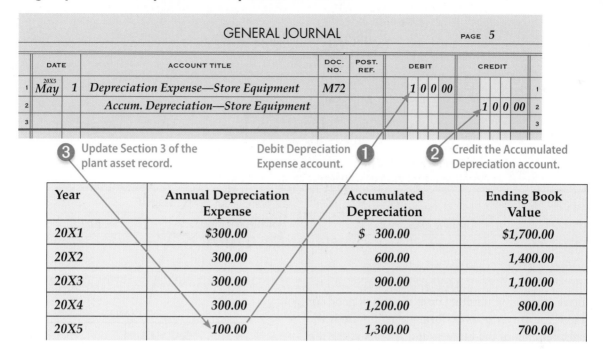

Year	Annual Depreciation Expense	Accumulated Depreciation	Ending Book Value
20X1	$300.00	$ 300.00	$1,700.00
20X2	300.00	600.00	1,400.00
20X3	300.00	900.00	1,100.00
20X4	300.00	1,200.00	800.00
20X5	100.00	1,300.00	700.00

Plant assets may be disposed of in different ways. They may be discarded, sold, or traded. A plant asset may be disposed of at any time during its useful life. When a plant asset that has not been fully depreciated is disposed of, its depreciation from the beginning of the current fiscal year to the date of disposal must be recorded.

On May 1, 20X5, Sun Treasures intends to sell a desk that was bought on January 10, 20X1, for $2,000.00. Annual depreciation expense for the desk is $300.00. Depreciation recorded through December 31, 20X4, is $1,200.00.

The method to calculate depreciation on disposal of a plant asset is the same as calculating depreciation for a partial year when an asset is bought during the fiscal year. The monthly depreciation expense is multiplied by the number of months the asset is used during the current fiscal year. Depreciation is calculated for each month prior to the month the plant asset is sold. Thus, Sun Treasures will depreciate the desk for four months, January through April.

> May 1, 20X5. Recorded a partial year's depreciation on a desk to be sold, $100.00. Memorandum No. 72.

The depreciation is also recorded on the plant asset record for the desk.

Recording a Partial Year's Depreciation on Disposal of a Plant Asset

1. Record a debit, $100.00, to Depreciation Expense—Store Equipment in the general journal.
2. Record a credit, $100.00, to Accum. Depreciation—Store Equipment in the general journal.
3. Record the depreciation expense in Section 3 of the plant asset record for the desk. Calculate and record accumulated depreciation and ending book value.

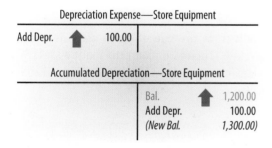

Annual Depreciation Expense	÷	Months in a Year	=	Monthly Depreciation Expense
$300.00	÷	12	=	$25.00

Monthly Depreciation Expense	×	Number of Months Asset Is Used	=	Partial Year's Depreciation Expense
$25.00	×	4	=	$100.00

Selling a Plant Asset for More Than Book Value LO10

						CASH RECEIPTS JOURNAL							PAGE 19	
						1	2	3	4	5	6	7		
					GENERAL		ACCOUNTS RECEIVABLE CREDIT	SALES CREDIT	SALES TAX PAYABLE CREDIT	SALES DISCOUNT DEBIT	CASH DEBIT			
	DATE	ACCOUNT TITLE	DOC. NO.	POST. REF.	DEBIT	CREDIT								
1	20X5 May 1	Accum. Depr.—Store Equip.	R582		1 3 0 0 00							8 5 0 00		1
2		Store Equipment				2 0 0 0 00								2
3		Gain on Plant Assets				1 5 0 00								3

1 Record an entry to remove the asset and its accumulated depreciation, record the gain, and record cash.

2 Complete Section 2 of the plant asset record.

Disposed of:		Discarded _____	Sold ✓	Traded _____
Date	*May 1, 20X5*		Disposal Amount	$850.00

An increase in equity resulting from the sale of goods or services is known as *revenue*. Revenue results from the normal operation of the business and appears at the top of the income statement under the heading Revenues. However, an increase in equity resulting from activity other than selling goods or services is called a **gain**. A gain is related to a supplemental activity, such as selling a plant asset. Gains are listed further down on the income statement, usually under the heading, Other Revenue.

Gain on Plant Assets

Debit **Decreases**	**Credit** **Increases**

An increase in equity that results when a plant asset is sold for more than book value is called **gain on plant assets**. Sun Treasures is selling a desk for $850.00. After the partial year's depreciation is recorded, a journal entry is made to record the sale of the desk.

> May 1, 20X5. Received cash from sale of desk, $850.00: original cost, $2,000.00; accumulated depreciation through May 1, 20X5, $1,300.00. Receipt No. 582.

The gain or loss on the sale of a plant asset is the book value subtracted from cash received.

Cash received		$850.00
Less book value of asset sold:		
Cost	$2,000.00	
Accumulated depreciation	1,300.00	700.00
Gain (loss) on sale of plant asset		$150.00

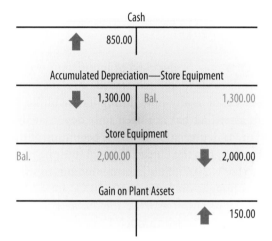

The gain realized on the disposal of a plant asset is credited to a revenue account titled Gain on Plant Assets.

A gain from the sale of plant assets is not operating revenue. Therefore, Gain on Plant Assets is listed in a classification titled Other Revenue in the chart of accounts.

Recording Sale of a Plant Asset for More Than Book Value

1 Record an entry in the cash receipts journal to remove the original cost, $2,000.00, from Store Equipment and $1,300.00 from Accum. Depr.—Store Equip. Record the gain on the sale, $150.00, as a credit to Gain on Plant Assets. Record the cash received from the sale, $850.00, as a debit to Cash.

2 Check the type of disposal, Sold, and write the date, May 1, 20X5, and disposal amount, $850.00, in Section 2 of the plant asset record for the desk.

Selling a Plant Asset for Less Than Book Value

					GENERAL		ACCOUNTS RECEIVABLE CREDIT	SALES CREDIT	SALES TAX PAYABLE CREDIT	SALES DISCOUNT DEBIT	CASH DEBIT
DATE		ACCOUNT TITLE	DOC. NO.	POST. REF.	DEBIT	CREDIT					

CASH RECEIPTS JOURNAL — PAGE 19

	DATE	ACCOUNT TITLE	DOC. NO.	POST. REF.	GENERAL DEBIT	GENERAL CREDIT	ACCOUNTS RECEIVABLE CREDIT	SALES CREDIT	SALES TAX PAYABLE CREDIT	SALES DISCOUNT DEBIT	CASH DEBIT	
1	20X6 Oct. 6	Accum. Depr.—Office Equip.	R645		3 3 0 0 00						2 0 0 00	1
2		Loss on Plant Assets			3 0 0 00							2
3		Office Equipment				3 8 0 0 00						3

1 Record an entry to remove the asset and its accumulated depreciation, record the loss, and record cash.

2 Complete Section 2 of the plant asset record.

Disposed of: Discarded _____ Sold ✓ Traded _____

Date October 6, 20X6 Disposal Amount $200.00

The cost of goods or services used to operate a business is known as an *expense*. Expenses result from the normal operation of the business and appear on the income statement under the heading, Operating Expenses. A decrease in equity resulting from activity other than selling goods or services is called a **loss**. A loss is related to a supplemental activity, such as selling a plant asset. Losses are listed further down on the income statement, usually under the heading, Other Expenses.

Loss on Plant Assets

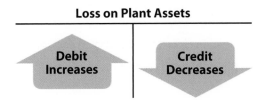

Debit Increases | Credit Decreases

The decrease in equity that results when a plant asset is sold for less than book value is called **loss on plant assets**. Sun Treasures sold a computer after three years of use. After the partial year's depreciation is recorded, a journal entry is made to record the sale of the computer.

October 6, 20X6. Received cash from sale of a computer, $200.00: original cost, $3,800.00; total accumulated depreciation through October 1, 20X6, $3,300.00. Receipt No. 645.

The gain or loss on the sale of a plant asset is the book value subtracted from cash received.

Cash received		$ 200.00
Less book value of asset sold:		
Cost	$3,800.00	
Accumulated depreciation	3,300.00	500.00
Gain (loss) on sale of plant asset		$(300.00)

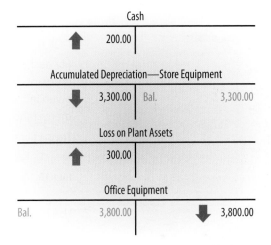

Cash
200.00

Accumulated Depreciation—Store Equipment
3,300.00 | Bal. 3,300.00

Loss on Plant Assets
300.00

Office Equipment
Bal. 3,800.00 | 3,800.00

The loss realized on the disposal of a plant asset is debited to another expense account titled Loss on Plant Assets. A loss from the sale of plant assets is not an operating expense. Therefore, Loss on Plant Assets is listed in a classification titled Other Expenses in the chart of accounts.

❯ Recording Sale of a Plant Asset for Less Than Book Value

1 Record an entry in the cash receipts journal to remove the original cost, $3,800.00, from Office Equipment and $3,300.00 from Accum. Depr.—Office Equip. Record the loss on the sale, $300.00, as a debit to Loss on Plant Assets. Record the cash received from the sale, $200.00, as a debit to Cash.

2 Check the type of disposal, Sold, and write the date, October 6, 20X6, and disposal amount, $200.00, in Section 2 of the plant asset record for the computer.

End of Lesson Review

LO9 Record the sale of a plant asset for book value.

LO10 Record the sale of a plant asset for more/less than book value.

Terms Review

gain

gain on plant assets

loss

loss on plant assets

Audit your understanding

1. What is recorded on plant asset records for plant assets that have been disposed of?

2. When an asset is disposed of after the beginning of the fiscal year, what entry may need to be recorded before an entry is made for the discarding of a plant asset?

3. What is the formula to calculate the gain or loss on the sale of a plant asset?

4. In which account classification is Loss on Plant Assets listed?

Work together 19-4

Recording the disposal of plant assets

Use the plant asset records from Work Together 19-3. Your instructor will guide you through the following examples.

1. For each of the following transactions completed in 20X4, journalize an entry for additional depreciation, if needed. Use page 15 of a general journal given in the *Working Papers*. Source documents are abbreviated as follows: memorandum, M; receipt, R.

   Transactions:

   Jan. 5. Received cash for sale of a display case, plant asset No. 105, $3,000.00. R217.

   Aug. 10. Received cash for sale of a work station, plant asset No. 106, $2,000.00. M61 and R281.

2. Use page 3 of a cash receipts journal to record the disposal of each plant asset.

3. Make appropriate notations in the plant asset records.

On your own 19-4

Recording the disposal of plant assets

Use the plant asset records from On Your Own 19-3. Work this problem independently.

1. For each of the following transactions completed in 20X4, journalize an entry for additional depreciation, if needed. Use page 10 of a general journal given in the *Working Papers*. Source documents are abbreviated as follows: memorandum, M; receipt, R.

   Transactions:

   Jan. 4. Received cash for sale of a stitching machine, plant asset No. 276, $1,300.00. R441.

   23. Received cash for sale of a notebook computer, plant asset No. 277, $850.00. M71 and R450.

2. Use page 2 of a cash receipts journal to record the disposal of each plant asset.

3. Make appropriate notations in the plant asset records.

19-5 Declining-Balance Method of Depreciation

LO11 Calculate depreciation using the double declining-balance method.

Calculating Depreciation Using the Double Declining-Balance Method LO11

Plant Asset: Automobile
Depreciation Method: Double Declining-Balance

Original Cost: $30,000.00
Estimated Salvage Value: $2,500.00
Estimated Useful Life: 5 years

Year	Beginning Book Value	Declining-Balance Rate	Annual Depreciation	Ending Book Value
1	$30,000.00	40%	$12,000.00	$18,000.00
2	18,000.00	40%	7,200.00	10,800.00

④ Transfer the book value to the following year. ① Calculate rate. ② Determine the annual depreciation expense. ③ Determine the ending book value.

The straight-line method charges an equal amount of depreciation expense each year. However, many plant assets depreciate more in the early years of useful life than in later years. For example, a truck's value will decrease more in the first year than in later years. Therefore, charging more depreciation expense in the early years may be more accurate than charging the same amount each year. [CONCEPT: Matching Expenses with Revenue] Any method of depreciation that records greater depreciation expense in the early years and less depreciation expense in the later years is called **accelerated depreciation**. GAAP allows the use of either straight-line or accelerated depreciation.

A common accelerated depreciation method bases its calculations on the book value of the asset, which declines each period. The **declining-balance method of depreciation** is a type of accelerated depreciation that multiplies the book value of an asset by a constant depreciation rate to determine annual depreciation. The declining-balance depreciation rate is some multiple of the straight-line rate. Many businesses use a declining-balance rate that is two times the straight-line rate. A declining-balance rate that is two times the straight-line rate is called the **double declining-balance method of depreciation**.

⭣ Calculating Depreciation Using the Double Declining-Balance Method

① Calculate the double declining-balance rate. An example of a plant asset with a five-year life is shown.

Estimated Depreciation Expense	÷	Years of Estimated Useful Life	=	Straight-Line Rate of Depreciation
100%	÷	5	=	20%

Straight-Line Rate of Depreciation	×	Multiply by Two	=	Double Declining-Balance Rate of Depreciation
20%	×	2	=	40%

② Multiply the double declining-balance rate by the beginning book value to determine the annual depreciation expense for a given year ($30,000.00 × 40% = $12,000.00).

③ Subtract the annual depreciation expense from the beginning book value to determine the ending book value ($30,000.00 − $12,000.00 = $18,000.00).

④ Transfer the ending book value to the beginning book value for the following year. Calculating the depreciation expense in the last year of an asset's life is described on the next page.

Calculating Depreciation Expense in the Final Year

Plant Asset: Automobile
Depreciation Method: Double Declining-Balance

Original Cost: $30,000.00
Estimated Salvage Value: $2,500.00
Estimated Useful Life: 5 years

Year	Beginning Book Value	Declining-Balance Rate	Annual Depreciation	Ending Book Value
1	$30,000.00	40%	$12,000.00	$18,000.00
2	18,000.00	40%	7,200.00	10,800.00
3	10,800.00	40%	4,320.00	6,480.00
4	6,480.00	40%	2,592.00	3,888.00
5	3,888.00	—	1,388.00	2,500.00
Total Depreciation			$27,500.00	

① Transfer the book value.

② Determine the last year's depreciation.

③ Verify the ending book value.

Although the depreciation rate is the same each year, the annual depreciation expense declines from one year to the next. A plant asset is never depreciated below its estimated salvage value. Therefore, in the final year, only enough depreciation expense is recorded to reduce the book value of the plant asset to its salvage value.

Sometimes, the formula for the declining-balance method results in an ending book value that is greater than the estimated salvage value in the final year of a plant asset's useful life. In other words, the depreciation formula does not create enough depreciation to reduce the asset's book value down to its estimated salvage value.

When this situation occurs, the amount of depreciation recorded should be more than the amount calculated using the double declining-balance method. The amount of depreciation in the final year of an asset's life should be the amount needed to make the book value of the asset equal to the estimated salvage value of the asset.

⊘ Calculating the Last Year's Depreciation Expense

❶ Transfer the ending book value from Year 4 to the beginning book value of Year 5.

❷ Subtract the salvage value of the plant asset from the beginning book value to determine the depreciation expense for the final year of useful life ($3,888.00 − $2,500.00 = $1,388.00).

❸ Verify that the ending book value is equal to the salvage value.

Accelerated Depreciation Methods

The double declining-balance method of depreciation is one method of accelerated depreciation. Other methods are also acceptable. All accelerated methods have one thing in common—more depreciation is charged in the first year than in the later years. GAAP allows each business to choose either straight-line or accelerated depreciation for financial reporting. But, once chosen, the business should use the same method from year to year. [CONCEPT: Consistent Reporting]

The U.S. Internal Revenue Service has published rules that must be applied when calculating the amount of depreciation expense that is used to compute a business's federal income tax obligation. Those rules are called the Modified Accelerated Cost Recovery System (MACRS). MACRS is an accelerated depreciation method. If a business chooses a different method of calculating depreciation for financial reporting, it must maintain two sets of financial records, one to support its financial reports and one to substantiate its federal income tax return. Some businesses choose to use MACRS for their financial reporting as well, allowing them to keep just one set of books. For more information about the differences between GAAP and IRS tax rules, see Explore Accounting on page 400.

remember Unlike the straight-line method, the declining-balance method does not use the estimated salvage value to calculate depreciation. The estimated salvage value is used only to limit the last year's depreciation expense.

Comparing Two Methods of Depreciation

Plant Asset:
Depreciation Method: Comparison of Two Methods

Original Cost: $6,000.00
Estimated Salvage Value: $500.00
Estimated Useful Life: 5 years

Year	Straight-Line Method			Double Declining-Balance Method		
	Beginning Book Value	Annual Depreciation	Ending Book Value	Beginning Book Value	Annual Depreciation	Ending Book Value
1	$6,000.00	$1,100.00	$4,900.00	$6,000.00	$2,400.00	$3,600.00
2	4,900.00	1,100.00	3,800.00	3,600.00	1,440.00	2,160.00
3	3,800.00	1,100.00	2,700.00	2,160.00	864.00	1,296.00
4	2,700.00	1,100.00	1,600.00	1,296.00	518.40	777.60
5	1,600.00	1,100.00	500.00	777.60	277.60	500.00
Total Depreciation		$5,500.00			$5,500.00	

Regardless of the depreciation method used, the total depreciation expense over the useful life of a plant asset is the same. The accounts used in the journal entries to record depreciation expense and the sale of plant assets are also the same.

Since both straight-line and accelerated depreciation methods are acceptable under GAAP, the company must decide which method to use. The straight-line method is easy to calculate. The same amount of depreciation expense is recorded for each year of estimated useful life.

An accelerated method is more complicated to use. A different depreciation expense amount must be calculated each year. One advantage of an accelerated method is that it records more depreciation expense in the earlier years. The result is lower income in the early years, which reduces the taxes paid on the income. However, this advantage is only true in the earlier years. In the later years of the asset, less depreciation will be recorded, which will increase net income and the taxes paid on the income.

WHY ACCOUNTING?

Resource Allocation

Every company has a limited amount of resources (human, monetary, and material) to invest. Therefore, when a company invests in a plant asset, it wants to choose the investment that yields the biggest return. Finance is the branch of business that looks at investments and returns. Larger businesses have finance departments that analyze cost and payback information to decide between investment opportunities.

Resource allocation is planning which items or projects should be funded and what level of funding each should receive. *Funding* in this analysis refers to providing resources, whether human, monetary, or material. The plan would rank items or projects recommended for funding. Therefore, if fewer resources are available, items with the lowest rankings would be removed from the list. The plan would also include a ranking of items that are not recommended for funding. If more funds become available, the next highest-ranking item would be funded.

For example, a company may have the following five projects under consideration: buy a new cutting machine, buy an air purifier system, add a second shift of production, retool the factory to be more efficient, or buy robots to perform some tasks. The finance department recommends that the company resources be used to (1) buy an air purifier system and (2) buy a new cutting machine. The projects not recommended for funding are ranked as follows: (3) remodel the factory, (4) add a second shift of production, and (5) buy robots. If more resources become available, they should be used to remodel the factory. If fewer resources become available, the new cutting machine would not be funded.

CRITICAL THINKING

As a class, using the five projects listed above, brainstorm a list of factors that the resource allocation team may consider when choosing which projects to recommend for funding.

LO11 Calculate depreciation using the double declining-balance method.

Terms Review

acelerated depreciation

declining-balance method of depreciation

double declining-balance method of depreciation

Audit your understanding

1. When calculating depreciation expense using the declining-balance method, what number stays constant each fiscal period?

2. What is the declining-balance method that uses twice the straight-line rate?

3. What change occurs in the annual depreciation expense calculated using the declining-balance method?

4. An asset is never depreciated below what amount?

Work together 19-5

Calculating depreciation using the double declining-balance depreciation method

Forms are given in the *Working Papers*. Your instructor will guide you through the following example.

Calculate beginning book value, annual depreciation, and ending book value for each of the following plant assets bought during the current year. Use the double declining-balance depreciation method. Round amounts to the nearest cent.

Date	Description	Original Cost	Estimated Salvage Value	Estimated Useful Life
Jan. 4	Painting Machine	$27,000.00	$1,000.00	4 years
Jan. 6	Office Computer	2,200.00	200.00	5 years
Jan. 7	Sander	800.00	80.00	8 years

On your own 19-5

Calculating depreciation using the double declining-balance depreciation method

Forms are given in the *Working Papers*. Work this problem independently.

Calculate beginning book value, annual depreciation, and ending book value for each of the following plant assets bought during the current year. Use the double declining-balance depreciation method. Round amounts to the nearest cent.

Date	Description	Original Cost	Estimated Salvage Value	Estimated Useful Life
Jan. 2	Skate Rack	$ 3,000.00	$ 200.00	5 years
Jan. 4	Delivery Truck	75,000.00	8,000.00	8 years
Jan. 6	Office Shredder	600.00	50.00	4 years

©CANDICE CUSACK, ISTOCK

19-6 Buying Intangible Assets and Calculating Amortization Expense

LO12 Record the buying of an intangible asset.
LO13 Calculate and record amortization expense.

Recording the Buying of an Intangible Asset LO12

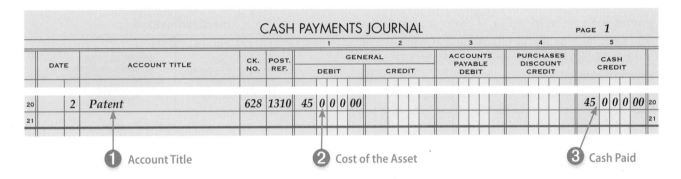

CASH PAYMENTS JOURNAL									PAGE 1	

① Account Title **② Cost of the Asset** **③ Cash Paid**

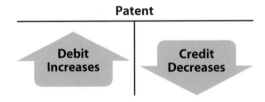

Patent

Debit Increases	Credit Decreases

An asset that does not have physical substance is called an **intangible asset**. Intangible assets include patents, copyrights, trademarks, and other similar items. The value of an intangible asset such as a patent comes from the rights it gives to the patent holder, not from the piece of paper that ensures those rights.

Some intangible assets have an easily determined legal life. For example, most patents are granted for 20 years. During those 20 years, no other company or individual can copy that product. However, after the patent expires, any individual or company can reproduce and sell that product.

Recording the buying of an intangible asset is very similar to buying any other asset. Sharp Company wishes to buy a patent from another company. The patent's legal remaining life is 14 years. However, Sharp

Company feels that the patent will only be useful for ten years. After that time, other new technology will exist that will reduce the patent's value to zero.

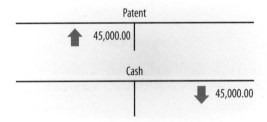

Patent	
↑ 45,000.00	

Cash	
	↓ 45,000.00

> January 2, 20X1. Paid cash for a patent, $45,000.00. Check No. 628.

⤵ Journalizing the Buying of a Plant Asset

❶ Write the intangible asset account, Patent, in the Account Title column of the cash payments journal.

❷ Enter the cost of the patent, $45,000.00, in the General Debit column.

❸ Enter the same amount, $45,000.00, in the Cash Credit column.

Calculating and Recording Amortization Expense LO13

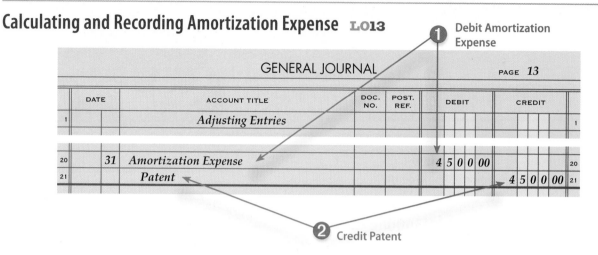

1 Debit Amortization Expense

2 Credit Patent

Amortization is the spreading of the cost of an intangible asset over its useful life. Amortization is similar to depreciation, which applies only to physical assets. Some intangible assets have a legal life, such as a patent. If an intangible asset has a useful or legal life that can be determined, the asset should be amortized. Amortization is based on an estimate of the useful, or legal, life of the intangible asset, whichever is less. Unlike the depreciation of a physical asset, there is no estimated salvage value of an intangible asset. Amortization is recorded as an adjusting entry each fiscal period until the value is zero.

The patent bought by Sharp Company will expire in 14 years. Therefore, the patent's legal life is 14 years.

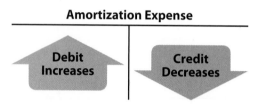

Amortization Expense

Debit Increases | **Credit** Decreases

However, Sharp Company feels that new technology will mean that its patent will only have a useful life of ten years. Sharp Company must amortize the patent over no more than ten years. Amortization Expense will be debited for $4,500.00 to record one year of amortization. The asset account, Patent, is credited for $4,500.00.

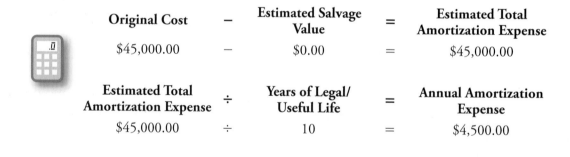

Original Cost	−	Estimated Salvage Value	=	Estimated Total Amortization Expense
$45,000.00	−	$0.00	=	$45,000.00

Estimated Total Amortization Expense	÷	Years of Legal/ Useful Life	=	Annual Amortization Expense
$45,000.00	÷	10	=	$4,500.00

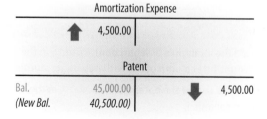

The balance in the **Patent** account represents the cost of the patent that has not yet been amortized.

Intangible assets appear on the balance sheet, usually as the last category of assets. The Amortization Expense account will appear on the income statement, as an operating expense.

⤵ Recording Amortization Expense

1 Debit Amortization Expense for the amount of amortization expense, **$4,500.00**.

2 Credit Patent for the same amount, **$4,500.00**.

End of Lesson Review

LO12 Record the buying of an intangible asset.

LO13 Calculate and record amortization expense.

Terms Review

intangible asset

amortization

Audit your understanding

1. Which account is debited when recording amortization on a patent?
2. Which account is credited when recording amortization on a patent?

Work together 19-6

Journalizing buying intangible assets and calculating amortization expense

The cash payments journal for River Falls Publishing is given in the *Working Papers*. Your instructor will guide you through the following examples.

1. Journalize the following transactions completed during the current year. Use page 1 of a cash payments journal. The abbreviation for a check is C.

   Transactions:

   Jan. 4. Paid cash for a patent, $18,000.00. C532.

   6. Paid cash for a trademark, $30,000.00. C538.

2. Use the following data to record amortization expense for December 31, 20X1. Use page 1 of a general journal.

Asset	Estimated Useful Life	Estimated Legal Life	Estimated Salvage Value
Patent	9 years	12 years	$0.00
Trademark	14 years	10 years	$0.00

On your own 19-6

Journalizing buying intangible assets and calculating amortization expense

The cash payments journal for High Tech, Inc., is given in the *Working Papers*. Work this problem independently.

1. Journalize the following transactions completed during the current year. Use page 1 of a cash payments journal. The abbreviation for a check is C.

   Transactions:

   Jan. 4. Paid cash for a trademark, $35,000.00. C112.

   6. Paid cash for a patent, $98,000.00. C115.

2. Use the following data to record amortization expense for December 31, 20X1. Use page 1 of a general journal.

Asset	Estimated Useful Life	Estimated Legal Life	Estimated Salvage Value
Trademark	8 years	10 years	$0.00
Patent	9 years	7 years	$0.00

A Look at Accounting Software
Accounting for Plant Assets

Plant (fixed) asset management, which includes calculation of depreciation, is an important part of the accounting responsibility in a corporation. That is especially true for companies with big investments in furniture, fixtures, and equipment. To facilitate plant asset management, specialized programs (usually called *fixed asset management* software) are available. Some *off-the-shelf* accounting software programs include plant asset management utilities. Built-in utilities, however, usually have limited capability. Large corporations generally choose software uniquely designed for plant asset management.

Sun Treasures, Inc., as described in this chapter, uses a manual accounting system and manages its plant assets using plant asset record forms. The company uses straight-line depreciation. In reality, even a company the size of Sun Treasures would certainly use a computerized accounting system, including some type of plant asset utility. It's likely that accelerated depreciation would be

Reports

New   Open   Save   Undo   Redo   Delete   Print   Export   Help

Select Report [Plant Assets ▼] ❶   Modify   New   Sort by [Item ▼] ❷

❸ ◉ All   ○ Active   ○ Inactive   [Add New Item]❺   Date [Apr. 10, 20X2]

Item	Activate or Inactivate	Location	In-service Date	Acct. No.	Cost	Accum. Depr.	Book Value	Disposal Date	Disposal Value	Memo
Display case - 1	A	Daytona Beach	12/20/20X0	1215	550.00	166.84	383.16			
Display case - 2	I	Daytona Beach	12/20/20X0	1215	598.00	160.83	0.00	12/20/20X2	0.00	Damaged
File cabinet - 11	A	Daytona Beach	10/14/20X1	1205	629.98	84.81	545.17			
Multifunction copier - 1	A	Daytona Beach	1/30/20X1	1205	3,199.99	1,209.21	1,990.78			
Network server - 1	A	Daytona Beach	12/19/20X0	1205	1,468.00	141.96	1,326.04			
Office chair - 10	A	Daytona Beach	1/10/20X1	1205	289.59	87.85	201.74			
Office chair - 11	A	Daytona Beach	10/14/20X1	1205	289.59	38.98	250.61			
Office chair - 12	A	Daytona Beach	3/8/20X2	1205	395.00	9.40	385.60			
Office color printer - 1	A	Daytona Beach	7/12/20X1	1205	349.49	91.90	257.59			
Office computer - 12	A	Daytona Beach	9/3/20X1	1205	3,000.00	989.26	2,010.74			
Office desk -10	A	Daytona Beach	1/10/20X1	1205	979.00	296.97	682.03			
Office desk -11	A	Daytona Beach	10/3/20X1	1205	979.00	131.79	847.21			
Office desk -12	A	Daytona Beach	3/1/20X2	1205	1,549.50	36.89	1,512.61			
Office laser printer - 1	A	Daytona Beach	1/5/20X1	1205	225.87	90.04	135.83			
Self unit - 1	A	Daytona Beach	12/20/20X0	1215	3,084.00	935.51	2,148.49			
Self unit - 2	A	Daytona Beach	12/20/20X0	1215	3,322.00	1,007.71	2,314.29			
Self unit - 3	A	Daytona Beach	1/2/20X1	1215	8,500.00	4,010.81	4,489.19			
Store desk - 1	A	Daytona Beach	1/10/20X1	1215	2,000.00	689.27	1,310.73			

[ ] Entered by user   [ ] Entered automatically

❶ To view the current list of plant assets, the user selects Plant Assets from the drop-down list in the Reports window.

❷ The user chooses the way the list is sorted by making a selection from the Sort by drop-down list.

❸ If the user wishes to see all the plant assets the company has ever owned, the All button would be clicked. Clicking on Active omits plant assets no longer owned or in use. Clicking Inactive lists only inactive items.

❹ To edit an item, the user double-clicks on the item name. Here, Office color printer - 1 has been selected for editing.

❺ If the user wants to add a new item, he or she would click on Add New Item on the Reports window or on New in the Add/Edit Plant Asset pop-up window. In either case, a blank pop-up window like the one shown here would allow the user to set up the new item.

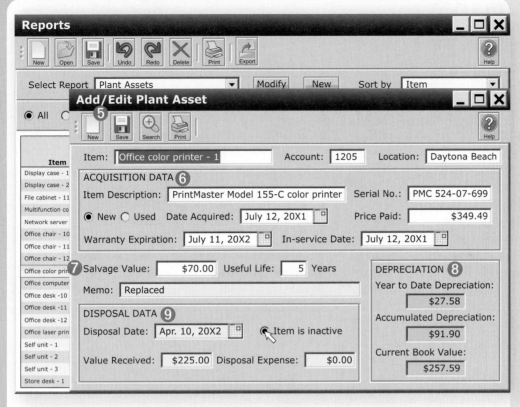

Entered by user   Entered automatically

⑥ After naming the new item, assigning the general ledger account number, and entering its location, the user would enter the acquisition data. All dates are entered by clicking the calendar button and selecting the appropriate date. Some information, such as the price paid and in-service date, are used by the system to calculate depreciation. Other data, such as the serial number and warranty expiration, are helpful in managing the use of the item.

⑦ The user would enter estimates of the salvage value and useful life. The Memo field is used to note any information about the purchase, use, or disposal of the item that may be helpful at a later date. Clicking Save would add the new item to the list of plant assets.

⑧ The Depreciation section displays three system-calculated fields. It is for information only. No user entry is enabled.

⑨ The user has opened this window to record the disposal of the office color printer. After entering the disposal date, value received, and the disposal expense ($0.00 in this example), the user has keyed "Replaced" in the Memo field to note the reason for the item's disposal. Finally, the user clicks the button to set the item to inactive and then clicks Save to record the changes.

used as well because it allows businesses to reduce taxable income in the short term.

If Sun Treasures used a computerized accounting system, its plant asset list, when selected in the Reports window, might appear as it does here. The accountant has double-clicked on Office color printer - 1 to select it for editing. Much of the information in the Add/Edit Plant Asset pop-up window is the same as would be found on a plant asset record. Notice that this window does not show the method of depreciation nor the depreciation schedule.

To set, change, or view depreciation data, the user would go to the System Manager and open the Manage Depreciation window. For this example, double declining-balance is the default depreciation method applied to all new plant assets. To change an asset from double declining-balance to straight-line, the user would access the Manage Depreciation window and select the asset to be changed. The user could also view and print a depreciation schedule from the Manage Depreciation window.

Chapter Summary

Plant assets are assets that will be used in the operation of a business for a number of years. Plant assets are recorded at cost. The cost of a plant asset must be spread out over its useful life. This is recorded each year as depreciation expense. If a group of assets is bought for one price, the cost of each asset must be allocated so that each asset can be depreciated separately. When recording depreciation for a plant asset, the plant asset account is not credited. A separate accumulated depreciation account is used to record the total depreciation for that plant asset.

Plant assets are depreciated using one of a variety of methods. Straight-line depreciation spreads the cost of the asset equally over its useful life. Accelerated methods, such as the declining-balance method, charge more depreciation expense in the early years of the asset's life, with the amount of depreciation decreasing each year. Over the life of the asset, both methods record the same total amount of depreciation expense. During the life of the plant asset,

its book value can be calculated by subtracting accumulated depreciation from the cost of the asset.

When a company sells a plant asset, it must determine if a gain or loss was incurred on the sale. The cash received for the asset is subtracted from the book value of the asset. If the cash received is more than the book value, the asset is sold for a gain. If the cash received is less than the book value, the asset is sold for a loss. The gain or loss is recorded at the time of the sale and is reported on the income statement under the heading, Other Revenues or Other Expenses.

Intangible assets are assets that have no physical substance, such as a patent. Intangible assets are amortized over the lesser of their legal or useful life. There is no estimated salvage value of an intangible asset and no accumulated amortization account. When an intangible asset is amortized, the asset's account is credited. Amortization expense decreases net income.

EXPLORE ACCOUNTING

Natural Resource Assets

Assets can be categorized into several subdivisions: current assets, plant assets, and intangible assets. An additional category of assets is natural resources. Natural resources include assets such as gold mines, timber forests, and oil wells.

When a natural resource is purchased, it is recorded at its historical cost plus any related expenses needed to make the natural resource useable. Assume that Coal Company bought a coal mine for $4,000,000. In addition, Coal Company estimates that it will spend $200,000 getting the land ready for mining to begin. The asset Coal Mine would be debited for the total, $4,200,000, as follows:

Coal Mine   4,200,000
    Cash   4,200,000

Natural resource assets are not depreciated or amortized. As coal is mined, a depletion expense will be recorded. Coal Company estimates that it will be able to mine 2,000,000 tons of coal from the mine and sell the land for $400,000 once all mining

is finished. A depletion rate is calculated as follows:

Depletion Rate = (Cost of Asset – Salvage Value) ÷ Estimated Units to Be Mined

Depletion Rate = ($4,200,000 – $400,000) ÷ 2,000,000

Depletion Rate = $3,800,000 ÷ 2,000,000

Depletion Rate = $1.90 per ton

Coal Company mines 450,000 tons of coal in 20X1. The annual depletion expense would be calculated as:

Annual Depletion Expense = Depletion Rate × Tons Mined

Annual Depletion Expense = $1.90 × 450,000

Annual Depletion Expense = $855,000

The expense would be recorded as follows:

Depletion Expense   855,000
    Coal Mine   855,000

As with amortization, an accumulated depletion account is not used.

Rather, the asset account is decreased. The depletion expense will appear on the income statement under the heading Operating Expenses. The asset account, Coal Mine, is decreased by the entry and will appear on the balance sheet under the heading Natural Resources.

INSTRUCTIONS

1. List five types of natural resource assets. For each asset, suggest which unit of measure would be used to measure the depletion of the natural resource.

2. On January 2, 20X1, Big Coal Company bought a coal mine for $5,500,000. Big Coal expects to mine 2,750,000 tons of coal from the mine. By December 31, 20X1, Big Coal has extracted 356,000 tons of coal.

   Using T accounts, record the effect of the purchase of the mine and any depletion expense Big Coal Company should record for the year.

Apply Your Understanding

INSTRUCTIONS: Download problem instructions for Excel, QuickBooks, and Peachtree from the textbook companion website at www.C21accounting.com.

19-1 Application Problem: Journalizing buying plant assets and paying property tax LO1, 2, 3

The cash payments journal for White Cleaners is given in the *Working Papers*.

Instructions:

Journalize the following transactions completed during the current year. Use page 1 of a cash payments journal. The abbreviation for a check is C.

Transactions:

Jan.   4.   Paid cash for office computer, $600.00. C226.
       5.   Paid cash for a pressing machine, $4,200.00. C230.
Feb. 24.   Paid property taxes on real property with an assessed value of $360,000.00. The tax rate in the city where the property is located is 1.2% of assessed value. C278.
May 12.   Paid cash for office desk (office equipment) and display rack (store equipment), $3,800.00. The office desk has an estimated value of $1,000.00, and the display rack has an estimated value of $3,000.00. C354.

19-2 Application Problem: Calculating straight-line depreciation LO4, 5, 6

AAONLINE

1. Go to www.cengage.com/login
2. Click on **AA Online** to access.
3. Go to the online assignment and follow the instructions.

1. Create and key formulas using the straight-line method to complete the depreciation table.
2. Print the worksheet.

Forms are given in the *Working Papers*.

Instructions:

Quick Mart bought the following assets during 20X1. Quick Mart uses the straight-line depreciation method. Calculate beginning book value, annual depreciation, accumulated depreciation, and ending book value for each asset for each year of estimated useful life. If the asset was not bought at the beginning of 20X1, calculate the depreciation expense for the part of 20X1 in which the company owned the asset. Save your work to complete Problem 19-3.1.

Transactions:

Jan.   4.   Bought a freezer costing $15,000.00; estimated salvage value, $600.00; estimated useful life, 6 years; plant asset No. 561; serial number, 674-653B.
Mar. 30.   Bought a conference table (office equipment), $3,000.00; estimated salvage value, $250.00; estimated useful life, 5 years; plant asset No. 562; serial number, FX27J482.
Aug.   2.   Bought a microwave oven (store equipment), $2,200.00; estimated salvage value, $100.00; estimated useful life, 5 years; plant asset no. 563; serial number, 7-ST1-003.

19-3.1 Application Problem: Preparing plant asset records LO7

Instructions:

Quick Mart records plant assets in two accounts: Office Equipment, Account No. 1210, and Store Equipment, Account No. 1220. Using the transaction data and depreciation calculations from Problem 19-2, prepare a plant asset record for each plant asset. Plant asset records are given in the *Working Papers*. Record the depreciation and book values for 20X1–20X4. Save the plant asset records for use in Problem 19-4.

19-3.2 Application Problem: Journalizing annual depreciation expense LO8

Instructions:

On December 31, 20X4, Pierce, Inc., determined that total depreciation expense for office equipment for the year was $19,358.00 and total depreciation expense for store equipment was $38,954.00. Record the adjusting entries on page 23 of a general journal given in the *Working Papers*.

19-4 Application Problem: Recording the disposal of plant assets LO9, 10

During 20X5, Quick Mart had the following transactions involving the sale of plant assets. Use the plant asset records completed in Problem 19-3.1. Journals are given in the *Working Papers*.

Instructions:

1. For each plant asset disposed of in 20X5, journalize an entry for additional depreciation, if needed. Use page 3 of a general journal. Source documents are abbreviated as follows: check, C; memorandum, M; receipt, R.

2. Use page 3 of a cash receipts journal to record the disposal of each plant asset.

3. Make appropriate notations in the plant asset records.

Transactions:

Jan.   6.   Received cash for sale of a conference table, plant asset No. 562, $1,200.00. R375.
Mar. 29.   Received cash for sale of a microwave oven, plant asset No. 563, $660.00. M35 and R398.
July   8.   Received cash for sale of a freezer, plant asset No. 561, $3,000.00. M78 and R421.

19-5 Application Problem: Calculating depreciation using the double declining-balance depreciation method LO11

Peachtree

1. Journalize and post depreciation related to the disposal of plant assets to the general journal.
2. Journalize and post cash received for the disposal of assets to the cash receipts journal.
3. Print the cash receipts journal, general journal, and trial balance.

Quick Books

1. Journalize and post transactions related to the disposal of plant assets to the journal.
2. Print the journal and trial balance.

Instructions:

Forms are given in the *Working Papers*. Calculate beginning book value, annual depreciation, and ending book value for each of the following plant assets bought during 20X1. Use the double declining-balance depreciation method. Round amounts to the nearest cent.

Date	Description	Original Cost	Estimated Salvage Value	Estimated Useful Life
Jan. 3	Forklift	$20,000.00	$2,500.00	8 years
Jan. 5	Cutting Machine	$40,000.00	$3,000.00	4 years
Jan. 8	Scale	$16,000.00	$1,000.00	5 years

19-6 Application Problem: Accounting for intangible assets LO12, 13

The cash payments journal for Tobie Industries is given in the *Working Papers*.

Instructions:

1. Journalize the following transactions completed during the current year. Use page 1 of a cash payments journal. The abbreviation for a check is C.

Transactions:

Jan.   5.   Paid cash for a patent, $700,000. C315.
         6.   Paid cash for a trademark, $85,000. C320.

2. Use the following data to record amortization expense for December 31, 20X1. Use page 1 of a general journal.

Asset	Estimated Useful Life	Estimated Legal Life	Estimated Salvage Value
Patent	10 years	13 years	$0.00
Trademark	10 years	5 years	$0.00

Hillside Resort records plant assets in two accounts: Furniture, Account No. 1205, and Equipment, Account No. 1215. Furniture is depreciated using the double declining-balance method. Equipment is depreciated using the straight-line method. Forms are given in the *Working Papers*.

Instructions:

1. Record the following transactions completed during 20X1 on page 1 of a cash payments journal.

Transactions:

Jan.   5.   Bought an X-ray machine and a supply cabinet: cost, $30,000.00. C521. X-ray machine: estimated value, $22,000.00; estimated salvage value, $0.00; estimated useful life, 5 years; plant asset No. 715; serial number, ZYX487-6. Supply cabinet: estimated value, $11,000.00; estimated salvage value, $800.00; estimated useful life, 5 years; plant asset No. 716; serial number, 74-3554-L8.

Feb.   26.   Paid property taxes on plant assets assessed at $600,000.00. The tax rate is 1.1%. C560.

Apr.   5.   Bought a testing machine for the exam room: cost, $6,500.00; estimated salvage value, $500.00; estimated useful life, 6 years; plant asset No. 717; serial number, 7-H256. C602.

2. Complete Section 1 of a plant asset record for each new plant asset.

3. Use the forms provided in the *Working Papers* to calculate beginning book value, annual depreciation, accumulated depreciation, and ending book value for the life of each new plant asset.

4. Complete Section 3 of the plant asset records for 20X1–20X4.

5. Record the following transactions completed during 20X5. Use page 2 of a cash receipts journal and page 1 of a general journal.

Transactions:

Jan.   6.   Received cash for sale of a supply cabinet, plant asset No. 716, $1,500.00. R321.

July   2.   Received cash for sale of an X-ray machine, plant asset No. 715, $1,700.00. M112 and R382.

Dec.   31.   Recorded the adjusting entry for depreciation. Total 20X5 depreciation expense of furniture was $29,500.00. Total 20X5 depreciation expense of equipment was $65,750.00.

6. Complete the plant asset records for each plant asset sold during 20X5.

7. Complete Section 3 of the plant asset record for the testing machine for 20X5.

AAONLiNE	Peachtree	QB Quick Books
1. Go to www.cengage.com/login 2. Click on **AA Online** to access. 3. Go to the online assignment and follow the instructions.	1. Journalize and post transactions related to plant assets to the cash disbursements journal. 2. Journalize and post transactions related to plant assets to the cash receipts journal and general journal. 3. Print the cash disbursements journal, cash receipts journal, general journal, and trial balance.	1. Journalize and post transactions related to plant assets in the Write Checks window. 2. Journalize and post transactions related to plant assets to the journal. 3. Print the check detail, journal, and trial balance.

19-C Challenge Problem: Calculating a partial year's depreciation using the double declining-balance method LO4, 5, 6, 11

Quick Repair, Inc., uses the double declining-balance depreciation method for its equipment. Because many items are bought during the year, Quick Repair must calculate a partial year's depreciation in the first year. Quick Repair uses the same method to calculate a partial year's depreciation as was described for Sun Treasures on page 591. The annual depreciation expense is calculated then divided by 12 to get the monthly depreciation. The monthly depreciation is then multiplied by the number of months the plant asset was owned during the year. For subsequent years, the annual depreciation is calculated using the normal method—book value multiplied by the depreciation rate.

Instructions:

Forms are given in the *Working Papers*. Calculate beginning book value, annual depreciation, accumulated depreciation, and ending book value for the following assets bought in 20X1. Round to the nearest cent.

Transactions:

Apr. 2. Bought an extension ladder, $3,000.00; estimated salvage value, $200.00; estimated useful life, 5 years.
July 24. Bought a power sprayer, $4,800.00; estimated salvage value, $250.00; estimated useful life, 4 years.

1. Create and key formulas using the double declining-balance method to complete the depreciation tables.
2. Print the worksheet.

21st Century Skills

Green Advantage

Theme: Financial, Economic, Business, and Entrepreneurial Literacy

Skills: Creativity and Innovation, Critical Thinking and Problem Solving, Communication and Collaboration, ICT Literacy

PARTNERSHIP FOR
21ST CENTURY SKILLS

It is often said, "If something is worth copying, it is worth protecting." This philosophy is what drives a company or individual to protect an invention by having it patented. In the United States, a patent is an exclusive right issued by the U.S. Patent and Trademark Office (USPTO) that legally excludes others from making, using, or selling an invention or a new process within the United States.

By some estimates, 45% to 75% of the wealth of market-leading companies like Procter & Gamble and Sony is made up of intangible assets such as patents and trademarks. These companies are acutely aware of the role patents and trademarks play in maintaining a competitive edge and maximizing revenues.

The patent process can be complex, taking an average of 40 months for review and approval by the USPTO. In December 2009, the U.S. government expedited the application process to an average of 49 days for patents involving "green" technology, reducing the review and approval time by about a year. In addition to promoting U.S. competitiveness and creating "green" jobs, the goal was to also encourage innovations that benefit the environment.

Many companies recognize the advantages of using green technology. To them, conserving energy to protect the environment is just as motivating as saving money. Bank of America (BOA) is one example of an eco-friendly business. Its internal paper recycling program saves approximately 200,000 trees each year. BOA was also able to reduce paper use by 32% while generating a 24% increase in customers.

We all can do some simple things to reduce energy consumption. The World Watch Institute, a global environmental organization, is just one resource for information on the environment. Its purpose is to educate and inform individuals on how to create an environmentally sustainable society.

APPLICATION

1. Go to www.worldwatch.org or an eco-friendly website of your choice and create a list of ten ways that an individual or a company can "Go Green and Save Green." Inform others by displaying posters in your classroom or throughout the school.

2. Using the above list, create a "Top Ten Tweets" to inform others on how they can help the environment.

Sources: www.uspto.gov/news/pr/2009/09_33.jsp, www.wipo.int/sme/en/documents/valuing_patents.htm, and www.businesspundit.com/25-big-companies-that-are-going-green/.

Clausen, Inc., recently bought two new plant assets. David Hetland, accounting clerk, has prepared the following depreciation schedule for the assets.

Plant Asset: Refrigerator Case
Depreciation Method: Straight-line

Original Cost: $12,000.00
Estimated Salvage Value: $2,000.00
Estimated Useful Life: 5 years

Year	Beginning Book Value	Annual Depreciation	Accumulated Depreciation	Ending Book Value
20X1	$12,000.00	$2,400.00	$ 2,400.00	$9,600.00
20X2	9,600.00	2,400.00	4,800.00	7,200.00
20X3	7,200.00	2,400.00	7,200.00	4,800.00
20X4	4,800.00	2,400.00	9,600.00	2,400.00
20X5	2,400.00	2,400.00	12,000.00	0.00

Plant Asset: Freezer
Depreciation Method: Declining-balance

Original Cost: $16,000.00
Estimated Salvage Value: $2,000.00
Estimated Useful Life: 5 years

Year	Beginning Book Value	Annual Depreciation	Accumulated Depreciation	Ending Book Value
20X1	$16,000.00	$5,600.00	$ 5,600.00	$10,400.00
20X2	10,400.00	4,160.00	9,760.00	6,240.00
20X3	16,240.00	2,496.00	12,256.00	3,744.00
20X4	3,744.00	1,497.60	13,753.60	2,246.40
20X5	2,246.40	898.56	14,652.16	1,347.84

REVIEW AND ANSWER

Determine the accuracy of each depreciation schedule. Identify any corrections that David should make.

Analyzing Nike's financial statements

Merchandising businesses often rent buildings from companies that specialize in building management. Any modifications made to the building become the property of the building owner at the end of the lease. These fixed assets are known as *leasehold improvements*.

INSTRUCTIONS

1. Review Nike's annual report in Appendix B. Referring to Note 3 on page B-12, what was the amount of leasehold improvements for 2011 and 2010?

2. Referring to Note 1 on page B-10, what method of depreciation does Nike use to depreciate property, plant and equipment?

3. What range of years does Nike use for the estimated useful life of leasehold improvements?

Chapter 20

Accounting for Inventory

LEARNING OBJECTIVES

After studying Chapter 20, in addition to defining key terms, you will be able to:

LO1 Prepare a stock record.

LO2 Calculate the cost of merchandise inventory using the first-in, first-out (FIFO) inventory costing method.

LO3 Calculate the cost of merchandise inventory using the last-in, first-out (LIFO) inventory costing method.

LO4 Calculate the cost of merchandise inventory using the weighted-average inventory costing method.

LO5 Estimate the cost of merchandise inventory using the gross profit method of estimating inventory.

Accounting In The Real World
OfficeMax

For any retail company, inventory makes up a large percentage of its current assets. The larger the store, the more inventory it has on hand. Think of a typical OfficeMax store. It offers hundreds of different products. Each product must be sufficiently stocked so that it is available when the customer wants it. The OfficeMax mission is: We help our customers do their best work. In order to fulfill this mission, OfficeMax must maintain up-to-date inventory that is wanted by its customers.

However, too much inventory is not desirable. Excess inventory takes space, either on the shelves or in a warehouse. Excess inventory uses capital that could be used for other revenue-generating projects. Inventory that takes a long time to sell could become obsolete.

OfficeMax recently won an award for its inventory management. Its website states that "OfficeMax has used greater forecast accuracy to reduce inventory while improving customer service levels." The annual reports for OfficeMax support the claim of reduction in inventory level. In 2005, inventory was over $1.1 billion. In 2010, inventory had dropped to $846 million. Not only did actual levels of inventory decrease, but inventory as a percentage of total current assets also decreased. In 2005, inventory was 57% of total current assets. By 2010, inventory was only 42% of total current assets.

CRITICAL THINKING

1. The companies from which OfficeMax purchases its inventory are called vendors. These vendors may offer OfficeMax a high volume purchase rebate program. This means that the more OfficeMax buys of that product, the lower the cost will be per unit. What action would this encourage on the part of OfficeMax?

2. If OfficeMax takes advantage of these high volume purchase rebate programs and purchases some items in high volume, what is the risk for OfficeMax?

Source: officemax.com.

Key Terms

- inventory record
- stock record
- stock ledger
- first-in, first-out inventory costing method (FIFO)

- last-in, first-out inventory costing method (LIFO)
- weighted-average inventory costing method

- market value
- lower of cost or market inventory costing method (LCM)

- gross profit method of estimating inventory

20-1 Determining the Quantity of Merchandise Inventory

LO1 Prepare a stock record.

Why Merchandise Inventory Is Important

Merchandise inventory on hand is typically the largest asset of a merchandising business. Successful businesses must have merchandise available for sale that customers want. A business therefore needs controls that help managers to maintain a merchandise inventory of sufficient quantity, variety, and price.

The cost of merchandise inventory is reported on both the balance sheet and the income statement. An accurate cost of merchandise inventory is required to correctly report current assets and retained earnings on the balance sheet. The accuracy of the inventory cost will also ensure that gross profit and net income are reported correctly on the income statement. [CONCEPT: Adequate Disclosure]

Hotlines

The accounting scandals of the early 21st century led the U.S. Congress to pass legislation designed to protect investors by improving the accuracy and reliability of financial reporting. The bill, known as the Sarbanes-Oxley Act of 2002 (SOX), contains a section that requires management to make a written statement about the effectiveness of its internal control system.

In an effective internal control system, employees and other stakeholders must be able to communicate possible ethics violations. A phone number called a *hotline* may be provided to allow an individual to provide confidential information about possible ethics violations. An effective ethics hotline must ensure an individual that:

1. Management takes hotline calls seriously.
2. The information provided will be maintained on an anonymous or confidential basis.
3. No retaliation or harassment will be tolerated.

INSTRUCTIONS

HealthSouth's compliance hotline is available to HealthSouth employees to report possible violations of its *Standards of Business Conduct*. Describe how the compliance hotline is designed to meet the three criteria presented above. You may also do a Google search for HealthSouth's *Standards of Business Conduct*.

©LUCA DI FILIPPO, ISTOCK

The Most Efficient Quantity of Inventory

To determine the most efficient quantity of inventory, a business makes frequent analysis of purchases, sales, and inventory records. Many businesses fail because too much or too little merchandise inventory is kept on hand. A business that stocks merchandise that does not satisfy the demand of its customers is also likely to fail.

A merchandise inventory that is larger than needed may decrease the net income of a business for several reasons.

1. Excess inventory requires a business to spend money for expensive store and warehouse space.
2. Excess inventory uses capital that could be invested in other assets to earn a profit for the business.
3. Excess inventory requires a business to spend money for expenses, such as taxes and insurance premiums, which increase with the cost of the merchandise inventory.
4. Excess inventory may become obsolete and unsalable.

Merchandise inventory that is smaller than needed may also decrease the net income of a business for several reasons.

1. Sales may be lost to competitors if items wanted by customers are not on hand.
2. Sales may be lost to competitors if there is an insufficient variety of merchandise to satisfy customers.
3. When a business frequently orders small quantities of an item, the price paid is often more per unit than when merchandise is ordered in large quantities.

Methods Used to Determine the Quantity of Merchandise Inventory

To control their inventory, businesses may take a physical count monthly, quarterly, semiannually, or annually. Usually, the volume of items on hand and the volume of sales determines how frequently a physical inventory is taken. However, the quantity of items in inventory at the end of a fiscal year must be determined in order to calculate the cost of merchandise sold.

As described in Chapter 9, two principal methods are used to determine the quantity of each item of merchandise on hand.

1. A merchandise inventory evaluated at the end of a fiscal period is known as a *periodic inventory*.
2. A merchandise inventory determined by keeping a continuous record of increases, decreases, and the balance on hand of each item of merchandise is known as a *perpetual inventory*. A perpetual inventory is also referred to as a *book inventory*.

Because controlling the quantity of merchandise inventory is so important to a business's success, many methods of keeping inventory records are used. Today, most companies use computers to keep track of the inventory on hand.

Keeping track of merchandise inventory also involves knowing the ideal quantity for each kind of merchandise in inventory. To ensure having the appropriate quantity, companies frequently establish an ideal minimum quantity and an ideal reorder quantity. When the minimum quantity is reached, new merchandise is ordered.

Minimum quantity levels must be established with consideration for how long it may take to receive new inventory. Otherwise, merchandise may not be available when a customer wants to buy it. Those who order new merchandise must also be aware of the ideal quantities to order to get the best prices and trade discounts.

A business usually determines the order in which products are sold, based on the type of inventory. A grocery store, for example, must sell its earliest purchases first. A hardware store, on the other hand, could sell its most recent purchases first. The inventory costing method used to calculate the cost of merchandise sold should not be determined by the order in which items are sold. A business should choose the inventory costing method that provides its managers with the best accounting information.

©EASTWEST IMAGING/FOTOLIA.COM

Inventory Record

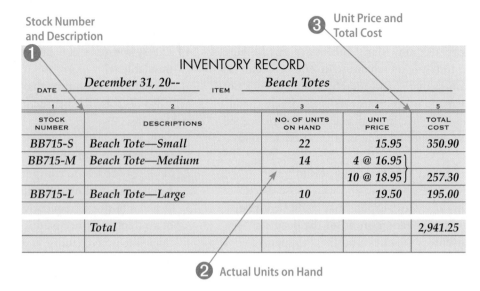

Stock Number and Description **①**

③ Unit Price and Total Cost

INVENTORY RECORD

DATE — December 31, 20--   ITEM — Beach Totes

1 STOCK NUMBER	2 DESCRIPTIONS	3 NO. OF UNITS ON HAND	4 UNIT PRICE	5 TOTAL COST
BB715-S	Beach Tote—Small	22	15.95	350.90
BB715-M	Beach Tote—Medium	14	4 @ 16.95	
			10 @ 18.95	257.30
BB715-L	Beach Tote—Large	10	19.50	195.00
	Total			2,941.25

② Actual Units on Hand

As described in Chapter 9, a periodic inventory conducted by counting, weighing, or measuring items of merchandise on hand is known as a physical inventory. Employees count each item of inventory and record the quantities on special forms. To ensure an accurate and complete count, a business will typically be closed during the physical inventory.

A business frequently establishes its fiscal year to end when inventory is at a minimum because it takes less time to count a smaller inventory. For example, a department store may take an inventory at the end of December. The amount of merchandise on hand is smaller because of holiday sales. Few purchases of additional merchandise are made in December after the holiday sales. All of these activities make the merchandise inventory smaller at the end of December.

A form used during a physical inventory to record information about each item of merchandise on hand is called an **inventory record**. The inventory record has space to record the stock number, description, number of units on hand, unit price, and total cost of each item. Columns 1–3 are completed when the business is taking a physical inventory. Columns 4–5 are completed after the physical inventory. The methods used to determine the unit prices are discussed later in this chapter.

> **Preparing an Inventory Record**
>
> **①** Write the stock number and description before the physical inventory begins.
>
> **②** Write the actual count in the No. of Units on Hand column.
>
> **③** Write the unit price and calculate the total cost after the physical inventory is completed. These columns are usually completed by the accounting department.

fyi

Taking an inventory is an involved and expensive task. An efficient inventory count requires extensive management planning and employee training. Some businesses hire independent companies that specialize in taking inventories to assist in planning for and counting the inventory.

Stock Record LO1

STOCK RECORD						
Description **_Beach Tote—Small_**			Stock No. **_BB715-S_**			
Reorder **_20_**			Minimum **_10_**		Location **_Rack 45_**	
1	2	3	4	5	6	7
INCREASES			DECREASES			BALANCE
DATE	PURCHASE INVOICE NO.	QUANTITY	DATE	SALES INVOICE NO.	QUANTITY	QUANTITY
			Oct. 10		2	9
Nov. 2	410	20				29
			Nov. 12	1531	2	27
			Nov. 29	1601	4	23
			Dec. 6	1647	1	22

Purchase Information   Sales Information   New Balance on Hand

Some businesses keep inventory records that show continuously the quantity on hand for each kind of merchandise. A form used to show the kind of merchandise, quantity received, quantity sold, and balance on hand is called a **stock record**. A separate stock record is prepared for each kind of merchandise on hand. A file of stock records for all merchandise on hand is called a **stock ledger**.

A perpetual inventory system provides day-to-day information about the quantity of merchandise on hand. The minimum balance allowed before a reorder must be placed is also shown on each stock record. The minimum balance is the quantity that will typically last until the ordered merchandise can be received from the vendors. When the quantity falls below the minimum, additional merchandise is ordered in the quantity shown on the reorder line of the stock record. A stock record shows the quantity but usually not the cost of the merchandise.

Purchase information is recorded in the Increases columns when additional merchandise is received. Sales information is recorded in the Decreases columns when merchandise is sold. The new balance on hand is recorded after each purchase and sale.

When a perpetual inventory is kept, errors may be made in recording or calculating amounts. Also, some stock records may be incorrect because merchandise is taken from stock and not recorded on stock records. A business should at least take a physical inventory at the end of its fiscal year. The perpetual records are then corrected to reflect the actual quantity on hand as determined by the physical inventory.

Perpetual Inventory Using a Computer

VEF/SHUTTERSTOCK.COM

UPC (Universal Product Code) symbol on merchandise is scanned to enter data into a point-of-sale (POS) terminal

Many merchandising businesses use a computer to keep perpetual inventory records. The point-of-sale terminals at the customer check-out counters are connected to the computer. The terminals read the Universal Product Codes (UPC) marked on products.

The stock ledger is stored in the computer. When a UPC is read at the terminal, the product description and the sales price are retrieved from the stock ledger and displayed on the terminal. The computer reduces the units on hand to reflect the item sold. The computer may also periodically check the quantities in the stock ledger and print a list of items that need to be reordered. Even with a computerized system, errors may occur. Therefore, companies that use a product's UPC code and a point-of-sale terminal should at least take a physical inventory at the end of the fiscal year.

Periodic Physical Inventory Counts

Classic Furniture counts its inventory at the end of each fiscal year. The physical inventory is an expensive and time-consuming undertaking. A special team of 40 temporary workers is employed. The physical inventory is actually performed on New Year's Day before any sales occur in the new year.

The company's inventory manager, Renee Schaeffer, is not satisfied with having only one physical count per year. She would like to have a monthly count to ensure she is making accurate buying decisions. But closing the store for a day, once a month, is not an option.

Instead, the inventory manager would like to perform daily counts of a few inventory items. Differences between the actual quantity on hand and the quantity stored in the accounting system could be investigated. Any loss of inventory could be entered in the accounting system to revise the recorded quantity of inventory.

OPEN THE SPREADSHEET TLA_CH20

The inventory manager has e-mailed the accounting manager asking for assistance in creating these daily lists. The worksheet contains a list of nearly 500 inventory items downloaded from the accounting system. Use the list to create two random lists of the inventory items.

1. Create a list of 5 inventory items.

2. Create a list consisting of 2% of the inventory items.

Click on the Instructions tab and follow the instructions.

End of Lesson **Review**

LO1 Prepare a stock record.

Terms Review

inventory record

stock record

stock ledger

Audit your understanding

1. Identify four reasons why a merchandise inventory that is larger than needed may decrease the net income of a business.

2. When are physical inventories normally taken?

3. How do inventory levels affect the period a business selects for its fiscal year? Why?

4. How is the accuracy of a perpetual inventory checked?

Work together 20-1

Preparing a stock record

A stock record for Green Gardens is given in the *Working Papers*. Your instructor will guide you through the following example.

Enter the following transactions on the stock record of Stock No. GL764-3, soaker hose. Source documents are abbreviated as follows: purchase invoice, P; sales invoice, S.

Transactions:

Oct. 3. Sold 3 of GL764-3 soaker hose. S835.

27. Purchased 40 of GL764-3 soaker hose. P1121.

29. Sold 5 of GL764-3, soaker hose. S886.

Dec. 4. Sold 3 of GL764-3, soaker hose. S912.

On your own 20-1

Preparing a stock record

A stock record for Plumbing World is given in the *Working Papers*. Work this problem independently.

Enter the following transactions on the stock record of Stock No. 7461XG, O-rings. Source documents are abbreviated as follows: purchase invoice, P; sales invoice, S.

Transactions:

Nov. 4. Sold 10 7461XG, O-rings. S237.

16. Sold 20 7461XG, O-rings. S286.

17. Sold 18 7461XG, O-rings. S312.

Dec. 9. Purchased 150 7461XG, O-rings. P323.

20-2 Determining the Cost of Merchandise Inventory

LO2 Calculate the cost of merchandise inventory using the first-in, first-out (FIFO) inventory costing method.

LO3 Calculate the cost of merchandise inventory using the last-in, first-out (LIFO) inventory costing method.

LO4 Calculate the cost of merchandise inventory using the weighted-average inventory costing method.

First-In, First-Out Inventory Costing Method LO2

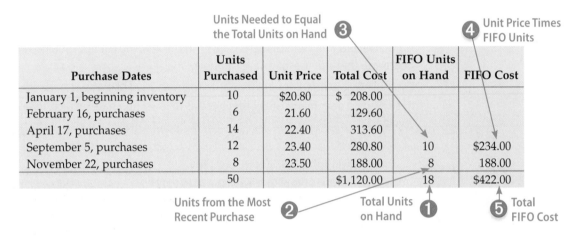

Purchase Dates	Units Purchased	Unit Price	Total Cost	FIFO Units on Hand	FIFO Cost
January 1, beginning inventory	10	$20.80	$ 208.00		
February 16, purchases	6	21.60	129.60		
April 17, purchases	14	22.40	313.60		
September 5, purchases	12	23.40	280.80	10	$234.00
November 22, purchases	8	23.50	188.00	8	188.00
	50		$1,120.00	18	$422.00

After the quantities of merchandise on hand are counted, purchase invoices are used to find merchandise unit prices. The total costs are then calculated using the quantities and unit prices recorded on the inventory records. Most businesses use one of three inventory costing methods: (1) first-in, first-out, (2) last-in, first-out, or (3) weighted-average.

Sun Treasures, Inc., uses the most recent invoices for purchases to determine the unit price of an item in inventory. The earliest invoices for purchases, therefore, are used to determine the cost of merchandise sold. Using the price of merchandise purchased first to calculate the cost of merchandise sold first is called the **first-in, first-out inventory costing method (FIFO)**. The first-in, first-out method is frequently abbreviated as *FIFO*.

On December 31, a physical inventory of Extra Large Beach Totes, Model No. BB715-XL, showed 18 units on hand. Using the FIFO method, the 18 units would show a total cost of $422.00.

Costing Inventory Using the FIFO Method

❶ Enter the total number of units on hand, **18.**

❷ From the most recent purchase, November 22, enter the number of units purchased, **8.** In some cases, the number of units of the most recent purchase will be greater than or equal to the total number of units on hand. In such a case, enter the total number of units on hand and do not complete Step 3 below.

❸ From the next most recent purchase, September 5, enter the number of units, **10,** needed for the FIFO units to equal the total number on hand, 18. Continue with the next invoices as needed.

❹ Multiply the unit price of each appropriate purchase by the FIFO units on hand to determine the FIFO cost.

❺ Add the individual FIFO costs to determine the FIFO cost of the total number of units in ending inventory.

Last-In, First-Out Inventory Costing Method LO3

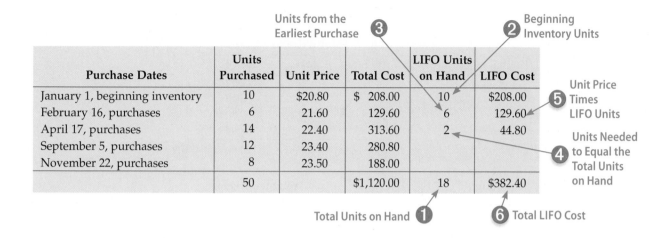

Units from the Earliest Purchase ③

Beginning ② Inventory Units

Unit Price ⑤ Times LIFO Units

Units Needed ④ to Equal the Total Units on Hand

Purchase Dates	Units Purchased	Unit Price	Total Cost	LIFO Units on Hand	LIFO Cost
January 1, beginning inventory	10	$20.80	$ 208.00	10	$208.00
February 16, purchases	6	21.60	129.60	6	129.60
April 17, purchases	14	22.40	313.60	2	44.80
September 5, purchases	12	23.40	280.80		
November 22, purchases	8	23.50	188.00		
	50		$1,120.00	18	$382.40

Total Units on Hand ①

⑥ Total LIFO Cost

Using the price of merchandise purchased last to calculate the cost of merchandise sold first is called the **last-in, first-out inventory costing method (LIFO)**. The last-in, first-out method is frequently abbreviated as *LIFO*. This method is based on the idea that the most recent costs of merchandise should be charged against current revenue. [CONCEPT: Matching Expenses with Revenue]

Using the LIFO method, each item on the inventory records is recorded at the earliest prices paid for the merchandise.

The earliest prices for the 18 beach totes would consist of the 10 units in the January 1 beginning inventory. The next earliest purchase, February 16, of 6 units is then used to cost 6 units in ending inventory. The remaining 2 units in ending inventory are costed using the next earliest purchase, April 17. On the inventory record, the 18 units would show a total cost of $382.40.

Costing Inventory Using the LIFO Method

① Enter the total number of units on hand, 18.

② Enter the number of units in beginning inventory, 10. In some cases, the number of units of beginning inventory will be greater than or equal to the total number of units on hand. In such a case, enter the total number of units on hand and do not complete Steps 3 and 4 below.

③ From the earliest purchase, February 16, enter the number of units purchased, 6.

④ From the next earliest purchase, April 17, enter the number of units, 2, needed for the LIFO units to equal the total number of units on hand, 18.

⑤ Multiply the unit price of the beginning inventory by the LIFO units on hand to determine the LIFO cost for beginning inventory. Repeat this process for each appropriate purchase.

⑥ Add the LIFO cost for the beginning inventory and each appropriate purchase to determine the LIFO cost of the total number of units in ending inventory.

remember

In the LIFO method, the latest purchases are assumed to be sold first (first-out). Therefore, ending inventory consists of the units purchased the earliest, and the earliest purchase invoice costs are used to value the ending inventory.

Weighted-Average Inventory Costing Method LO4

Purchases			Total
Date	Units	Unit Price	Cost
January 1, beginning inventory	10	$20.80	$ 208.00
February 16, purchases	6	21.60	129.60
April 17, purchases	14	22.40	313.60
September 5, purchases	12	23.40	280.80
November 22, purchases	8	23.50	188.00
	50		$1,120.00

1 Total Cost of Inventory Available

Total of Beginning Inventory and Purchases	÷	Total Units	=	Weighted-Average Price per Unit
$1,120.00	÷	50	=	$22.40

2 Weighted-Average Price per Unit

Units in Ending Inventory	×	Weighted-Average Price per Unit	=	Cost of Ending Inventory
18	×	$22.40	=	$403.20

3 Cost of Ending Inventory

Using the average cost of beginning inventory plus merchandise purchased during a fiscal period to calculate the cost of merchandise sold is called the **weighted-average inventory costing method**. The average unit price of the total inventory available is calculated. This average unit price is used to calculate both ending inventory and cost of merchandise sold. The average cost of merchandise is then charged against current revenue. [CONCEPT: Matching Expenses with Revenue]

Using the weighted-average method, the inventory is costed at the average price per unit of the beginning inventory plus the cost of all purchases during the fiscal year. On the inventory record, the 18 units would show a total cost of $403.20.

> **Costing Inventory Using the Weighted-Average Method**
>
> **1** Calculate the total cost of beginning inventory and each purchase, $1,120.00, by multiplying the units by each unit price.
>
> **2** Calculate the weighted-average price per unit, $22.40, by dividing the total cost, $1,120.00, by the total number of units available, 50.
>
> **3** Calculate the cost of ending inventory, $403.20, by multiplying the weighted-average price per unit, $22.40, by the units in ending inventory, 18.

Inventory Costing Method and Actual Flow of Inventory

The actual flow of inventory in a company does not have to match the inventory costing method a company chooses. For example, a grocery store will usually stock to the back so that the first goods purchased are the first goods sold. Therefore, the actual flow of the groceries is on a FIFO basis. A hardware store may decide to stock its new inventory in front of its older inventory. Therefore, the actual flow of the hardware is on a LIFO basis. A gas station, where all the gas is put into a large underground tank, sells its gas on a weighted-average basis. However, each of these three kinds of businesses can decide which inventory method (FIFO, LIFO, or weighted-average) it uses. The inventory method chosen by a company to determine the cost of merchandise sold does not have to match the actual flow of inventory for that company.

The Rise and Fall of WorldCom

Telecommunications giant WorldCom collapsed in 2003. What could have caused the failure of the nation's second largest long-distance service provider, boasting over $100 billion in assets?

The roots of WorldCom were planted during the historic breakup of AT&T in 1984. AT&T dominated the long-distance and local phone service market. To increase competition, the Federal Trade Commission (FTC) forced AT&T to divest itself of its local phone service companies. The seven new independent local phone companies were dubbed the "Baby Bells."

Long-distance phone service instantly became a commodity that could be bought and sold. WorldCom was one of several corporations created to take advantage of this new business opportunity. WorldCom bought a huge volume of long-distance service from AT&T and resold the minutes to small businesses.

From its humble beginnings, WorldCom embarked on a path of growth through acquisitions. WorldCom bought a variety of telecom businesses, most often paying for the acquisitions with WorldCom stock. Its most notable acquisition was its 1997 merger with MCI Communications. The $37 billion price tag was triple the size of WorldCom. The new MCI WorldCom then set its sights on Sprint Corporation, announcing in 1999 a staggering $129 billion merger. Fearing that a combined Sprint and MCI WorldCom would decrease competition, the government did not approve the merger.

But hidden behind by the smoke screen of its merger activity, WorldCom was experiencing decreasing sales and incurring losses. To hide the losses, WorldCom began recording fraudulent journal entries. The fraud involved the accounting for line costs, the fees paid to other telecom companies. The journal entries reduced line cost expenses and recorded the expenses as plant assets.

WorldCom's internal auditors were suspicious that a fraud was occurring. During their investigation, one auditor noted an unusual transaction to a plant asset account. It wasn't so much that the amount was large. After all, WorldCom was often involved in acquisitions in the billions of dollars. But it was the amount, exactly $500,000,000.00, that caught the internal auditor's attention. Why would the amount of an addition to plant assets be a rounded number? When all the investigations were complete, it was revealed that WorldCom had reported $3.8 billion of line costs as plant assets.

ACTIVITY

The board of directors of Royal Imports has launched an internal investigation. The board suspects an accounting fraud at its foreign operations. Begin the investigation by analyzing the corporation's journal entries for any signs of a fraud. At the direction of the manager of internal audit, complete the following steps.

INSTRUCTIONS

Open the spreadsheet FA_CH20 and complete the steps on the Instructions tab.

1. Prepare a list of transactions greater than $25,000.00 that end in 000.00.

2. Identify any transaction that appears unusual. Support your conclusion.

3. What would you suggest as the next step in your investigation?

Sources: Richard B. Lanza and Scott Gilbert, "A Risk-Based Approach to Journal Entry Testing," *Journal of Accountancy* (July 2007) and Cecil W. Jackson, *Business Fairy Tales* (Thomson, 2006).

Calculating the Cost of Merchandise Sold

The cost of ending inventory determined using any of the three inventory costing methods can be used to calculate the cost of merchandise sold. The cost of ending inventory is subtracted from the total cost of units available for sale. Although the formula is the same, under each inventory costing method the amount determined will be different. Sun Treasures uses the FIFO method. Therefore, the FIFO cost of $422.00 is subtracted from the total cost of merchandise available for sale, $1,120.00, to calculate the cost of merchandise sold of $698.00.

Cost of Merchandise Available for Sale	−	FIFO Cost of Ending Inventory	=	Cost of Merchandise Sold
$1,120.00	−	$422.00	=	$698.00

Comparison of Inventory Methods

	FIFO	LIFO	Weighted-Average
Cost of merchandise sold:			
Merchandise inventory, Jan. 1............	$ 208.00	$ 208.00	$ 208.00
Net purchases	912.00	912.00	912.00
Merchandise available for sale	$1,120.00	$1,120.00	$1,120.00
Less ending inventory, Dec. 31	422.00	382.40	403.20
Cost of merchandise sold..............	$ 698.00	$ 737.60	$ 716.80
In a period of rising prices: Relative cost of ending inventory	highest	lowest	intermediate
Relative cost of merchandise sold	lowest	highest	intermediate

In a *period of rising prices*, the FIFO method gives the highest possible ending inventory cost and the lowest cost of merchandise sold. The LIFO method gives the lowest possible ending inventory cost and the highest cost of merchandise sold. The weighted-average method gives ending inventory cost and cost of merchandise sold between FIFO and LIFO. As the cost of merchandise sold increases, gross profit and net income decrease. Thus, net income is highest under the FIFO method, lowest under the LIFO method, and intermediate under the weighted-average method.

In a *period of declining prices*, the results for the FIFO and LIFO methods are reversed.

All three inventory costing methods are acceptable accounting practices. A business should select one method and use that same method continuously for each fiscal period. If a business changed inventory costing methods, part of the difference in gross profit and net income would be caused by the change in methods. To provide financial statements that can be analyzed and compared with statements of other fiscal periods, the same inventory costing method must be used for each fiscal period. [CONCEPT: Consistent Reporting]

Lower of Cost or Market Inventory Costing Method

The price that must be paid to replace an asset is called the **market value**. Using the lower of cost or market price to calculate the cost of ending merchandise inventory is called the **lower of cost or market inventory costing method (LCM)**. In this context, *cost* refers to the actual amount paid for the unit of inventory on hand. *Market* refers to the amount that must be paid to replace the unit of inventory. For example, assume that a permanent change in market conditions means that Sun Treasures may currently have to pay a vendor $22.50 to purchase the extra large beach tote.

Two amounts are needed to apply the lower of cost or market method:

1. The cost of the inventory using the FIFO, LIFO, or weighted-average method.
2. The current market value of the inventory.

These two amounts are then compared and the lower of the two is used to cost the inventory. For example, Sun Treasures uses the FIFO method of costing inventory. The FIFO cost and the current market value for 18 beach totes are shown below. The FIFO cost is $422.00, and the current market value is $405.00. Using the lower of cost or market method, the market value of the beach totes is lower than the FIFO cost. Therefore, the market value of $405.00 is used as the cost of the totes.

If Sun Treasures used the LIFO method, the LIFO cost would be $382.40. The LIFO cost of $382.40 is lower than the market value, so the LIFO cost would be used instead of the market value. If Sun Treasures used the weighted-average method, the weighted-average cost would be $403.20. The weighted-average cost of $403.20 is lower than the market value, so the weighted-average cost would be used instead of the market value.

The LCM method is designed to prevent inventory values from being overstated. This is especially important in industries where the cost of component parts tends to decrease rather than increase. Without the LCM method, these inventories would be stated at older, higher prices. The use of the LCM method ensures that the inventory value will not be reported at a value higher than current market value.

Lower of Cost or Market Inventory Costing Method			
Costing Method	Cost	Market Value (18 units × $22.50 current market price)	Lower of Cost or Market
FIFO	$422.00	$405.00	$405.00
LIFO	382.40	405.00	382.40
Weighted-average	403.20	405.00	403.20

Calculate the cost Calculate the market price Determine the smaller number to use as the lower of cost or market

Inventory Management

The cost of inventory is usually a large portion of a retail, manufacturing, or wholesale company's current assets. The efficient management of inventory, therefore, can lead to major cost savings for many companies. Inventory management deals with the fine line between having too much inventory and running out of inventory. It is broad in nature, starting with identifying inventory requirements and covering each step until the inventory is received at the correct location. It requires trying to forecast demand, price levels, defective goods, available space, and handling costs.

Many of the decisions made by an inventory manager will have an effect on the financial statements of a company. Too much inventory will tie up capital that could be used for other projects. Inventory requires storage space and handlers, which decrease profit. Excess inventory may have to be sold at below cost prices, which further decreases profits.

Too little inventory also has an effect on financial statements. Lost sales will decrease net income.

WHY ACCOUNTING?

Business Management & Administration

CRITICAL THINKING

1. Inventory management companies help their clients manage inventory. Search the Internet for an inventory management company and write a one-sentence summary of the services it provides.

2. Search the Internet for an inventory management software program. List the name of the software and write a one-sentence summary of its features.

Source: Inventory Management, published by the U.S. Small Business Administration.

End of Lesson Review

Terms Review

Audit your understanding

1. On what idea is the FIFO method based?

2. When the LIFO method is used, at what price is each item in ending merchandise inventory recorded?

3. In a period of rising prices, which inventory costing method gives the lowest cost of merchandise sold?

4. Why should a business select one inventory costing method and use that same method continuously for each fiscal period?

Work together 20-2

Determining the cost of inventory using the FIFO, LIFO, and weighted-average inventory costing methods

Inventory costing information for Sunshine Spas is given in the *Working Papers*. Your instructor will guide you through the following example.

Calculate the cost of ending inventory using the FIFO, LIFO, and weighted-average methods. There are 15 units in ending inventory.

On your own 20-2

Determining the cost of inventory using the FIFO, LIFO, and weighted-average inventory costing methods

Inventory costing information for Electronics Plus is given in the *Working Papers*. Work this problem independently.

Calculate the cost of ending inventory using the FIFO, LIFO, and weighted-average methods. There are 26 units in ending inventory.

20-3 Estimating Inventory

LO5   Estimate the cost of merchandise inventory using the gross profit method of estimating inventory.

Gross Profit Method of Estimating Inventory   LO5

STEP 1: Beginning inventory, January 1 .... $ 331,235.20

     Plus   net purchases for January 1 to January 31. ....   +64,516.21

     Equals   cost of merchandise available for sale .... $ 395,751.41

STEP 2: Net sales for January 1 to January 31 .... $ 122,367.00

     Times   previous year's gross profit percentage. ....   ×   40.00%

     Equals   estimated gross profit on operations .... $ 48,946.80

STEP 3: Net sales for January 1 to January 31 .... $ 122,367.00

     Less   estimated gross profit on operations ....   −48,946.80

     Equals   estimated cost of merchandise sold .... $ 73,420.20

STEP 4: Cost of merchandise available for sale .... $ 395,751.41

     Less   estimated cost of merchandise sold ....   −73,420.20

     Equals   estimated ending merchandise inventory............ $ 322,331.21

Restaurant Supply Co.
Income Statement
For Month Ended January 31, 20--

		% of Net Sales
Operating Revenue:		
Net Sales	$122,367.00	100.0
Cost of Merchandise Sold:		
Beginning Inventory, January 1 .... $331,235.20		
Net Purchases........................ 64,516.21		
Merchandise Available for Sale $395,751.41		
Less Est. Ending Inv., January 31........ 322,331.21		
Cost of Merchandise Sold..............	73,420.20	60.0
Gross Profit on Operations..............	$ 48,946.80	40.0
Operating Expenses....................	43,807.39	35.8
Net Income	$ 5,139.41	4.2

Estimating inventory by using the previous year's percentage of gross profit on operations is called the **gross profit method of estimating inventory**. The gross profit method is often used to estimate the cost of the ending inventory reported on monthly financial statements. The gross profit method is a less expensive method of calculating inventory costs than taking a physical inventory or maintaining a perpetual inventory system.

Four values are needed to perform this four-step process. Actual net sales and net purchases amounts are obtained from the general ledger. The beginning inventory amount is obtained from the prior period's financial statements. The gross profit percentage is estimated by management based on the previous year's actual percentage, adjusted for any significant changes in economic conditions.

Estimating Inventory for Other Months

When the gross profit method of estimating inventory is used for months other than the first month of the fiscal year, the process is the same as that just illustrated. Net sales and purchases amounts are obtained from the general ledger. For the sales account, the previous month's ending balance is subtracted from the current month's ending balance to calculate the amount of sales for just the current month. The same process is used for the purchases account. The beginning inventory for the month is the same as the ending inventory from the previous month. Note that both the beginning and ending inventory amounts will be based on estimated amounts.

Accounting in Ancient Civilizations

Five thousand years before the appearance of double-entry accounting, Mesopotamian scribes were among the few people who could read and write. These scribes became the equivalent of today's accountants.

Public scribes would meet business partners at the gates of the city. The scribe would listen as the partners described their agreement. The scribe would then record the contract on moist clay tablets. The business partners would sign their names by pressing their seals into the clay. The tablets were then dried in the sun or a kiln. The development of accounting in Egypt was similar, except that the Egyptians used papyrus rather than clay tablets, allowing for more details to be recorded.

The major problem with these systems was the lack of a single unit of valuation to use in measuring the value of each transaction. This issue was solved when the Greeks introduced coined money about 600 BC. Although it took many years for the usage of coins to spread, this is often identified as a major event in the development of accounting records.

The Babylonians in Asia Minor used an early form of banking. They transferred funds with a system resembling our checking accounts, one of the first uses of business documents.

These early practices provided the foundation for today's financial system and recordkeeping methods.

CRITICAL THINKING

1. Estimate how many transactions might occur in a single day in a mid-sized bank.

2. List the number of different methods of payment that are accepted by a local department store.

Sources: www.accountancystudents.co.uk and John R. Alexander, *History of Accounting,* Association of Chartered Accountants in the United States.

End of Lesson Review

▼·········

LO5 Estimate the cost of merchandise inventory using the gross profit method of estimating inventory.

Term Review

gross profit method of estimating inventory

Audit your understanding

1. When neither a perpetual system is maintained nor a physical inventory is taken, how can an ending merchandise inventory be determined that is accurate enough for a monthly income statement?

2. What amounts are needed to estimate ending merchandise inventory?

3. What amount is used for beginning inventory for a month that is not the first month of a fiscal year?

Work together 20-3

Estimating ending inventory using the gross profit method

A form for making estimated inventory calculations and a form for completing an income statement are given in the *Working Papers*. Your instructor will guide you through the following examples.

1. Use the following information obtained from the records and management of Goldsmith Company to estimate the cost of the ending inventory on June 30.

Estimated beginning inventory, June 1	$77,400.00
Actual net purchases for June	$23,900.00
Actual net sales for June	$122,500.00
Estimated gross profit percentage	45.0%
Actual operating expenses for June	$38,465.00

2. Prepare an income statement for the month ended June 30 of the current year.

On your own 20-3

Estimating ending inventory using the gross profit method

A form for making estimated inventory calculations and a form for completing an income statement are given in the *Working Papers*. Work this problem independently.

1. Use the following information obtained from the records and management of Leah Enterprises to estimate the cost of the ending inventory on April 30.

Estimated beginning inventory, April 1	$49,000.00
Actual net purchases for April	$24,200.00
Actual net sales for April	$112,000.00
Estimated gross profit percentage	55.0%
Actual operating expenses for April	$35,840.00

2. Prepare an income statement for the month ended April 30 of the current year.

A Look at Accounting Software

Managing Inventory

The inventory management module of a computerized accounting system is very complex. It has links to accounts payable, accounts receivable, and the general ledger. It must receive data from, and pass data to, each of those modules. Computerized inventory systems today are so powerful they can track the sales of specific items to specific customers. That data can be used to send targeted sales offers to those customers. Inventory systems are also capable of issuing automatic reorders when stock levels drop to designated reorder quantities.

The illustration shows a new inventory stock item being entered. This window would also be used to edit information for an existing stock item. In that case, the user would double-click one of the stock items in the report to open the window. Then the user could, for example, change the preferred vendor, the location of the item, or the reorder quantity. By clicking the Inactive button, the user would prevent the item from being reordered.

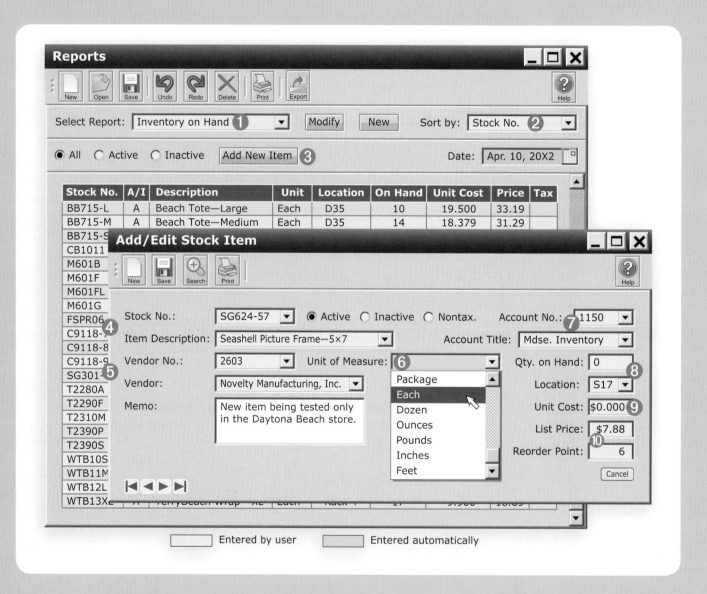

1. To view an inventory report, the user opens the Reports window and selects Inventory on Hand from the drop list.

2. The user has chosen to have this report sorted by stock number.

3. The user has clicked on the Add New Item button to open the Add/Edit Stock Item pop-up window.

4. The user enters the new stock number and description. The Active button is on by default. States determine which types of products are exempt from sales tax. When Nontax is selected, point-of-sale (POS) terminals will print the item on the customer receipt with an NT, and no sales tax will be charged for it.

5. The user may enter a preferred vendor (by vendor number or name). This can speed up order entry when creating a purchase order, although the vendor could be changed in the Write Purchase Orders window.

6. The user must select a unit of measure. Here, the user is selecting Each from the drop list.

7. The system automatically selects the Merchandise Inventory account—number 1150. In the manual system used by Sun Treasures, Inc., inventory is maintained using the periodic system. When a computer system is used, inventory is maintained using a perpetual system, so inventory purchases are debited to Merchandise Inventory rather than to Purchases.

8. The quantity on hand for this new item is zero because no orders have been entered yet. The system will update this number as new orders increase it and sales decrease it. The user would select the storage location for the item. That information helps salespeople know where to look for replacement items when stock is depleted on the sales floor. It also is helpful when counting the inventory.

9. The system computes an average unit cost of all the items currently in inventory. Sun Treasures uses LIFO, so as items are sold, the most recently purchased items will be deducted from inventory first. The system then computes a new average cost of the remaining items in inventory.

10. The user enters the list price. The POS terminals use this price to compute the value of each sale. Finally, the user enters a reorder quantity. If the accounting system is not programmed to do an automatic reorder, the purchasing department would reorder the item when the stock level dropped to this quantity.

Chapter Summary

The quantity of inventory on hand can be kept on a perpetual or periodic basis. The perpetual basis provides an up-to-date balance in the **Merchandise Inventory** account throughout the period. The periodic basis does not update inventory throughout the period. Both methods require that a physical inventory be taken at least once a year. Once the quantity of inventory is determined, a cost must be applied to each unit of inventory. This can be done using the FIFO, LIFO, or weighted-average methods. Each method results in different amounts for the cost of ending inventory and the cost of merchandise sold. In times of rising prices, the FIFO method will result in the highest net income amount. When the ending inventory cannot be counted, ending inventory can be estimated using the gross profit method.

EXPLORE ACCOUNTING

Activity-Based Costing

A company must accurately calculate the cost of a product in order to determine the selling price of that product. The materials and labor costs for most products are not difficult to determine. Other costs that must be measured include custodial services in the factory, machine maintenance costs, supervisory labor costs, and the cost of factory supplies. All expenses other than direct materials and direct labor that apply to making products are called **factory overhead**.

Several methods can be used to calculate factory overhead costs. A method commonly used is to relate factory overhead costs to the number of hours of labor that each product requires. Using this method, a product using one hour of labor per unit would be allocated four times more factory overhead costs than a product using 15 minutes of labor per unit. This method was more practical when production was labor intensive. Today, many automated manufacturing processes involve little, if any, direct labor. Therefore, a newer method of allocating factory overhead costs is one based on activities. Major activities in the manufacturing process are identified and factory overhead costs are allocated based on these activities. Allocating factory overhead based on the level of major activities is referred to as **activity-based costing (ABC)**.

For example, the production of a pizza at a local pizza parlor involves two significant activities: assembling the ingredients and cooking the pizza. The first activity involves direct labor, but the second activity involves only cooking time in the oven. In contrast, the production of a sub sandwich involves three times as much direct labor as a pizza but no cooking in the oven. If factory overhead were applied based solely on direct labor, the sub sandwich would improperly receive three times as much overhead cost as the pizza.

Using ABC, the accountant recognizes that a significant amount of overhead costs of the pizza parlor results from the ovens: the cost of the ovens, heating the ovens, and cooling the kitchen from the heat that escapes from the ovens. These overhead costs should be allocated to those products that require cooking. Thus, factory overhead costs related to the ovens would be applied to pizza production based on cooking time.

ABC is also used by service businesses to determine the cost of providing various services. ABC results in more accurate estimates on the cost of producing individual products and services. Managers can use this information to assist them in making better decisions, such as the price of products and the profitability of different product lines.

INSTRUCTIONS

The challenge of implementing ABC is to match costs with related activities that are easy to measure. Identify the measurable activities in two different lawn maintenance services: mowing a lawn and cutting down a tree.

Apply Your Understanding

INSTRUCTIONS: Download problem instructions for Excel, QuickBooks, and Peachtree from the textbook companion website at www.C21accounting.com.

20-1 Application Problem: Preparing a stock record LO1

A stock record for Electronics World is given in the *Working Papers*.

Instructions:

Enter the following transactions on the stock record of a 42-inch flat-screen television, Stock No. 891DC-5. Source documents are abbreviated as follows: purchase invoice, P; sales invoice, S.

Transactions:

Feb. 4. Sold 2 Model No. 891DC-5 televisions to Country Motel, n/30. S910.
28. Sold 1 Model No. 891DC-5 television to Janice Olson, 2/10, n/30. S984.
Mar. 10. Received 10 units of Model No. 891DC-5 televisions from GLC Electronics, 2/10, n/30. P1012.
24. Sold 2 Model No. 891DC-5 televisions to Seaside Restaurant, n/30. S1062.

20-2 Application Problem: Determining the cost of inventory using the FIFO, LIFO, and weighted-average inventory costing methods LO2, 3, 4

Forms for costing inventory for Oakland Supply are given in the *Working Papers*. There are 192 units in ending inventory.

Purchase Date	Quantity	Unit Price
January 1, beginning inventory	100	$4.00
March 13, purchases	88	4.10
June 8, purchases	90	4.25
September 16, purchases	94	4.30
December 22, purchases	98	4.40

Instructions:

Calculate the cost of ending inventory using the FIFO, LIFO, and weighted-average methods.

Peachtree
1. Journalize and post purchases of inventory on account in the Purchases/ Receive Inventory window.
2. Journalize and post sales of inventory on account in the Sales/Invoicing window.
3. Print the purchases journal, sales journal, inventory valuation report, and trial balance.

QuickBooks
1. Journalize and post purchases of inventory on account in the Enter Bills window.
2. Journalize and post sales of inventory on account in the Create Invoices window.
3. Print the vendor balance detail, inventory valuation summary, and trial balance.

Excel
1. Key the inventory-related transactions on the stock record.
2. Use the inventory costing methods to calculate year-end inventory.
3. Print the worksheet.

AA ONLINE
1. Go to www.cengage.com/login
2. Click on **AA Online** to access.
3. Go to the online assignment and follow the instructions.

20-3 Application Problem: Estimating ending inventory using the gross profit method LO5

Use the following information obtained from the records and management of Lee Industries. A form for making inventory calculations and a form for completing an income statement are given in the *Working Papers*.

Instructions:

1. Estimate the cost of the ending inventory on March 31.

Estimated beginning inventory, March 1	$49,350.00
Actual net purchases for March	$22,900.00
Actual net sales for March	$93,000.00
Estimated gross profit percentage	55.0%
Actual operating expenses for March	$40,176.00

2. Prepare an income statement for the month ended March 31 of the current year.

20-M Mastery Problem: Determining the cost of inventory using the FIFO, LIFO, and weighted-average inventory costing methods LO2, 3, 4

Computer Supply Company began the year with 16 units of its model 120-HP print cartridge in beginning inventory. Each unit sells for $39.95. The following transactions involving model 120-HP occurred during the year. Forms are given in the *Working Papers*. Source documents are abbreviated as follows: purchase invoice, P; sales invoice, S.

Transactions:

Jan.   6.   Purchased 40 units from Printers Plus for $10.24 per unit, 2/10, n/30. P361.
Apr.   5.   Sold 44 units to Glenville Hospital, n/30. S812.
       14.   Purchased 40 units from Printers Plus for $10.36 per unit, 2/10, n/30. P437.
July   5.   Sold 50 units to Hills Department Store, n/30. S971.
Aug.   3.   Purchased 40 units from Printers Plus for $10.46 per unit, 2/10, n/30. P512.
Dec.   2.   Sold 30 units to ABC Company, n/30. S1186.
       12.   Purchased 40 units from Printers Plus for $10.54 per unit, 2/10, n/30. P556.

Instructions:

1.   Enter the transactions on the stock record and determine the number of units in ending inventory.

2.   Calculate the cost of ending inventory using the FIFO, LIFO, and weighted-average methods.

3.   Which of the inventory costing methods resulted in the lowest cost of merchandise sold? Merchandise available for sale is the total cost of beginning inventory plus all purchases during the year.

Peachtree

1. Journalize and post purchases of inventory on account in the Purchases/Receive Inventory window.
2. Journalize and post sales of inventory on account in the Sales/Invoicing window.
3. Print the purchases journal, sales journal, inventory valuation report, and trial balance.

QB Quick Books

1. Journalize and post purchases of inventory on account in the Enter Bills window.
2. Journalize and post sales of inventory on account in the Create Invoices window.
3. Print the vendor balance detail, inventory valuation summary, and trial balance.

X

1. Key the inventory-related transactions on the stock record.
2. Use the inventory costing methods to calculate year-end inventory.
3. Print the worksheet.

AAONLiNE

1. Go to www.cengage.com/login
2. Click on **AA Online** to access.
3. Go to the online assignment and follow the instructions.

20-C Challenge Problem: Determining the cost of merchandise inventory destroyed in a fire LO5

A fire completely destroyed the warehouse of Albertson Painting Company on the night of May 12 of the current year. The accounting records of the company and $945.00 of merchandise inventory were salvaged. The company does not maintain a perpetual inventory system. The insurance company therefore has requested an estimate of the merchandise inventory destroyed in the fire. Forms are given in the *Working Papers*. The following income statement is for the previous fiscal year.

Albertson Painting Company
Income Statement
For Year Ended April 30, 20--

Operating Revenue:		
Net Sales		$316,308.00
Cost of Merchandise Sold:		
Beginning Inventory, May 1 (Prior Year) .	$ 15,348.27	
Net Purchases.	156,282.02	
Merchandise Available for Sale	$171,630.29	
Less Est. Ending Inv., April 30	17,271.99	
Cost of Merchandise Sold.		154,358.30
Gross Profit on Operations.		$161,949.70
Operating Expenses.		142,267.61
Net Income		$ 19,682.09

The following additional financial information is obtained from the current year's accounting records.

Net purchases, May 1 to May 12	$ 3,377.02
Net sales, May 1 to May 12	11,216.44
Operating expenses, May 1 to May 12	4,937.70

Instructions:

1. Calculate the prior year's gross profit on operations as a percentage of net sales. Round the percentage calculation to the nearest 0.1%.

2. Use the percentage calculated in part (1) and the current year's financial information to calculate an estimate of the total merchandise inventory as of May 12.

3. To calculate the cost of the inventory destroyed in the fire, subtract the cost of the merchandise inventory that was not destroyed from the estimate of the total merchandise inventory as of May 12.

4. Prepare an income statement for the period May 1 through May 12.

The insurance company maintains that it is liable for paying only the book value of the inventory destroyed by fire. Albertson Painting Company maintains that the insurance company should pay the replacement cost of the destroyed inventory.

5. What is meant by the book value and the replacement value of the inventory?

6. Albertson Painting Company uses the FIFO inventory costing method. How does using FIFO affect the difference between the book value and the replacement value of the destroyed inventory?

7. What should determine which value the insurance company uses?

21st Century Skills

Piggly Wiggly—Just In Time!

Theme: Financial, Economic, Business, and Entrepreneurial Literacy

Skills: Critical Thinking and Problem Solving, Communication and Collaboration

PARTNERSHIP FOR
21ST CENTURY SKILLS

For a small business, inventory is often the most important asset. If not managed properly, inventory costs can also become the greatest expense on the income statement keeping a business from being profitable. The cost of inventory consists of more than just the cost of the actual item and its shipping. One of the greatest costs associated with inventory is the cost of storing, or holding the merchandise, as well as having excessive inventory.

To keep inventory costs down, many companies have implemented an inventory strategy called just-in-time delivery (JIT). Toyota, now a leader in the automotive industry, developed JIT as part of its management strategy after its delegates observed the Piggly Wiggly grocery store while on a visit to the United States to view auto manufacturers. While not all that impressed with the Ford manufacturing processes, the delegates were fascinated with how the supermarket only reordered and restocked goods after customers had made purchases. The JIT strategy maintains that inventory is not reordered until stock is close to depletion. This saves warehouse space and costs.

While JIT may save costs, a business must not underestimate the risks involved. The products must arrive exactly when needed. Uncontrollable circumstances such as natural disasters, untimely weather, supplier misfortunes, and political risks can damage business credibility and reduce revenue. The best intentions to become more profitable can leave a company vulnerable. Management must carefully develop a risk management plan to implement if using the JIT strategy.

When planning an event to occur on a specific date, one must assess the risks involved so proactive measures can be taken to offset the risks, deliver the product, and make a profit.

Your business has been asked to design and provide t-shirts for a local benefit sponsored by your school. Individuals in your school will be participating in the event as well as some members from the local community. Your supplier needs five days to complete and deliver the order. The organizer of the event estimates that approximately 1,000 t-shirts will be needed. The shirts will cost you $5.00 each to purchase. The organizer will only pay for the number of shirts for those participating. You must make a profit.

1. Create a table with two columns. Label with the following: (1) Risks, (2) Measures.

2. Create a bulleted list with at least five risks associated with this order.

3. Create a bulleted list next to the risks, under the heading Measures, and explain measures you will take to offset the risks in order to make a profit. Present your risk assessment to the class.

Analyzing Nike's financial statements

The managers at Nike need to constantly monitor the amount of inventory available for sale. Having too little inventory can result in products running out of stock, which can cause the company to lose sales. Holding too much inventory increases the company's operating expenses. A financial ratio that evaluates the amount of inventory available for sale is known as the inventory turnover ratio. The ratio is calculated as follows:

$$\text{Inventory Turnover} = \frac{\text{Cost of Goods Sold}}{(\text{Beginning Inventory} + \text{Ending Inventory}) \div 2}$$

Dividing the sum of the beginning and ending inventory by 2 approximates the average inventory for the fiscal year. As one example, the inventory turnover for Domino's Pizza, Inc., based on its 2011 fiscal year financial statements (www.dominos.com), is calculated below.

$$\text{Inventory Turnover} = \frac{\$1,181,677,000}{(\$26,998,000 + \$30,702,000) \div 2} = 41.17$$

Dividing 365 by the turnover ratio yields a financial ratio known as *number of days' sales in inventory*. Domino's number of days' sales in inventory is 8.87 days. Thus, the average item remains in its inventory for approximately 9 days.

INSTRUCTIONS

1. Using the financial information in Appendix B of this text, calculate Nike's inventory turnover ratio and number of days' sales in inventory for 2011.

2. Why would the inventory turnover ratios for Nike and Domino's differ?

Reinforcement Activity 3—Part A

An Accounting Cycle for a Corporation: Journalizing and Posting Transactions

 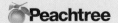 QB Quick Books   AAONLiNE

Reinforcement Activity 3 reinforces learning from Parts 2 and 3. Activities cover a complete accounting cycle for a merchandising business organized as a corporation. Reinforcement Activity 3 is a single problem divided into two parts. Part A includes learning from Part 2 and Chapters 18 through 20 of Part 3. Part B includes learning from Chapters 21 and 22.

The accounting work of a single merchandising business for the last month of a fiscal year is used in this reinforcement activity. The records kept and reports prepared, however, illustrate the application of accounting concepts for all merchandising businesses.

Restaurant Warehouse, Inc.

Restaurant Warehouse, Inc., a merchandising business, is organized as a corporation. The business sells a complete line of restaurant supplies, mostly to business customers. Restaurant Warehouse is located within an industrial park and is open for business Monday through Saturday. A monthly rent is paid for the building. Restaurant Warehouse subleases some of its warehouse space. Restaurant Warehouse sells to some businesses on account and accepts cash or credit cards from small business owners.

Chart of Accounts

Restaurant Warehouse uses the chart of accounts shown on the next page.

Journals and Ledgers

The journals, ledgers, and forms used by Restaurant Warehouse are listed below. Models of these items are shown in the textbook chapters indicated.

Journals and Ledgers	Chapter(s)
Purchases journal	9
Cash payments journal	9
Accounts payable ledger	9 and 11
Sales journal	10
Cash receipts journal	10
Accounts receivable ledger	10 and 11
General journal	11
General ledger	11
Plant asset record	19

Reinforcement Activity 3—Part A (Cont.)

An Accounting Cycle for a Corporation: Journalizing and Posting Transactions

Restaurant Warehouse, Inc., Chart of Accounts
General Ledger

Balance Sheet Accounts

(1000) ASSETS

<u>1100   Current Assets</u>
1105   Cash
1110   Petty Cash
1115   Accounts Receivable
1120   Allowance for Uncollectible Accounts
1125   Notes Receivable
1130   Interest Receivable
1135   Merchandise Inventory
1140   Supplies
1145   Prepaid Insurance
<u>1200   Plant Assets</u>
1205   Office Equipment
1210   Accumulated Depreciation—Office Equipment
1215   Warehouse Equipment
1220   Accumulated Depreciation—Warehouse Equipment

(2000) LIABILITIES

<u>2100   Current Liabilities</u>
2105   Accounts Payable
2110   Sales Tax Payable
2115   Notes Payable
2120   Interest Payable
2125   Unearned Rent Income
2130   Employee Income Tax Payable
2135   Social Security Tax Payable
2140   Medicare Tax Payable
2145   Medical Insurance Payable
2150   Unemployment Tax Payable—State
2155   Unemployment Tax Payable—Federal
2160   Federal Income Tax Payable
2165   Dividends Payable
<u>2200   Long-Term Liabilities</u>
2205   Bonds Payable

(3000) STOCKHOLDERS' EQUITY

3105   Capital Stock—Common
3110   Paid-in Capital in Excess of Par—Common
3115   Capital Stock—Preferred

3120   Paid-in Capital in Excess of Par—Preferred
3205   Retained Earnings
3210   Dividends
3215   Income Summary

Income Statement Accounts

(4000) OPERATING REVENUE

4105   Sales
4110   Sales Discount
4115   Sales Returns and Allowances

(5000) COST OF GOODS SOLD

5105   Purchases
5110   Purchases Discount
5115   Purchases Returns and Allowances

(6000) OPERATING EXPENSES

6105   Advertising Expense
6110   Cash Short and Over
6115   Credit Card Fee Expense
6120   Depreciation Expense—Office Equipment
6125   Depreciation Expense—Warehouse Equipment
6130   Insurance Expense
6135   Miscellaneous Expense
6140   Payroll Taxes Expense
6145   Rent Expense
6150   Repairs Expense
6155   Salary Expense
6160   Supplies Expense
6165   Uncollectible Accounts Expense
6170   Utilities Expense
<u>6200   Income Tax Expense</u>
6205   Federal Income Tax Expense

(7000) OTHER REVENUE

7105   Interest Income
7110   Rent Income
7115   Gain on Plant Assets

(8000) OTHER EXPENSES

8105   Interest Expense
8110   Loss on Plant Assets

Subsidiary Ledgers

Accounts Receivable Ledger

110   Bakery Depot
120   Ferndale Café
130   Hilltop Hospital
140   Huang Restaurant
150   Northside Catering
160   Rao Deli

Accounts Payable Ledger

210   Bok Supply Company
220   Dreyfus Company
230   Glommen Company
240   Hilton Supply
250   Sarr Corp.
260   Winona Manufacturing

Recording Transactions

The December 1, 20X4, account balances for the general and subsidiary ledgers are given in the *Working Papers*. Transactions from the period December 1 through December 23 have already been journalized and individual items have been posted.

INSTRUCTIONS

1. Journalize the following transactions completed during the last week in December of the current year. Restaurant Warehouse offers sales terms of 2/10, n/30. The sales tax rate is 6%. Post the following transactions when journalized: (1) transactions affecting the accounts receivable or accounts payable subsidiary ledgers, (2) transactions recorded in the general journal, and (3) amounts entered in a general amount column of the cash payments and cash receipts journals. Source documents are abbreviated as follows: check, C; memorandum, M; purchase invoice, P; receipt, R; sales invoice, S; terminal summary, TS; debit memorandum, DM; credit memorandum, CM; note payable, NP.

Dec. 26. Received cash for the maturity value of NR28, a 90-day, 12% note for $11,600.00. R454.

27. Recorded cash and credit card sales, $4,674.00, plus sales tax, $280.44; total, $4,954.44. TS40.

28. Sold merchandise on account to Huang Restaurant, $5,000.00, plus sales tax. S428.

28. Purchased merchandise on account from Dreyfus Company, $12,296.00. P190.

28. Signed a 90-day, 10% note, for $12,000.00 with Northstar National Bank. NP22 and R455.

28. Received cash for sale of a computer, plant asset No. 284, $300.00. M29 and R456. Update the plant asset record and record the sale.

28. Received cash in full payment of Bakery Depot's account, previously written off as uncollectible, $1,896.00. M30 and R457.

29. Paid $1,000.00 on the outstanding balance of the Sarr Corp. account. C343.

29. Issued 500 shares of $10.00 par value common stock at $50.00 per share. R458.

29. Issued 300 shares of 5%, $50.00 par value preferred stock at par value, $15,000.00. R459.

30. Rao Deli dishonored NR29, a 60-day, 12% note, for $6,000.00. M31.

Dec. 30. Recorded payment of credit card fee expense, $836.00. M32.

30. Purchased a work station for use in the office and a forklift for use in the warehouse in a lump-sum transaction, $30,000.00. The work station has an estimated value of $11,000, and the forklift has an estimated value of $22,000.00. C344. Open a plant asset record for each item. Work station: plant asset No. 452; serial number, M251; useful life, 4 years; estimated salvage value, $1,000.00. Forklift: plant asset No. 453; serial number, 124XYG; useful life, 5 years; estimated salvage value, $3,000.00.

31. Paid cash to replenish the petty cash fund, $169.92: supplies, $25.00; advertising, $100.00; miscellaneous, $44.74; cash short, $0.18. C345.

31. Paid cash for semimonthly payroll, $4,413.72 (total payroll, $5,520.00, less deductions: employee income tax, $304.00; social security tax, $342.24; Medicare tax, $80.04; medical insurance, $380.00). C346.

31. Recorded employer payroll taxes, $484.28, for the semimonthly pay period ended December 31. Taxes owed are: social security tax, $342.24; Medicare tax, $80.04; state unemployment tax, $54.00; and federal unemployment tax, $8.00. M33.

31. Recorded cash and credit card sales, $930.00, plus sales tax, $55.80; total, $985.80. TS41.

31. Paid semiannual interest on bonds payable, $1,200.00. C347.

2. Prove and rule the sales journal. Post the totals of the special columns.

3. Total and rule the purchases journal. Post the total.

4. Prove the equality of debits and credits for the cash receipts and cash payments journals.

5. Prove cash. The balance on the next unused check stub is $25,001.40.

6. Rule the cash receipts journal. Post the totals of the special columns.

7. Rule the cash payments journal. Post the totals of the special columns.

8. Prepare a schedule of accounts receivable and a schedule of accounts payable. Prove the accuracy of the subsidiary ledgers by comparing the schedule totals with the balances of the controlling accounts in the general ledger. If the totals are not the same, find and correct the errors.

The ledgers and plant asset records used in Reinforcement Activity 3—Part A are needed to complete Reinforcement Activity—3 Part B.

Chapter 21

Accounting for Accruals, Deferrals, and Reversing Entries

LEARNING OBJECTIVES

After studying Chapter 21, in addition to defining key terms, you will be able to:

LO1 Record the reversing entry for accrued revenue.

LO2 Record an entry to receive payment on a note receivable with accrued interest.

LO3 Calculate accrued interest expense.

LO4 Record the adjusting entry for an accrued expense.

LO5 Record the reversing entry for an accrued expense.

LO6 Record an entry to pay an installment on a note payable with accrued interest.

LO7 Record an entry to receive cash on deferred revenue.

LO8 Calculate the amount and record the entry for deferred revenue when earned.

LO9 Record an entry to pay cash on a deferred expense.

LO10 Calculate the amount and record the entry for a deferred expense when incurred.

©DANIEL KOUREY, ISTOCK/©JIM PRUITT, ISTOCK

PIERREDESVARRE/ISTOCKPHOTO.COM

Accounting In The Real World
USA Today

You've probably heard someone ask, "Did you read *USA Today* today?" *USA Today* is a national newspaper with an average daily circulation of over 1.8 million, not including online subscriptions. *USA Today* is published Monday through Friday. It is known for color-coding its four sections: News (blue), Money (green), Sports (red), and Life (purple).

USA Today has two major sources of revenue: advertising and subscriptions. Both kinds of revenue are collected in advance. *USA Today* collects fees for advertising before the advertisements appear. Customers pay subscriptions for paper delivery or online editions as much as a year in advance. Receiving these fees does not, however, mean that *USA Today* can record the amounts as current revenue.

In accordance with GAAP, advertising fees are recorded as revenue when the advertising is printed or placed on a website. In the same manner, subscription fees are recorded as revenue when purchased newspapers are delivered. When preparing financial statements, accountants at *USA Today* must analyze the money collected from advertising and subscriptions to determine what amount should be recorded as revenue.

CRITICAL THINKING

1. Suppose you purchase a $150 annual subscription to *USA Today* on November 1. How much should *USA Today* recognize as revenue on its December financial statements?

2. Would your answer to question 1 differ if the customer selected online delivery of *USA Today*?

Sources: www.gannett.com; www.wikipedia.com.

Key Terms

- accrual
- deferral
- reversing entry
- accrued expenses
- accrued interest expense
- deferred revenue
- deferred expenses

LO1 Record the reversing entry for accrued revenue.
LO2 Record an entry to receive payment on a note receivable with accrued interest.
LO3 Calculate accrued interest expense.
LO4 Record the adjusting entry for an accrued expense.
LO5 Record the reversing entry for an accrued expense.
LO6 Record an entry to pay an installment on a note payable with accrued interest.

Accruals and Deferrals

Generally accepted accounting principles (GAAP) require that revenue and expenses be recorded in the accounting period in which revenue is earned and expenses are incurred. [CONCEPT: Matching Expenses with Revenue] However, some revenues, such as interest income, are earned each day but are recorded only when the interest is actually received. Likewise, some expenses may be incurred before they are actually paid. For example, a note payable incurs interest expense each day the note is outstanding, but the interest may not be paid until the note's maturity date. An entry recording revenue before the cash is received, or an expense before the cash is paid, is called an **accrual**. An accrual can be illustrated as follows:

Accrual

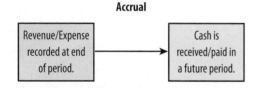

Some revenues, such as rental income, are received before they are earned. Some expenses, such as rent expense, are paid before they are incurred. An entry recording the receipt of cash before the related revenue is earned, or payment of cash before the related expense is incurred, is called a **deferral**. A deferral can be illustrated as follows:

Deferral

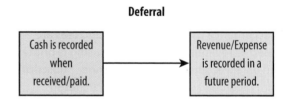

Guarding Intellectual Property

Is it ethical to use file-sharing software to download music from the Internet? Is it ethical to purchase a DVD that you know has been pirated? If you purchase software that allows for three installations, is it ethical to install the software on a friend's computer?

Anything, or any process, that is protected by patent, trademark, or copyright is called **intellectual property**. Music, videos, and computer software are examples of intellectual property. The individual or business that creates intellectual property retains the exclusive right to control the use of the property. The authorized use is stated in the terms of service, often called the terms of use. When installing computer software, the consumer must agree to the terms of service to proceed with the installation. Violating the terms of service, including the sharing or purchasing of unauthorized copies, is illegal.

Businesses recognize the need to comply with the licensing agreements of computer software. Many companies address this issue in their code of conduct.

INSTRUCTIONS

Do an Internet search to access "Everyday Values," the code of conduct for Harley-Davidson, Inc. What guidance does Harley-Davidson provide its employees about copying software for both business and personal use?

©LUCA DI FILIPPO, ISTOCK

Reversing Entry for Accrued Interest Income LO1

GENERAL JOURNAL							PAGE 13	
DATE	ACCOUNT TITLE	DOC. NO.	POST. REF.	DEBIT		CREDIT		
1		*Adjusting Entries*						1
4	31	*Interest Receivable*			1 7 5 00			4
5		*Interest Income*				1 7 5 00		5

In Chapter 15, ThreeGreen Products, Inc., made an adjusting entry to record accrued interest income. Sun Treasures makes a similar entry for accrued interest income. On December 31, Sun Treasures has one note receivable on hand, a 90-day, 7%, $15,000.00 note dated November 1. Accrued interest on this note is $175.00. **Interest Receivable** is debited, and **Interest Income** is credited for this amount, as shown above.

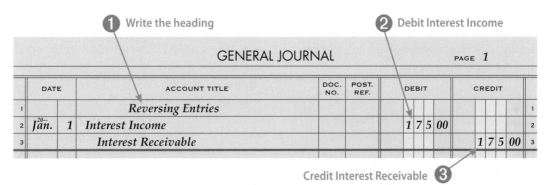

1 Write the heading

2 Debit Interest Income

GENERAL JOURNAL							PAGE 1	
DATE	ACCOUNT TITLE	DOC. NO.	POST. REF.	DEBIT		CREDIT		
1		*Reversing Entries*						1
2	Jan. 20-- 1	*Interest Income*			1 7 5 00			2
3		*Interest Receivable*				1 7 5 00		3

Credit Interest Receivable **3**

On December 31, **Interest Income** is closed as part of the regular closing entry for income statement accounts with credit balances. **Interest Income** is debited for $2,512.80 to reduce the account balance to zero.

Interest Income

Dec. 31 Closing	2,512.80	Dec. 31 Unadj. Bal.	2,337.80
Jan. 1 Rev.	175.00	Dec. 31 Adj.	175.00
(New Bal.	175.00)		

Interest Receivable

Dec. 31 Adj.	175.00	Jan. 1 Rev.	175.00
(New Bal.	0.00)		

Adjusting entries for accrued revenues have an effect on transactions that will be recorded in the following fiscal period. On the maturity date of the outstanding 90-day note receivable, Sun Treasures will receive interest of $262.50.

However, an adjusting entry was made to record the amount of interest earned last year, $175.00. Thus, $175.00 of the $262.50 total interest income has already been recorded as revenue. The remaining $87.50 of the $262.50 total interest will be earned during the current fiscal period.

It is not convenient to determine how much, if any, of cash received from notes receivable relates to interest accrued during the prior fiscal period. To avoid this inconvenience, an entry is made at the beginning of the new fiscal period to reverse the adjusting entry. An entry made at the beginning of one fiscal period to reverse an adjusting entry made in the previous fiscal period is called a **reversing entry**.

The reversing entry is the opposite of the adjusting entry. The entry creates a debit balance of $175.00 in **Interest Income**. A debit balance is the opposite of the normal balance of **Interest Income**. When the full amount of interest is received, the $262.50 will be credited to **Interest Income**, resulting in an $87.50 credit balance ($262.50 credit – $175.00 debit), the amount of interest earned in the new year.

The reversing entry reduced the balance in **Interest Receivable** to zero. When the interest is received, no entry will be made to **Interest Receivable**. Instead, the total amount of interest received will be credited to **Interest Income**.

> **Reversing an Adjusting Entry for Accrued Interest Income**
>
> **1** Write the heading, **Reversing Entries**, in the middle of the general journal's Account Title column. This heading explains all the reversing entries that follow. There is no source document.
>
> **2** Record a debit, **$175.00**, to **Interest Income**.
>
> **3** Record a credit, **$175.00**, to **Interest Receivable**.

Collecting a Note Receivable with Accrued Interest LO2

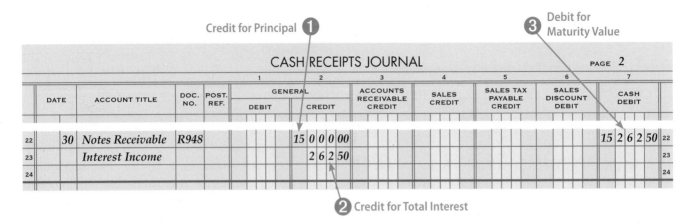

① Credit for Principal

③ Debit for Maturity Value

	DATE	ACCOUNT TITLE	DOC. NO.	POST. REF.	GENERAL DEBIT (1)	GENERAL CREDIT (2)	ACCOUNTS RECEIVABLE CREDIT (3)	SALES CREDIT (4)	SALES TAX PAYABLE CREDIT (5)	SALES DISCOUNT DEBIT (6)	CASH DEBIT (7)	
22	30	Notes Receivable	R948			15 0 0 0 00					15 2 6 2 50	22
23		Interest Income				2 6 2 50						23
24												24

CASH RECEIPTS JOURNAL   PAGE 2

② Credit for Total Interest

On January 30, Sun Treasures received the maturity value of the only note receivable on hand on December 31, the end of the previous fiscal year.

> **January 30. Received cash for the maturity value of a 90-day, 7% note: principal, $15,000.00, plus interest, $262.50; total, $15,262.50. Receipt No. 948.**

The total interest, $262.50, was earned during two fiscal periods—$175.00 during the previous fiscal period and $87.50 during the current fiscal period. The reversing entry created a $175.00 debit balance in Interest Income. After the $262.50 credit is posted, Interest Income has a credit balance of $87.50, the amount of interest earned during the current fiscal period. After the $15,000.00 credit is posted, Notes Receivable has a zero balance.

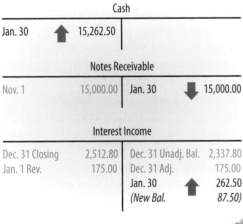

Cash

Jan. 30 ⬆ 15,262.50	

Notes Receivable

Nov. 1 15,000.00	Jan. 30 ⬇ 15,000.00

Interest Income

Dec. 31 Closing 2,512.80	Dec. 31 Unadj. Bal. 2,337.80
Jan. 1 Rev. 175.00	Dec. 31 Adj. 175.00
	Jan. 30 ⬆ 262.50
	(New Bal. 87.50)

⮌ Collecting a Note Receivable with Accrued Interest

① Record a credit to **Notes Receivable** in the General Credit column of the cash receipts journal for the principal of the note, **$15,000.00**.

② Record a credit to **Interest Income** in the General Credit column for the total interest, **$262.50**.

③ Record a debit in the Cash Debit column for the maturity value of the note, **$15,262.50**.

ANDREW TAYLOR/SHUTTERSTOCK.COM

IMAGE SOURCE/JUPITER IMAGES

Careers In Accounting

Jonathon Lopez
ACCOUNTING INSTRUCTOR

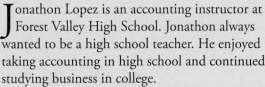

Jonathon Lopez is an accounting instructor at Forest Valley High School. Jonathon always wanted to be a high school teacher. He enjoyed taking accounting in high school and continued studying business in college.

As a secondary teacher, Mr. Lopez develops daily lesson plans and prepares materials for classroom activities. He presents accounting concepts via lectures, discussions, and demonstrations. He also guides students through activities and helps students as they independently complete problems and assignments. Mr. Lopez evaluates his students' growing knowledge of accounting and adjusts his teaching as necessary. Other tasks include grading assignments, administering and grading tests, assigning grades for reporting purposes, coordinating fund-raising activities, and serving as advisor to the Business Professionals of America Club.

Forest Valley School is publically supported, so Mr. Lopez is required by his local administration and by state and federal law to maintain accurate student records. He must plan his teaching so that students fulfill stated objectives for each course he teaches. In addition, he is responsible for establishing and enforcing rules for student behavior and maintaining a good learning environment.

The accounting classroom has an interactive white board and other up-to-date technology. To complete their accounting assignments, students use spreadsheet and accounting software as well as the Internet. Mr. Lopez has been trained on all the technology used in his classroom.

Mr. Lopez teaches both first-year and advanced accounting. He works with local two- and four-year colleges so that when his advanced students finish the course they are allowed to take a college-level test. If the student passes the test, he or she receives college credit for the course.

To keep himself up to date in the accounting field, Mr. Lopez attends conferences and seminars.

He can learn about new accounting rules, discover new resource materials for teaching, and interact with other teachers to exchange ideas.

All members of the Forest Valley High School faculty serve on a school-wide committee and chaperone various student activities. Mr. Lopez also meets with parents for conferences and communicates with parents via e-mail and phone.

Salary Range: The national median range for a secondary teacher in vocational education is $53,000. However, individual salaries vary greatly. Salaries are dependent on local school contracts, level of education completed, and years of teaching experience.

Qualifications: Most states require a four-year bachelor's degree in order to be certified to teach, but there are exceptions to this standard. In order to teach business courses, most degree programs require extensive coursework in the business area. In addition, most states require continuing education units in order to renew a state teaching license.

Occupational Outlook: The growth for secondary vocational educators is projected to be average (7 to 13% for the period from 2008 to 2018).

ACTIVITY

Use the Internet to research the qualifications required in your state to be a secondary teacher. Write a one-page report summarizing your findings.

Source: www.online.onetcenter.org.

©MILENNY, ISTOCK

Analyzing an Adjustment for Accrued Interest Expense LO3, 4

Sun Treasures, Inc. Unadjusted Trial Balance December 31, 20--		
ACCOUNT TITLE	DEBIT	CREDIT
Interest Payable		
Long-term Notes Payable		106 625 67
Interest Expense	17 636 26	

Debit Interest Expense **1**

GENERAL JOURNAL PAGE 13

	DATE	ACCOUNT TITLE	DOC. NO.	POST. REF.	DEBIT	CREDIT	
1		*Adjusting Entries*					1
18	31	Interest Expense			710 84		18
19		Interest Payable				710 84	19

Credit Interest Payable **2**

Expenses incurred in one fiscal period, but not paid until a later fiscal period, are called **accrued expenses**. At the end of a fiscal period, an accrued expense is recorded by an adjusting entry. [CONCEPT: Matching Expenses with Revenue] The adjusting entry increases an expense account. The adjusting entry also increases a payable account.

Interest incurred but not yet paid is called **accrued interest expense**. On December 31, Sun Treasures has one long-term note payable outstanding. On April 1,

Sun Treasures signed a five-year, 8.0% note payable for $120,000. The terms of the note state that Sun Treasures must make a payment of $2,433.17 on the first of each month. The payment is first applied to the interest for the prior month. Any additional amount reduces the principal of the note. The balance of the note after the December 31 payment is $106,625.67. On December 31, Sun Treasures owes 30 days of accrued interest expense and must make an adjusting entry for this amount.

Principal	×	Interest Rate	×	Time as Fraction of Year	=	Accrued Interest Expense
$106,625.67	×	8%	×	30/360	=	$710.84

Before the adjusting entry is made, Interest Expense has a balance of $17,636.26, which represents the interest expense incurred throughout the year on all other debt. In the adjusting entry, Interest Expense is debited for $710.84 to show the increase in the

balance of this Other Expense account. The credit to Interest Payable creates a $710.84 account balance that represents the interest owed on December 31 that will be paid in the next fiscal period, on January 1, 20X2.

After posting, **Interest Payable** has a credit balance of $710.84 and will appear on the December 31 balance sheet as a current liability. This credit balance is the accrued interest expense incurred but not yet paid at the end of the year. The new balance of **Interest Expense**, $18,347.10, is the total amount of interest expense incurred during the fiscal period and will appear on the income statement for the year ended December 31 as an Other Expense.

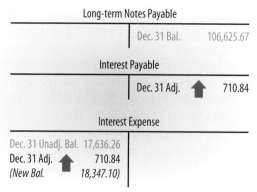

Long-term Notes Payable	
	Dec. 31 Bal. 106,625.67

Interest Payable	
	Dec. 31 Adj. ⬆ 710.84

Interest Expense	
Dec. 31 Unadj. Bal. 17,636.26	
Dec. 31 Adj. ⬆ 710.84	
(New Bal. 18,347.10)	

> **↗↗↗ remember**
>
> The **Interest Payable** account appears in the Current Liabilities section of the balance sheet. The **Interest Expense** account appears in the Other Expenses section of the income statement.

> **⊘ Recording an Adjusting Entry for Accrued Interest Expense**
>
> ❶ Record a debit, **$710.84**, to **Interest Expense**.
>
> ❷ Record a credit, **$710.84**, to **Interest Payable**.

Reversing Entry for Accrued Interest Expense LO5

Debit Interest Payable ❶

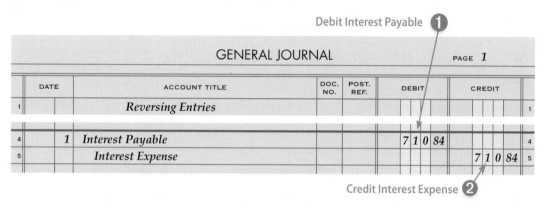

	DATE		ACCOUNT TITLE	DOC. NO.	POST. REF.	DEBIT	CREDIT	
1			*Reversing Entries*					1
4	1		*Interest Payable*			7 1 0 84		4
5			*Interest Expense*				7 1 0 84	5

GENERAL JOURNAL   PAGE **1**

Credit Interest Expense ❷

On December 31, **Interest Expense** is closed as part of the regular closing entries. **Interest Expense** is credited for $18,347.10 to reduce the account balance to zero. After the closing entry is posted, the **Interest Expense** account is closed.

Interest Expense	
Dec. 31 Unadj. Bal. 17,636.26	Dec. 31 Closing 18,347.10
Dec. 31 Adj. 710.84	Jan. 1 Rev. ⬇ 710.84
	(New Bal. ⬇ 710.84)

Interest Payable	
Jan. 1 Rev. ⬇ 710.84	Dec. 31 Adj. 710.84
(New Bal. 0.00)	

Adjusting entries for accrued expenses have an effect on transactions to be recorded in the following fiscal period. For example, on January 1, Sun Treasures will pay the monthly payment which will decrease the principal balance and pay the interest of $710.84.

However, an adjusting entry was made to record the amount of accrued interest expense last year, $710.84. Thus, the total interest expense was incurred and recorded in the previous year.

Having to remember that the cash paid for interest is for accrued interest expense is an inconvenience. To avoid the inconvenience, a reversing entry is made at the beginning of the new fiscal period.

The reversing entry is the opposite of the adjusting entry. The entry creates a credit balance of $710.84 in **Interest Expense**. A credit balance is the opposite of the normal balance of the **Interest Expense** account. When the interest is paid, $710.84 will be debited to **Interest Expense**. The account will then have a zero balance.

The reversing entry to **Interest Payable** reduces that account to a zero balance. Thus, when the interest is paid, no debit entry will be required to recognize payment of the balance of **Interest Payable**. The total amount of interest paid will be debited to **Interest Expense**.

> **⊘ Reversing an Adjusting Entry for Accrued Interest Expense**
>
> ❶ Record a debit, **$710.84**, to **Interest Payable** in the general journal.
>
> ❷ Record a credit, **$710.84**, to **Interest Expense**.

Effect of Not Using Reversing Entries

Reversing entries are not required in accounting. A company can choose to use reversing entries or not. If Sun Treasures did not use a reversing entry for accrued interest expense, there is a possibility that the interest could be reported twice. The $710.84 amount is recorded once as an adjusting entry to Interest Expense in the previous fiscal period. The amount could be recorded a second time as a debit to Interest Expense in the current fiscal period when the note is paid. The double charge will be avoided only if accounting personnel remember that the interest chargeable to the previous fiscal period should be recorded as a debit to Interest Payable, not to Interest Expense. In large companies with hundreds of accounts, making sure that these double charges do not occur can be difficult.

Companies that choose to use reversing entries do not want to force their accountants to have to go back and check prior entries when notes are paid or received in the next period. Like other companies that use reversing entries, Sun Treasures records a reversing entry whenever an adjusting entry creates a balance in an asset or a liability account that initially had a zero balance.

Paying an Installment Note Payable with Accrued Interest LO6

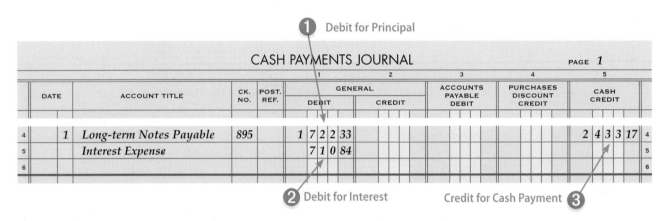

1 Debit for Principal

CASH PAYMENTS JOURNAL   PAGE **1**

	DATE	ACCOUNT TITLE	CK. NO.	POST. REF.	GENERAL DEBIT	GENERAL CREDIT	ACCOUNTS PAYABLE DEBIT	PURCHASES DISCOUNT CREDIT	CASH CREDIT	
4	1	Long-term Notes Payable	895		1 7 2 2 33				2 4 3 3 17	4
5		Interest Expense				7 1 0 84				5
6										6

2 Debit for Interest   Credit for Cash Payment **3**

> **January 1. Paid cash for the monthly payment on the long-term note payable: principal, $1,722.33, plus interest, $710.84; total, $2,433.17. Check No. 895.**

Sun Treasures is required to make monthly cash payments of $2,433.17. The difference between the total cash paid and the amount of interest expense is the amount by which the principal is reduced. The principal balance of the notes payable will be reduced $1,722.33 by the January 1 payment.

Payment Amount	−	Interest Expense	=	Reduction of Principal
$2,433.17	−	$710.84	=	$1,722.33

The total interest, $710.84, was incurred during the previous fiscal period. The reversing entry created a $710.84 credit balance in Interest Expense. After the $710.84 debit is recorded, Interest Expense has a zero balance.

Not all notes payable require a monthly payment, which covers interest expense for the month plus a reduction in principal. Some notes payable are paid in full on the maturity date of the note. If the maturity date is in a different fiscal period than when the note was signed, an adjusting entry is required at the end of the fiscal period to record accrued interest expense. The accrued interest expense would cover the number of days between the issue date of the note and the end of the period. The reversing entry and the entry to show the payment of the maturity value would be the same as the note payable illustrated in this lesson.

> **Paying an Installment Note Payable with Accrued Interest**
>
> **1** Record a debit to Long-term Notes Payable in the General Debit column for the reduction of principal, $1,722.33.
>
> **2** Record a debit to Interest Expense in the General Debit column for the total interest, $710.84.
>
> **3** Record a credit to Cash in the Cash Credit column for the monthly payment amount, $2,433.17.

Analyzing Accruals

The adjusting entries for accrued revenue and accrued expenses must be recorded at the end of a fiscal period in order for the financial statements to be accurate. Each accrual entry affects a balance sheet account and an income statement account. If an accrual entry is not recorded, both the balance sheet and the income statement will be incorrect.

Since accrual entries do not involve an outside business or customer, Sun Treasures must remember to record these entries. When determining its accrued revenue, Sun Treasures must include all forms of revenue earned but not yet received. This lesson illustrated accrued interest income. There are many other forms of accrued revenue. A utility company that bills its customers in January for utilities it supplied in December records an entry for estimated revenue earned in December even though the cash will not be received until January. Some rental agreements allow the renter to pay in the following month. The company renting the property must record rent earned in December even though the cash will not be received until January.

In a similar manner, when determining its accrued expenses, Sun Treasures must include all forms of expenses incurred but not yet paid. This lesson illustrated accrued interest expense. There are many other forms of accrued expenses. Payroll is an accrued expense for many companies. If a company pays its employees two weeks after the end of a payroll period, on December 31, that company will owe two weeks of wages. An accrued expense must be recorded. If a renter is allowed to pay December rent on January 15, the renter must record an accrued expense for the December rent incurred but not yet paid.

remember The adjusting entry for accrued interest income affects both the income statement and the balance sheet. The income statement will report all income for the period even though some of the income has not yet been received. The balance sheet will report all assets, including the accrued income receivable.

remember The adjusting entry for accrued interest expense affects both the income statement and the balance sheet. The income statement will report all expenses for the period even though some of the expenses have not yet been paid. The balance sheet will report all liabilities, including the accrued expenses payable. [CONCEPT: Adequate Disclosure]

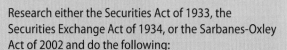

WHY ACCOUNTING?

Government's Role in Regulating Accounting Practices

Government, both federal and state, plays a very important role in the regulation of the field of accounting. From the establishment of GAAP to the criteria for becoming a CPA, federal and/or state laws must be followed. It is critical that lawmakers and policy setters have an understanding of accounting in order to make laws that enable the desired outcome.

Sometimes laws are a result of an event that had a tremendous impact on society. The Securities Act of 1933 was the first federal legislation to regulate the offer and sale of securities. The Securities Exchange Act of 1934 established the Securities and Exchange Commission. Both of these acts were enacted in response to the stock market crash of 1929. The Sarbanes-Oxley Act of 2002 (SOX) set new standards for boards of directors, company management, and public accounting firms. The law was enacted in direct response to a number of major accounting scandals. SOX addresses many issues including auditor independence, internal control, and financial disclosure. It is the intent of the government that these laws will prevent stock market crashes and accounting scandals in the future.

Government & Public Administration

CRITICAL THINKING

Research either the Securities Act of 1933, the Securities Exchange Act of 1934, or the Sarbanes-Oxley Act of 2002 and do the following:

1. Formulate questions to analyze the event that led to the formation of the law.
2. Gather and list relevant sources of information to answer the questions.
3. Determine the reliability of the sources.
4. Present an oral or written report stating how the law serves to prevent the same event from happening in the future.

©ANEKCEN KOWEBHNKOB, ISTOCK

Audit your understanding

1. Which accounting concept is being applied when an adjusting entry is made at the end of the fiscal period to record accrued revenue?

2. Why does a business use reversing entries as part of its procedures for accounting for accrued interest expense?

Work together 21-1

Journalizing entries for accruals

Accounting forms and a partial unadjusted trial balance for Kufas Corporation are given in the *Working Papers*. After each journal entry, update the T accounts given in the *Working Papers*. Your instructor will guide you through the following examples.

On December 31, 20X1, Kufas Corporation has one note receivable outstanding, a 120-day, 6%, $10,000.00 note dated November 16, and one note payable outstanding, a 90-day, 6%, $12,000.00 note dated December 1.

1. Journalize the adjusting entries for accrued interest income and accrued interest expense on December 31. Use page 14 of a general journal.

2. Journalize the closing entries for interest income and interest expense using page 14 of a general journal.

3. Journalize the January 1, 20X2, reversing entries for accrued interest income and accrued interest expense on page 15 of a general journal.

4. Journalize the payment of cash for the maturity value of the note payable on March 1, 20X2. Check No. 478. Use page 25 of a cash payments journal.

5. Journalize the receipt of cash for the maturity value of the note receivable on March 16, 20X2. Receipt No. 278. Use page 16 of a cash receipts journal.

6. List the amount of interest income from this note receivable that will be shown on the income statements for 20X1 and 20X2.

7. List the amount of interest expense from this note payable that will be shown on the income statements for 20X1 and 20X2.

On your own 21-1

Journalizing entries for accruals

Accounting forms and a partial unadjusted trial balance for Craven, Inc., are given in the *Working Papers*. After each journal entry, update the T accounts given in the *Working Papers*. Work this problem independently.

On December 31, 20X1, Craven, Inc., has one note receivable outstanding, a 90-day, 10%, $12,000.00 note dated December 1, and one note payable outstanding, a 180-day, 5%, $20,000.00 note dated October 17.

1. Journalize the adjusting entries for accrued interest income and accrued interest expense on December 31. Use page 14 of a general journal.

2. Journalize the closing entries for interest income and interest expense using page 14 of a general journal.

▶ **On your own 21-1 (Continued)**

3. Journalize the January 1, 20X2, reversing entries for accrued interest income and accrued interest expense on page 15 of a general journal.

4. Journalize the receipt of cash for the maturity value of the note receivable on March 1, 20X2. Receipt No. 241. Use page 19 of a cash receipts journal.

5. Journalize the payment of cash for the maturity value of the note payable on April 15, Check No. 512. Use page 30 of a cash payments journal.

6. List the amount of interest income from this note receivable that will be shown on the income statements for 20X1 and 20X2.

7. List the amount of interest expense from this note payable that will be shown on the income statements for 20X1 and 20X2.

LO7 Record an entry to receive cash on deferred revenue.

LO8 Calculate the amount and record the entry for deferred revenue when earned.

LO9 Record an entry to pay cash on a deferred expense.

LO10 Calculate the amount and record the entry for a deferred expense when incurred.

Recording Revenue Received in Advance LO7

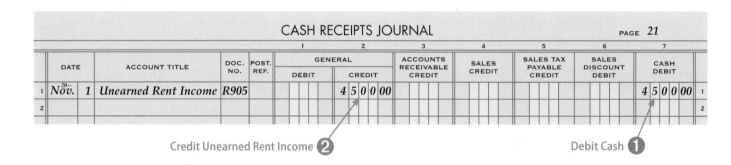

					GENERAL		ACCOUNTS RECEIVABLE CREDIT	SALES CREDIT	SALES TAX PAYABLE CREDIT	SALES DISCOUNT DEBIT	CASH DEBIT
DATE	ACCOUNT TITLE	DOC. NO.	POST. REF.	DEBIT	CREDIT						
				1	2	3	4	5	6	7	
Nov. 1	Unearned Rent Income	R905			4 5 0 0 00						4 5 0 0 00

Credit Unearned Rent Income **2**   Debit Cash **1**

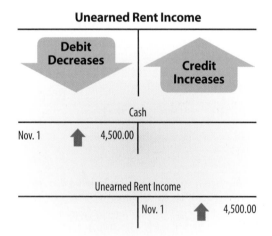

Unearned Rent Income

Debit Decreases / Credit Increases

Cash

Nov. 1 ⬆ 4,500.00

Unearned Rent Income

Nov. 1 ⬆ 4,500.00

Sun Treasures rents its store space. The lease allows Sun Treasures to sublease extra space. In November, Sun Treasures signs an agreement to sublease a portion of the store space to Cones N More, an ice cream business.

> November 1. Received cash for three months' rent in advance, $4,500.00. Receipt No. 905.

Sun Treasures has received cash, but has not yet earned income. Cash received for goods or services which have not yet been provided is called **deferred revenue**. Deferred revenue is sometimes called *unearned revenue*. Deferred revenue is a liability until the services have been provided. Sun Treasures has incurred a liability to provide store space to Cones N More. Therefore, a liability account, **Unearned Rent Income**, is used to record the cash received in advance. Unearned Rent Income is a liability account with a normal credit balance. It is increased by a credit and decreased by a debit.

> ### ⬎ Recording Revenue Received in Advance
>
> **1** Record a debit to Cash in the Cash Debit column of the cash receipts journal for the cash received, $4,500.00.
>
> **2** Record a credit to Unearned Rent Income in the General Credit column for the total liability, $4,500.00.

Recording Adjusting Entry for Deferred Revenue Earned LO8

Debit Unearned Rent Income ❶

GENERAL JOURNAL   PAGE 13

	DATE		ACCOUNT TITLE	DOC. NO.	POST. REF.	DEBIT	CREDIT	
1			*Adjusting Entries*					1
20		31	*Unearned Rent Income*			3 0 0 0 00		20
21			*Rent Income*				3 0 0 0 00	21

Credit Rent Income ❷

Sun Treasures will earn rent income each day that it allows Cones N More to use its store space. It is not practical to record this revenue every day. However, any rent income earned by the end of the fiscal period must be shown on the financial statements. Therefore, Sun Treasures makes an adjusting entry on December 31 to show how much rent income has been earned to date. Sun Treasures has earned two months' rent and must make an adjusting entry for this amount.

Total Rent Received	÷	Number of Months	=	Rent per Month
$4,500.00	÷	3	=	$1,500.00

Rent per Month	×	Months Earned	=	Amount of Adjustment
$1,500.00	×	2	=	$3,000.00

Sun Treasures will record this income in a separate income account, **Rent Income**. **Rent Income** increases with a credit and decreases with a debit. **Unearned Rent Income** is debited for $3,000.00 to reduce this liability account by the amount of rent income earned. **Rent Income** is credited for the same amount, $3,000.00.

After this entry is posted, **Unearned Rent Income** will have a balance of $1,500.00, which represents one month of rent that is still unearned. Because this entry does not establish a balance in a payable or receivable account, no reversing entry will be necessary.

> **▶ Recording the Adjusting Entry for Deferred Revenue Earned**
>
> ❶ Record a debit, **$3,000.00**, to **Unearned Rent Income** in the general journal.
>
> ❷ Record a credit, **$3,000.00**, to **Rent Income**.

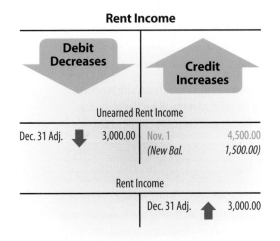

Rent Income

Debit Decreases	Credit Increases

Unearned Rent Income	
Dec. 31 Adj. 3,000.00	Nov. 1 4,500.00
	(New Bal. 1,500.00)

Rent Income	
	Dec. 31 Adj. 3,000.00

When cash is received before the related revenue has been earned, the revenue must be deferred until it is earned.

Recording an Expense Paid in Advance LO9

Debit Prepaid Rent ①   Credit Cash ②

					GENERAL		ACCOUNTS PAYABLE DEBIT	PURCHASES DISCOUNT CREDIT	CASH CREDIT	
					1	2	3	4	5	
DATE	ACCOUNT TITLE	CK. NO.	POST. REF.	DEBIT	CREDIT					
¹ Nov. 1	Prepaid Rent	231		4 5 0 0 00					4 5 0 0 00	¹

CASH PAYMENTS JOURNAL   PAGE 1

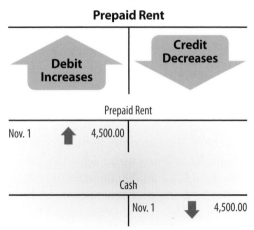

Prepaid Rent

Prepaid Rent

Nov. 1   ↑   4,500.00

Cash

Nov. 1   ↓   4,500.00

When Cones N More paid $4,500.00 to Sun Treasures for three months' rent in advance, it was deferred revenue for Sun Treasures. This required Sun Treasures to record the amount initially as a liability and to defer calling it income until it was earned. Cones N More also records an entry for the transaction.

November 1. Paid cash for three months' rent in advance, $4,500.00. Check No. 231.

Cones N More will eventually record the rent as an expense. But the rent is not an expense at the time of payment because the expense will be incurred over the three-month period. Payments for goods or services which have not yet been received are called **deferred expenses**. Deferred expenses are often listed as *prepaid expenses* (see page 163). Deferred expenses are assets until the services have been received. Therefore, Cones N More records an asset, Prepaid Rent, at the time the rent is paid. Prepaid Rent is increased on the debit side and decreased on the credit side.

❯ Recording an Expense Paid in Advance

① Record a debit to Prepaid Rent in the General Debit column of the cash payments journal for the rent paid in advance, $4,500.00.

② Record a credit to Cash in the Cash Credit column for the cash paid, $4,500.00.

What Is a Good Credit Risk?

When a creditor lends money, it wants to be sure it will get repaid. While each lender is unique, most use some variation of the five C's of credit to help determine the creditworthiness of the borrower before approving a loan.

1. **Character**—What is the borrower's general attitude about payment obligations? What is the educational background?

2. **Capacity**—What is the capacity to repay the loan? Checking previous payment history and comparing income against debt help assess the ability to repay.

3. **Capital**—What is the borrower's net worth—total assets minus total debt? Usually the greater the capital, the greater the ability to repay.

4. **Collateral**—What assets is the borrower willing to pledge as a guarantee of repayment?

5. **Conditions**—What are the current economic conditions? Is the borrower's source of income secure?

By determining creditworthiness, the lender reduces the likelihood of default on the debt and reduces the amount of its uncollectable accounts.

ACTIVITIES

1. Assume you are a small business owner. Create your own credit application including ten questions that would help you ensure creditworthiness.

2. If you had to pick the top three C's of credit, which three do you think are the best predictors of creditworthiness? Explain why.

©NOREBBO, ISTOCK

Recording Adjusting Entry for Deferred Expenses Incurred LO10

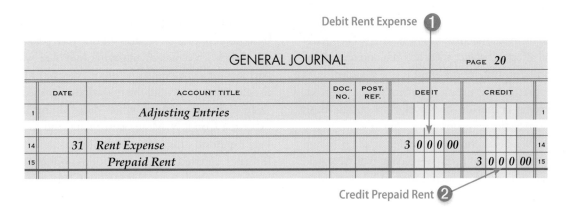

Debit Rent Expense ❶

GENERAL JOURNAL   PAGE 20

	DATE		ACCOUNT TITLE	DOC. NO.	POST. REF.	DEBIT	CREDIT	
1			*Adjusting Entries*					1
14		31	*Rent Expense*			3 0 0 0 00		14
15			*Prepaid Rent*				3 0 0 0 00	15

Credit Prepaid Rent ❷

Cones N More will incur rent expense each day it is allowed to use store space. It is not practical to record this expense every day. However, any rent expense incurred by the end of the fiscal period must be shown on the financial statements. Therefore, Cones N More makes an adjusting entry on December 31 to show how much rent expense has been incurred to date. Cones N More has *used* two months' rent and must make an adjusting entry for this amount.

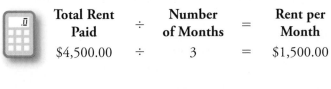

Total Rent Paid	÷	Number of Months	=	Rent per Month
$4,500.00	÷	3	=	$1,500.00

Rent per Month	×	Months Incurred	=	Amount of Adjustment
$1,500.00	×	2	=	$3,000.00

Cones N More will record this adjustment in the expense account, Rent Expense. Rent Expense is debited for $3,000.00 to show the amount of this adjustment for November and December. Prepaid Rent is credited for $3,000.00 to reduce this asset by the amount of rent expense incurred.

After this entry is posted, Prepaid Rent will have a balance of $1,500.00, which represents one month of rent that is still prepaid. Because this entry does not establish a balance in a payable or receivable account, no reversing entry will be necessary.

> **Recording the Adjusting Entry for Deferred Expenses Incurred**
>
> ❶ Record a debit, $3,000.00, to Rent Expense in the general journal.
>
> ❷ Record a credit, $3,000.00, to Prepaid Rent.

Rent Expense

Dec. 31 Adj. ⬆	3,000.00

Prepaid Rent

Nov. 1	4,500.00	Dec. 31 Adj. ⬇	3,000.00
(New Bal.	1,500.00)		

remember

When cash is paid in advance for a future expense, the expense is deferred until it is actually incurred.

Analyzing Deferrals

The adjusting entries for deferred revenue and deferred expenses must be recorded at the end of a fiscal period in order for the financial statements to be accurate. Each entry for a deferral affects a balance sheet account and an income statement account. If a deferral entry is not recorded, both the balance sheet and the income statement will be incorrect.

Since deferral entries do not involve an outside business or customer, the company must remember to record these entries. When determining its deferred revenue, Sun Treasures must include all forms of revenue that were paid for previously and have now been earned. While this lesson illustrated deferred rent revenue, there are many other kinds of deferred revenue. For example, a law firm that is retained by a business for legal services for one year, paid in advance, has deferred revenue. A magazine publisher who receives payment for a one-year subscription must record the receipt as deferred revenue until the magazines are issued.

In a similar manner, when determining its deferred expenses, Cones N More must include all forms of prepaid expenses. This lesson illustrated prepaid rent. Other forms of deferred expenses include supplies and prepaid insurance, which were discussed in Chapters 6 and 15.

THINK LIKE AN ACCOUNTANT

Estimating Product Costs

In the comedy classic *Father of the Bride*, actor Steve Martin's character, George Banks, has had enough. Faced with the reality of his daughter's extravagant wedding expenses, he escapes to the grocery store to buy hot dogs for dinner. Standing in front of the bread isle, he tears four buns from the package. The following interaction ensues.

Stock Boy: What are you doing?

George Banks: I'll tell you what I'm doing. I want to buy eight hot dogs and eight hot dog buns to go with them. But no one sells eight hot dog buns. They only sell twelve hot dog buns. So I end up paying for four buns I don't need. So I am removing the superfluous buns.

Stock Boy: But I'm sorry sir, you're going to have to pay for all twelve buns. They're not marked individually.

George Banks: Yeah. And you want to know why? Because some big-shot over at the wiener company got together with some big-shot over at the bun company and decided to rip off the American public.

George Banks' dilemma is not that uncommon in business. Merchandise is often packaged in a quantity that results in unneeded extras. When those extras go unused, their cost has to be considered when making business decisions.

Dave's Dogs is a local institution and favorite with local college students. Alumni returning for football games dream of devouring one of Dave's special hot dogs. So Dave rents concession booths at football games. But Dave faces some of the same problems as George Banks. Hot dogs come in packages of 100. Hot dog buns are packaged by the dozen.

Based on the weather, the opponent, and the success of the team, Dave estimates how many hot dogs he will sell. But Dave has asked you to help determine a better way of determining the quantity of merchandise he needs to order as well as the number of employees he must hire.

OPEN THE SPREADSHEET TLA_CH21

The worksheet contains an incomplete schedule containing relevant assumptions. Comments provide detailed explanation of each assumption. Use the data to answer following questions:

1. Determine Dave's operating income if he estimates game attendance at 28,000, 30,000, and 32,000, assuming he sells every hot dog.

2. What is the cost per hot dog if Dave estimates game attendance at 38,000, 40,000, and 42,000?

3. Provide Dave with an explanation of why the cost per hot dog changes. Support your answer.

©DAN BACHMAN, ISTOCK

End of Lesson Review

LO7 Record an entry to receive cash on deferred revenue.

LO8 Calculate the amount and record the entry for deferred revenue when earned.

LO9 Record an entry to pay cash on a deferred expense.

LO10 Calculate the amount and record the entry for a deferred expense when incurred.

Terms Review

deferred revenue

deferred expenses

Audit your understanding

1. When a business receives cash for services that will be performed in the future, what type of account is credited?

2. The adjusting entry for deferred expenses that have now been incurred includes a debit to what type of account?

Work together 21-2

Journalizing entries for deferrals

The appropriate accounting forms are given in the *Working Papers*. After each journal entry, update the T accounts given in the *Working Papers*. Your instructor will guide you through the following examples.

1. Journalize the following transactions for Boje Law Firm.

   Sept. 1. Signed a contract to provide legal services to Johnson Corporation for six months. Received cash in advance, $12,000.00. R345.

   Dec. 31. Journalized the adjusting entry for legal services performed for Johnson Corporation.

2. Journalize the following transactions for Johnson Corporation.

   Sept. 1. Signed a contract to receive legal services from Boje Law Firm for six months. Paid cash in advance, $12,000.00. C672.

   Dec. 31. Journalized the adjusting entry for expense incurred for legal services provided by Boje Law Firm.

3. What is the balance in the Prepaid Legal Fees account? What does it represent?

On your own 21-2

Journalizing entries for deferrals

The appropriate accounting forms are given in the *Working Papers*. After each journal entry, update the T accounts given in the *Working Papers*. Work this problem independently.

1. Journalize the following transactions for Smythe Manufacturing.

   Nov. 1. Signed a contract to lease excess warehouse space to Fredrickson Company for six months. Received cash in advance, $9,000.00. R487.

   Dec. 31. Journalized the adjusting entry for rent earned.

2. Journalize the following transactions for Fredrickson Company.

   Nov. 1. Signed a contract to lease a warehouse from Smythe Manufacturing for six months. Paid cash in advance, $9,000.00. C212.

   Dec. 31. Journalized the adjusting entry for rent expense.

3. What is the balance in the Prepaid Rent account? What does it represent?

A Look at Accounting Software

Maintaining Vendor Information and Setting up a Loan

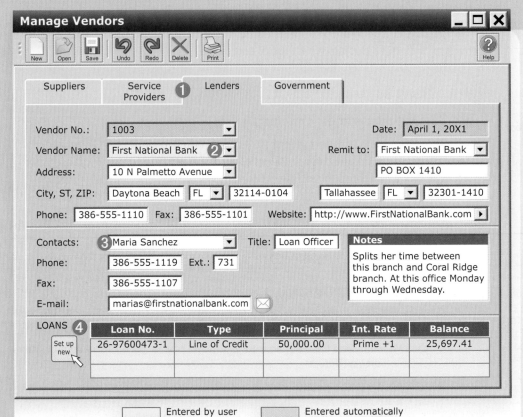

Entered by user ☐   Entered automatically ▨

① Different types of vendors require different kinds of information. The user has selected the Lenders tab in the Manage Vendors window. The top two sections of the tab are similar for all vendor types; however, the bottom section is unique to lenders.

② The user has selected First National Bank from the Vendor Name drop-down menu. The system enters the vendor number automatically. The vendor could also have been selected by number. When a new vendor is added, the system enters the same information in the Remit to cells by default. However, if the vendor has a different address for receiving payments, the information can be changed as it has been for First National Bank.

③ Multiple contacts, each with their own contact information, can be entered for each vendor. Contacts are selected from the drop-down menu. Clicking the button at the end of the e-mail address opens a new message to the contact in the user's e-mail program.

④ Loans owed to this vendor are listed in this section. Currently, Sun Treasures has a $50,000.00 line of credit with First National Bank. As of April 1, there is a $25,697.41 balance drawn on the line of credit. Sun Treasures has just signed a new loan with the bank and is now setting it up in the accounting system.

In a manual accounting system, customer and vendor information might be kept in a file cabinet. Since many individuals in the business might need access to that information, it is often duplicated and kept in several different offices. Computerized accounting systems make it easy to provide customer and vendor information to everyone in the organization who has access to the accounting system.

To protect the integrity of the data in a computerized accounting system, users are assigned limited rights to access it. For example, sales reps might be given the right to view customer and vendor information but have no authority to enter or change it. An accounting clerk in the payroll department can be given the authority to enter or edit payroll data, but not purchasing or sales data. The controller would likely have full access to the system.

This feature focuses on maintaining vendor information. Businesses rely on different kinds of vendors. Suppliers provide the merchandise and supplies that merchandising businesses need to operate. Service providers include advertisers, insurance companies, utilities, maintenance personnel, financial services, data services, etc. Lenders are a type of service provider, but the need to track individual loans and their repayment requirements makes lenders unique. There are several types of vendors that fall into the general category of government. These are taxing authorities, as well as licensing and regulatory agencies, at federal, state, and local levels.

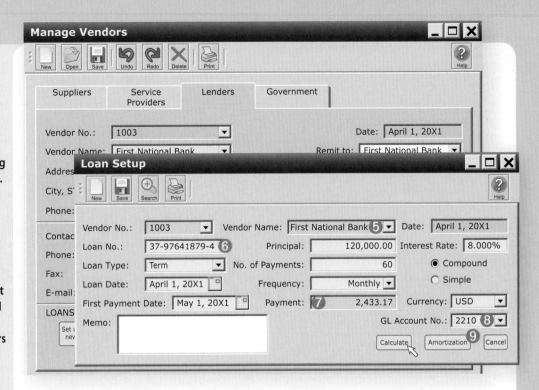

⑤ Because the user launched the Loan Setup pop-up window from the First National Bank vendor tab, the system automatically fills in the vendor name and number. If Loan Setup had been launched from the Banking module, the user would then select the lender from the drop-down menu.

⑥ The user completes all the other fields in the pop-up window except for the amount of the payment. This loan is a $120,000.00, five-year, 8% compound interest term loan requiring monthly payments beginning on May 1. USD is the international banking symbol for the U.S. dollar.

⑦ After entering the loan information, the user clicks the Calculate button. The system computes and enters the payment amount, $2,433.17. This amount would be confirmed with the loan document. If the amount were different, the user could overwrite the amount to match the loan document.

⑧ The user must enter a general ledger account number before the system will complete the loan setup.

⑨ If the user wants an amortization schedule for this loan, clicking the Amortization button will open the schedule, which can then be printed, saved, and even e-mailed, if desired. A recurring transaction could be set up to partially or fully automate the monthly payment on the loan. Monthly payments can be made either through the Write Checks window or by electronic funds transfer from the Banking module.

Chapter Summary

Accrued revenue must be recorded as an adjusting entry at the end of a fiscal period. The adjusting entry increases a receivable account and a revenue account. The adjusting entry for accrued interest income can be reversed by a reversing entry. A reversing entry makes it easier for accounting personnel to record the receipt of the interest, which could come many months later. The reversing entry establishes a debit balance in the Interest Income account. When the interest is received, the total interest received is credited to the Interest Income account. The new balance in the account reflects the amount of interest income earned in the current period.

An accrued expense must also be recorded as an adjusting entry at the end of a fiscal period. The adjusting entry increases a payable account and an expense account. The adjusting entry for accrued interest expense can be reversed by a reversing entry. The reversing entry establishes a credit balance in the Interest Expense account. When the interest is paid, the total interest paid is debited to the Interest Expense account. The new balance in the account reflects the amount of interest expense incurred in the current period.

Deferred revenue and deferred expenses occur when money is transferred before goods or services are provided. The company receiving the cash records a liability representing unearned income. The company paying the cash records an asset representing a prepaid expense. Both companies must record an adjusting entry at the end of the fiscal period. The company providing the goods or service will decrease the liability account and increase an income account. The company receiving the goods or service will decrease the asset account and increase an expense account.

DLEWIS33/ISTOCKPHOTO.COM

The Annual Report and the 10-K—
Financial Information and More

Corporations publish annual reports to communicate the results of operations to interested parties, such as stockholders, creditors, and government agencies. Most companies post a copy of this report on their website. An annual report has two main sections:

1. *Management's Discussion and Analysis*. This section provides management with an opportunity to promote the corporation. Through the use of pictures, graphs, and narrative, management can highlight the achievements of the past fiscal year and present its plans for the future. Discussions of environmental and recycling programs, for example, could demonstrate how the corporation is socially responsible.

2. *Financial Statements*. The financial statements section contains several items in addition to basic financial statements. Most of the additional items are required by GAAP or the Securities and Exchange Commission. As a result, these items are similar among corporations.

   a. *Notes to the Financial Statements*. The notes contain additional, detailed information about items presented on the financial statements. For example, the note related to long-term debt would include the projected loan repayments for the next five years.

   b. *Auditor's Report*. The report of the independent auditor states that a public accounting firm has tested the financial statements for accuracy and fair presentation. The report gives the reader confidence to use the financial statements to make business decisions.

   c. *Financial Analysis*. Summary financial information, such as total assets, net income, and common financial ratios, are presented for several years. Company management is responsible for preparing and issuing the annual report.

Corporations are also required to file a yearly report to the Securities and Exchange Commission (SEC), called the 10-K. The SEC, in its role as regulator, sets forth specific requirements as to what is included in a 10-K filing. Besides the financial statements, the 10-K also includes detailed information about the business, its properties, executive compensation, fixed assets, organizational structure, and subsidiaries. Many companies are combining the annual report and the 10-K into one document which is given to all stockholders.

INSTRUCTIONS

Access an annual report using a library or the Internet and prepare a detailed outline of its contents. Summarize the major topics in *Management's Discussion and Analysis*. Did management do a good job of "putting its best foot forward?" Would you recommend that a friend purchase the corporation's stock? Support your answers.

Apply Your Understanding

INSTRUCTIONS: Download problem instructions for Excel, QuickBooks, and Peachtree from the textbook companion website at www.C21accounting.com.

21-1 Application Problem: Journalizing entries for accruals LO1, 2, 3, 4, 5, 6

 Peachtree

1. Journalize and post adjusting and closing entries to the general journal.
2. Print the general journal and trial balance.
3. Journalize and post reversing entries.
4. Journalize and post notes payable and notes receivable transactions.

Quick Books

1. Journalize and post adjusting and closing entries to the journal.
2. Print the journal and trial balance.
3. Journalize and post reversing entries.
4. Journalize and post notes payable and notes receivable transactions.

![Excel icon]

1. Journalize and post adjusting, closing and reversing entries to the general journal.
2. Journalize and post notes payable and notes receivable transactions.
3. Print the worksheets.

Accounting forms and a partial unadjusted trial balance for Spano Corporation are given in the *Working Papers*. After each journal entry, update the T accounts given in the *Working Papers*. Your instructor will guide you through the following examples.

On December 31, 20X1, Spano Corporation has one note receivable outstanding, a 120-day, 6%, $16,000.00 note dated November 16, and one note payable outstanding, a 90-day, 6%, $18,000.00 note dated December 1.

Instructions:

1. Journalize the adjusting entries for accrued interest income and accrued interest expense on December 31. Use page 14 of a general journal.
2. Journalize the closing entries for interest income and interest expense using page 14 of a general journal.
3. Journalize the January 1, 20X2, reversing entries for accrued interest income and accrued interest expense on page 15 of a general journal.
4. Journalize the payment of cash for the maturity value of the note payable on March 1, 20X2. Check No. 321. Use page 25 of a cash payments journal.
5. Journalize the receipt of cash for the maturity value of the note receivable on March 16, 20X2. Receipt No. 587. Use page 16 of a cash receipts journal.
6. List the amount of interest income from this note receivable that will be shown on the income statements for 20X1 and 20X2.
7. List the amount of interest expense from this note payable that will be shown on the income statements for 20X1 and 20X2.

21-2 Application Problem: Journalizing entries for deferrals LO7, 8, 9, 10

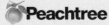
1. Go to www.cengage.com/login
2. Click on **AA Online** to access.
3. Go to the online assignment and follow the instructions.

The appropriate accounting forms are given in the *Working Papers*. After each journal entry, update the T accounts given in the *Working Papers*.

Instructions:

1. Journalize the following transactions for Deegs Company.
   Oct. 1. Signed a contract to lease excess space to Sheldon Company for six months. Received cash in advance, $12,000.00. R164.
   Dec. 31. Journalized the adjusting entry for rent earned.

2. Journalize the following transactions for Sheldon Company.
   Oct. 1. Signed a contract to lease space from Deegs Company for six months. Paid cash in advance, $12,000.00. C377.
   Dec. 31. Journalized the adjusting entry for rent expense.

3. What is the balance in the Prepaid Rent account? What does it represent?

Accounting forms and a partial unadjusted trial balance for Figlmiller Corporation are given in the *Working Papers*. Figlmiller Corporation collected $30,000 on November 1 for six months' rent. On December 31, 20X1, Figlmiller Corporation has one note receivable outstanding, a 90-day, 5%, $13,000.00 note dated December 1, and one note payable outstanding, a 120-day, 4%, $8,000.00 note dated November 16.

Instructions:

1. Journalize the adjusting entries for accrued interest income, accrued interest expense, and rent earned on December 31. Use page 14 of a general journal.

2. Journalize the closing entries for all income and expense accounts using page 14 of a general journal. Record the closing entry for both income accounts in one entry.

3. Journalize the January 1, 20X2, reversing entries for accrued interest income and accrued interest expense on page 15 of a general journal.

4. Journalize the receipt of cash for the maturity value of the note receivable on March 1, 20X2. Receipt No. 125. Use page 16 of a cash receipts journal.

5. Journalize the payment of cash for the maturity value of the note payable on March 16, 20X2. Check No. 185. Use page 25 of a cash payments journal.

6. List the amount of interest income from this note receivable that will be shown on the income statements for 20X1 and 20X2.

7. List the amount of interest expense from this note payable that will be shown on the income statements for 20X1 and 20X2.

8. What is the balance in the Prepaid Rent account on December 21, 20X1? What does it represent?

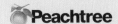

Peachtree	QuickBooks	X
1. Journalize and post adjusting and closing entries to the general journal.	1. Journalize and post adjusting and closing entries to the journal.	1. Journalize and post adjusting, closing, and reversing entries to the general journal.
2. Print the general journal and trial balance.	2. Print the journal and trial balance.	2. Journalize and post notes payable and notes receivable transactions.
3. Journalize and post reversing entries.	3. Journalize and post reversing entries.	3. Print the worksheets.
4. Journalize and post notes payable and notes receivable transactions.	4. Journalize and post notes payable and notes receivable transactions.	

21-C Challenge Problem: Journalizing entries for deferred revenue LO7, 8

The appropriate accounting forms are given in the *Working Papers*. After each journal entry, update the T accounts given in the *Working Papers*.

Marboe Fitness Center began operations on November 1, 20X1. It sells yearly memberships for $600, which allow the member full access to all exercise equipment in the center. By November 1, Marboe Fitness Center had sold 500 one-year memberships. Marboe Fitness Center also publishes a monthly magazine. By the end of November, Marboe had sold 1,000 one-year magazine subscriptions for $36.00 each. The first issue of the magazine was distributed on December 1, 20X1.

Instructions:

1. Journalize the adjusting entries for membership fees and magazine subscriptions earned.
2. What is the balance in the Unearned Membership Fees account? What does it represent?
3. What is the balance in the Unearned Magazine Subscriptions account? What does it represent?
4. GAAP requires that deferred revenue be recorded as it is earned. Revenue earned from a one-year magazine subscription is relatively easy to calculate. Each month, when a magazine is published, one-twelfth of the one-year subscription fee is earned for each subscription. Other forms of unearned revenue are not as easy to calculate and may not be earned evenly over time. A fitness center that sells one-year memberships can assume that the membership revenue is earned equally over time. However, if the fitness center feels that the membership is not earned equally over time, another method may be used to calculate the amount of revenue earned each month. Assume that Marboe Fitness Center does not believe membership revenue is earned equally over time. Develop a method for Marboe Fitness Center to calculate the amount of revenue earned each month.

21st Century Skills

FICO Scores—What's Your Number?

Theme: Financial, Economic, Business, and Entrepreneurial Literacy

Skills: Creativity and Innovation, Critical Thinking and Problem Solving, Communication and Collaboration, ICT Literacy

PARTNERSHIP FOR
21ST CENTURY SKILLS

Banks and other lenders provide consumer loans for cars, homes, home furnishings, etc. They also provide business loans. These lenders are well aware of the risks of not being repaid on time, and they take steps to minimize those risks. So, how do lenders determine if a business or individual is creditworthy (i.e., willing and able to repay a loan)?

Banks use credit scores to help predict the likelihood that individuals or businesses will repay their debt. The credit score is a numerical rating assigned to the borrower's credit information, which includes the way credit has been managed in the past.

For individuals, the most well-known type of credit score is FICO. FICO is named for the Fair Isaac Company, which developed the mathematical model in the 1950s. It calculates a score based on a person's credit report. It is important to remember that negative information remains on your credit report for seven to ten years. The three major credit bureaus that keep the credit history for scoring are Experian, Equifax, and TransUnion. Different scoring systems are used for rating businesses.

Many factors are taken into consideration to determine your FICO score. Among these are the amount you owe each month, your late-payment history, the length of your credit history, and the number of your recent credit applications. Income is not a factor because ability to pay is not necessarily an indicator of willingness to pay. The score, ranging from 300–850, often determines whether a person gets a loan and the interest rate they are charged. Many lenders consider someone with a FICO score over 720 to be a very good credit risk. A good score might also help someone get approved for an apartment, obtain employment, secure better insurance rates, or reduce deposits with utility companies. That is because a credit score is often seen as an indicator of character.

Your credit report should be reviewed regularly to uncover and correct any mistakes that might affect your FICO score. The Fair and Accurate Transactions Act of 2003 entitles everyone to a free report from each of the three agencies once a year. Students can begin a positive credit history by applying for a small amount of credit and paying on time and in full each month. Even your cell phone bill counts towards your credit history!

APPLICATION

1. Go to www.myfico.com. Determine the categories and percentages used to calculate your FICO score. Which category is the most important in determining the FICO score?

2. Create a table or spreadsheet with headings like the one below. Based on what you have learned, read the following scenarios and determine (a) if the impact is positive or negative on the FICO score, (b) the reason for the change, and (c) what needs to be done to improve the score if a negative impact was made. *Note*: If the impact was positive, only write "N/A".

   Example:

Scenario	Impact	Reason for Change	Action to Remedy
Pays cell phone bill on time	+	*Timely Payments*	*N/A*
Overdue payment			
Obtains new car loan			
Pays off credit card			
Missed or late payment			

3. With a partner, create a one-minute public service announcement (poster, radio commercial, or video) informing other students of the FICO score and the impact it can have on their future.

Analyzing Nike's financial statements

Like most companies, Nike, Inc., records accrued liabilities at the end of a fiscal period in order for the financial statements to be accurate and up to date. Nike's accrued liabilities are often the largest single item in current liabilities. By looking at Nike's balance sheet, you cannot determine the makeup of its accrued liabilities. However, the notes to the financial statements usually give additional information about items such as accrued liabilities. Use the Consolidated Balance Sheets on page B-6 of Nike's 10-K report in Appendix B.

INSTRUCTIONS

1. What is the dollar amount of Nike's accrued liabilities as of May 31, 2011?

2. Find Note 5 on page B-14. Ignoring the Other category, list the names and amounts of the two largest accrued liabilities.

Chapter 22

End-of-Fiscal-Period Work for a Corporation

LEARNING OBJECTIVES

After studying Chapter 22, in addition to defining key terms, you will be able to:

LO1 Plan and record end-of-fiscal-period adjustments for a merchandising business organized as a corporation.

LO2 Prepare an income statement for a merchandising business organized as a corporation.

LO3 Prepare a statement of stockholders' equity for a merchandising business organized as a corporation.

LO4 Prepare a balance sheet for a merchandising business organized as a corporation.

LO5 Prepare a statement of cash flows for a merchandising business organized as a corporation.

LO6 Record closing entries for a merchandising business organized as a corporation.

LO7 Record reversing entries for a merchandising business organized as a corporation.

©DANIEL KOUREY, ISTOCK/©JIM PRUITT, ISTOCK

BLEND IMAGES/JUPITER IMAGES

Accounting In The Real World
Bank of America

Bank of America (BoA) is one of the largest financial services companies in the country. According to a recent annual report, BoA serves half of all U.S. households and operates in more than 40 countries. Chances are, you have a Bank of America branch office or ATM machine near you.

The recession that began in 2008 had a dramatic impact on financial institutions. One hard-hit area was the housing market. Housing prices plummeted, and many home mortgages were higher than the value of the mortgaged home. A mortgage that has a balance higher than the value of the property mortgaged is called an **underwater mortgage**. By the end of the first quarter of 2011, approximately 22.7% of all U.S. home mortgages were estimated to be underwater.

With a high percentage of mortgages underwater, mortgage lenders were faced with a greatly increased risk that homeowners would stop making their mortgage payments. Not making payments on a loan when they are due is called **defaulting** on the loan. When a mortgage is in default, the bank or finance company has the right to take possession of the property. When the bank or finance company takes possession of mortgaged property, it is called a **foreclosure**.

Foreclosures usually mean a loss for the mortgage holder, who must sell the property at a price less than the amount owed on the property. What is the impact of these foreclosures on the financial statements of the mortgage holder? Remember that GAAP requires a business to estimate the amount of receivables that will not be collected. Mortgages financed by BoA are listed as receivables on its balance sheet. Therefore, BoA must estimate the amount of these receivables that will not be paid in the future. This estimate is recorded in an account titled Allowance for Loans and Lease Losses.

BoA reported the following balances on its balance sheet:

2010: Loans and leases, $940,440,000,000; Allowance for loans and lease losses, $41,885,000,000

2009: Loans and leases, $900,128,000,000; Allowance for loans and lease losses, $37,200,000,000

CRITICAL THINKING

1. For 2010 and 2009, calculate what percent the allowance account is of the Loans and Leases account.

2. For which year was the percentage higher? What does this indicate about what Bank of America thinks about the rate of foreclosures?

Sources: www.credit.com/blog/2011/06 and CoreLogic.com.

Key Terms

- cash flow
- statement of cash flows
- operating activities
- investing activities
- financing activities

22-1 Preparing Adjusting Entries

LO1 Plan and record end-of-fiscal-period adjustments for a merchandising business organized as a corporation.

End-of-Fiscal-Period Work LO1

The end of a fiscal period is a busy time for a corporation. It begins with preparing an unadjusted trial balance to ensure that debits equal credits in the general ledger. The unadjusted trial balance and other financial data are used to plan and record adjusting entries. Once the adjusting entries are posted, an adjusted trial balance is prepared.

The adjusted trial balance is used to prepare the financial statements. The income statement is the first statement prepared. The amount of net income, selected balance sheet accounts, and other accounting information are used to prepare the statement of stockholders' equity. Summary amounts on this statement and the adjusted trial balance are used to prepare a balance sheet.

In preparation for recording transactions during the next period, closing and reversing entries are recorded and posted. The accounts are then ready to record transactions for the next fiscal period. Sun Treasures may prepare financial statements any time they are needed. However, Sun Treasures always prepares financial statements at the end of a fiscal year. [CONCEPT: Accounting Period Cycle]

Setting the Tone at the Top

A certain company's code of conduct prohibits employees from accepting gifts, favors, or entertainment that would influence their sound business decisions. Despite the rule, the company president is known to accept lavish gifts from suppliers. Do you think the employees will be motivated to adhere to the code of conduct?

The employees at the top of a company—managers, officers, and directors—must provide leadership in making ethical decisions. Among the many ways companies can "set the tone at the top" is to have a special code of conduct for members of the board of directors.

INSTRUCTIONS

Access the *Board of Directors Code of Conduct for Kellogg Company*. Determine whether directors can personally invest in the stock of companies that do business with Kellogg Company.

©LUCA DI FILIPPO, ISTOCK

Unadjusted Trial Balance

Sun Treasures' unadjusted trial balance prepared from the general ledger is shown below.

ACCOUNT TITLE	DEBIT	CREDIT
Cash	43 8 4 8 68	
Petty Cash	4 5 0 00	
Accounts Receivable	52 4 8 1 37	
Allowance for Uncollectible Accounts		6 7 5 56
Notes Receivable	15 0 0 0 00	
Interest Receivable	—	
Merchandise Inventory	331 2 3 5 20	
Supplies—Office	89 6 4 0 00	
Supplies—Store	158 1 0 0 00	
Prepaid Insurance	54 8 7 2 35	
Office Equipment	325 6 4 8 16	
Accumulated Depreciation—Office Equipment		79 7 2 7 00
Store Equipment	1099 6 3 8 43	
Accumulated Depreciation—Store Equipment		337 9 0 2 00
Accounts Payable		15 4 6 2 50
Sales Tax Payable		6 4 7 31
Notes Payable		—
Interest Payable		—
Line of Credit		7 5 0 0 00
Unearned Rent Income		4 5 0 0 00
Employee Income Tax Payable		1 5 7 3 00
Social Security Tax Payable		3 0 0 0 80
Medicare Tax Payable		7 0 1 80
Medical Insurance Payable		3 2 1 24
Retirement Benefits Payable		4 7 5 00
Unemployment Tax Payable—State		3 5 00
Unemployment Tax Payable—Federal		2 3 6 25
Federal Income Tax Payable		—
Dividends Payable		—
Long-term Notes Payable		106 6 2 5 67
Bonds Payable		180 0 0 0 00
Capital Stock—Common ($10 par, 40,000)		400 0 0 0 00
Paid-in Capital in Excess of Par—Common		480 0 0 0 00
Capital Stock—Preferred ($50 par, 400)		20 0 0 0 00
Paid-in Capital in Excess of Par—Preferred		—
Retained Earnings		82 5 2 5 10
Dividends	21 2 0 0 00	
Income Summary	—	

Sun Treasures, Inc.
Unadjusted Trial Balance
December 31, 20--

(Continued on next page)

Unadjusted Trial Balance *(continued)*

ACCOUNT TITLE	DEBIT	CREDIT
Sun Treasures, Inc.		
Unadjusted Trial Balance		
December 31, 20--		
Sales		2576 3 2 1 45
Sales Discount	15 4 5 7 93	
Sales Returns and Allowances	113 5 2 3 11	
Purchases	1307 1 6 0 50	
Purchases Discount		15 6 8 5 93
Purchases Returns and Allowances		1 1 5 0 40
Advertising Expense	58 0 0 0 00	
Cash Short and Over	2 4 1 7 25	
Credit Card Fee Expense	23 7 6 3 21	
Depreciation Expense—Office Equipment	—	
Depreciation Expense—Store Equipment	—	
Insurance Expense	—	
Miscellaneous Expense	38 0 1 0 66	
Payroll Taxes Expense	27 4 2 3 60	
Rent Expense	143 0 0 0 00	
Salary Expense	290 4 0 0 00	
Supplies Expense—Office	—	
Supplies Expense—Store	—	
Uncollectible Accounts Expense	—	
Utilities Expense	66 8 8 6 10	
Federal Income Tax Expense	23 0 0 0 00	
Interest Income		2 3 3 7 80
Rent Income		—
Gain on Plant Assets		18 2 3 1 00
Interest Expense	17 6 3 6 26	
Loss on Plant Assets	16 8 4 2 00	
Totals	4335 6 3 4 81	4335 6 3 4 81

Adjusting Entries for Uncollectible Accounts and Merchandise Inventory

ACCOUNT TITLE	DEBIT	CREDIT
Sun Treasures, Inc.		
Unadjusted Trial Balance		
December 31, 20--		
Accounts Receivable	52 4 8 1 37	
Allowance for Uncollectible Accounts		6 7 5 56
Merchandise Inventory	331 2 3 5 20	
Income Summary		
Uncollectible Accounts Expense		

Some general ledger accounts need to be brought up to date before financial statements are prepared. An unadjusted trial balance is used to plan and record the adjusting entries. Accounts are brought up to date by recording the adjustments in the general journal and then posting them to the general ledger.

Two methods are used to determine the amount of each adjustment. For some accounts, the calculated estimate of the account is also the amount used in the adjustment. These adjustments include interest income, depreciation expense, and interest expense.

Other accounts require estimating the end-of-period balance. The current balance is typically subtracted from the estimated end-of-period account balance to determine the amount of the adjustment. These adjustments include uncollectible accounts expense, merchandise inventory, supplies, prepaid insurance, and federal income tax expense.

Examples of both types of adjustments are shown on the following pages. Other adjustments were illustrated earlier in Part 3. Adjustments generally are made in the order that accounts are listed in the general ledger.

UNCOLLECTIBLE ACCOUNTS ADJUSTMENT

Sun Treasures estimates that $2,099.25 of its accounts receivable will not be collected. On December 31, the balance in the **Allowance for Uncollectible Accounts**

account is $675.56. The amount of the adjusting entry is calculated as shown.

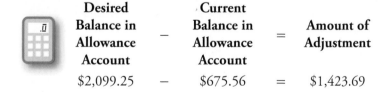

	Desired Balance in Allowance Account	−	Current Balance in Allowance Account	=	Amount of Adjustment
	$2,099.25	−	$675.56	=	$1,423.69

Uncollectible Accounts Expense is debited and **Allowance for Uncollectible Accounts** is credited for $1,423.69.

MERCHANDISE INVENTORY ADJUSTMENT

If the current balance in the Merchandise Inventory account is more than the actual inventory on hand at the end of the period, Income Summary is debited and Merchandise Inventory is credited. On December 31, the balance in the Merchandise Inventory account is $331,235.20. The actual inventory on hand on December 31 is $307,613.20. The amount of the adjusting entry is calculated as shown.

Current Balance in Merchandise Inventory Account	−	Desired Balance in Merchandise Inventory Account	=	Amount of Adjustment
$331,235.20	−	$307,613.20	=	$23,622.00

Income Summary is debited and Merchandise Inventory is credited for $23,622.00. If the current balance in Merchandise Inventory is less than the actual inventory on hand at the end of the period, Merchandise Inventory is debited and Income Summary is credited.

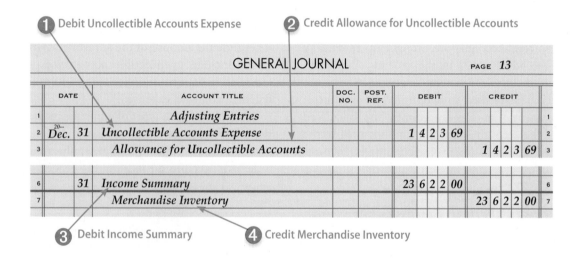

1 Debit Uncollectible Accounts Expense   **2** Credit Allowance for Uncollectible Accounts

GENERAL JOURNAL   PAGE *13*

	DATE		ACCOUNT TITLE	DOC. NO.	POST. REF.	DEBIT	CREDIT	
1			*Adjusting Entries*					1
2	*Dec.* 20--	*31*	*Uncollectible Accounts Expense*			1 4 2 3 69		2
3			*Allowance for Uncollectible Accounts*				1 4 2 3 69	3
6		*31*	*Income Summary*			23 6 2 2 00		6
7			*Merchandise Inventory*				23 6 2 2 00	7

3 Debit Income Summary   **4** Credit Merchandise Inventory

⤵ Journalizing Adjustments for Uncollectible Accounts and Merchandise Inventory

1 Debit Uncollectible Accounts Expense for $1,423.69.

2 Credit Allowance for Uncollectible Accounts for $1,423.69.

3 Debit Income Summary for $23,622.00.

4 Credit Merchandise Inventory for $23,622.00.

Adjusting Entries for Supplies and Insurance

Sun Treasures, Inc.
Unadjusted Trial Balance
December 31, 20--

ACCOUNT TITLE	DEBIT	CREDIT
Supplies—Store	158 1 0 0 00	
Prepaid Insurance	54 8 7 2 35	
Insurance Expense		
Supplies Expense—Store		

1 Debit Supplies Expense—Store

2 Credit Supplies—Store

GENERAL JOURNAL   PAGE 13

	DATE	ACCOUNT TITLE	DOC. NO.	POST. REF.	DEBIT	CREDIT	
1		*Adjusting Entries*					1
10	31	Supplies Expense—Store			109 8 0 0 00		10
11		Supplies—Store				109 8 0 0 00	11
12	31	Insurance Expense			36 2 2 5 00		12
13		Prepaid Insurance				36 2 2 5 00	13

3 Debit Insurance Expense

4 Credit Prepaid Insurance

SUPPLIES—STORE ADJUSTMENT

The balance of **Supplies—Store** in the trial balance, $158,100.00, is the cost of supplies on hand at the beginning of the year plus the supplies purchased during the year. The supplies on hand on December 31 are counted and determined to be $48,300.00. To bring the account up to date, the balance of **Supplies—Store** needs to be decreased by $109,800.00 ($158,100.00 − $48,300.00), the cost of supplies used during the year. **Supplies Expense—Store** is debited and **Supplies—Store** is credited for the amount of the decrease.

PREPAID INSURANCE ADJUSTMENT

The balance of **Prepaid Insurance** in the trial balance, $54,872.35, is the cost of prepaid insurance remaining at the beginning of the year plus the cost of insurance

purchased during the period. An analysis of the account determined that $18,647.35 of prepaid insurance premiums remain on December 31. To bring the account up to date, the balance of **Prepaid Insurance** needs to be decreased by $36,225.00 ($54,872.35 − $18,647.35), the cost of insurance that expired during the year. **Insurance Expense** is debited and **Prepaid Insurance** is credited for the amount of the decrease.

> **Journalizing Adjustments for Supplies and Insurance**
>
> **1** Debit Supplies Expense—Store for $109,800.00.
> **2** Credit Supplies—Store for $109,800.00.
> **3** Debit Insurance Expense for $36,225.00.
> **4** Credit Prepaid Insurance for $36,225.00.

Federal Income Tax Adjustment

Sun Treasures, Inc.
Unadjusted Trial Balance
December 31, 20--

ACCOUNT TITLE	DEBIT	CREDIT
Federal Income Tax Payable		
Federal Income Tax Expense	23 0 0 0 00	

		GENERAL JOURNAL				PAGE 13	
	DATE	ACCOUNT TITLE	DOC. NO.	POST. REF.	DEBIT	CREDIT	
1		*Adjusting Entries*					1
22	31	Federal Income Tax Expense			2 9 9 2 22		22
23		Federal Income Tax Payable				2 9 9 2 22	23

① Debit Federal Income Tax Expense   **②** Credit Federal Income Tax Payable

Detailed instructions for preparing the federal income tax adjustment were presented in Chapter 15. The first step is to calculate the corporation's net income before federal income tax. Sun Treasures' net income before federal income tax expense is $109,595.43.

The amount of federal income tax is calculated using tax rates provided by the Internal Revenue Service. The tax rate varies, depending on the amount of net income earned. The tax rates are given in the table below.

Tax Rate Schedule

If taxable income (line 30, Form 1120, or line 26, Form 1120-A) is:

Over—	But not over—	Tax is:	Of the amount over—
$0	50,000	15%	-0-
50,000	75,000	$7,500 + 25%	$50,000
75,000	100,000	13,750 + 34%	75,000
100,000	335,000	22,250 + 39%	100,000
335,000	10,000,000	113,900 + 34%	335,000
10,000,000	15,000,000	3,400,000 + 35%	10,000,000
15,000,000	18,333,333	5,150,000 + 38%	15,000,000
18,333,333	—	35%	-0-

CALCULATING FEDERAL INCOME TAX

The amount of taxable income is $109,595.43.
The amount over $100,000 is $9,595.43.
39% of $9,595.43 is $3,742.22
$22,250.00 + $3,742.22 = $25,992.22 Total Federal Income Tax

Sun Treasures has already paid $23,000.00. Therefore, the amount of federal income tax still due is $25,992.22 – $23,000.00 = $2,992.22. The estimated tax payments already made are subtracted from the total federal income tax expense to calculate the adjustment for federal income tax expense.

Total Federal Income Tax Expense	–	Estimated Federal Income Tax Already Paid	=	Accrued Federal Income Tax Expense
$25,992.22	–	$23,000.00	=	$2,992.22

Federal Income Tax Expense is debited and Federal Income Tax Payable is credited for the amount of the accrued taxes.

> **Journalizing Adjustment for Federal Income Tax Expense**
>
> ❶ Debit Federal Income Tax Expense for $2,992.22.
>
> ❷ Credit Federal Income Tax Payable for $2,992.22.

Adjusting Entries

GENERAL JOURNAL   PAGE 13

	DATE		ACCOUNT TITLE	DOC. NO.	POST. REF.	DEBIT	CREDIT	
1			*Adjusting Entries*					1
2	Dec.²⁰⁻⁻	31	Uncollectible Accounts Expense			1 4 2 3 69		2
3			Allowance for Uncollectible Accounts				1 4 2 3 69	3
4		31	Interest Receivable			1 7 5 00		4
5			Interest Income				1 7 5 00	5
6		31	Income Summary			23 6 2 2 00		6
7			Merchandise Inventory				23 6 2 2 00	7
8		31	Supplies Expense—Office			76 4 4 0 00		8
9			Supplies—Office				76 4 4 0 00	9
10		31	Supplies Expense—Store			109 8 0 0 00		10
11			Supplies—Store				109 8 0 0 00	11
12		31	Insurance Expense			36 2 2 5 00		12
13			Prepaid Insurance				36 2 2 5 00	13
14		31	Depreciation Exp.—Office Equip.			25 1 4 6 00		14
15			Accum. Depr.—Office Equip.				25 1 4 6 00	15
16		31	Depreciation Exp.—Store Equip.			113 4 1 8 00		16
17			Accum. Depr.—Store Equip.				113 4 1 8 00	17
18		31	Interest Expense			7 1 0 84		18
19			Interest Payable				7 1 0 84	19
20		31	Unearned Rent Income			3 0 0 0 00		20
21			Rent Income				3 0 0 0 00	21
22		31	Federal Income Tax Expense			2 9 9 2 22		22
23			Federal Income Tax Payable				2 9 9 2 22	23

Sun Treasures' adjusting entries are shown above. The entries are posted to the general ledger to bring each account up to date. An adjusted trial balance is prepared. The adjusted trial balance is used to prepare financial statements.

Adjusted Trial Balance

After all adjusting entries are journalized and posted, another trial balance is prepared to prove the general ledger. The adjusted trial balance is shown below.

	Sun Treasures, Inc. Adjusted Trial Balance December 31, 20--		
ACCOUNT TITLE		**DEBIT**	**CREDIT**
Cash		43 848 68	
Petty Cash		450 00	
Accounts Receivable		52 481 37	
Allowance for Uncollectible Accounts			2 099 25
Notes Receivable		15 000 00	
Interest Receivable		175 00	
Merchandise Inventory		307 613 20	
Supplies—Office		13 200 00	
Supplies—Store		48 300 00	
Prepaid Insurance		18 647 35	
Office Equipment		325 648 16	
Accumulated Depreciation—Office Equipment			104 873 00
Store Equipment		1099 638 43	
Accumulated Depreciation—Store Equipment			451 320 00
Accounts Payable			15 462 50
Sales Tax Payable			6 473 1
Notes Payable			—
Interest Payable			710 84
Line of Credit			7 500 00
Unearned Rent Income			1 500 00
Employee Income Tax Payable			1 573 00
Social Security Tax Payable			3 000 80
Medicare Tax Payable			701 80
Medical Insurance Payable			321 24
Retirement Benefits Payable			475 00
Unemployment Tax Payable—State			35 00
Unemployment Tax Payable—Federal			236 25
Federal Income Tax Payable			2 992 22
Dividends Payable			
Long-term Notes Payable			106 625 67
Bonds Payable			180 000 00

Sun Treasures, Inc.
Adjusted Trial Balance
December 31, 20--

ACCOUNT TITLE	DEBIT	CREDIT
Capital Stock—Common ($10 par, 40,000)		400 000 00
Paid-in Capital in Excess of Par—Common		480 000 00
Capital Stock—Preferred ($50 par, 400)		20 000 00
Paid-in Capital in Excess of Par—Preferred		—
Retained Earnings		82 525 10
Dividends	21 200 00	
Income Summary	23 622 00	
Sales		2576 321 45
Sales Discount	15 457 93	
Sales Returns and Allowances	113 523 11	
Purchases	1307 160 50	
Purchases Discount		15 685 93
Purchases Returns and Allowances		1 150 40
Advertising Expense	58 000 00	
Cash Short and Over	2 417 25	
Credit Card Fee Expense	23 763 21	
Depreciation Expense—Office Equipment	25 146 00	
Depreciation Expense—Store Equipment	113 418 00	
Insurance Expense	36 225 00	
Miscellaneous Expense	38 010 66	
Payroll Taxes Expense	27 423 60	
Rent Expense	143 000 00	
Salary Expense	290 400 00	
Supplies Expense—Office	76 440 00	
Supplies Expense—Store	109 800 00	
Uncollectible Accounts Expense	1 423 69	
Utilities Expense	66 886 10	
Federal Income Tax Expense	25 992 22	
Interest Income		2 512 80
Rent Income		3 000 00
Gain on Plant Assets		18 231 00
Interest Expense	18 347 10	
Loss on Plant Assets	16 842 00	
Totals	4479 500 56	4479 500 56

End of Lesson Review

. . . .

LO1 Plan and record end-of-fiscal-period adjustments for a merchandising business organized as a corporation.

Audit your understanding

1. Describe the two methods used to determine the amount of an adjustment.
2. Which accounts are used to adjust the Supplies account?

Work together 22-1

Recording adjusting entries and preparing an adjusted trial balance

Travel Lite Corporation's unadjusted trial balance and accounting forms are given in the *Working Papers*. Your instructor will guide you through the following example.

1. Using the following information, journalize the adjusting entries for the current year ended December 31.

Estimated uncollectible accounts based on aging accounts receivable	$ 3,697.32
Accrued interest income	137.50
Merchandise inventory	45,058.15
Supplies inventory	126.00
Value of prepaid insurance	1,535.80
Annual depreciation expense—equipment	2,250.00
Accrued interest expense	277.58
Prepaid rent income earned	1,000.00

2. Post the adjusting entries to the T accounts.
3. Using the tax table shown in this chapter, calculate federal income tax expense and journalize the income tax adjustment.
4. Post the federal income tax adjusting entry to the T accounts.
5. Using the unadjusted trial balance and the T accounts, complete the adjusted trial balance. Save your work to complete Work Together 22-2.

On your own 22-1

Recording adjusting entries and preparing an adjusted trial balance

Williams Corporation's unadjusted trial balance and accounting forms are given in the *Working Papers*. Work this problem independently.

1. Using the following information, journalize the adjusting entries for the current year ended December 31.

Estimated uncollectible accounts based on aging accounts receivable	$ 3,796.00
Accrued interest income	80.00
Merchandise inventory	98,996.13
Supplies inventory	401.25
Value of prepaid insurance	600.00
Annual depreciation expense—equipment	7,345.00
Accrued interest expense	150.00
Prepaid rent income earned	2,000.00

2. Post the adjusting entries to the T accounts.
3. Using the tax table shown in this chapter, calculate federal income tax expense and journalize the income tax adjustment.
4. Post the federal income tax adjusting entry to the T accounts.
5. Using the unadjusted trial balance and the T accounts, complete the adjusted trial balance. Save your work to complete On Your Own 22-2.

22-2 Preparing an Income Statement, Statement of Stockholders' Equity, and Balance Sheet

LO2 Prepare an income statement for a merchandising business organized as a corporation.

LO3 Prepare a statement of stockholders' equity for a merchandising business organized as a corporation.

LO4 Prepare a balance sheet for a merchandising business organized as a corporation.

Income Statement LO2

				% OF SALES
Sun Treasures, Inc.				
Income Statement				
For Year Ended December 31, 20--				
Operating Revenue:				
Sales		2576 32 1 45		
Less: Sales Discount	15 45 7 93			
Sales Returns and Allowances	113 52 3 11	128 98 1 04		
Net Sales			2447 34 0 41	100.0
Cost of Merchandise Sold:				
Merchandise Inventory, Jan. 1, 20--		331 23 5 20		
Purchases	1307 16 0 50			
Less: Purchases Discount	15 68 5 93			
Purch. Returns and Allowances	1 15 0 40	16 83 6 33		
Net Purchases		1290 32 4 17		
Total Cost of Mdse. Avail. for Sale		1621 55 9 37		
Less Mdse. Inventory, Dec. 31. 20--		307 61 3 20		
Cost of Merchandise Sold			1313 94 6 17	53.7
Gross Profit			1133 39 4 24	46.3
Operating Expenses:				
Advertising Expense		58 00 0 00		
Cash Short and Over		2 41 7 25		
Credit Card Fee Expense		23 76 3 21		
Depr. Expense—Office Equipment		25 14 6 00		
Depr. Expense—Store Equipment		113 41 8 00		
Insurance Expense		36 22 5 00		
Miscellaneous Expense		38 01 0 66		
Payroll Taxes Expense		27 42 3 60		
Rent Expense		143 00 0 00		
Salary Expense		290 40 0 00		
Supplies Expense—Office		76 44 0 00		
Supplies Expense—Store		109 80 0 00		
Uncollectible Accounts Expense		1 42 3 69		
Utilities Expense		66 88 6 10		
Total Operating Expenses			1012 35 3 51	41.4

(Continued on next page)

Income Statement (*continued*)

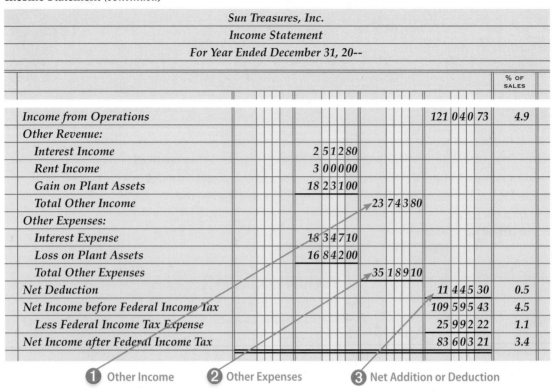

		% OF SALES
Income from Operations	121 040 73	4.9
Other Revenue:		
Interest Income	2 512 80	
Rent Income	3 000 00	
Gain on Plant Assets	18 231 00	
Total Other Income	23 743 80	
Other Expenses:		
Interest Expense	18 347 10	
Loss on Plant Assets	16 842 00	
Total Other Expenses	35 189 10	
Net Deduction	11 445 30	0.5
Net Income before Federal Income Tax	109 595 43	4.5
Less Federal Income Tax Expense	25 992 22	1.1
Net Income after Federal Income Tax	83 603 21	3.4

Sun Treasures, Inc.
Income Statement
For Year Ended December 31, 20--

① Other Income   **②** Other Expenses   **③** Net Addition or Deduction

Additional Items on an Income Statement

Sun Treasures' income statement is very similar to ThreeGreen's income statement, shown in Part 2. Both companies report net sales, net purchases, gross profit, income from operations, and other revenue (interest income). However, Sun Treasures lists the following additional items on its income statement:

(1) Rent income
(2) Gains and losses from the sale of plant assets
(3) Accruals for interest payable (interest expense)

These accounts are reported after income from operations. To help make decisions about current and future operations, Sun Treasures also analyzes relationships between revenue and expense items. Based on this analysis, Sun Treasures reports vertical analysis ratios for all major income statement items. Detailed procedures for preparing an income statement were presented in Chapter 16. The new items are highlighted in the illustration.

New Elements on the Income Statement for Sun Treasures

① Income from operations, $121,040.73, is the income earned only from normal business activities. Sun Treasures' normal business activities are selling souvenirs and tourist items. Interest earned on notes receivable, $2,512.80, rent income, $3,000.00, and gain from the sale of plant assets, $18,231.00, are not normal operating activities. Therefore, these accounts are reported after income from operations in a section labeled *Other Revenue*. The total of these Other Revenue accounts is $23,743.80.

② The interest expense on notes payable and lines of credit, $18,347.10, and the loss from the sale of plant assets, $16,842.00, are not normal operating activities. Therefore, these accounts are reported after income from operations in a section labeled *Other Expenses*. The total of these two Other Expenses accounts is $35,189.10.

③ The difference between other revenue and other expenses, $11,445.30, is reported as a net addition or net deduction. The difference is added to or deducted from income from operations to determine the net income before federal income tax.

Statement of Stockholders' Equity LO3

Sun Treasures, Inc. Statement of Stockholders' Equity For Year Ended December 31, 20--			
Capital Stock—Common:			
$10.00 Par Value			
January 1, 20--, 39,400 Shares Issued		394 0 0 0 00	
Issued during Current Year, 600 Shares		6 0 0 0 00	
Bal., December 31, 20--, 40,000 Shares Issued			400 0 0 0 00
Paid-in Capital in Excess of Par—Common:			
Balance, January 1, 20--		462 0 0 0 00	
Issued during Current Year		18 0 0 0 00	
Balance, December 31, 20--			480 0 0 0 00
Capital Stock—Preferred:			
$50.00 Par Value, 6%			
January 1, 20--, 0 Shares Issued		—	
Issued during Current Year, 400 Shares		20 0 0 0 00	
Balance, December 31, 20--, 400 Shares Issued			20 0 0 0 00
Retained Earnings:			
Balance, January 1, 20--		82 5 2 5 10	
Net Income after Federal Income Tax for 20--	83 6 0 3 21		
Less Dividends Declared during 20--	21 2 0 0 00		
Net Increase during 20--		62 4 0 3 21	
Balance, December 31, 20--			144 9 2 8 31
Total Stockholders' Equity, December 31, 20--			1044 9 2 8 31

1 Paid-in Capital in Excess of Par—Common section

2 Preferred Stock section

The statement of stockholders' equity for Sun Treasures is similar to that for ThreeGreen in Part 2. Both companies report changes in the **Capital Stock** and **Retained Earnings** accounts. However, Sun Treasures has two additional equity accounts, so its statement of stockholders' equity has two additional sections: (1) Paid-in Capital in Excess of Par—Common and (2) Preferred Stock.

Detailed instructions for preparing the statement of stockholders' equity were presented in Chapter 16. The new sections are highlighted in the illustration.

New Elements on the Statement of Stockholders' Equity for Sun Treasures

1 Changes in Paid-in Capital in Excess of Par—Common are listed in section 2. The ending balance, $480,000.00, is included in total stockholders' equity.

2 Changes in Preferred Stock are listed in section 3. The ending balance, $20,000.00, is included in total stockholders' equity.

Major corporations, especially those listed on the New York Stock Exchange (NYSE), publish lavish annual reports on their operations for the year. These annual reports are intended to summarize operations for their stockholders. They are also used to encourage investors to buy new issues of a company's stock. Most annual reports are available online as well.

Balance Sheet LO4

① New current liability accounts

Sun Treasures, Inc.

Balance Sheet

December 31, 20--

Assets			
Current Assets:			
Cash		43 8 4 8 68	
Petty Cash		4 5 0 00	
Accounts Receivable	52 4 8 1 37		
Less Allowance for Uncollectible Accounts	2 0 9 9 25	50 3 8 2 12	
Notes Receivable		15 0 0 0 00	
Interest Receivable		1 7 5 00	
Merchandise Inventory		307 6 1 3 20	
Supplies—Office		13 2 0 0 00	
Supplies—Store		48 3 0 0 00	
Prepaid Insurance		18 6 4 7 35	
Total Current Assets			497 6 1 6 35
Plant Assets:			
Office Equipment	325 6 4 8 16		
Less Accumulated Depr.—Office Equipment	104 8 7 3 00	220 7 7 5 16	
Store Equipment	1099 6 3 8 43		
Less Accumulated Depr.—Store Equipment	451 3 2 0 00	648 3 1 8 43	
Total Plant Assets			869 0 9 3 59
Total Assets			1366 7 0 9 94
Liabilities			
Current Liabilities:			
Accounts Payable		15 4 6 2 50	
Sales Tax Payable		6 4 7 31	
Interest Payable		7 1 0 84	
Line of Credit		7 5 0 0 00	
Unearned Rent Income		1 5 0 0 00	
Employee Income Tax Payable		1 5 7 3 00	
Social Security Tax Payable		3 0 0 0 80	
Medicare Tax Payable		7 0 1 80	
Medical Insurance Payable		3 2 1 24	
Retirement Benefits Payable		4 7 5 00	
Unemployment Tax Payable—State		3 5 00	
Unemployment Tax Payable—Federal		2 3 6 25	
Federal Income Tax Payable		2 9 9 2 22	
Total Current Liabilities			35 1 5 5 96
Long-term Liabilities:			
Long-term Notes Payable		106 6 2 5 67	
Bonds Payable		180 0 0 0 00	
Total Long-term Liabilities			286 6 2 5 67
Total Liabilities			321 7 8 1 63
Stockholders' Equity			
Capital Stock—Common		400 0 0 0 00	
Paid-in Capital in Excess of Par—Common		480 0 0 0 00	
Capital Stock—Preferred		20 0 0 0 00	
Retained Earnings		144 9 2 8 31	
Total Stockholders' Equity			1044 9 2 8 31
Total Liabilities and Stockholders' Equity			1366 7 0 9 94

② Long-term Liabilities section

③ Expanded Stockholders' Equity section

The balance sheet for Sun Treasures is similar to that for ThreeGreen in Part 2. Both balance sheets report assets, liabilities, and equity on a specific date. However, Sun Treasures has more current liability accounts, a new section, Long-term Liabilities, and more equity accounts. ThreeGreen only had current liabilities. Sun Treasures has both current and long-term liabilities. Each type of liability is listed separately and subtotaled. Total liabilities is also presented. Detailed procedures for preparing a balance sheet were presented in Chapter 16. The new items are highlighted in the illustration.

New Elements on the Balance Sheet for Sun Treasures

1 Several new current liabilities appear in the Current Liabilities section.

2 A new Long-term Liabilities section follows the Current Liabilities section. Each long-term liability account is listed, along with total long-term liabilities and total liabilities.

3 New stockholders' equity accounts are listed in the Stockholders' Equity section.

THINK LIKE AN ACCOUNTANT

Formatting Amounts in Financial Statements

The board of directors of Blanc Corporation is reviewing its financial statements. The president begins her presentation to the board by discussing sales trends. Which of these statements would the board members better understand?

1. Our sales for May were $542,349.31, an increase of $23,136.89 over April.
2. Our sales for May were $542 thousand, an increase of $23 thousand over April.

Does the board need to know the exact amount of sales? Will knowing about that extra $349.31 of sales cause the board to make any different decisions? Most people will better understand the second statement.

Amounts rounded to two, three, or four digits can provide an adequate level of information.

This level of accuracy is common in other areas of our daily living. Consider these examples. Speed limit signs have only two digits. Baseball batting averages are stated in three digits, such as .325. College grade point averages are also presented with three digits, such as 3.68.

Most corporations present their financial statements in thousands or millions. Notations such as *in thousands of dollars* or *$000s* are included in the statement headings. These notations inform the reader that the amounts are stated in thousands of dollars. A corporation can also replace digits with zeros. For example, the statement could round $12,345 to $12,000.

OPEN THE SPREADSHEET TLA_CH22
Follow the steps on the Instructions worksheet. Each worksheet contains a financial statement. Format each financial statement assuming it will be presented to a board of directors.

End of Lesson Review

LO2 Prepare an income statement for a merchandising business organized as a corporation.

LO3 Prepare a statement of stockholders' equity for a merchandising business organized as a corporation.

LO4 Prepare a balance sheet for a merchandising business organized as a corporation.

Audit your understanding

1. Why are other revenue and other expenses reported separately from sales, cost of merchandise sold, and operating expenses on the income statement?

2. What is an example of a long-term liability?

Work together 22-2

Preparing an income statement, statement of stockholders' equity, and balance sheet for a corporation

Use the adjusted trial balance from Work Together 22-1. Forms are given in the *Working Papers*. Your instructor will guide you through the following examples.

1. Complete the income statement for the current year. Calculate and record the following vertical analysis ratios: (a) cost of merchandise sold; (b) gross profit on operations; (c) total operating expenses; (d) income from operations; (e) net addition or deduction resulting from other revenue and expenses; and (f) net income before federal income tax. Round percentage calculations to the nearest 0.01%.

2. Complete the statement of stockholders' equity for the current year. As of January 1, Travel Lite Corporation had issued 4,500 shares of common stock with a par value of $1.00 per share. During the fiscal year, the corporation issued 500 additional shares of common stock. The balance in Paid-in Capital in Excess of Par—Common on January 1, 20--, was $8,000.00. As of January 1, Travel Lite had not issued any shares of preferred stock. During the fiscal year, it issued 500 shares of $10.00 par, 5% preferred stock at par value.

3. Complete the balance sheet for the current year. Save your work to complete Work Together 22-3.

On your own 22-2

Preparing an income statement, statement of stockholders' equity, and balance sheet for a corporation

Use the adjusted trial balance from On Your Own 22-1. Forms are given in the *Working Papers*. Your instructor will guide you through the following examples.

1. Complete the income statement for the current year. Calculate and record the following vertical analysis ratios: (a) cost of merchandise sold; (b) gross profit on operations; (c) total operating expenses; (d) income from operations; (e) net addition or deduction resulting from other revenue and expenses; and (f) net income before federal income tax. Round percentage calculations to the nearest 0.01%.

2. Complete the statement of stockholders' equity for the current year. As of January 1, Williams Corporation had issued 2,000 shares of common stock with a par value of $5.00 per share. During the fiscal year, the corporation issued 1,000 additional shares of common stock. The balance in Paid-in Capital in Excess of Par—Common on January 1, 20--, was $2,000. As of January 1, Williams Corporation had not issued any shares of preferred stock. During the fiscal year, it issued 1,000 shares of $10.00 par, 5% preferred stock at par value.

3. Complete the balance sheet for the current year. Save your work to complete On Your Own 22-3.

©CANDICE CUSACK, ISTOCK

22-3 Preparing a Statement of Cash Flows

LO5 Prepare a statement of cash flows for a merchandising business organized as a corporation.

Statement of Cash Flows LO5

ThreeGreen, the company in Part 2, prepared three financial statements: income statement, statement of stockholders' equity, and balance sheet. Corporations are required to prepare one additional statement which addresses the changes in the business's cash for the period. The cash receipts and cash payments of a company are called **cash flow**. A financial statement that summarizes cash receipts and cash payments resulting from business activities during a fiscal period is called a **statement of cash flows**.

The statement of cash flows is different than the other financial statements in one major way—the basis it uses. The income statement, the statement of stockholders' equity, and the balance sheet are prepared using the accrual basis of accounting. This means that revenues are recorded when earned, not when cash is received and expenses are included when incurred, not when cash is paid. The statement of cash flows is prepared using the cash basis of accounting. This means that the statement of cash flows only reports inflows and outflows of cash and excludes business transactions that do not affect cash. For example, interest accrued on a note receivable would not affect cash. Similarly, wages accrued but not paid during the period would not affect cash.

The purpose of the statement of cash flows is to provide important information to external parties such as stockholders and creditors. A business may have impressive profits, but may experience a cash shortage and have difficulty paying its bills. The statement of cash flows allows the reader to more fully understand how cash is acquired and how it is used by a company.

GLOBAL AWARENESS

Working in a Foreign Country

Does working in a foreign country appeal to you? Are you willing to pack your clothes and a few personal belongings and fly off for new adventures? Before you go, you will need to do some advance planning.

Many countries do not allow foreign workers. Those that do allow foreign workers may require a work permit. In some countries, you can only get a work permit if it can be proven that the position cannot be filled by a citizen of that country because of lack of skills or other reasons.

If you go to a country that does not require a work permit, you may be required to apply for and be granted a visa before you can enter the country. In addition, you may be required to provide proof of specific immunizations. Visas are often issued for a limited time span, after which you must leave the country.

Perhaps the most important thing to consider is the culture and customs of the country, which may be very different than those to which you are accustomed. Understanding and tolerating these customs may be the ultimate test of your ability to live happily and successfully abroad.

CRITICAL THINKING

Choose a country in which you are interested. Search the Internet for suggestions on what is needed to work in that country, including work permits and visas. Also include what language is spoken in this country and what kind of climate you can tolerate. Summarize your findings in a one-paragraph written report.

©FONTMONSTER, ISTOCK

Cash Flows from Operating, Investing, and Financing Activities

The statement of cash flows is divided into three sections. The cash flows for each of these sections are calculated by analyzing the information presented in the ledger accounts and the other financial statements of the company.

CASH FLOWS FROM OPERATING ACTIVITIES

The cash receipts and payments necessary to operate a business on a day-to-day basis are called **operating activities**. Creditors, owners, and potential investors examine the operating activities to determine if the company generates sufficient cash to support future investments and long-term profitability.

CASH FLOWS FROM INVESTING ACTIVITIES

Cash receipts and cash payments involving the sale or purchase of assets used to earn revenue over a period of time are called **investing activities**. Financial analysts examine the investing activities to assess the future financial strength and profitability of a business. If a company is forced to sell buildings and equipment to raise cash for operations, there would soon be no more assets to use in operations.

CASH FLOWS FROM FINANCING ACTIVITIES

Cash receipts and payments involving debt or equity transactions are called **financing activities**. These activities usually involve borrowing money from creditors and repaying the principal or selling stock and paying dividends. Financing activities are often used to ensure that an adequate balance exists in the **Cash** account. If a business uses more cash than it receives, it must obtain additional financing. This often happens as a business expands operations, as Sun Treasures is doing. Extra cash is required to obtain inventory and assets for the new stores. If a business has excess cash, it can use it to repay loans, notes, and bonds.

A list of Sun Treasures' common inflows and outflows from operating, investing, and financing activities is presented.

Activity	Cash Inflows	Cash Outflows
Operating	Sale of merchandise Receipt of interest income Receipt of rent income	Payment for daily operations (advertising, insurance, interest, inventory, rent, salaries, taxes, utilities)
Investing	Sale of office equipment Sale of store equipment Sale of other investments	Purchase of office equipment Purchase of store equipment Purchase of other investments
Financing	Issuance of stock Issuance of long-term notes payable Issuance of bonds Borrowing cash against line of credit	Payment of dividends Payment of principal from long-term notes payable Payment of bond principal Making principal payments on line of credit

Companies often establish a line of credit with a bank. This credit can be used to pay invoices or make cash purchases, especially for urgent business needs that require an immediate cash payment. A line of credit is a short-term loan to the company, and interest must be paid on the loan. The advantage of having a line of credit is that the company will not need to take out a new loan every time cash is needed to operate the business.

Operating Activities Section of a Statement of Cash Flows

Sun Treasures' statement of cash flows is shown on the next page.

The operating activities section of the statement of cash flows can be prepared using one of two methods: the direct method or the indirect method. Sun Treasures uses the direct method to prepare the operating activities section of the statement of cash flows. The indirect method begins with net income and makes adjustments for noncash expenditures and other cash differences. Regardless of the method used, the net cash provided or used by operating activities is the same amount.

Sun Treasures has three sources of cash from operating activities: sales, interest, and rent. The amount of cash received for each of these items is not the same as the amount of sales, interest income, and rent income listed on Sun Treasures' income statement. Since the statement of cash flows is prepared on a cash basis, the amount listed is the total amount of cash received this period for each item. For example, Sun Treasures received $4,500.00 for three months' rent on November 1. The amount listed on the statement of cash flows for rent received is $4,500.00. By December 31, Sun Treasures only earned $3,000.00 of rent income. Only the amount of rent income earned, $3,000.00, is reported on Sun Treasures' income statement. Likewise, other amounts on the statement of cash flows may not be the same as related amounts on the income statement or the statement of stockholders' equity.

The amount listed for sales and interest income is the actual amount of cash received for each item during this fiscal period. The amount is determined by examining the general ledger accounts and the financial statements.

The payments section is prepared in a similar manner. The actual amount of cash paid for each item must be determined. Sun Treasures lists the major operating items separately and adds smaller operating items together in a category called Other operating expenses.

DMITRIY SHIRONOSOV/SHUTTERSTOCK.COM

Completed Statement of Cash Flows

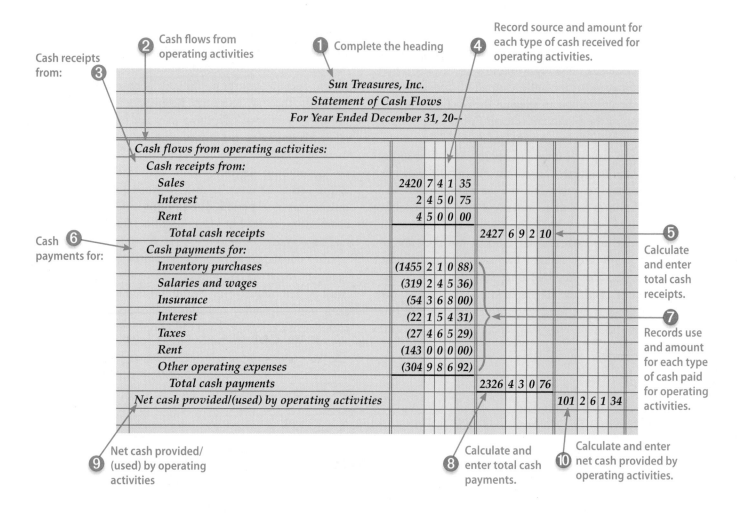

2 Cash flows from operating activities

1 Complete the heading

Record source and amount for each type of cash received for operating activities.

Cash receipts from: **3**

Sun Treasures, Inc.
Statement of Cash Flows
For Year Ended December 31, 20--

Cash flows from operating activities:		
Cash receipts from:		
Sales	2420 7 4 1 35	
Interest	2 4 5 0 75	
Rent	4 5 0 0 00	
Total cash receipts		2427 6 9 2 10
Cash payments for:		
Inventory purchases	(1455 2 1 0 88)	
Salaries and wages	(319 2 4 5 36)	
Insurance	(54 3 6 8 00)	
Interest	(22 1 5 4 31)	
Taxes	(27 4 6 5 29)	
Rent	(143 0 0 0 00)	
Other operating expenses	(304 9 8 6 92)	
Total cash payments		2326 4 3 0 76
Net cash provided/(used) by operating activities		101 2 6 1 34

6 Cash payments for:

5 Calculate and enter total cash receipts.

7 Records use and amount for each type of cash paid for operating activities

9 Net cash provided/(used) by operating activities

8 Calculate and enter total cash payments.

10 Calculate and enter net cash provided by operating activities.

◆ **Preparing the Operating Activities Section of a Statement of Cash Flows**

1 Prepare the heading of the statement. The statement is prepared for the same period of time as the income statement.

2 Write the name of the first section, Cash flows from operating activities, on the first line.

3 Write the words Cash receipts from: on the next line.

4 Write the name and amount of each type of cash receipt for operating activities.

5 Calculate and enter total cash receipts.

6 Write the words Cash payments for: on the next line.

7 Write the name and amount of each type of cash payment for operating activities.

8 Calculate and enter total cash payments.

9 Write the words Net cash provided/(used) by operating activities on the next line.

10 Calculate and enter the net cash provided by operating activities, $101,261.34 ($2,427,692.10 − $2,326,430.76).

Investing Activities Section of a Statement of Cash Flows

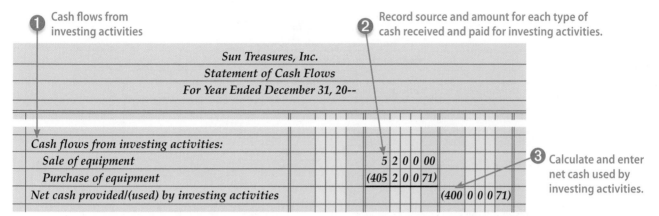

① Cash flows from investing activities

② Record source and amount for each type of cash received and paid for investing activities.

Sun Treasures, Inc.
Statement of Cash Flows
For Year Ended December 31, 20--

Cash flows from investing activities:		
Sale of equipment	5 2 0 0 00	
Purchase of equipment	(405 2 0 0 71)	
Net cash provided/(used) by investing activities		(400 0 0 0 71)

③ Calculate and enter net cash used by investing activities.

The remaining two sections of the statement of cash flows are prepared the same, regardless of the method used to prepare the operating activities section. The accountant for Sun Treasures examines the ledger accounts and other financial data to determine the actual cash received by investing activities and the actual cash paid for investing activities.

> **⤵ Preparing the Investing Activities Section of a Statement of Cash Flows**
>
> ① Leaving one line blank, write the name of the second section, **Cash flows from investing activities**.
>
> ② Write the name and amount of each type of cash receipt and cash payment for investing activities.
>
> ③ Calculate and enter the net cash used by investing activities, **$(400,000.71)** ($5,200.00 – $405,200.71).

Financing Activities Section of a Statement of Cash Flows

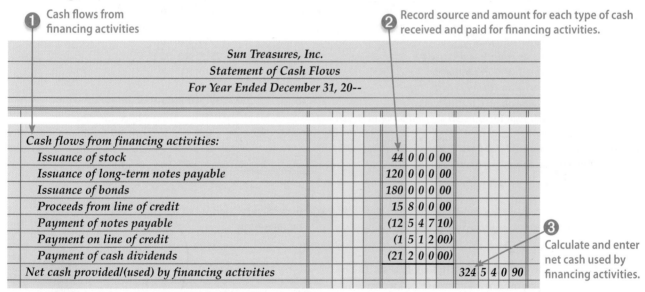

① Cash flows from financing activities

② Record source and amount for each type of cash received and paid for financing activities.

Sun Treasures, Inc.
Statement of Cash Flows
For Year Ended December 31, 20--

Cash flows from financing activities:		
Issuance of stock	44 0 0 0 00	
Issuance of long-term notes payable	120 0 0 0 00	
Issuance of bonds	180 0 0 0 00	
Proceeds from line of credit	15 8 0 0 00	
Payment of notes payable	(12 5 4 7 10)	
Payment on line of credit	(1 5 1 2 00)	
Payment of cash dividends	(21 2 0 0 00)	
Net cash provided/(used) by financing activities		324 5 4 0 90

③ Calculate and enter net cash used by financing activities.

The financing activities section is prepared in a manner similar to the investing activities section. Actual cash received by financing activities and actual cash paid for financing activities is determined and recorded on the statement of cash flows.

> **⤵ Preparing the Financing Activities Section of a Statement of Cash Flows**
>
> ① Leaving one line blank, write the name of the third section, **Cash flows from financing activities**.
>
> ② Write the name and amount of each type of cash receipt and cash payment for financing activities.
>
> ③ Calculate and enter the net cash provided by financing activities, **$324,540.90** ($44,000.00 + $120,000.00 + $180,000.00 + $15,800.00 – $12,547.10 – $1,512.00 – $21,200.00).

Completing the Statement of Cash Flows

Sun Treasures, Inc. Statement of Cash Flows For Year Ended December 31, 20--					
Cash flows from operating activities:					
Cash receipts from:					
Sales	2420 7 4 1 35				
Interest	2 4 5 0 75				
Rent	4 5 0 0 00				
Total cash receipts		2427 6 9 2 10			
Cash payments for:					
Inventory purchases	(1455 2 1 0 88)				
Salaries and wages	(319 2 4 5 36)				
Insurance	(54 3 6 8 00)				
Interest	(22 1 5 4 31)				
Taxes	(27 4 6 5 29)				
Rent	(143 0 0 0 00)				
Other operating expenses	(304 9 8 6 92)				
Total cash payments		(2326 4 3 0 76)			
Net cash provided/(used) by operating activities			101 2 6 1 34		
Cash flows from investing activities:					
Sale of equipment		5 2 0 0 00			
Purchase of equipment		(405 2 0 0 71)			
Net cash provided/(used) by investing activities			(400 0 0 0 71)		
Cash flows from financing activities:					
Issuance of stock		44 0 0 0 00			
Issuance of long-term notes payable		120 0 0 0 00			
Issuance of bonds		180 0 0 0 00			
Proceeds from line of credit		15 8 0 0 00			
Payment of notes payable		(12 5 4 7 10)			
Payment on line of credit		(1 5 1 2 00)			
Payment of cash dividends		(21 2 0 0 00)			
Net cash provided/(used) by financing activities			324 5 4 0 90		
Net change in cash			25 8 0 1 53		
Cash balance, January 1, 20--			18 0 4 7 15		
Cash balance, December 31, 20--			43 8 4 8 68		

(1) Calculate net change in cash.

(2) Record cash balance on January 1.

(3) Record cash balance on December 31. Verify change in cash balance.

The last three lines of the statement of cash flows show and verify the amount of increase or decrease in cash during the fiscal period. The net change in cash is calculated by netting out the totals of the three activities: Net cash provided by operating activities, $101,261.34, minus net cash used by investing activities, $400,000.71, plus net cash provided by financing activities, $324,540.90, equals net change in cash, $25,801.53.

The net change in cash is verified by adding it to the cash balance at the beginning of the period. The total should equal the ending balance in the **Cash** account.

Completing the Statement of Cash Flows

(1) Calculate and record the net change in cash, $25,801.53.

(2) Record the beginning cash balance, $18,047.15.

(3) Record the ending cash balance, $43,848.68, and verify the net change in cash ($25,801.53 + $18,047.15 = $43,848.68).

The Enron Legacy

There was a time when Enron Corporation was an iconic symbol of American capitalism. The company was a leader in the production and trading of energy. Enron owned pipelines, power plants, natural gas distributors, and paper mills all over the world. Enron occupied a stunning office complex in Houston. For a short time, its famous crooked E logo adorned the home of Major League Baseball's Houston Astros.

Enron's growth and political power were headline news. Enron's revenue grew an astonishing 750% from 1996 to 2000. Its revenue of $101 billion in 2000 ranked it as one of the world's largest companies. *Fortune* magazine named Enron its "most innovative" company for six years. Enron was also well connected in national politics. Chief executive officer Ken Lay was a personal friend of President George W. Bush.

But underneath its pristine image was a corporate culture that motivated employees to take advantage of any situation to increase revenue and earnings. Enron's role in the 2000–2001 California energy crisis brought this culture to light. Legislation in California designed to control the energy prices charged to consumers had an unintended effect. California power companies had to pay market prices for extra energy while being limited to what they could charge the public. Enron schemed to inflate energy costs, causing wholesale electricity prices to skyrocket from $30 to $1,500 per megawatt hour. Enron was making huge profits while Californians were dealing with rolling blackouts. It certainly didn't help when president and chief operating officer Jeffrey Skilling was quoted as saying "What's the difference between California and the *Titanic*? At least when the *Titanic* went down … the lights were on."

A victim of accounting fraud and high debt, Enron filed for bankruptcy just over a year after its stock reached an all-time high of $90 per share. The accounting fraud included the abuse of revenue recognition rules, mark-to-market accounting, and special-purpose entities. These topics are well beyond the scope of this textbook. In fact, the complexity of these topics may have been beyond the ability or willingness of the financial community to understand.

Neither Enron nor its auditor, Arthur Andersen, survived the fraud. Numerous Enron officers were convicted of federal charges and sentenced to substantial jail terms. In a scene out of a Hollywood movie, Arthur Andersen staff shredded thousands of documents and e-mails related to its Enron audit. The accounting firm was convicted of obstruction of justice, an action that resulted in the firm's demise.

The Enron story has been told by numerous books and the documentary *The Smartest Guys in the Room*. The combined size and spectacular nature of the Enron and WorldCom frauds led to the passage of the Sarbanes-Oxley Act. The Act requires corporations to exert a higher level of internal control and executive responsibility over the fair presentation of financial information.

ACTIVITY

BelCorp Furniture has hired you to examine its purchases of materials. The company has reason to believe that its purchasing employees are favoring certain vendors.

INSTRUCTIONS

Open the spreadsheet FA_CH22 and complete the steps on the Instructions tab.

Sources: http://en.wikipedia.org; *Called to Account*, Paul M. Clikeman, Rutledge (New York and London), 2009; and *Business Fairy Tales*, Cecil W. Jackson, Thomson (Mason, Ohio), 2006.

End of Lesson Review

LO5 Prepare a statement of cash flows for a merchandising business organized as a corporation.

Terms Review

cash flow

statement of cash flows

operating activities

investing activities

financing activities

Audit your understanding

1. What basis is used to prepare the statement of cash flows?
2. List the three categories of activities used on the statement of cash flows.

Work together 22-3

Preparing a statement of cash flows for a corporation

Use the balance sheet from Work Together 22-2 and the information below. A form is given in the *Working Papers*. Your instructor will guide you through the following example.

Prepare a statement of cash flows for the current year.

Cash balance at the beginning of the period	$ 39,522.51

Cash receipts during the year:

Cash from sales	$598,236.31
Cash from interest	635.21
Cash from rent	4,000.00
Cash from sale of equipment	1,200.00
Cash from issuance of stock	17,500.00
Cash from issuance of bonds	10,000.00

Cash payments during the year:

Cash for inventory	$375,623.54
Cash for salaries and wages	85,807.14
Cash for insurance	4,254.35
Cash for interest	1,587.35
Cash for taxes	12,885.00
Cash for rent	16,248.65
Cash for other operating expenses	95,412.88
Cash for purchase of equipment	10,549.00
Cash for payment of notes payable	2,500.00
Cash for payment of dividends	21,200.00

▶ ## On your own 22-3

Preparing a statement of cash flows for a corporation

Use the balance sheet from On Your Own 22-2 and the information below. A form is given in the *Working Papers*. Work the following problem independently.

Prepare a statement of cash flows for the current year.

Cash receipts during the year:

Cash from sales	$1,226,425.41
Cash from interest	377.00
Cash from rent	13,000.00
Cash from sale of equipment	13,200.00
Cash from issuance of stock	18,000.00
Cash from issuance of bonds	10,000.00

Cash payments during the year:

Cash for inventory	$ 805,412.20
Cash for salaries and wages	220,147.25
Cash for insurance	8,200.00
Cash for interest	915.00
Cash for taxes	28,000.00
Cash for rent	28,210.00
Cash for other operating expenses	95,214.20
Cash for purchase of equipment	75,000.00
Cash for payment of notes payable	7,500.00
Cash for payment of dividends	10,000.00
Cash balance at the beginning of the period	$ 6,023.29

22-4 Preparing Closing and Reversing Entries

LO6 Record closing entries for a merchandising business organized as a corporation.

LO7 Record reversing entries for a merchandising business organized as a corporation.

Closing Entry for Accounts with Credit Balances LO6

				GENERAL JOURNAL						PAGE 14	
	DATE		ACCOUNT TITLE	DOC. NO.	POST. REF.	DEBIT			CREDIT		
1			*Closing Entries*								1
2	Dec. 31		Sales			2576 3 2 1 45					2
3			Purchases Discount			15 6 8 5 93					3
4			Purchases Returns and Allowances			1 1 5 0 40					4
5			Interest Income			2 5 1 2 80					5
6			Rent Income			3 0 0 0 00					6
7			Gain on Plant Assets			18 2 3 1 00					7
8			Income Summary						2616 9 0 1 58		8

1 Debit the balance of every income statement account with a credit balance.

2 Enter the total of the debit entries as a credit to Income Summary.

After financial statements are prepared, the adjusted trial balance is used to journalize the closing entries for a corporation. The income statement accounts with credit balances consist of the revenue accounts (Sales, Interest Income, Rent Income, and Gain on Plant Assets) and the contra cost accounts (Purchases Discount and Purchases Returns and Allowances). Closing entries are recorded on a new page of the general journal.

> **Journalizing a Closing Entry for Income Statement Accounts with Credit Balances**
>
> **1** Debit the balance of every income statement account with a credit balance.
>
> **2** Enter the total of the debit entries, **$2,616,901.58**, as a credit to **Income Summary**.

fyi

In most commercial computerized accounting systems, year-end closing is performed by the software. The accountant selects a menu item to close the accounting records for the year, and the software automatically updates its database. In some systems, year-end closing cannot be undone.

Closing Entry for Accounts with Debit Balances

1 Enter Income Summary

3 Enter the total of the credit entries as a debit to Income Summary.

	DATE	ACCOUNT TITLE	DOC. NO.	POST. REF.	DEBIT	CREDIT	
1		*Closing Entries*					1
9	31	Income Summary			2509 6 7 6 37		9
10		Sales Discount				15 4 5 7 93	10
11		Sales Returns and Allowances				113 5 2 3 11	11
12		Purchases				1307 1 6 0 50	12
13		Advertising Expense				58 0 0 0 00	13
14		Cash Short and Over				2 4 1 7 25	14
15		Credit Card Fee Expense				23 7 6 3 21	15
16		Depreciation Expense—Office Equipment				25 1 4 6 00	16
17		Depreciation Expense—Store Equipment				113 4 1 8 00	17
18		Insurance Expense				36 2 2 5 00	18
19		Miscellaneous Expense				38 0 1 0 66	19
20		Payroll Taxes Expense				27 4 2 3 60	20
21		Rent Expense				143 0 0 0 00	21
22		Salary Expense				290 4 0 0 00	22
23		Supplies Expense—Office				76 4 4 0 00	23
24		Supplies Expense—Store				109 8 0 0 00	24
25		Uncollectible Accounts Expense				1 4 2 3 69	25
26		Utilities Expense				66 8 8 6 10	26
27		Federal Income Tax Expense				25 9 9 2 22	27
28		Interest Expense				18 3 4 7 10	28
29		Loss on Plant Assets				16 8 4 2 00	29

GENERAL JOURNAL — PAGE *14*

2 Credit the balance of every income statement account with a debit balance.

The income statement accounts with debit balances consist of the contra revenue accounts (Sales Discount and Sales Returns and Allowances), the cost (Purchases), and all expense accounts. Information needed for closing income statement debit balance accounts is obtained from the adjusted trial balance Debit column.

Because Cash Short and Over has a debit balance in this fiscal period, the account balance amount is closed to Income Summary with the debit balance accounts.

> **Journalizing a Closing Entry for Income Statement Accounts with Debit Balances**
>
> **1** Enter the account title Income Summary.
>
> **2** Credit the balance of every income statement account with a debit balance.
>
> **3** Enter the total of the credit entries, $2,509,676.37, as a debit to Income Summary.

Closing Entry to Record Net Income

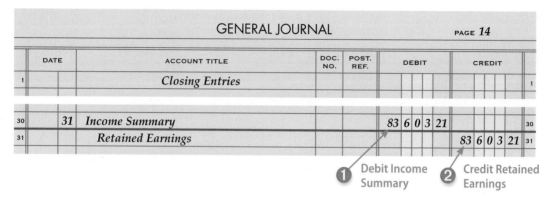

After closing entries for the income statement accounts are posted, Income Summary has a credit balance of $83,603.21. This credit balance equals the net income for the period.

As reported on the statement of stockholders' equity, the net income of a corporation increases Retained Earnings. Closing the balance of Income Summary actually increases the Retained Earnings account by the amount of net income. After the closing entry is posted, Income Summary has a zero balance.

A corporation having a net loss will have a debit balance in Income Summary. Retained Earnings would then be debited and Income Summary credited for the net loss amount. The entry would reduce the balance of Retained Earnings.

> **↘ Journalizing a Closing Entry to Record Net Income in Retained Earnings**
>
> **1** Record a debit to Income Summary for the amount of net income, $83,603.21.
>
> **2** Record a credit to Retained Earnings for the same amount, $83,603.21.

Closing Entry for Dividends

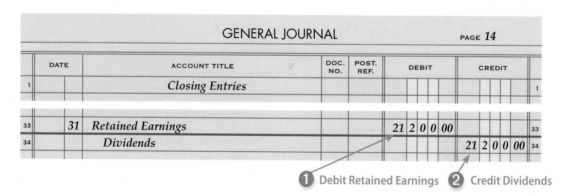

Dividends reduce the earnings retained by a corporation, as reported on the statement of stockholders' equity. The closing entry reduces the balance in the Retained Earnings account by the amount of the dividends.

> **↘ Journalizing a Closing Entry for Dividends**
>
> **1** Record a debit to Retained Earnings for the amount of dividends, $21,200.00.
>
> **2** Record a credit to Dividends for the same amount, $21,200.00.

Reversing Entries LO7

GENERAL JOURNAL

	DATE	ACCOUNT TITLE	DOC. NO.	POST. REF.	DEBIT	CREDIT	
1		*Adjusting Entries*					1
4	31	Interest Receivable			1 7 5 00		4
5		Interest Income				1 7 5 00	5
18	31	Interest Expense			7 1 0 84		18
19		Interest Payable				7 1 0 84	19
22	31	Federal Income Tax Expense			2 9 9 2 22		22
23		Federal Income Tax Payable				2 9 9 2 22	23

1 Reverse the entry that created a balance in Interest Receivable.

GENERAL JOURNAL

	DATE	ACCOUNT TITLE	DOC. NO.	POST. REF.	DEBIT	CREDIT	
1		*Reversing Entries*					1
2	Jan. 1	Interest Income			1 7 5 00		2
3		Interest Receivable				1 7 5 00	3
4	1	Interest Payable			7 1 0 84		4
5		Interest Expense				7 1 0 84	5
6	1	Federal Income Tax Payable			2 9 9 2 22		6
7		Federal Income Tax Expense				2 9 9 2 22	7
8							8

2 Reverse the entry that created a balance in Interest Payable.

3 Reverse the entry that created a balance in Federal Income Tax Payable.

If an adjusting entry creates a balance in an asset or a liability account, the adjusting entry should be reversed. A review of Sun Treasures' adjusting entries shows that three adjusting entries created a balance in an asset or a liability account.

1. The adjusting entry for accrued interest income created a balance in the Interest Receivable account.
2. The adjusting entry for accrued interest expense created a balance in the Interest Payable account.
3. The adjusting entry for federal income tax expense created a balance in the Federal Income Tax Payable account.

↘ Journalizing Reversing Entries

1 Reverse the entry that created a balance in Interest Receivable.

2 Reverse the entry that created a balance in Interest Payable.

3 Reverse the entry that created a balance in Federal Income Tax Payable.

Accounting Cycle for a Merchandising Business Organized as a Corporation

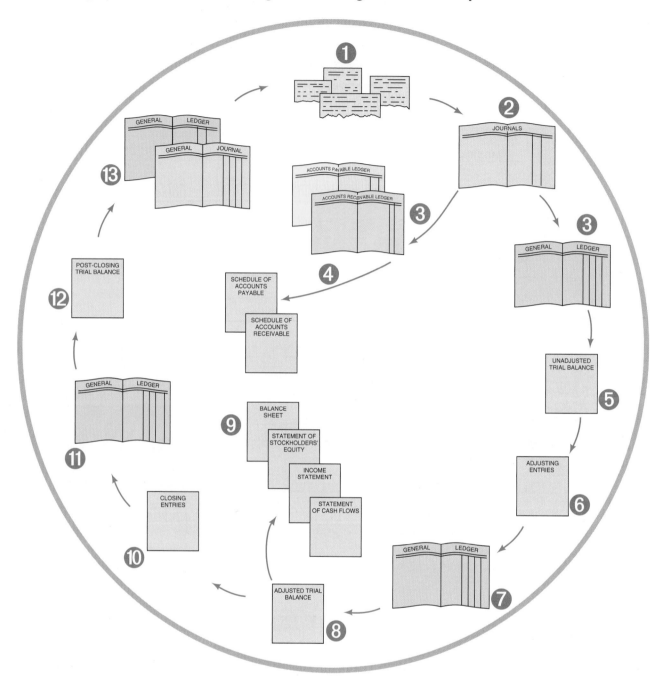

The accounting cycles are similar for merchandising businesses, regardless of how the businesses are organized. Variations occur in preparing financial statements. Variations also occur when reversing entries are recorded.

1. Source documents are checked for accuracy, and transactions are analyzed into debit and credit parts.

2. Transactions, from information on source documents, are recorded in journals.

3. Journal entries are posted to the accounts payable, accounts receivable, and general ledgers.

4. Schedules of accounts payable and accounts receivable are prepared from the subsidiary ledgers.

5. An unadjusted trial balance is prepared from the general ledger.

6. Adjusting entries are journalized.

7. Adjusting entries are posted to the general ledger.

8. An adjusted trial balance is prepared from the general ledger.

9. Financial statements are prepared from the adjusted trial balance.

10. Closing entries are journalized.

11. Closing entries are posted to the general ledger.

12. A post-closing trial balance is prepared from the general ledger.

13. Reversing entries are journalized and posted to the general ledger.

WHY ACCOUNTING?

Information Technology Departments

Most companies use some form of automated accounting software to record transactions, generate reports, and analyze financial results. For a small business, this software is usually a generic system that can easily be used by thousands of other businesses. These "one-size-fits-all" packages allow the user a few choices, but not great flexibility.

Larger companies, with information technology (IT) departments, may either develop their own accounting software programs internally or make major revisions in purchased programs to meet the company's needs. In addition to standard financial statements, company management may need unique reports for decision-making purposes. A standard accounting program assists in preparing the financial statements but is not programmed to gather data for the special reports. In this case, the IT department may attempt to revise the program.

These reports will only be helpful if they are accurate. The IT personnel must have at least a basic understanding of accounting. They will have to work closely with accounting department personnel to ensure that the revised accounting software is measuring and reporting the data accurately. The more accounting knowledge the IT workers have, the easier it will be to communicate the needs of the accounting department and company management.

CRITICAL THINKING

1. As a class, identify a local business or government agency that has an information technology department. Choose a student to contact that organization to arrange an interview with a member of that department and two or three class representatives.

2. As a class, develop a list of questions that the class representatives should ask the IT representative.

3. After the interview, have the class representatives share their findings with the class.

LO6 Record closing entries for a merchandising business organized as a corporation.

LO7 Record reversing entries for a merchandising business organized as a corporation.

Audit your understanding

1. What is used to prove the equality of debits and credits in the general ledger after closing entries are posted?

2. What are the four closing entries for a corporation?

3. Which accounts are closed to Retained Earnings?

Work together 22-4

Journalizing closing and reversing entries for a corporation

Use the accounting forms and financial statements from Work Together 22-1. General journal pages are given in the *Working Papers*. Your instructor will guide you through the following examples.

1. For the current year, journalize the closing entries using page 13 of a general journal.

2. For the following year, journalize the reversing entries using page 14 of a general journal.

On your own 22-4

Journalizing closing and reversing entries for a corporation

Use the accounting forms and financial statements from On Your Own 22-1. General journal pages are given in the *Working Papers*. Work this problem independently.

1. For the current year, journalize the closing entries using page 13 of a general journal.

2. For the following year, journalize the reversing entries using page 14 of a general journal.

A Look at Accounting Software
Recurring Reversing Entries

A Look at Accounting Software in Chapter 15 showed the procedure for fully or partially automating transactions. This feature shows what happens when a recurring entry is set up for adjustments.

In this chapter, you learned about the need to accrue some types of revenue and expenses. You learned that accountants often prefer to reverse some adjusting entries. It was explained that reversing entries are not required, but doing so makes the accounting easier and less prone to error.

Reversing entries in a computerized accounting system are very easy to do. It is as simple as clicking a button on the Make Journal Entries window. The system does all the work.

When recurring entries and reversing entries work together, much of the work is reduced for the accounting staff and the chances for error are greatly reduced. It is important to remember, however, that accountants still need to determine which accounts to adjust and by what amounts.

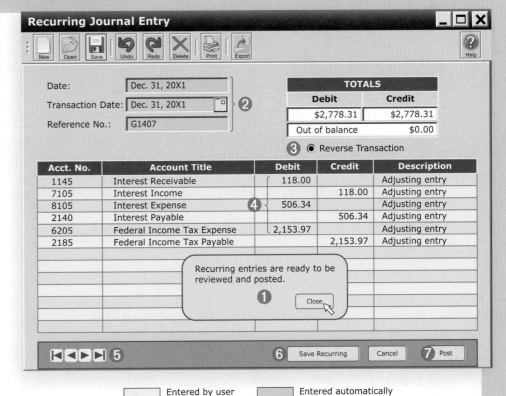

Entered by user ☐   Entered automatically ☐

❶ At the end of 20X0, Sun Treasures made the adjusting entries shown in the window and saved them as a recurring entry (Chapter 15). The posting option of "Edit before posting" was selected. Now, on December 31, 20X1, the system presents the recurring entries for review.

❷ The system automatically enters the system date, the transaction date, and the transaction reference number.

❸ When these adjustments were entered in 20X0, the accountant chose to reverse the entries and clicked the reverse transaction button. The system automatically posted a reversing entry on January 1, 20X1.

❹ These amounts were used for the adjustments on December 31, 20X0. The user will change them to the 20X1 amounts: Interest Receivable, $175.00; Interest Expense, $710.84; and Federal Income Tax Expense, $2,992.22.

❺ Other recurring transactions will have been presented by the system as well, including the adjusting entries that will not be reversed. The user can use the forward and back arrows to view those transactions.

❻ After the entries have been edited, the user can elect to save the edited recurring entry. That would be very helpful if adjusting entries were added or deleted with this year's adjustments.

❼ The user clicks Post to post the adjustments. The system will automatically post a reversing entry on January 1, 20X2.

Chapter Summary

Each adjusting entry affects an income statement account and a balance sheet account. Therefore, all adjusting entries must be accurately calculated and recorded. Any errors will affect the accuracy of both the income statement and the balance sheet.

Once the adjusting entries are journalized and posted, financial statements are prepared. The income statement is prepared first. The amount of net income is used in the statement of stockholders' equity, which is prepared second. The totals from the statement of stockholders' equity are used to prepare the balance sheet.

The statement of cash flows is also prepared. It contains three main sections: operating activities, investing activities, and financing activities. The statement of cash flows is prepared on a cash basis, meaning that it shows actual cash inflows and outflows.

Next, the closing entries are prepared and posted. The closing entries close all temporary accounts and transfer the balances through **Income Summary** to the **Retained Earnings** account. Only assets, liabilities, and equity accounts will have a balance going into the next fiscal period. A post-closing trial balance is completed to ensure that debits equal credits.

If a company chooses to use reversing entries, these entries are recorded as the first entries of the new fiscal period. Every adjusting entry that established a balance in a receivable or payable account is reversed.

EXPLORE ACCOUNTING

Audits Provide Stockholders with Positive Assurance

The financial statements are the responsibility of the company management. Stockholders want assurance that the financial statements of their corporation accurately present its financial condition and results of operations. To provide this assurance, corporations hire independent public accountants to audit the financial statements. Public accountants referred to as *auditors* provide the assurance of the accuracy of the financial statements. They also provide a written opinion that informs stockholders whether the financial statements can be relied upon for making informed business decisions.

Auditors examine accounting records to collect evidence that supports amounts in the financial statements. The auditors then form an opinion, which is the basis for a letter to the stockholders and directors. There are four types of audit opinions that the letter can communicate: unqualified, qualified, adverse, and disclaimer.

An unqualified opinion means the auditors feel that the financial statements fairly represent the financial position of the company without any exceptions (qualifications). This is the best opinion that an auditor can issue. It means that the auditor believes the company followed GAAP to prepare its financial statements—without exceptions.

A qualified opinion means the auditors feel that the financial statements fairly represent the financial position of the company, except for one or more minor issues (or qualifications).

An adverse opinion means the auditors feel the financial statements do not fairly represent the financial position of the company or that the financial statements do not follow GAAP.

A disclaimer means the auditors could not form an opinion as to whether the financial statements fairly represent the financial position of the company. This may happen because the company did not provide enough information to the auditors. It can also happen when the information needed to support the financial statements is not available because it has been destroyed by fire or natural disaster.

INSTRUCTIONS

Access an annual report using a library or the Internet. Read the opinion letter written by the company auditors. In a written report, list the name of the company, the date of the opinion, and which type of audit opinion the auditors gave the company. Include a copy of the auditors' letter with your report.

Apply Your Understanding

INSTRUCTIONS: Download problem instructions for Excel, QuickBooks, and Peachtree from the textbook companion website at www.C21accounting.com.

22-1 Application Problem: Recording adjusting entries and preparing an adjusted trial balance LO1

Handy Hardware Corporation's unadjusted trial balance and accounting forms are given in the *Working Papers*.

Instructions:

1. Using the following information, journalize the adjusting entries for the current year ended December 31.

Adjustment Information, December 31

Estimated uncollectible accounts based on aging accounts receivable	$ 13,832.96
Accrued interest income	630.00
Merchandise inventory	162,569.00
Supplies inventory	3,695.00
Value of prepaid insurance	8,360.00
Annual depreciation expense—equipment	13,034.00
Accrued interest expense	600.00
Prepaid rent income earned	4,000.00

2. Post the adjusting entries to the T accounts.
3. Using the tax table shown in this chapter, calculate federal income tax expense and journalize the income tax adjustment.
4. Post the federal income tax adjusting entry to the T accounts.
5. Using the unadjusted trial balance and the T accounts, complete the adjusted trial balance. Save your work to complete Problem 22-2.

22-2 Application Problem: Preparing an income statement, statement of stockholders' equity, and balance sheet for a corporation LO2, 3, 4

Use the adjusted trial balance from Problem 22-1. Forms are given in the *Working Papers*.

Instructions:

1. Complete the income statement for the current year. Calculate and record the following vertical analysis ratios: (a) cost of merchandise sold; (b) gross profit on operations; (c) total operating expenses; (d) income from operations; (e) net addition or deduction from other revenue and expenses; and (f) net income before federal income tax. Round percentage calculations to the nearest 0.01%.
2. Complete the statement of stockholders' equity for the current year. As of January 1, Handy Hardware Corporation had issued 15,000 shares of common stock with a par value of $1.00 per share. During the fiscal year, the corporation issued 5,000 additional shares of common stock. The balance in Paid-in Capital in Excess of Par—Common on January 1, 20--, was $20,000.00. As of January 1, Handy Hardware had not issued any shares of preferred stock. During the fiscal year, it issued 1,000 shares of $30.00 par, 5% preferred stock at par value.
3. Complete the balance sheet for Handy Hardware Corporation for the current year. Save your work to complete Problem 22-3.

22-3 Application Problem: Preparing a statement of cash flows for a corporation LO5

Use the balance sheet from Problem 22-2 and the information below. A form is given in the *Working Papers*.

Instructions:

Prepare a statement of cash flows for the current year.

Cash receipts during the year:

Cash from sales	$1,925,342.80
Cash from interest	754.14

Cash from rent	$ 12,000.00
Cash from sale of equipment	2,500.00
Cash from issuance of stock	65,000.00
Cash from issuance of bonds	8,000.00
Cash payments during the year:	
Cash for inventory	$1,371,254.10
Cash for salaries and wages	262,954.25
Cash for insurance	18,500.00
Cash for interest	7,050.50
Cash for taxes	25,650.00
Cash for rent	30,000.00
Cash for other operating expenses	171,501.54
Cash for purchase of equipment	40,000.00
Cash for payment of notes payable	20,000.00
Cash for payment of dividends	40,000.00
Cash balance at the beginning of the period	$ 11,010.61

22-4 Application Problem: Journalizing closing and reversing entries for a corporation LO6, 7

Use the accounting forms and financial statements from Problem 22-1 to complete this problem. General journal pages are given in the *Working Papers*.

Instructions:

1. For the current year, journalize the closing entries using page 13 of a general journal.
2. For the following year, journalize the reversing entries using page 14 of a general journal.

 Peachtree

1. Journalize and post closing entries to the general journal.
2. Print the general journal and trial balance.
3. Journalize and post reversing entries to the general journal.

 QuickBooks

1. Journalize and post closing entries to the journal.
2. Print the journal and trial balance.
3. Journalize and post reversing entries to the journal.

1. Journalize and post closing and reversing entries to the general journal.
2. Print the worksheets.

22-M Mastery Problem: Journalizing adjustments, preparing financial statements, and journalizing end-of-fiscal-period entries for a corporation LO1, 2, 3, 4, 5, 6, 7

Ramel Corporation's unadjusted trial balance and accounting forms are given in the *Working Papers*.

Instructions:

1. Using the following information, journalize the adjusting entries for the current year ended December 31.

Adjustment Information, December 31

Estimated uncollectible accounts based on aging accounts receivable	$ 11,020.00
Accrued interest income	160.00
Merchandise inventory	581,489.16
Supplies inventory	620.01
Value of prepaid insurance	4,000.00
Annual depreciation expense—office equipment	10,960.00
Annual depreciation expense—store equipment	10,120.00
Accrued interest expense	625.00
Prepaid rent income earned	6,000.00

2. Post the adjusting entries to the T accounts.

3. Using the tax table presented in this chapter, calculate the federal income tax expense and journalize the income tax adjustment.

4. Post the federal income tax adjusting entry to the T accounts.

5. Using the unadjusted trial balance and the T accounts, complete the adjusted trial balance.

6. Complete the income statement for the current year. Calculate and record the following vertical analysis ratios: (a) cost of merchandise sold; (b) gross profit on operations; (c) total operating expenses; (d) income from operations; (e) net addition or deduction from other revenue and expenses; and (f) net income before federal income tax. Round percentage calculations to the nearest 0.01%.

7. Analyze the corporation's income statement by determining if vertical analysis ratios are within acceptable levels. If any vertical analysis ratio is not within an acceptable level, suggest steps that the company should take. The corporation considers the following ratios acceptable.

Cost of merchandise sold	Not more than 65.00%
Gross profit on operations	Not less than 35.00%
Total operating expenses	Not more than 30.00%
Income from operations	Not less than 5.00%
Net deduction from other revenue and expenses	Not more than 0.10%
Net income before federal income tax	Not less than 4.90%

8. Complete the statement of stockholders' equity for the current year. As of January 1, Ramel Corporation had issued 10,000 shares of common stock with a par value of $5.00 per share. During the fiscal year, the corporation issued 6,000 additional shares of common stock. The balance in Paid-in Capital in Excess of Par—Common on January 1, 20--, was $130,000.00. As of January 1, Ramel Corporation issued 1,500 shares of $20.00 par, 5% preferred stock. During the year, it issued 500 additional shares of preferred stock at par value.

9. Complete the balance sheet for Ramel Corporation for the current year.

10. Calculate the corporation's (a) working capital and (b) current ratio. Determine if these items are within acceptable levels. The corporation considers the following levels acceptable.

Working capital	Not less than $600,000.00
Current ratio	Between 5.0 to 1 and 6.0 to 1

11. Using the balance sheet and the following information, prepare a statement of cash flows for the current year.

Cash receipts during the year:

Cash from sales	$4,211,326.34
Cash from interest	1,510.00
Cash from rent	9,000.00
Cash from sale of store equipment	3,500.00
Cash from issuance of stock	90,000.00

Cash payments during the year:

Cash for inventory	$2,645,507.48
Cash for salaries and wages	844,521.30
Cash for insurance	30,000.00
Cash for interest	8,000.00
Cash for taxes	50,000.00
Cash for rent	90,000.00
Cash for other operating expenses	312,884.13
Cash for purchase of office equipment	48,651.87
Cash for purchase of store equipment	15,500.00
Cash for payment of notes payable	68,000.00
Cash for payment of bonds payable	150,000.00
Cash for payment of dividends	70,000.00
Cash balance at the beginning of the period	$ 72,764.94

12. Journalize the closing entries using page 16 of a general journal.

13. Journalize the reversing entries using page 17 of a general journal.

Peachtree

1. Journalize and post adjusting and closing entries to the general journal.
2. Print the general journal and trial balance.
3. Journalize and post reversing entries to the general journal.

QB Quick Books

1. Journalize and post adjusting and closing entries to the journal.
2. Print the journal and trial balance.
3. Journalize and post reversing entries to the journal.

1. Journalize and post adjusting, closing, and reversing entries to the general journal.
2. Print the worksheets.

AAONLiNE

1. Go to www.cengage.com/login
2. Click on **AA Online** to access.
3. Go to the online assignment and follow the instructions.

22-C Challenge Problem: Reversing entries L07

Elert Company's blank journals and T accounts are given in the *Working Papers*. On December 31, 20X1, Elert Company has one note receivable on its records. It is a $10,000.00, 90-day, 9% note. The accountant recorded the following adjusting entry related to this note:

	DATE	ACCOUNT TITLE	DOC. NO.	POST. REF.	DEBIT	CREDIT	
1		*Adjusting Entries*					1
4	31	Interest Receivable			7 5 00		4
5		Interest Income				7 5 00	5

GENERAL JOURNAL PAGE 24

After closing entries were posted, the related accounts had the balances reflected in the following T accounts.

Notes Receivable	
Dec. 31 Bal. 10,000.00	

Interest Income	
Dec. 31 Closing 75.00	Dec. 31 Adj. 75.00

Interest Receivable	
Dec. 31 Adj. 75.00	

Instructions:

1. Assume that Elert Company uses reversing entries.
   a. Journalize the reversing entry and post the entry to the T accounts.
   b. Journalize the receipt of the note and interest on its due date, March 1, 20X2, using Check No. 441 as the source document. Post the entry to the T accounts.
   c. Complete the statements regarding how much interest income was recognized in 20X1 and 20X2.

2. Assume that Elert Company does not use reversing entries.
   a. Journalize the receipt of the note and interest on its due date, March 1, 20X2, using Check No. 441 as the source document. Post the entry to the T accounts.
   b. Complete the statements regarding how much interest income was recognized in 20X1 and 20X2.

3. Why would Elert choose to use reversing entries?

The Ins and Outs of Cash Flow

**PARTNERSHIP FOR
21ST CENTURY SKILLS**

Theme: Financial, Economic, Business, and Entrepreneurial Literacy

Skills: Critical Thinking and Problem Solving, ICT Literacy

One of the first things to do in managing personal finances is to understand the inflow and outflow of cash for a period of time. While a budget provides a plan for spending, a cash flow statement actually shows where the money came from and how it was spent. Learning to manage cash flow will prevent overspending and allow personal wealth-building.

A cash flow statement for personal use contains three parts: sources of income (inflows of cash), expenditures (outflows of cash), and the difference between the two amounts, the net cash flow.

Sources of income are more than just your salary. Income can be gifts, scholarships, and investment income. Basically, anything that brings in money is considered income.

Outflows of cash consist of all of your expenditures, both fixed and variable. Fixed expenditures are those costs that remain unchanged from one period to the next. These include rent, car payments, savings, and investments. Variable expenditures might include food, charitable contributions, gas, and clothing.

The last component of the cash flow statement is calculating the net cash flow. This is the cash inflow minus cash outflow. A positive number is good and means you have extra cash to invest toward financial goals and build personal wealth or even pay down debt. A negative balance is bad and means outflow is greater than inflow. A plan must be created to spend less or generate more income. One cannot become a millionaire if there is a deficit of cash.

Managing your cash flow allows you to direct the cash. Understanding money flow keeps you in control!

APPLICATION

1. Julia, a recent college graduate, just prepared a cash flow statement after her first month of employment at Hickman's Hometown Cuisine. Her cash flow statement showed the following for the month of August: cash inflow, $3,269.27 and cash outflow, $2,975.00. Julia also has student loan debt totaling $12,425.00. Julia would like to purchase a new computer. She does not have a savings plan or a retirement plan. Determine the amount of net cash at the end of August. What suggestions would you make for Julia to help her achieve her financial goals? Explain.

2. Elias works at Harmon's Historical Village, a living history museum. He received $4,971.65 during May for tips and wages earned by providing tours at the museum. His cash outflow for May was $5,325.19. Explain how Elias could have a negative cash flow, yet be able to make his payments.

3. Create an Excel spreadsheet with the following headings down the side (rows): Cash Inflow, Cash Outflow, and Net Cash Flow. The following headings should be placed at the top (columns): Recent College Graduate, Newly Married, Married with 3 Kids.

   a. Assume that you are a recent college graduate, newly married, and married with three children. Anticipate your sources of cash inflow and a list of expenditures (cash outflow) for the different stages in your life. Record your sources and estimations. Calculate your net cash flow.

   b. Explain how the various stages of your life might affect your cash flow statement.

Analyzing Nike's financial statements

As stated in this chapter, the Operating Activities section of the statement of cash flows can be prepared using the direct method or the indirect method. Sun Treasures used the direct method to prepare its statement of cash flows. Nike uses the indirect method. The only difference is in the operating activities section. Look at Nike's Consolidated Statements of Cash Flows on page B-7 in Appendix B. The "Cash provided by operations" section begins with net income and then makes adjustments not affecting cash and changes in certain other accounts. The Operating Activities section of Sun Treasures' statement of cash flows lists cash receipts and cash payments. Both companies arrive at an amount of cash flow from operating activities.

INSTRUCTIONS

1. List the cash provided by operations for Nike for the fiscal year 2011.
2. Did Nike's cash increase or decrease during the fiscal year ended 2011? By what amount?
3. What was the largest use of cash for financing activities for the fiscal year ended 2011?

Reinforcement Activity 3—Part B

An Accounting Cycle for a Corporation: End-of-Fiscal-Period Work

 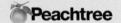Peachtree QB Quick Books AAONLiNE

The plant asset records and ledgers used in Reinforcement Activity 3—Part A are needed to complete Reinforcement Activity 3—Part B.

Reinforcement Activity 3—Part B includes those accounting activities needed to complete the accounting cycle of Restaurant Warehouse, Inc.

INSTRUCTIONS

9. Record the 20X4 depreciation on the plant asset record of plant asset no. 422. (Plant assets 452 and 453 will not have depreciation in 20X4 because they were purchased at the end of the year.)

10. Prepare an unadjusted trial balance.

11. Use the information below, collected on December 31, to journalize the adjusting entries.

   a. Estimated uncollectible accounts based on aging accounts receivable, $1,261.20.

   b. Outstanding notes receivable consist of NR30, a 60-day, 11% note accepted from Northside Catering on December 7, 20X4, for an extension of time on its account, $7,200.00.

   c. Merchandise inventory, $150,983.90.

   d. Supplies inventory, $850.00.

   e. Value of prepaid insurance, $9,200.00.

   f. Estimate of office equipment depreciation, $15,040.00.

   g. Estimate of warehouse equipment depreciation, $28,420.00.

   h. Outstanding notes payable consist of (1) NP19, a 100-day, 9% note for $20,000.00 signed on October 31, 20X4, and (2) NP22, a 90-day, 10% note for $12,000.00 signed on December 28, 20X4.

   i. Rent earned, $3,000.00.

12. Post the adjusting entries in the general ledger.

13. Prepare an adjusted trial balance and total the columns.

14. Using the tax table shown in Chapter 22, calculate the federal income tax owed for the fiscal year.

15. Journalize and post the adjusting entry for federal income tax payable.

16. Complete the adjusted trial balance.

17. Prepare an income statement for the current year. Prepare a vertical analysis of each amount in the fourth column. Round calculations to the nearest 0.1%.

18. Prepare a statement of stockholders' equity. The company had 6,000 shares of $10.00 par value common stock and no shares of $50.00, 5% preferred stock outstanding on January 1. The company issued 500 shares of common stock and 300 shares of preferred stock during the year.

19. Prepare a balance sheet for the current year.

20. Use the Cash account and the information below to prepare a statement of cash flows for the current year.

Cash balance at the beginning of the period:	$ 15,250.25
Cash receipts during the year:	
Cash from sales	$1,534,072.65
Cash from interest	875.00
Cash from rent	10,000.00
Cash from sale of equipment	33,000.00
Cash from issuance of stock	40,000.00

An Accounting Cycle for a Corporation: End-of-Fiscal-Period Work

Cash payments during the year:

Cash for inventory	$1,024,273.20
Cash for salaries and wages	210,573.25
Cash for insurance	15,000.00
Cash for interest	6,851.23
Cash for taxes	16,412.88
Cash for rent	48,000.00
Cash for other operating expenses	174,585.94
Cash for purchase of equipment	25,500.00
Cash for payment of bonds	40,000.00
Cash for payment of notes payable	17,000.00
Cash for payment of dividends	30,000.00

21. Journalize and post the closing entries.

22. Prepare a post-closing trial balance.

23. Journalize and post the reversing entries.

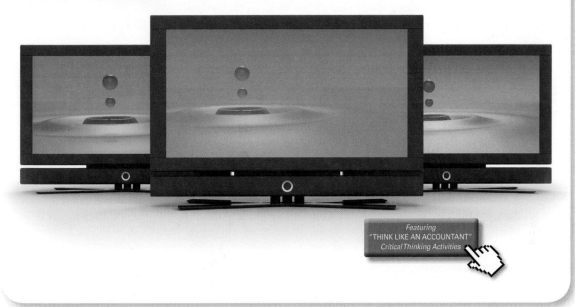

DIGITAL
DIVERSIONS

Featuring
"THINK LIKE AN ACCOUNTANT"
Critical Thinking Activities

© MUSTAFA DELIORMANLI/ISTOCKPHOTO

This company covers an online merchandising business organized as a corporation with its company offices in Bradenton, Florida. Digital Diversions sells televisions, cell phones, MP3 players, computers, video games, and other electronics goods.

The business sells merchandise for cash and also subscribes to a national credit card service.

In addition, some sales are made on account to certain customers. In this simulation, you will do accounting work for Digital Diversions.

This real-life business simulation comes with source documents. It is available in manual and automated versions. The automated version is used with Automated Accounting Online software.

The following activities are included in this simulation:

1. Recording transactions in special journals from source documents.

2. Posting items to be posted individually to a general ledger and subsidiary ledger.

3. Posting column totals to a general ledger.

4. Preparing schedules of accounts receivable and accounts payable from subsidiary ledgers.

5. Preparing a trial balance on a work sheet.

6. Planning adjustments and completing a work sheet.

7. Preparing financial statements.

8. Journalizing and posting adjusting entries.

9. Journalizing and posting closing entries.

10. Preparing a post-closing trial balance.

11. Journalizing and posting reversing entries.

12. Completing the Think Like an Accountant Financial Analysis activities.

Part 4

Additional
Accounting Procedures

Chapter 23 Accounting for Partnerships

Chapter 24 Recording International and Internet Sales

©OLGALIS, ISTOCK

MUST-HAVE GADGETS

Sarah Hatcher and Parker O'Reilly own a partnership called Must-Have Gadgets. The business sells accessories for electronic devices. The company accepts orders through its website and has customers in other countries.

Must-Have Gadgets rents the building that it uses for its operations. There are no employees; the partners do all the work in the company. Partners are not employees, and the money that partners receive from a partnership is not considered salaries. Therefore, Must-Have Gadgets does not need accounts for recording salaries and payroll taxes. Must-Have Gadgets will be used in Chapters 23 and 24 in Part 4 to illustrate the chapter concepts.

Chart of Accounts
MUST-HAVE GADGETS

GENERAL LEDGER

Balance Sheet Accounts

(1000) ASSETS
1100   Current Assets
1110   Cash
1120   Petty Cash
1130   Accounts Receivable
1135   Allowance for Uncollectible Accounts
1137   Time Drafts Receivable
1140   Merchandise Inventory
1150   Supplies
1160   Prepaid Insurance
1200   Plant Assets
1210   Office Equipment
1215   Accumulated Depreciation—Office Equipment

(2000) LIABILITIES
2100   Current Liabilities
2110   Accounts Payable

(3000) OWNERS' EQUITY
3110   Sarah Hatcher, Capital
3120   Sarah Hatcher, Drawing
3130   Parker O'Reilly, Capital
3140   Parker O'Reilly, Drawing
3150   Income Summary

Income Statement Accounts

(4000) OPERATING REVENUE
4110   Sales
4115   Sales Returns and Allowances
4120   Sales Discount

(5000) COST OF MERCHANDISE
5110   Purchases
5115   Purchases Returns and Allowances
5120   Purchases Discount

(6000) OPERATING EXPENSES
6110   Advertising Expense
6120   Credit Card Fee Expense
6130   Depreciation Expense—Office Equipment
6135   Insurance Expense
6140   Miscellaneous Expense
6150   Rent Expense
6160   Supplies Expense
6170   Uncollectible Accounts Expense

The chart of accounts for Must-Have Gadgets is illustrated above for ready reference as you study Part 4 of this textbook.

Chapter 23

Accounting for Partnerships

LEARNING OBJECTIVES

After studying Chapter 23, in addition to defining key terms, you will be able to:

LO1 Journalize entries to record investments by partners.

LO2 Journalize entries to record withdrawals by partners.

LO3 Prepare a distribution of net income statement for a partnership.

LO4 Prepare an owners' equity statement for a partnership.

LO5 Calculate and record a gain on realization.

LO6 Calculate and record a loss on realization.

LO7 Journalize entries to liquidate a partnership.

©DANIEL KOUREY, ISTOCK/©JIM PRUITT, ISTOCK

ROB MARMION/SHUTTERSTOCK.COM

Background: © JACK PUCCIO/ISTOCKPHOTO; Real World: SCOTT OLSON/GETTY IMAGES

Accounting In The Real World

Subway

More than 35,000 restaurants in 98 countries, easy-to-remember advertising slogans, and one of the fastest growing food chains in the world—that's Subway! But what else is there to know about Subway?

The first Subway shop was opened in 1965 by Fred DeLuca, a 17-year-old, recent high-school graduate. Fred had hopes of becoming a medical doctor but needed to earn money to pay for college. A family friend and doctor, Peter Buck, encouraged Fred to open a submarine sandwich shop. In addition, Dr. Buck handed Fred a $1,000 check and offered to become his partner. The first two shops were not successful, but the two partners continued to expand. In 1974, they decided to allow others to participate in the expansion of the company through franchising.

A franchise is a right granted to an individual or business to sell the products or services of another, larger business within a defined geographic area. The company granting the franchise is called the *franchisor*, and the holder of the franchise is called the *franchisee*. Franchisees typically receive support services from the franchisor, gain the advantage of national advertising, and receive rights to the use of the franchisor's trademarks.

Subway is a franchise company, which means that many local shops are owned by franchisees. To become a Subway franchisee, you must pay $15,000 up front, plus the cost of obtaining and preparing a shop. As a franchisee, you are able to take advantage of Subway's training programs and support, use its trademarks, and take advantage of nationwide purchase programs. Currently, a franchise pays 12.5% of weekly sales to Subway, which covers franchise royalties and advertising. The franchisee keeps any additional profit. A franchise is one way to own your own business while sharing in benefits that only large corporations can offer.

As with many franchise opportunities, Subway franchises are available to partners. Owning a franchise with a partner allows you to enter into business ownership with a smaller capital investment. It also allows you to benefit from the expertise of your partner(s).

CRITICAL THINKING

1. If you were going to start a business with someone else, how would you choose your partner?

2. Search the Internet for a franchise that is for sale. Write a report including the name of the franchise, the amount of investment required, the amount and kind of ongoing fees that must be paid, and what services are provided for these fees.

Key Terms

- partnership
- partner
- partnership agreement
- distribution of net income statement
- owners' equity statement
- liquidation of a partnership
- realization

LESSON
23-1 Forming a Partnership

LO1 Journalize entries to record investments by partners.
LO2 Journalize entries to record withdrawals by partners.

Partnerships

Delgado Web Services, the business described in Part 1, is a proprietorship, a small business owned by one person. ThreeGreen Products, Inc., and Sun Treasures, Inc., the businesses described in Parts 2 and 3, are organized as corporations. Businesses that require the skills and capital of more than one person, but that do not wish to be organized as a corporation, may choose another form of business. A business in which two or more persons combine their assets and skills is called a **partnership**. Each member of a partnership is called a **partner**. As in other forms of ownership, reports and financial records of the business are kept separate from the personal records of the partners. [CONCEPT: Business Entity] Each form of ownership has its advantages and disadvantages. Some of these are listed below.

Form	Advantages	Disadvantages
Sole Proprietorship	1. Ease of formation 2. Retention of all profits 3. Total control 4. Simple tax structure	1. Unlimited liability 2. Less capital available 3. Limited vision and skills 4. Terminates with life of owner
Partnership	1. Ease of formation 2. More capital available 3. Share work; each partner can operate in their area of expertise 4. Simple tax structure	1. Unlimited liability 2. Liable for partner's actions 3. Must share profits 4. Hard to dissolve 5. Terminates with life of one partner
Corporation	1. Limited liability 2. Ease of transfer of ownership 3. Unlimited life of the organization; does not terminate with death of investor	1. Harder/more expensive to form 2. Less control 3. Double taxation 4. More government regulations

Partnership Agreements

A written agreement setting forth the conditions under which a partnership is to operate is called a **partnership agreement**. Legally, a partnership agreement may be either written or oral. However, a written agreement may limit misunderstandings in the future; therefore, a partnership agreement should be in writing. It should include the name of the business and the partners, the investments of each partner, the duties and responsibilities of each partner, how profits and losses are to be divided, what happens if a partner dies, how the partnership is to be dissolved, and the duration of the agreement.

PARTNERSHIP AGREEMENT

THIS CONTRACT is made and entered into this _____1st_____ day of _January, 20--_, by and between ___Sarah Hatcher___ of _____Plano, TX_____, and ___Parker O'Reilly___ of _____Allen, TX_____.

WITNESSETH: That the said parties have this date formed a partnership to engage in and conduct a business under the following stipulations which are part of this contract. The partnership will begin operation on _January, 1, 20--_.

FIRST: The business shall be conducted under the name ___Must-Have Gadgets___, located initially at _2310 Premier Drive, Plano, TX 75075-2511_.

SECOND: The investment of each partner is: (first partner) _____Sarah Hatcher_____: Cash of $___20,000.00___. (second partner) _____Parker O'Reilly_____: Cash of $___20,000.00___ and total investment, $___40,000.00___.

THIRD: Both partners are to (a) participate in all general policy-making decisions, (b) devote full time and attention to the partnership business, and (c) engage in no other business enterprise without the written consent of the other partner. _____Sarah Hatcher_____ to be general manager of the business's operations.

FOURTH: Neither partner is to become a surety bonding agent for anyone without the written consent of the other partner.

FIFTH: The partners will share equally in all profits and losses of the partnership.

SIXTH: No partner is to withdraw assets without the other partner's written consent.

SEVENTH: All partnership transactions are to be recorded in accordance with standard and generally accepted accounting procedures and concepts. The partners' records are to be open at all times for inspection by either partner.

EIGHTH: In case of either partner's death or legal disability, the equity of the partners is to be determined as of the time of the death or disability of the one partner. The continuing partner is to have first option to buy the deceased/disabled partner's equity at recorded book value.

NINTH: This partnership agreement is to continue indefinitely unless (a) terminated by death of one partner, (b) terminated by either partner giving the other partner written notice at least ninety (90) days prior to the termination date; or (c) terminated by written mutual agreement signed by both partners.

TENTH: At the termination of this partnership agreement, the partnership's assets, after all liabilities are paid, will be distributed according to the balance in partners' capital accounts.

IN WITNESS WHEREOF, the parties to this contract have set their hands and seals on the date and year written.

Signed: _Sarah Hatcher_   (Seal) Date: _January 1, 20--_

Signed: _Parker O'Reilly_   (Seal) Date: _January 1, 20--_

Initial Investments by Owners LO1

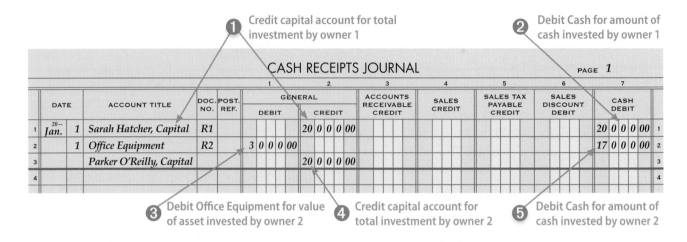

① Credit capital account for total investment by owner 1

② Debit Cash for amount of cash invested by owner 1

CASH RECEIPTS JOURNAL   PAGE 1

					GENERAL		ACCOUNTS RECEIVABLE CREDIT	SALES CREDIT	SALES TAX PAYABLE CREDIT	SALES DISCOUNT DEBIT	CASH DEBIT	
	DATE		ACCOUNT TITLE	DOC. NO.	POST. REF.	DEBIT	CREDIT					
1	20-- Jan.	1	Sarah Hatcher, Capital	R1			20 0 0 0 00					20 0 0 0 00	1
2		1	Office Equipment	R2		3 0 0 0 00						17 0 0 0 00	2
3			Parker O'Reilly, Capital				20 0 0 0 00						3
4													4

③ Debit Office Equipment for value of asset invested by owner 2

④ Credit capital account for total investment by owner 2

⑤ Debit Cash for amount of cash invested by owner 2

Must-Have Gadgets' partnership agreement calls for Sarah Hatcher to contribute cash and for Parker O'Reilly to contribute cash and office equipment to the new partnership. A separate journal entry is made for each partner's initial investment.

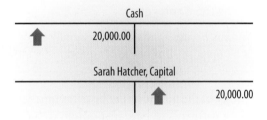

Cash
20,000.00

Sarah Hatcher, Capital
20,000.00

> **January 1.** Received cash from partner, Sarah Hatcher, as an initial investment, $20,000.00. Receipt No. 1.

The asset account, Cash, increases by a debit, $20,000.00. The owner's capital account, Sarah Hatcher, Capital, increases by a credit, $20,000.00.

> **January 1.** Received cash, $17,000.00, and office equipment valued at $3,000.00, from partner, Parker O'Reilly, as an initial investment. Receipt No. 2.

remember A partnership can consist of two or more partners. Partnerships are usually thought of as having only a few partners, but a partnership could have hundreds of partners.

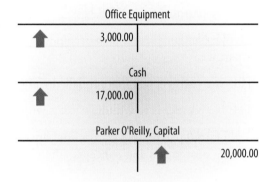

Office Equipment
3,000.00

Cash
17,000.00

Parker O'Reilly, Capital
20,000.00

The asset account, Cash, increases by a debit, $17,000.00. The asset account, Office Equipment, increases by a debit, $3,000.00. The owner's capital account, Parker O'Reilly, Capital, increases by a credit, $20,000.00.

↘ Journalizing Receipt of Partners' Initial Investment

① Credit Sarah Hatcher, Capital for the amount invested, $20,000.00.

② Debit Cash for the same amount.

③ Debit Office Equipment for its value, $3,000.00.

④ Credit Parker O'Reilly, Capital for the total amount invested, $20,000.00.

⑤ Debit Cash for the amount invested, $17,000.00.

Withdrawal of Cash by Partner LO2

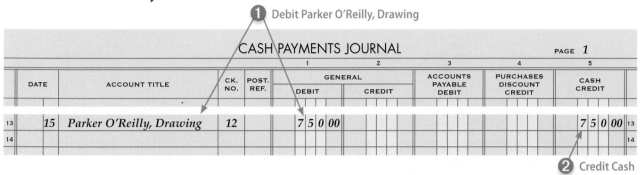

① Debit Parker O'Reilly, Drawing

CASH PAYMENTS JOURNAL PAGE 1

	DATE	ACCOUNT TITLE	CK. NO.	POST. REF.	GENERAL DEBIT	GENERAL CREDIT	ACCOUNTS PAYABLE DEBIT	PURCHASES DISCOUNT CREDIT	CASH CREDIT	
13	15	Parker O'Reilly, Drawing	12		7 5 0 00				7 5 0 00	13
14										14

② Credit Cash

During a fiscal period, partners may take assets out of the partnership in anticipation of the net income for the period. As in a proprietorship, assets taken out of a business for the personal use of an owner are known as *withdrawals*. The three types of assets generally taken out of a merchandising business are cash, supplies, and merchandise. The partnership agreement may limit the amount of assets that may be withdrawn.

Partner's Drawing Account

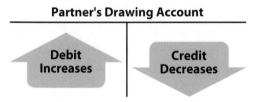

| Debit Increases | Credit Decreases |

While income increases the capital in the business, withdrawals reduce the amount of capital. The account titles of the partners' drawing accounts are Sarah Hatcher, Drawing and Parker O'Reilly, Drawing. Since capital accounts have credit balances, partners' drawing accounts have normal debit balances. Therefore, the drawing accounts increase by a debit and decrease by a credit, as shown in the T accounts.

> **January 15. Parker O'Reilly, partner, withdrew cash for personal use, $750.00. Check No. 12.**

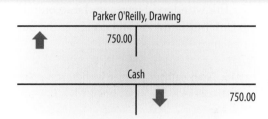

Parker O'Reilly, Drawing	
↑ 750.00	

Cash	
	↓ 750.00

The owner's drawing account, Parker O'Reilly, Drawing, has a normal debit balance because withdrawals decrease owner's equity. Therefore, increases in withdrawals are recorded by a debit, $750.00. The asset account, Cash, decreases by a credit, $750.00.

> **↘ Journalizing Withdrawals of Cash by Partners**
>
> ① **Debit Parker O'Reilly, Drawing** for the amount withdrawn, **$750.00.**
>
> ② **Credit Cash for the same amount.**

ETHICS IN ACTION

Can You Share Client Names?

After working six years with a national public accounting firm, Raymond Steele decided to venture out on his own. Raymond's new firm, Steele Consulting, specializes in helping companies that are facing severe financial difficulties. When delivering proposals to potential clients, Raymond proudly lists the names of his current clients.

The Code of Professional Conduct for the American Institute of Certified Public Accountants

"prohibits a member in public practice from disclosing confidential information without the client's consent." Raymond is aware of this rule but believes he is not violating it.

INSTRUCTIONS

Access the AICPA Code of Professional Conduct. Determine if Raymond's actions violate the confidentiality rule. (*Hint:* Remember that the Code includes rules, interpretations, and ethics rulings.)

Withdrawal of Supplies by Partner

1 Debit Sarah Hatcher, Drawing

	DATE		ACCOUNT TITLE	DOC. NO.	POST. REF.	DEBIT	CREDIT	
1	Jan.	15	*Sarah Hatcher, Drawing*	M1		4 5 0 00		1
2			*Supplies*				4 5 0 00	2
3								3
4								4

GENERAL JOURNAL PAGE *1*

2 Credit Supplies

A partner usually withdraws cash for personal use. However, a partner may also withdraw supplies for personal use. This withdrawal increases the account balance of Sarah Hatcher, Drawing and decreases the Supplies account balance.

> **January 15. Sarah Hatcher, partner, withdrew supplies for personal use, $450.00. Memorandum No. 1.**

Sarah Hatcher's drawing account increases by a debit of $450.00. The asset account, Supplies, decreases by a credit of $450.00. This transaction is recorded in the general journal.

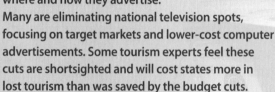

Sarah Hatcher, Drawing
450.00

Supplies
450.00

Journalizing Withdrawals of Merchandise by Partners

1 Debit **Sarah Hatcher, Drawing for $450.00.**

2 Credit **Supplies for the same amount.**

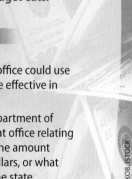

End of Lesson Review

L01 Journalize entries to record investments by partners.

L02 Journalize entries to record withdrawals by partners.

Terms Review

partnership

partner

partnership agreement

Audit your understanding

1. List at least three items that should be included in a partnership agreement.

2. Which accounts are debited and credited when a partner withdraws supplies from the partnership?

Work together 23-1

Journalizing partners' investments and withdrawals

Cash receipts, cash payments, and general journals are given in the *Working Papers*. Your instructor will guide you through the following examples.

Journalize the following transactions completed by Carpet World during April of the current year:

Transactions:

Apr. 1. Received cash of $15,000.00 and supplies valued at $4,000.00 from partner, Sofie Pavlov, as an initial investment. Receipt No. 1.

1. Received cash from partner, Noah Mancini, as an initial investment, $22,000.00. Receipt No. 2.

30. Sofie Pavlov, partner, withdrew cash for personal use, $1,000.00. Check No. 18.

30. Noah Mancini, partner, withdrew supplies for personal use, $1,200.00. Memorandum No. 6.

On your own 23-1

Journalizing partners' investments and withdrawals

Cash receipts, cash payments, and general journals are given in the *Working Papers*. Work this problem independently.

Journalize the following transactions completed by Ballo Brothers during October of the current year:

Transactions:

Oct. 1. Received cash of $30,000.00 and equipment valued at $10,000.00 from partner, Abdalla Ballo, as an initial investment. Receipt No. 1.

1. Received cash from partner, Rashad Ballo, as an initial investment, $36,000.00 Receipt No. 2.

30. Abdalla Ballo, partner, withdrew cash for personal use, $1,500.00. Check No. 47.

30. Rashad Ballo, partner, withdrew supplies for personal use, $1,900.00. Memorandum No. 8.

LO3 Prepare a distribution of net income statement for a partnership.

LO4 Prepare an owners' equity statement for a partnership.

Distribution of Net Income Statement LO3

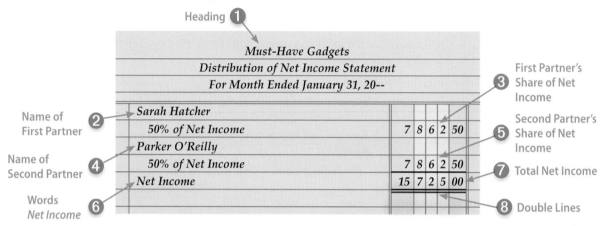

A partnership's net income or net loss may be divided in any way agreed upon by the partners in their partnership agreement. Sarah Hatcher and Parker O'Reilly, partners in Must-Have Gadgets, agreed to share net income or net loss equally.

A partnership's distribution of net income or net loss is usually shown on a separate financial statement. A partnership financial statement showing net income or loss distribution to partners is called a **distribution of net income statement**.

The income statement for a partnership is prepared in the same way as an income statement for a proprietorship, described in Chapter 7. Must-Have Gadgets' income statement shows a net income of $15,725.00 for the month ended January 31. This net income is used to prepare the distribution of net income statement.

🔽 Preparing a Distribution of Net Income Statement

1 Write the heading of the distribution of net income statement on three lines.

2 Write one partner's name, Sarah Hatcher, on the first line at the extreme left.

3 Indent about one centimeter on the next line, and write Sarah Hatcher's share of net income as a percentage, 50.0% of Net Income. Write Ms. Hatcher's share of net income, $7,862.50 (50.0% × $15,725.00), in the amount column on the same line.

4 Write the other partner's name, Parker O'Reilly, on the next line.

5 Indent about one centimeter on the next line, and write Parker O'Reilly's share of net income as a percentage, 50.0% of Net Income. Write Mr. O'Reilly's share of net income, $7,862.50 (50.0% × $15,725.00), in the amount column on the same line.

6 Write Net Income on the next line at the extreme left of the wide column.

7 Add the distribution of net income and write the total amount, $15,725.00, in the amount column. Verify accuracy by comparing the total amount, $15,725.00, with the net income reported on the income statement, $15,725.00. The two amounts must be the same.

8 Rule double lines across the amount column to show that the distribution of net income statement has been verified as correct.

Distribution of Net Income Statement with Unequal Distribution

Computer Consulting						
Distribution of Net Income Statement						
For Year Ended December 31, 20--						
Ling Wang						
70% of Net Income	47	2	5	0	00	
Lucas Fornier						
30% of Net Income	20	2	5	0	00	
Net Income	67	5	0	0	00	

Regardless of how earnings are shared, the steps in preparing a distribution of net income statement are the same. The only difference is the description of how the earnings are to be shared by the partners.

Ling Wang and Lucas Fornier are partners in a business. Because Ms. Wang spends more time in the business than Mr. Fornier, the partners agree to share net income or loss unequally. Ms. Wang gets 70.0% of net income or loss. Mr. Fornier gets 30.0% of net income or loss. With a net income of $67,500.00, Ms. Wang receives 70.0%, or $47,250.00. Mr. Fornier receives 30.0%, or $20,250.00.

Lease Agreements

Consumers should review their personal finances at least once a year to assess income and spending. It is a good time to review the cost of your living arrangements. Most financial experts recommend that no more than 30% of net pay be spent on housing.

While home ownership comes with tax advantages, privacy, and fewer restrictions, many find renting more appealing. The flexibility to relocate quickly and the benefit of maintenance-free living are two advantages to renting that many find attractive. Renters are sometimes tempted by luxuries, such as pools and clubhouses that come with the rental unit, to rush into a lease agreement without a full understanding of the costs or properly budgeting for them. A lease agreement is a binding legal contract for both the tenant and the landlord. It should not be rushed into.

In addition to listing the names of the lessor and the lessee and the address of the property, a lease agreement will also contain: the amount of the rent, when rent is due, additional fees for pets and/or parking, restrictions (including noise and visitors), lease start and end dates, amount of notice needed for termination, conditions upon which the landlord can enter the property, and signatures. A security deposit is almost always required. It is paid in advance to the landlord to cover possible damage to the property. It is reimbursed if the property is left as described in the lease agreement. The amount of the deposit is usually equivalent to one month's rent.

ACTIVITIES

Read and respond to the following items. Be sure to give reasons.

1. Brandon's lease just ended, and he moved to another apartment. Several months ago, Brandon allowed his friend Brady to stay with him temporarily. Now, Brandon's landlord will not return his $500 security deposit because of damage caused by his friend's dog. The landlord claims that the $500 will partially cover the cost of replacing carpeting in three rooms due to soiling and tears. Brandon disagrees because pets were allowed by the lease agreement, and he feels if anyone should incur the charges it should be Brady. Who is correct, Brandon or the landlord?

2. If you were the landlord, indicate at least five rules and/or restrictions that you would place in your lease agreement to protect yourself in the situations described in number 1.

3. Research the Federal Fair Housing Act and Fair Housing Amendments to determine what types of housing discrimination are legal.

©NOREBBO, ISTOCK

Partners' Capital and Drawing Accounts

ACCOUNT *Sarah Hatcher, Capital*   ACCOUNT NO. *3110*

DATE	ITEM	POST. REF.	DEBIT	CREDIT	BALANCE DEBIT	BALANCE CREDIT
Jan. 1		CR1		20 0 0 0 00		20 0 0 0 00

ACCOUNT *Sarah Hatcher, Drawing*   ACCOUNT NO. *3120*

DATE	ITEM	POST. REF.	DEBIT	CREDIT	BALANCE DEBIT	BALANCE CREDIT
Jan. 15		G1	4 5 0 0 00		4 5 0 0 00	

ACCOUNT *Parker O'Reilly, Capital*   ACCOUNT NO. *3130*

DATE	ITEM	POST. REF.	DEBIT	CREDIT	BALANCE DEBIT	BALANCE CREDIT
Jan. 1		CR1		20 0 0 0 00		20 0 0 0 00

ACCOUNT *Parker O'Reilly, Drawing*   ACCOUNT NO. *3140*

DATE	ITEM	POST. REF.	DEBIT	CREDIT	BALANCE DEBIT	BALANCE CREDIT
Jan. 15		CP1	7 5 0 00		7 5 0 00	

The amount of net income earned is important to business owners. Owners are also interested in changes that occur in owners' equity during a fiscal period. A financial statement that summarizes the changes in owners' equity during a fiscal period is called an owners' equity statement. Business owners can review an owners' equity statement to determine if owners' equity is increasing or decreasing and what is causing the change. Three factors can change owners' equity:

1. Additional investments.
2. Withdrawals.
3. Net income or net loss.

An owners' equity statement shows information about changes in each partner's capital during a fiscal period. Information needed to prepare an owners' equity statement is obtained from the distribution of net income statement, shown on page 728, and the general ledger capital and drawing accounts shown above. The distribution of net income statement shows each partner's share of net income or net loss. Three kinds of information are obtained from each partner's capital and drawing account:

1. Beginning capital amount.
2. Any additional investments made during the fiscal period.
3. Each partner's withdrawal of assets during the fiscal period.

Owners' Equity Statement LO4

② Name of First Partner   ① Heading

		Must-Have Gadgets		
		Owners' Equity Statement		
		For Month Ended January 31, 20--		
Sarah Hatcher				
Capital, January 1, 20--			20 0 0 0 00	
Share of Net Income	7 8 6 2 50			
Less Withdrawals	4 5 0 00			
Net Increase in Capital			7 4 1 2 50	
Capital, January 31, 20--				27 4 1 2 50
Parker O'Reilly				
Capital, January 1, 20--			20 0 0 0 00	
Share of Net Income	7 8 6 2 50			
Less Withdrawals	7 5 0 00			
Net Increase in Capital			7 1 1 2 50	
Capital, January 31, 20--				27 1 1 2 50
Total Owners' Equity, January 31, 20--				54 5 2 5 00

Labels pointing to the statement:
- First Partner's Ending Capital ③
- Name of Second Partner ④
- Second Partner's Ending Capital ⑤
- ⑥ Total Owners' Equity
- ⑦ Double Lines

Neither Sarah Hatcher nor Parker O'Reilly invested any additional capital during the month ended January 31 after the initial investments on January 1. Both partners withdrew either cash or supplies during the month.

Some businesses include the owners' equity statement information as part of the balance sheet. An example of this method of reporting changes in owner's equity is shown in Chapter 7.

↘ Preparing an Owners' Equity Statement

① Write the heading of the owners' equity statement on three lines.

② Write the name Sarah Hatcher on the first line at the extreme left.

③ Calculate the net increase in capital and ending capital amount for Sarah Hatcher.

  a. Indent about one centimeter on the next line, and write Capital, January 1, 20--. Write the amount $20,000.00 in the second amount column. (This amount is obtained from the capital account.)

  b. Indent about one centimeter on the next line, and write Share of Net Income. Write the amount $7,862.50 in the first amount column. (This amount is obtained from the distribution of net income statement.)

  c. Indent about one centimeter on the next line, and write Less Withdrawals. Write the amount $450.00 in the first amount column. (This amount is obtained from the drawing account.)

  d. Indent about one centimeter on the next line, and write Net Increase in Capital. Write the amount $7,412.50 in the second amount column. ($7,862.50 – $450.00 = $7,412.50)

  e. Indent about one centimeter on the next line, and write Capital, January 31, 20--. Write the amount $27,412.50 in the third amount column. ($20,000.00 + $7,412.50 = $27,412.50)

④ Write the name Parker O'Reilly on the next line at the extreme left of the wide column.

⑤ Calculate the net increase in capital and ending capital amount for Parker O'Reilly. Follow Step 3.

⑥ Write Total Owners' Equity, January 31, 20-- on the next line at the extreme left of the wide column. Write the amount $54,525.00 in the third amount column.

⑦ Rule double lines across the three amount columns to show that the totals have been verified as correct.

Owners' Equity Statement with an Additional Investment and a Net Loss

J & J Tree Service				
Owners' Equity Statement				
For Year Ended December 31, 20--				
Markus Jensen				
Capital, January 1, 20--	100 1 6 0 00			
Plus Additional Investment	9 6 0 0 00			
Total		109 7 6 0 00		
Share of Net Loss	2 2 7 2 00			
Plus Withdrawals	14 2 0 8 00			
Net Decrease in Capital		16 4 8 0 00		
Capital, December 31, 20--			93 2 8 0 00	
Emma Johansen				
Capital, January 1, 20--	98 7 2 0 00			
Plus Additional Investment	9 6 0 0 00			
Total		108 3 2 0 00		
Share of Net Loss	2 2 7 2 00			
Plus Withdrawals	14 4 9 6 00			
Net Decrease in Capital		16 7 6 8 00		
Capital, December 31, 20--			91 5 5 2 00	
Total Owners' Equity, December 31, 20--			184 8 3 2 00	

On December 31, the capital accounts of Markus Jensen and Emma Johansen showed additional investments of $9,600.00 each. Also, the income statement for their company, J & J Tree Service, showed a net loss of $4,544.00. The partners agreed to share net income or net loss equally. The owners' equity statement above shows the net loss as a deduction from the owners' capital.

Balance Sheet for a Partnership

Must-Have Gadgets				
Balance Sheet				
January 31, 20--				
Total Liabilities			32 8 4 1 00	
Owners' Equity				
Sarah Hatcher, Capital		27 4 1 2 50		
Parker O'Reilly, Capital		27 1 1 2 50		
Total Owners' Equity			54 5 2 5 00	
Total Liabilities and Owners' Equity			87 3 6 6 00	

The Asset and Liability sections of a balance sheet for a partnership are prepared in the same way as the Asset and Liability sections of a balance sheet for a proprietorship. The only section that is different is the Equity section. The Equity section lists the capital account for each partner. The balances of these two accounts are added together and listed as Total Owners' Equity. Total Liabilities and Total Owners' Equity are added together to determine Total Liabilities and Owners' Equity.

Careers In Accounting

Jenna Fitch
GOVERNMENTAL ACCOUNTANT

Jenna Fitch is an accountant for a midsized city in the state of Washington. A city government is not expected to make a profit. Therefore, the records kept by Ms. Fitch do not focus on revenues and expenses. Instead, the emphasis is on making sure that monies spent by the city are within specific limits. Each year, the city council presents and approves a budget for the coming year. Once approved, the budget must be followed. One of Ms. Fitch's major tasks is to make sure that the city does not spend more money in any budget category than was approved in the budget.

As a governmental accountant, Ms. Fitch follows different guidelines than would be followed by an accountant for a corporation. Instead of having one general ledger, Ms. Fitch keeps financial records for several separate funds, including a fire department fund, a water department fund, a fund for a street repaving project, and a general fund. She must keep separate records of revenues and expenditures for each fund.

Governmental accountants use a modified accrual basis of accounting as opposed to the accrual basis of accounting used by corporations. In the accrual basis, revenue is recognized when it is earned. In the modified accrual basis, revenue is recognized when it becomes both available and measurable.

Salary Range: Salaries vary depending on the type and size of government agency. The average salary for state and local agencies is $55,700. Federal agencies tend to be higher, with an average salary of $88,190.

Qualifications: A governmental accountant has to have many of the same qualifications as most other accountants. Minimum education for an entry-level position is a basic knowledge of accounting with some classes in not-for-profit accounting. Promotion to a manager-level position usually requires a bachelor's degree in accounting. Good communications skills are required, especially when working with donors or taxpayers.

Occupational Outlook: The growth for governmental accounting positions is projected to be in the average range (between 7% and 13%).

ACTIVITY

Research job openings for governmental accountants in your area. Record the educational requirements and the salary range for the position(s) listed. Summarize your findings in a written report.

Source: www.accountingedu.org.

LO3 Prepare a distribution of net income statement for a partnership.

LO4 Prepare an owners' equity statement for a partnership.

Terms Review

distribution of net income statement

owners' equity statement

Audit your understanding

1. What information used to prepare an owners' equity statement is obtained from the distribution of net income statement?

2. What information used to prepare an owners' equity statement is obtained from the partners' capital and drawing accounts?

3. What is the procedure for calculating an owner's end-of-year capital when the partnership earned a net income for the year?

Work together 23-2

Preparing distribution of net income and owners' equity statements

Carpet World is a partnership owned by Sofie Pavlov and Noah Mancini. Information from Carpet World's general ledger and income statement is given below. Forms for completing this problem are given in the *Working Papers*. Your instructor will guide you through the following examples.

Net income for the month ended April 30	$32,600.00
Sofie Pavlov, Capital April 1 balance	19,000.00
Noah Mancini, Capital April 1 balance	22,000.00
Sofie Pavlov, Drawing April 30 balance	1,000.00
Noah Mancini, Drawing April 30 balance	1,200.00

1. Prepare a distribution of net income statement for Carpet World. Net income or loss is to be shared equally.

2. Using the balances of the general ledger capital and drawing accounts, prepare an owners' equity statement for Carpet World. No additional investments were made.

On your own 23-2

Preparing distribution of net income and owners' equity statements

Ballo Brothers is a partnership owned by Abdalla Ballo and Rashad Ballo. Information from Ballo Brothers' general ledger and income statement is given below. Forms for completing this problem are given in the *Working Papers*. Work this problem independently.

Net income for the month ended October 31	$62,500.00
Abdalla Ballo, Capital October 1 balance	40,000.00
Rashad Ballo, Capital October 1 balance	36,000.00
Abdalla Ballo, Drawing October 31 balance	1,500.00
Rashad Ballo, Drawing October 31 balance	1,900.00

1. Prepare a distribution of net income statement for Ballo Brothers. Net income or loss is to be distributed 60% to Abdalla Ballo and 40% to Rashad Ballo.

2. Using the balances of the general ledger capital and drawing accounts, prepare an owners' equity statement for Ballo Brothers. No additional investments were made.

23-3 Dissolving a Partnership

LO5 Calculate and record a gain on realization.
LO6 Calculate and record a loss on realization.
LO7 Journalize entries to liquidate a partnership.

Account Balances Before Realization

Cash	
Bal.	28,000.00

Supplies	
Bal.	2,000.00

Machinery	
Bal.	25,000.00

Accumulated Depreciation—Machinery	
	Bal. 5,000.00

Accounts Payable	
	Bal. 8,500.00

Gerald Bakken, Capital	
	Bal. 22,000.00

Jon Bakken, Capital	
	Bal. 19,500.00

If a partnership goes out of business, its assets are distributed to the creditors and partners. The process of paying a partnership's liabilities and distributing remaining assets to the partners is called **liquidation of a partnership**.

Cash received from the sale of assets during liquidation of a partnership is called **realization**. Typically, when a partnership is liquidated, the noncash assets are sold, and the available cash is used to pay the creditors.

Any remaining cash is distributed to the partners according to each partner's total equity.

On June 30, Gerald and Jon Bakken liquidated their partnership. At that time, adjusting entries were made and financial statements were prepared; then closing entries were journalized and posted. After the end-of-fiscal-period work was completed, the partnership had account balances as shown in the T accounts above.

A partnership usually tries to sell the business before it begins the process of liquidation.

Calculating Gain on Realization L05

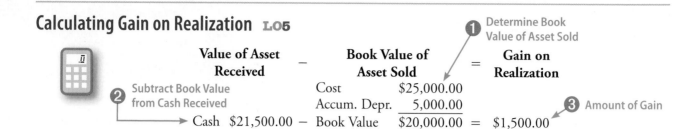

| Value of Asset Received | − | Book Value of Asset Sold | = | Gain on Realization |

① Determine Book Value of Asset Sold

② Subtract Book Value from Cash Received

Cost $25,000.00
Accum. Depr. 5,000.00

③ Amount of Gain

Cash $21,500.00 − Book Value $20,000.00 = $1,500.00

Noncash assets might be sold for more than the recorded book value. When this happens, the amount received in excess of the book value is recorded as a gain on realization.

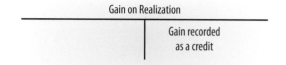

Gain on Realization
Gain recorded as a credit

A gain on realization is calculated as shown above. The account, Gain on Realization, is used to record the amount of the gain. Most companies will have to add this account to their charts of account. Gain on Realization is usually included in the Other Revenue section of the chart of accounts.

↻ Calculating a Gain on Realization

① Determine the book value of the asset sold.

② Subtract the book value from the cash received.

③ Record the amount of gain on realization.

Recording a Gain on Realization

① Debit Accumulated Depreciation—Machinery

② Credit Machinery

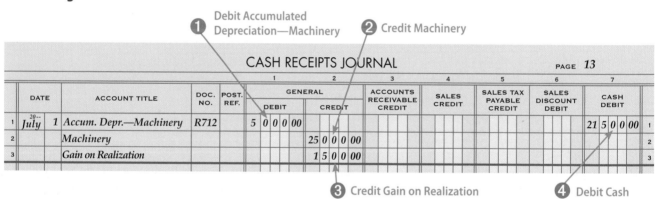

CASH RECEIPTS JOURNAL
PAGE 13

	DATE	ACCOUNT TITLE	DOC. NO.	POST. REF.	GENERAL DEBIT	GENERAL CREDIT	ACCOUNTS RECEIVABLE CREDIT	SALES CREDIT	SALES TAX PAYABLE CREDIT	SALES DISCOUNT DEBIT	CASH DEBIT	
1	July 1	Accum. Depr.—Machinery	R712		5 000 00						21 500 00	1
2		Machinery				25 000 00						2
3		Gain on Realization				1 500 00						3

③ Credit Gain on Realization

④ Debit Cash

The transaction is recorded in the cash receipts journal. After the transaction is posted, the Machinery and the Accumulated Depreciation—Machinery accounts will have a zero balance.

↻ Recording a Gain on Realization

① Debit Accumulated Depreciation—Machinery for $5,000.00.

② Credit Machinery for $25,000.00, the original cost of the machinery sold.

③ Credit Gain on Realization for $1,500.00, the amount of the gain.

④ Debit Cash for $21,500.00, the amount of cash received.

July 1. Received cash from sale of machinery, $21,500.00: original cost, $25,000.00; total accumulated depreciation recorded to date, $5,000.00. Receipt No. 712.

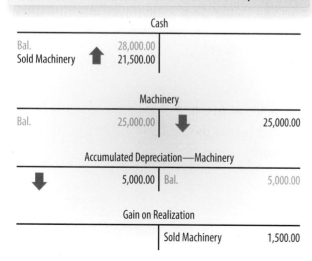

Cash	
Bal. 28,000.00	
Sold Machinery 21,500.00	

Machinery	
Bal. 25,000.00	25,000.00

Accumulated Depreciation—Machinery	
5,000.00	Bal. 5,000.00

Gain on Realization	
	Sold Machinery 1,500.00

Calculating Loss on Realization LO6

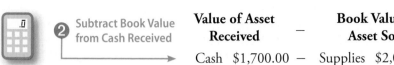

① Determine Book Value of Asset Sold

② Subtract Book Value from Cash Received

Value of Asset Received	−	Book Value of Asset Sold	=	Loss on Realization
Cash $1,700.00	−	Supplies $2,000.00	=	$(300)

③ Amount of Loss

Noncash assets might be sold for less than the recorded book value. When that happens, the amount by which the book value exceeds the amount received is recorded as a loss on realization.

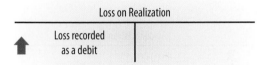

Loss on Realization

Loss recorded as a debit

A loss on realization is calculated as shown above. The account, Loss on Realization, is used to record the amount of the loss. Most companies will have to add this account to their charts of account. Loss on Realization is usually included in the Other Expenses section of the chart of accounts.

> **Calculating a Loss on Realization**
> ① Determine the book value of the asset sold.
> ② Subtract the book value from the cash received.
> ③ Record the amount of loss on realization.

Recording a Loss on Realization

① Debit Loss on Realization

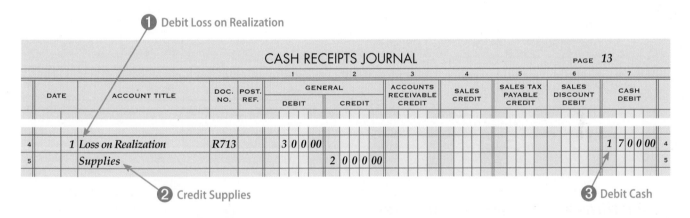

CASH RECEIPTS JOURNAL   PAGE 13

	DATE	ACCOUNT TITLE	DOC. NO.	POST. REF.	GENERAL DEBIT	GENERAL CREDIT	ACCOUNTS RECEIVABLE CREDIT	SALES CREDIT	SALES TAX PAYABLE CREDIT	SALES DISCOUNT DEBIT	CASH DEBIT	
4	1	Loss on Realization	R713		3 0 0 00						1 7 0 0 00	4
5		Supplies				2 0 0 0 00						5

② Credit Supplies   ③ Debit Cash

> July 1. Received cash from sale of supplies, $1,700.00; balance of Supplies account, $2,000.00. Receipt No. 713.

The transaction is recorded in the cash receipts journal. After the transaction is posted, the Supplies account will have a zero balance.

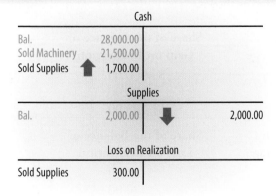

Cash

Bal.	28,000.00	
Sold Machinery	21,500.00	
Sold Supplies	1,700.00	

Supplies

| Bal. | 2,000.00 | 2,000.00 |

Loss on Realization

| Sold Supplies | 300.00 | |

> **Recording a Loss on Realization**
> ① Debit Loss on Realization for the amount of the loss, $300.00.
> ② Credit Supplies for $2,000.00, the book value of the supplies sold.
> ③ Debit Cash for $1,700.00, the amount of cash received.

Liquidating Liabilities LO7

				GENERAL		ACCOUNTS PAYABLE DEBIT	PURCHASES DISCOUNT CREDIT	CASH CREDIT	
	DATE	ACCOUNT TITLE	CK. NO.	POST. REF.	DEBIT	CREDIT			

CASH PAYMENTS JOURNAL   PAGE **13**

	DATE	ACCOUNT TITLE	CK. NO.	POST. REF.	GENERAL DEBIT	GENERAL CREDIT	ACCOUNTS PAYABLE DEBIT	PURCHASES DISCOUNT CREDIT	CASH CREDIT	
1	July 1	✔	825				8 5 0 0 00		8 5 0 0 00	1
2										2

The partnership's available cash is used to pay creditors. The entry is recorded in the cash payments journal as shown.

> **July 1. Paid cash to all creditors for the amounts owed, $8,500.00. Check No. 825.**

After this entry is posted, the Accounts Payable account will have a zero balance.

Cash

Bal.	28,000.00	Paid Accts. Pay.	8,500.00
Sold Machinery	21,500.00		
Sold Supplies	1,700.00		

Accounts Payable

	8,500.00	Bal.	8,500.00

ACCOUNT BALANCES AFTER LIQUIDATION OF NONCASH ASSETS AND PAYMENT OF LIABILITIES

When this transaction has been journalized and posted, the partnership has only five general ledger accounts with balances as shown.

Cash

Bal.	28,000.00	Paid Accts. Pay.	8,500.00
Sold Machinery	21,500.00		
Sold Supplies	1,700.00		
(New Bal.	42,700.00)		

Gerald Bakken, Capital

	Bal.	22,000.00

Jon Bakken, Capital

	Bal.	19,500.00

Gain on Realization

	Sold Machinery	1,500.00
	Bal.	1,500.00

Loss on Realization

Sold Supplies	300.00	
Bal.	300.00	

DISTRIBUTING LOSS OR GAIN ON REALIZATION

When all creditors have been paid, the balances of Gain on Realization and Loss on Realization are distributed to the partners based on the method of distributing net income or net loss as stated in the partnership agreement. The percentages for the Bakken partnership are Gerald Bakken, 60%, and Jon Bakken, 40%. The distribution of the balances of the two accounts is calculated as shown.

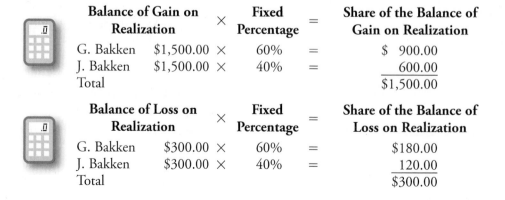

	Balance of Gain on Realization	×	Fixed Percentage	=	Share of the Balance of Gain on Realization
G. Bakken	$1,500.00	×	60%	=	$ 900.00
J. Bakken	$1,500.00	×	40%	=	600.00
Total					$1,500.00

	Balance of Loss on Realization	×	Fixed Percentage	=	Share of the Balance of Loss on Realization
G. Bakken	$300.00	×	60%	=	$180.00
J. Bakken	$300.00	×	40%	=	120.00
Total					$300.00

Close Gain on Realization account.

	DATE		ACCOUNT TITLE	DOC. NO.	POST. REF.	DEBIT	CREDIT	
1			*Closing Entries*					1
2	20-- July	6	*Gain on Realization*	M531		1 5 0 0 00		2
3			*Gerald Bakken, Capital*				9 0 0 00	3
4			*Jon Bakken, Capital*				6 0 0 00	4
5		6	*Gerald Bakken, Capital*	M532		1 8 0 00		5
6			*Jon Bakken, Capital*			1 2 0 00		6
7			*Loss on Realization*				3 0 0 00	7

GENERAL JOURNAL   PAGE 7

Close Loss on Realization account.

Each partner's capital account is debited for the partner's share of the loss on realization.

> July 6. Recorded distribution of gain on realization: to Gerald Bakken, $900; to Jon Bakken, $600. Recorded distribution of loss on realization: to Gerald Bakken, $180.00; to Jon Bakken, $120.00. Memorandum Nos. 531 and 532.

After this entry is posted, the balances of Gain on Realization and Loss on Realization are zero. The total of the two capital accounts equals the balance of the Cash account.

Gerald Bakken, Capital

Share of loss	180.00	Bal.	22,000.00
		Share of gain	900.00
		(New Bal.	*22,720.00)*

Jon Bakken, Capital

Share of loss	120.00	Bal.	19,500.00
		Share of gain	600.00
		(New Bal.	*19,980.00)*

Gain on Realization

Distribution	1,500.00	Sold Machinery	1,500.00

Loss on Realization

Sold Supplies	300.00	Distribution	300.00

USING ONE REALIZATION ACCOUNT

The partnership in this lesson uses two separate realization accounts: one for loss on realization and one for gain on realization. A partnership could choose to use only one realization account. This account is usually titled Loss and Gain on Realization. When only one realization account is used, losses on realization are recorded on the debit side of the account and gains on realization are recorded on the credit side of the account. After all assets have been liquidated, the balance in this account will be equal to the net loss or net gain on realization and is closed into the partners' capital accounts.

Partnerships must file tax returns with the IRS to report how income was divided among the partners. However, partnerships do not pay income taxes. Net income passes through to the partners according to the terms of their partnership agreement. That income must be reported on each partner's individual tax return.

Distributing Remaining Cash to Partners

			CASH PAYMENTS JOURNAL						PAGE 13	

						1	2	3	4	5
	DATE	ACCOUNT TITLE	CK. NO.	POST. REF.	GENERAL DEBIT	GENERAL CREDIT	ACCOUNTS PAYABLE DEBIT	PURCHASES DISCOUNT CREDIT	CASH CREDIT	
2	6	Gerald Bakken, Capital	826		22 7 2 0 00				22 7 2 0 00	2
3	6	Jon Bakken, Capital	827		19 9 8 0 00				19 9 8 0 00	3

Debit each partner's capital account for the amount of the account balance

Credit Cash for the amounts distributed

All remaining cash is distributed to the partners. The cash is distributed according to each partner's capital account balance, regardless of the method used to distribute net income or net loss.

July 6. Recorded final distribution of remaining cash to partners: to Gerald Bakken, $22,720.00; to Jon Bakken, $19,980.00. Check Nos. 826 and 827.

After these journal entries are journalized and posted as shown above, all of the partnership's general ledger accounts will have zero balances. The partnership is liquidated.

Cash

Bal.	42,700.00	22,720.00
(New Bal.	0.00)	19,980.00

Gerald Bakken, Capital

22,720.00	Bal.	22,720.00
	(New Bal.	0.00)

Jon Bakken, Capital

19,980.00	Bal.	19,980.00
	(New Bal.	0.00)

THINK LIKE AN ACCOUNTANT

Condensed Financial Statements

Large businesses have many levels of managers. Operational managers organize and monitor the daily activities of a business. Common tasks of an operational manager might include:

- Set employee work schedules.
- Purchase inventory and supplies.
- Plan advertising and promotions.

In contrast, strategic managers focus on the long-term operations of the business. Common tasks of a senior manager might include:

- Identify expansion opportunities.
- Make capital acquisition decisions.
- Determine dividends or partnership distributions.
- Hire and monitor operational managers.

The information needs of these managers differ. Operational managers need very detailed information. Senior managers prefer summarized information.

Even small businesses can have hundreds, even thousands, of general ledger accounts. This level of detail is necessary for operational managers to monitor daily activities. For example, a sales manager may use 30 or more accounts to classify the expenses of his department. In contrast, a strategic manager may only want to know the total of sales expenses.

A financial statement containing summarized amounts is referred to as a condensed financial statement. A condensed income statement might contain a single line for sales expenses. Strategic managers, investors, and government agencies require only condensed financial statements.

OPEN THE SPREADSHEET TLA_CH23

The worksheet contains the income statement of a partnership. Prepare the income statement so it can be used by any level of manager.

LO5 Calculate and record a gain on realization.

LO6 Calculate and record a loss on realization.

LO7 Journalize entries to liquidate a partnership.

Terms Review

liquidation of a partnership

realization

Audit your understanding

1. How is a gain on realization recorded?
2. How is a loss on realization recorded?
3. Which accounts are debited when distributing remaining cash to partners during liquidation?

Work together 23-3

Liquidation of a partnership

Johanna and Stefan Salo agreed to liquidate their partnership on March 31 of the current year. On that date, after financial statements were prepared and closing entries were posted, the general ledger accounts had the balances shown in the *Working Papers*.

A cash receipts journal, a cash payments journal, and a general journal are provided in the *Working Papers*. Your instructor will guide you through the following examples.

Journalize the following transactions:

Transactions:

Apr. 1. Received cash from sale of office equipment, $12,000.00. R421.
1. Received cash from sale of supplies, $1,900.00. R422.
3. Received cash from sale of truck, $15,000.00. R423.
5. Paid cash to all creditors for amounts owed. C547.
6. Distributed balance of Gain on Realization to Johanna Salo, 60%; to Stefan Salo, 40%. M65.
6. Distributed balance of Loss on Realization to Johanna Salo, 60%; to Stefan Salo, 40%. M66.
6. Distributed remaining cash to partners. C548 and C549.

On your own 23-3

Liquidation of a partnership

Carlo Diaz and Olivia Thompson agreed to liquidate their partnership on June 30 of the current year. On that date, after financial statements were prepared and closing entries were posted, the general ledger accounts had the balances shown in the *Working Papers*.

A cash receipts journal, a cash payments journal, and a general journal are provided in the *Working Papers*. Work this problem independently.

Journalize the following transactions:

Transactions:

July 1. Received cash from sale of office equipment, $1,600.00. R348.
1. Received cash from sale of supplies. $3,100.00. R349.
3. Received cash from sale of truck, $10,800.00. R350.
5. Paid cash to all creditors for amounts owed. C265.
6. Distributed balance of Gain on Realization to Carlo Diaz, 60%; to Olivia Thompson, 40%. M33.
6. Distributed balance of Loss on Realization to Carlo Diaz, 60%; to Olivia Thompson, 40%. M34.
6. Distributed remaining cash to partners. C266 and C267.

A Look at Accounting Software
Setting Up a New Partnership

You were first introduced to the Company Setup window in Chapter 1, where a proprietorship was started. Setting up a partnership requires more information. In this chapter, you saw that Must-Have Gadgets was created on January 1, 20--, with two partners having equal shares in the business. The window at the right illustrates how that partnership might be set up in a computerized accounting system.

There are different types of partnership organization. Some of those types allow "limited" partners. That is, partners with limited liability. Must-Have Gadgets is a general partnership. Accounting software programs differ greatly in how partner information is entered, but the information illustrated here would be the minimum required.

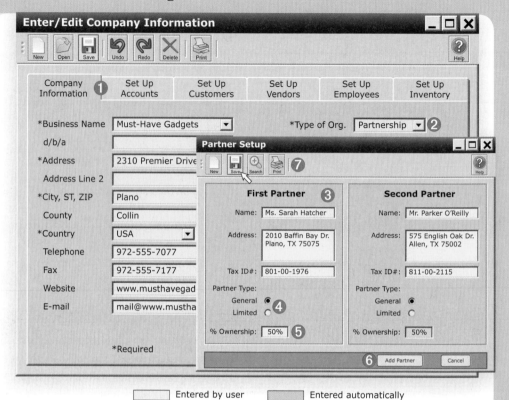

Entered by user □   Entered automatically ▨

① The Company Setup window is opened from the System Manager window. The Company Information tab opens by default. When this tab is completed, the user would open other tabs to set up the general ledger accounts, customer and vendor accounts, etc. Must-Have Gadgets has no employees, so there would be no need to open that tab.

② When the user selects Partnership from the drop-down list for the type of organization, the system knows that additional information is required, and a popup window opens to accept that information.

③ The minimum number of partners is two, so space is available to enter information for the two. The user would enter the names and addresses of both partners, along with their social security numbers (Tax ID#).

④ Must-Have Gadgets is a general partnership, so the user would click on the General button for both partners.

⑤ The percent ownership for each partner is entered. The system initially assumes that there are only two partners. As soon as the first percentage is entered, the system enters the balance of 100% for the other partner. The user can change the percentage if an entry error was made or if an additional partner is to be added. If these two percentages do not add up to 100%, the system will pop up a warning to the user to correct the entries or add another partner.

⑥ To add an additional partner, the user would click the Add Partner button. Clicking Cancel would close the window without saving, but the partnership cannot be set up in the system until this information is entered and saved.

⑦ The user clicks Save to exit the popup window. The popup will close and the user will continue entering information on the Company Information tab.

Chapter Summary

A partnership is one form of business ownership. It offers the advantage of sharing the work load, opportunity for more capital investment, and ease of formation. A written partnership agreement sets forth the conditions under which a partnership operates. Partners can invest cash or other assets in the partnership. A capital account is maintained for each partner. Investments by the partners are recorded in these capital accounts. Partners can also withdraw cash or merchandise from the partnership. Withdrawals by partners are recorded in temporary drawing accounts.

Partnership earnings are divided between the partners according to the terms of the partnership agreement. The ending capital balance for each partner reflects investments, share of earnings, and withdrawals. The balance sheet for a partnership is similar to that for a sole proprietorship except for the Equity section, which lists a capital account for each partner.

When a partnership is dissolved, several steps are required. First, noncash assets are sold, usually at either a gain or a loss. Then cash is used to pay any remaining liabilities. Finally, the remaining cash is distributed to the partners according to each partner's equity balance.

Is It Tax Avoidance or Tax Evasion?

EXPLORE ACCOUNTING

Once you start earning enough income, you will probably have to start paying some form of income tax to federal, state, and/or local governments. Some American taxpayers, both individuals and corporations, pay out a sizable percentage of their income for these taxes. However, we don't all pay out the same percent of our earnings in income tax. The United States has a graduated, or progressive, income tax system which increases the tax rate as income rises. However, due to provisions in the tax code, some individuals and corporations don't pay any income taxes at all.

Not paying taxes is not necessarily illegal. Using the provisions in the tax code to reduce one's taxes by legal means is known as *tax avoidance*, or more recently, *tax mitigation*. Not only can all tax-paying Americans apply tax laws to reduce the taxes they owe, but they are also encouraged to do so by the U.S. Legislature and courts of law. A judge who became famous for his decisions on tax avoidance versus tax evasion once said "… for nobody owes any public duty to pay more than the law demands: taxes are enforced exactions, not voluntary contributions." Some tax avoidance methods include contributing income to charitable organizations, delaying the receipt of income through the use of approved retirement accounts, and decreasing taxable income by the payment of mortgage interest.

In contrast, using illegal methods to reduce one's taxes is known as *tax evasion* and is punishable by a fine and/or a prison sentence. The news media often report on prominent individuals or companies that have been found guilty of some form of tax evasion. Some tax evasion practices include failure to report all income earned, overstating expenses so as to lower taxable income, and overstatement of charitable contributions.

The Internal Revenue Service has a name for the difference between the amount of tax legally owed and the amount actually collected. It is called the *tax gap*. A recent study estimated the tax gap to be $450 billion.

INSTRUCTIONS

1. Use the Internet to search for a recent case of tax evasion. Write a summary of your findings including the name of the person, the method used to evade tax, and the punishment given.

2. Interview five people, asking them to give their views on tax avoidance versus tax evasion. Summarize your findings in a short written report.

Sources: Helvering v. Gregory, 69 F.2d 809, 810 (2d Cir.1934), aff'd, 293 U.S. 465, 55 S.Ct. 266, 79 L.Ed. 596 (1935); http://www.irs.gov/newsroom/article/0,,id=252038,00.html

©MAKHNACH_M_iSTOCK

Apply Your Understanding

INSTRUCTIONS: Download problem instructions for Excel, QuickBooks, and Peachtree from the textbook companion website at www.C21accounting.com.

23-1 Application Problem: Journalizing partners' investments and withdrawals LO1, 2

Cash receipts, cash payments, and general journals are given in the *Working Papers*.

Instructions:

Journalize the following transactions completed during May of the current year:

Transactions:

May 1. Received cash of $4,000.00 and equipment valued at $66,000.00 from partner, Alka Wozniak, as an investment. Receipt No. 1.

  1. Received cash from partner, Florian Kaminski, as an initial investment, $60,000.00. Receipt No. 2.

  30. Florian Kaminski, partner, withdrew cash for personal use, $7,200.00. Check No. 42.

  30. Alka Wozniak, partner, withdrew supplies for personal use, $9,600.00. Memorandum No. 8.

23-2.1 Application Problem: Preparing distribution of net income and owners' equity statements (net income) LO3, 4

Agnes Carlsson and Viktor Lindberg are partners in Sharp Appliances, a merchandising business. Forms for completing this problem are given in the *Working Papers*. The following information was taken from the records on December 31 of the current year.

Partner	Balance of Capital Account January 1	Balance of Drawing Account	Distribution of Net Income/Loss
Carlsson	$79,500.00	$8,775.00	60.0%
Lindberg	$71,300.00	$9,400.00	40.0%

Instructions:

1. On December 31, the partnership had a net income of $41,630.00. Prepare a distribution of net income statement for the partnership.

2. Prepare an owners' equity statement for Sharp Appliances. No additional investments were made.

23-2.2 Application Problem: Preparing an owners' equity statement (net decrease in capital) LO4

Heather Graham and Travis Owens are partners in Evergreen Gardens, a merchandising business. Forms for completing this problem are given in the *Working Papers*. The following information was taken from the records on December 31 of the current year.

Partner	Balance of Capital Account January 1	Balance of Drawing Account	Distribution of Net Income/Loss
Graham	$62,150.00	$6,975.00	$1,875.00
Owens	$59,000.00	$7,450.00	$1,875.00

Instructions:

Prepare an owners' equity statement for Evergreen Gardens. Additional investments made during the year: Heather Graham, $6,000.00; Travis Owens, $5,000.00.

23-3 Application Problem: Liquidating a partnership LO5, 6, 7

Rebecca and Doris Dixon agreed to liquidate their partnership on March 31 of the current year. On that date, after financial statements were prepared and closing entries were posted, the general ledger accounts had the following balances.

Cash	$10,000.00
Supplies	1,000.00
Office Equipment	20,000.00
Accumulated Depreciation—Office Equipment	11,000.00
Truck	34,000.00
Accumulated Depreciation—Truck	24,400.00
Accounts Payable	1,000.00
Rebecca Dixon, Capital	14,600.00
Doris Dixon, Capital	14,000.00

Instructions:

Journalize the following transactions which occurred during April of the current year:

Transactions:

Apr. 1. Received cash from sale of office equipment, $8,000.00. R364.
1. Received cash from sale of supplies, $400.00. R365.
3. Received cash from sale of truck, $10,000.00. R366.
5. Paid cash to all creditors for amounts owed. C534.
6. Distributed balance of Gain on Realization to Rebecca Dixon, 65%; to Doris Dixon, 35%. M141.
6. Distributed balance of Loss on Realization to Rebecca Dixon, 65%; to Doris Dixon, 35%. M142.
6. Distributed remaining cash to partners. C535 and C536.

Peachtree

1. Journalize and post transactions related to liquidating a partnership to the general journal.
2. Journalize and post the distribution of remaining cash in the Write Checks window.
3. Print the general journal and trial balance.

QuickBooks

1. Journalize and post transactions related to liquidating a partnership to the journal.
2. Journalize and post the distribution of remaining cash in the Write Checks window.
3. Print the journal and trial balance.

Excel

1. Journalize transactions related to liquidating a partnership to the general journal.
2. Journalize and post the distribution of remaining cash to the cash payments journal.
3. Print the worksheets.

AAONLINE

1. Go to www.cengage.com/login
2. Click on **AA Online** to access.
3. Go to the online assignment and follow the instructions.

23-M Mastery Problem: Recording partners' investments and withdrawals, preparing financial statements, and liquidating a partnership LO1, 2, 3, 4, 5, 6, 7

Sean and Shannon Fleming are partners in a business called CarpetClean. Journals and forms for completing this problem are given in the *Working Papers*. CarpetClean completed the following transactions during the current year.

Transactions:

Jan. 15. Received cash as an investment from partner, Sean Fleming, $12,000.00. Receipt No. 110.

     15. Received cash of $3,000.00 and equipment valued at $10,000.00 from partner, Shannon Fleming, as an investment. Receipt No. 111.

Mar. 31. Shannon Fleming, partner, withdrew supplies for personal use, $2,000.00. Memorandum No. 81.

     31. Sean Fleming, partner, withdrew cash for personal use, $1,600.00. Check No. 212.

Instructions:

1. Journalize the investments on January 15.

2. Journalize the withdrawals on March 31.

Additional information is given below.

Sean Fleming, Capital, January 1 balance	$35,620.00
Shannon Fleming, Capital, January 1 balance	31,760.00
Net income for the year ended December 31	29,200.00

3. Prepare a distribution of net income statement for CarpetClean for the year ended December 31. Net income or loss is to be distributed equally to the partners.

4. Using the balances of the general ledger capital accounts, prepare an owners' equity statement for CarpetClean for the year ended December 31. The investments made on January 15 are the only additional investments made by the partners this year. The withdrawals made on March 31 are the only withdrawals made by the partners this year.

The Flemings decided to liquidate CarpetClean and retire on December 31. On that date, after financial statements were prepared and closing entries were posted, the general ledger accounts had the following balances:

Cash	$108,980.00
Merchandise Inventory	4,000.00
Equipment	30,000.00
Accumulated Depreciation—Equipment	20,000.00
Accounts Payable	5,000.00
Sean Fleming, Capital	60,620.00
Shannon Fleming, Capital	57,360.00

The following transactions occurred on December 31 of the current year:

Transactions:

a. Received cash from the sale of merchandise inventory, $3,600.00. R345.

b. Received cash from the sale of equipment, $14,000.00. R346.

c. Paid cash to all creditors for amounts owed. C575.

d. Distributed balance of Gain on Realization to the partners on an equal basis. M288.

e. Distributed balance of Loss on Realization to the partners on an equal basis. M289.

f. Distributed remaining cash to partners. C576 and C577.

5. Journalize the transactions. Continue on the next available line of the journals used in instructions 1 and 2.

Peachtree	**QuickBooks**	**X**	**AAONLINE**
1. Journalize and post transactions related to liquidating a partnership to the general journal.	1. Journalize and post transactions related to liquidating a partnership to the journal.	1. Journalize transactions related to liquidating a partnership to the general journal.	1. Go to www.cengage.com/login
			2. Click on **AA Online** to access.
2. Journalize and post the distribution of remaining cash in the Write Checks window.	2. Journalize and post the distribution of remaining cash in the Write Checks window.	2. Journalize and post the distribution of remaining cash to the cash payments journal.	3. Go to the online assignment and follow the instructions.
3. Print the general journal and trial balance.	3. Print the journal and trial balance.	3. Print the worksheets.	

23-C Challenge Problem: Preparing a distribution of net income statement and an owners' equity statement with unequal distribution of net loss and additional investment LO3, 4

Kalima Verma and Amar Tambe are partners in a merchandising business, Travel Trinkets. Forms for completing this problem are given in the *Working Papers*. The following information was taken from the records on December 31 of the current year.

Partner	Balance of Capital Account January 1	Balance of Drawing Account	Distribution of Net Income/Loss
Verma	$62,647.00	$9,000.00	65.0%
Tambe	$50,980.50	$8,150.00	35.0%

Instructions:

1. On December 31, the partnership had a net loss of $16,170.00. Prepare a distribution of net income statement for the partnership.

2. Prepare an owners' equity statement for Travel Trinkets. Additional investments made during the year: Kalima Verma, $5,500.00; Amar Tambe, $4,750.00.

21st Century Skills

Time Value of Money—The Power of Compounding

Theme: Financial, Economic, Business, and Entrepreneurial Literacy

Skills: Flexibility and Adaptability, Initiative and Self-Direction

PARTNERSHIP FOR
21ST CENTURY SKILLS

The value of a dollar today is not the same as the value of that dollar at some point in the future. If you were asked whether you would prefer to receive $100 today or $100 a year from now, you'd take it today. If you don't actually need the money today, you might agree to wait a year if you are offered $105. Why? Because money has a time value. The time value of money is expressed as a rate of interest.

There are many terms used in the discussion and calculation of the time value of money. You may be familiar with some of them: simple interest, compound interest, present value, and future value. Simple interest is easy to understand. If you save $100 at 6% annual interest, you will get $6 more for every year the money is on deposit. After two years, you'd get back $112. Compound interest is harder to grasp because it depends on the number of times during each year that interest is added. Suppose interest is added every three months (quarterly). The interest rate is divided by four, so after three months your $100 earns 1.5% and is worth $101.50. After six months, another 1.5% is added, not just to the original $100, but to the $101.50. Now, the value is $103.02. After nine months, it's worth $104.57; after one year, its value is $106.14, and at the end of the second year, its value is $112.65. So quarterly compounding increased your return by $0.65 over the simple interest amount.

Using the above example, the present value of $100 has a future value of $112.65 in two years. The future value is what it will be worth at some time in the future given a specific rate of interest, the amount of time, and the number of compounding periods in each year. In the example, the interest rate is 6%, the time is two years, and the number of compounding periods is four.

Most people take home more money than they need to live on. If you begin saving that extra money when you are young, the time value of money will work for you. Save as early as you can. The sooner you begin, the more time your money has to grow. If you saved that $100 at 6% interest for 40 years, and the interest compounded every month, you could withdraw $1,095.75, nearly 11 times what you saved.

APPLICATION

1. Calculate the future value of an investment with a present value of $10,000 compounded monthly for one year at 6% interest. *Hint:* An interest rate of 6% compounded monthly means 6% divided by 12 months. Calculate the future value of the same investment at 6% simple interest. Explain the impact of time when calculating future value.

2. Calculate the future value of an investment presently worth $10,000 compounded annually for 20 years with interest rates of 2%, 4%, 6%, and 8%. Create a line graph to illustrate the different interest rates. Explain the importance of the interest rate in growing wealth.

Auditing for errors

Dorothy Wizen and Jonathan Yates are partners in New Market Foods. The following information was taken from the records on December 31 of the current year.

Partner	Balance of Capital Account January 1	Balance of Drawing Account	Distribution of Net Income/Loss
Wizen	$30,000.00	$4,600.00	40.0%
Yates	$24,000.00	$2,200.00	60.0%

On December 31, the partnership had a net income of $29,000.00. No additional investments were made.

REVIEW AND ANSWER

The following statements were prepared using the information above. Audit the statements. Prepare a list that describes any errors you discover and how they should be corrected.

New Market Foods						
Distribution of Net Income Statement						
December 31, 20--						
Dorothy Wizen						
40% of Net Income	14	5	0	0	00	
Jonathan Yates						
60% of Net Income	14	5	0	0	00	
Net Income	29	0	0	0	00	

New Market Foods									
Owners' Equity Statement									
For Year Ended December 31, 20--									

Dorothy Wizen									
Capital, January 1, 20--				30 0 0 0 00					
Share of Net Income	14 5 0 0 00								
Less Withdrawals	4 6 0 0 00								
Net Increase in Capital				9 9 0 0 00					
Capital, December 31, 20--						39 9 0 0 00			
Jonathan Yates									
Capital, January 1, 20--				42 0 0 0 00					
Share of Net Income	14 5 0 0 00								
Less Withdrawals	2 2 0 0 00								
Net Increase in Capital				16 7 0 0 00					
Capital, December 31, 20--						58 7 0 0 00			
Total Owners' Equity, December 31, 20--						98 6 0 0 00			

Analyzing Nike's financial statements

Look at the Liabilities and Shareholders' Equity section of Nike's Consolidated Balance Sheets in Appendix B on page B-6.

INSTRUCTIONS

How would this section be different if Nike were a partnership owned by two partners instead of a corporation?

Chapter 24

Recording International and Internet Sales

LEARNING OBJECTIVES

After studying Chapter 24, in addition to defining key terms, you will be able to:

LO1 Explain the purpose of entering the export and import markets.

LO2 Describe issues that must be considered before making international sales.

LO3 Explain the documentation that must be produced to process international sales.

LO4 Account for international sales.

LO5 Account for time drafts.

LO6 Account for an Internet sale.

©DANIEL KOUREY, ISTOCK/©JIM PRUITT, ISTOCK

VALUELINE/JUPITER IMAGES

Accounting In The Real World
Under Armour

It started with a problem and a former athlete's determination to find an alternative to his sweat-soaked cotton shirt. Kevin Plank's solution was a shirt that wicked the sweat from the body to increase speed and comfort. Kevin named the company Under Armour.

After only 14 short years, the company surpassed the $1 billion revenue mark! The manufacturing has grown from Plank's grandmother's row house to 26 manufacturing facilities in 22 countries outside of the United States.

In spite of its explosive revenue earnings, Under Armour still considers itself in the "early stages" of growth. Future growth plans include a move to develop an international presence. Currently, international sales account for only 4% of revenues. In an effort to expand globally, Under Armour has enhanced its website and mobile commerce.

Under Armour seeks to drive consumer demand by building brand awareness as a leading athletic performance brand. This strategy is executed partly by outfitting sports teams for such colleges as Auburn University and The University of Maryland, Plank's alma mater. Under Armour also has an emerging presence in the National Football League.

By focusing on athletic teams and having its products worn by leaders in the industry, Under Armour intends to appeal to athletes and consumers with active lifestyles around the globe.

CRITICAL THINKING

Doing business internationally involves risk that may interfere with payment and/or transportation. To reduce this risk and focus on its products, Under Armour has entered into an agreement with a third party called FiftyOne to help sell products and engage with online customers around the world. The services provided by FiftyOne include no-risk payments, tailored websites, and customer returns.

1. Evaluate the risks in doing business internationally.

2. List the factors that must be considered when creating a website that will be used in other countries.

3. Why would companies like Under Armour pay a third-party company to manage their website, payments, and returns? Is there a risk associated with a third party? Explain why or why not.

Key Terms

- exports
- imports
- contract of sale
- letter of credit
- bill of lading
- commercial invoice
- draft
- sight draft
- time draft
- trade acceptance

24-1 Recording International Sales

LO1 Explain the purpose of entering the export and import markets.
LO2 Describe issues that must be considered before making international sales.
LO3 Explain the documentation that must be produced to process international sales.
LO4 Account for international sales.
LO5 Account for time drafts.

International Sales LO1

Sales in the international market have become a major source of revenue for both small and large businesses. The growth of information technology tools and trading relationships in the twenty-first century has made it easier and less expensive to transact business internationally. It is no longer necessary to talk to your vendor or customer via telephone. E-mail, the Internet, and mobile devices have made it possible to do business in an interconnected world without much concern about time zones and business hours around the world.

Goods or services shipped out of a seller's home country to another country are called **exports**. Goods or services shipped into the buyer's home country from another country are called **imports**.

A company that conducts business across national borders is an international company. The number of international companies continues to grow as businesses are able to import materials or services that are less expensive or not available within their own country. Many companies have entered the export and import markets not only to expand their sales and profits, but also to maintain global competitiveness and provide products and services to meet customer demand.

Must-Have Gadgets imports merchandise such as digital cameras and cell phones from a variety of countries. Must-Have Gadgets also exports electronic gadgets such as earphones and tablet covers to customers around the world. Merchandise sold to individuals or other businesses within one's own country is referred to as *domestic sales*.

ETHICS IN ACTION

He's Guilty!

A company that believes one of its employees is stealing may obtain the services of a Certified Fraud Examiner (CFE). The CFE is trained to examine accounting records and obtain other evidence related to the alleged theft. CFEs often serve as expert witnesses in court. The *Code of Professional Standards* of the Association of Certified Fraud Examiners provides its members with guidance on how to serve as an expert witness. The Code states that the CFE should obtain evidence that provides a reasonable basis for his or her opinion. However, the CFE should never express an opinion on the guilt or innocence of any person.

INSTRUCTIONS

Access the *Code of Professional Standards* of the Association of Certified Fraud Examiners. Citing the section, what other advice does the Code provide a CFE when serving as an expert witness?

International Sales Compared with Domestic Sales LO2

Most domestic sales are for cash or on account after the customer's credit has been reviewed and approved. Because all transactions in the United States are covered by the same universal commercial laws and the same accounting standards, many transactions are based on trust. A customer with approved credit orders merchandise, the merchandise is shipped, and an invoice is sent by the vendor. After receiving the merchandise and invoice, the customer pays the vendor.

However, because of the increased complexities of international sales, several issues must be considered. The lack of uniform commercial laws between countries makes settlement of disputes more difficult.

Greater distances and sometimes more complex transportation methods increase the time to complete the transaction. Because it may be difficult to determine a customer's financial condition and to take legal action if a customer does not pay, the risk of uncollected amounts is increased. Unstable political conditions in some countries may affect the ability to receive payments from customers in those countries. Therefore, most businesses dealing in exports and/or imports follow a general process in international trade to ensure that the vendor receives payment for merchandise sold and the customer receives the merchandise ordered.

Processing an International Sale LO3

A document that details all the terms agreed to by seller and buyer for a sales transaction is called a **contract of sale**. The contract includes a description and quantity of merchandise, price, point of delivery, packing and marking instructions, shipping information, insurance provisions, and method of payment. A detailed contract of sale makes sales straightforward and eliminates confusion.

Must-Have Gadgets, located in Plano, Texas, contracts to sell merchandise to Serrano Company in Sao Paulo, Brazil. The contract price is $6,000.00 in U.S. dollars, and merchandise is to be delivered to Sao Paulo. Serrano Company is to pay transportation charges.

A letter issued by a bank guaranteeing that a named individual or business will be paid a specified amount provided stated conditions are met is called a **letter of credit**. The contract of sale between Must-Have Gadgets and Serrano specified a letter of credit as the method of payment. A letter of credit is known worldwide as a risk management tool for international transactions.

Serrano prepared an application with its bank, Banco do Rio, to issue a letter of credit. Banco do Rio

approved Serrano's application and issued the letter of credit. Banco do Rio forwarded the letter of credit to Must-Have Gadgets' bank, First Bank in Plano.

First Bank delivered the letter of credit to Must-Have Gadgets. Must-Have Gadgets reviewed the letter of credit to ensure that the provisions in the letter agreed with the contract of sale. Must-Have Gadgets then shipped the merchandise.

LAARTIST/ISTOCKPHOTO.COM

The International Chamber of Commerce publishes "Incoterms" to attempt to coordinate international sales. This set of international rules interprets common sales terms used in foreign trade that are adopted by most international trade associations.

Collecting Payment for an International Sale

In order for Must-Have Gadgets to collect payment, three documents specified in the letter of credit must be submitted to First Bank: (1) a bill of lading, (2) a commercial invoice, and (3) a draft.

A receipt signed by the authorized agent of a transportation company for merchandise received that also serves as a contract for the delivery of the merchandise is called a **bill of lading**. The transportation company sends the bill of lading to Must-Have Gadgets when the merchandise is shipped. Must-Have Gadgets then prepares the other two documents. A statement prepared by the seller of merchandise addressed to the buyer showing a detailed listing and description of merchandise sold, including prices and terms, is called a **commercial invoice**. A written, signed, and dated order from one party ordering another party, usually a bank, to pay money to a third party is called a **draft**. A draft is sometimes referred to as a *bill of exchange*. A draft payable on sight when the holder presents it for payment is called a **sight draft**.

First Bank examines the documents submitted by Must-Have Gadgets to ensure that all terms of sale are in compliance with the letter of credit. First Bank then forwards the documents to Serrano's bank, Banco do Rio. Banco do Rio examines the documents to ensure they are in compliance with the terms and conditions of the letter of credit. When Banco do Rio determines that all documents are in compliance, it deducts the amount of the sight draft from Serrano's account and sends that amount, $6,000.00, to Must-Have-Gadgets' bank, First Bank in Plano.

Banco do Rio then forwards the documents to Serrano Company. By presenting the bill of lading and letter of credit to the transportation company, Serrano can receive the merchandise.

THINK LIKE AN ACCOUNTANT

Promoting Internet Sales

ArtCart is an Internet retail business that specializes in closeout art supplies. Similar to other Internet retail sites, selections are stored in an online shopping cart until the customer elects to check out.

To measure its success rate, ArtCart tracks the percentage of customers who complete their purchases. The company had been experiencing a success rate of approximately 82%. To encourage the remaining 18% of customers to complete their purchases, ArtCart introduced a discount program. Random customers are e-mailed a 10% discount offer one week after the items are entered in the shopping cart without being checked out. The 10% discount offer expires seven days later, thus encouraging immediate action by the customer.

Initial information seems to indicate that the discount program is working. Last December, over 70% of customers who received the discount offer checked out during the discount period. However, a new chief executive officer is questioning whether these sales would have been completed without the discount. She wonders whether the discount is simply changing when the customer checks out. If that is the case, the company is "giving away" 10% of its sales value on the discounted transactions.

OPEN THE SPREADSHEET TLA_CH24

The spreadsheet contains transaction information for January and February. Use the information to provide answers to the following questions:

1. After seven days, is there a significant difference between the success rates among customers who take the discount when checking out their shopping cart compared to those who aren't offered a discount?

2. What is the difference in the gross margin for discount sales versus nondiscount sales?

3. Apply the nondiscount success rate to the number of discount transactions. How many discount sales can be presumed to have been lost without the discount program?

4. Do you believe ArtCart's discount strategy is effective?

©DAN BACHMAN, ISTOCK

World Trade Organization

Decades ago, most U.S. businesses conducted their transactions within the boundaries of the United States. The majority of companies did not even consider going global for purchases or sales. U.S. laws governing patents, trade policies, and legal issues were in place to support a fair trade system. A company could expect its suppliers and customers to follow the laws.

Today, thousands of U.S. businesses either purchase or sell goods and services throughout the world. U.S. law does not apply to all international trade. There is a need for a set of international rules and guidelines to assist companies that wish to trade globally. The World Trade Organization (WTO) is attempting to negotiate these rules.

The WTO was formed in 1955 and is headquartered in Geneva, Switzerland. It is the only organization that focuses on rules for international trading. Currently, the WTO has 153 member countries and 30 "observer" governments, most of which are seeking membership. According to its website, the main function of the WTO "is to ensure that trade flows as smoothly, predictably and freely as possible."

The WTO has negotiated a variety of agreements with its member nations. It has a policy of one country, one vote. However, the consensus method is used and an actual vote has never taken place. Instead, member countries listen to opponents of an agreement and try to find ways to make the agreement acceptable to every member.

In addition to negotiating trade agreements, the WTO also implements and monitors agreements already in place. If a member country believes another country is not following the terms of an agreement, the WTO has a procedure for settling the dispute.

The WTO lists six principles that are fundamental to all WTO agreements: (1) non-discrimination, (2) more open trade, (3) predictable and transparent, (4) more competition, (5) benefits to less developed countries, and (6) protection of the environment.

The WTO publishes a variety of resources, many of which are available online. In addition to the legal texts of WTO agreements, the resources include economic research and analysis findings, the annual WTO report, international trade statistics, and the world trade report.

CRITICAL THINKING

1. Use the Internet to find three countries that fall into the following categories:
   a. Members of the WTO
   b. "Observers" of the WTO
   c. Neither members nor observers of the WTO
2. Find the top decision-making body on the WTO. In a few sentences, report the name of the body, when it meets, who attends, and what it does.

©FONTMONSTER, ISTOCK

Journalizing an International Sale LO4

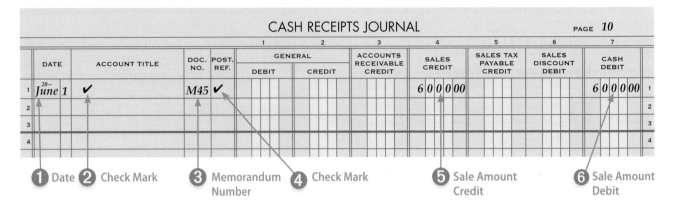

					GENERAL		ACCOUNTS RECEIVABLE CREDIT	SALES CREDIT	SALES TAX PAYABLE CREDIT	SALES DISCOUNT DEBIT	CASH DEBIT	
	DATE	ACCOUNT TITLE	DOC. NO.	POST. REF.	DEBIT	CREDIT						
1	20-- June 1	✔	M45	✔				6 0 0 0 00			6 0 0 0 00	1
2												2
3												3
4												4

CASH RECEIPTS JOURNAL   PAGE **10**

1 Date   **2** Check Mark   **3** Memorandum Number   **4** Check Mark   **5** Sale Amount Credit   **6** Sale Amount Debit

After receiving payment from Banco do Rio, First Bank deposits the payment for the sale in Must-Have Gadgets' account and sends Must-Have Gadgets a deposit slip for the amount deposited. After receiving the deposit slip from First Bank, Must-Have Gadgets prepares a memorandum as a source document for the cash received. The sale is then recorded as a cash sale.

Sales taxes are normally paid only on sales to the final consumer also referred to as the end user. Must-Have Gadgets' sale is to Serrano Company, a merchandising company. Therefore, sales tax is not collected.

The sales and collection process assured Must-Have Gadgets of receiving payment for its sale and Serrano Company of receiving the merchandise it ordered.

> **Recording an Entry for an International Sale**
>
> **1** Write the date, 20--, June 1, in the Date column.
>
> **2** Place a check mark in the Account Title column to indicate that no account title needs to be entered.
>
> **3** Write the source document number, M45, in the Doc. No. column.
>
> **4** Place a check mark in the Post. Ref. column to indicate that the amounts on this line are not posted individually.
>
> **5** Write the sale amount, $6,000.00, in the Sales Credit column.
>
> **6** Write the sale amount, $6,000.00, in the Cash Debit column.

June 1. Recorded international cash sale, $6,000.00. Memorandum 45.

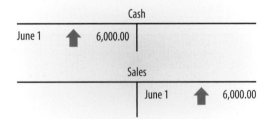

Cash		
June 1 ⬆ 6,000.00		

Sales		
	June 1 ⬆ 6,000.00	

Visitors to foreign countries with a value added tax (VAT) typically are required to pay the VAT. However, if items purchased exceed a specified amount, a refund of a portion of the VAT can be requested.

Journalizing Time Drafts LO5

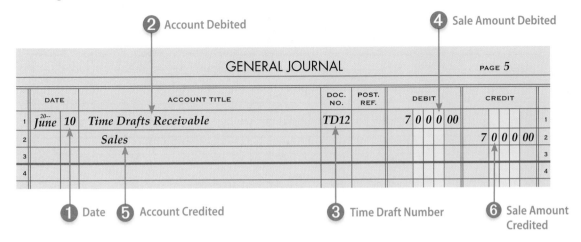

① Date   ⑤ Account Credited   ③ Time Draft Number   ⑥ Sale Amount Credited

Must-Have Gadgets sold $7,000.00 of merchandise to Ramirez Co., located in Guadalajara, Mexico. The contract of sale with Ramirez was similar to the contract with Serrano Company, with one exception. Must-Have Gadgets agreed to delay receipt of payment 60 days. A draft that is payable at a fixed or determinable future time after it is accepted is called a **time draft**.

The sales process with Ramirez is the same as with Serrano, except Must-Have Gadgets submits with the documentation a time draft due 60 days from the date the draft is accepted. On June 10, all documentation for the Ramirez sale is verified to be correct by the seller's and buyer's banks, and Must-Have Gadgets' time draft is accepted.

After verifying the documentation, Ramirez's bank, Banco Mexico, returns the accepted time draft to Must-Have Gadgets and forwards the other documents to Ramirez Co. Ramirez can receive the merchandise by presenting the bill of lading and letter of credit to the transportation company.

> June 10. Received a 60-day time draft from Ramirez Co. for an international sale, $7,000.00. Time Draft No. 12.

The minimum value added tax in the European Community is 15%; however, there is no additional local sales tax. The Philippines imposes a 12% VAT that applies to the sale, barter, or exchange of goods, properties, or services. Thailand applies a 7% VAT to selected beverages.

Journalizing a Time Draft

① Write the date, 20--, June 10, in the Date column.

② Write Time Drafts Receivable in the Account Title column.

③ Write the time draft number, TD12, in the Doc. No. column.

④ Write the sale amount, $7,000.00, in the Debit column.

⑤ On the next line, indent and write Sales in the Account Title column.

⑥ Write the sale amount, $7,000.00, in the Credit column.

Journalizing Cash Receipts from Time Drafts

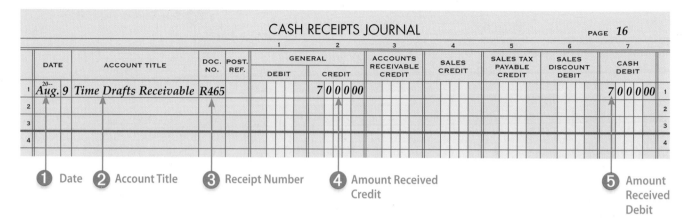

When Ramirez's time draft is due and presented to its bank, Banco Mexico, the bank pays the draft. The payment process is the same as the payment of Serrano Company's sight draft.

> **August 9. Received cash for the value of Time Draft No. 12, $7,000.00. Receipt No. 465.**

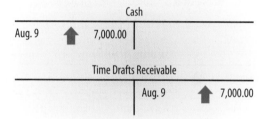

The process used by Must-Have Gadgets for international sales relies upon letters of credit from banks to assure receipt of payment for those sales. Occasionally, Must-Have Gadgets grants an extension of time for payment to long-time international customers by submitting a time draft.

TRADE ACCEPTANCES

A form signed by a buyer at the time of a sale of merchandise in which the buyer promises to pay the seller a specified sum of money, usually at a stated time in the future, is called a **trade acceptance**.

A trade acceptance is similar to a draft except a draft is generally paid by a bank and a trade acceptance is paid by the buyer. A seller generally has much more assurance of receiving payment from a bank than from a buyer. Because of the many complexities, few businesses use trade acceptances in international sales. Some businesses, however, use trade acceptances for domestic sales to very reliable customers.

Journalizing Cash Received from a Time Draft

1. Write the date, 20--, Aug. 9, in the Date column.
2. Write Time Drafts Receivable in the Account Title column.
3. Write the source document number, R465, in the Doc. No. column.
4. Write the amount received, $7,000.00, in the General Credit column.
5. Write the same amount, $7,000.00, in the Cash Debit column.

remember

A sight draft and a time draft are similar. Both methods of international sales require the buyer's bank to guarantee the cash payment for the sale. The primary difference between a sight draft and a time draft is the timing of the payment. Cash payment of a time draft is delayed for a period of time after the delivery of the goods to the buyer.

Benford's Law

In 1925, Frank Benford, a scientist for General Electric, observed that the front pages of his logarithm book were worn from use more than the back pages. Prior to the age of computers, handheld calculators, and smartphones, scientists used a logarithm book to assist them in multiplying and dividing numbers. Being a good scientist, Benford questioned why he was using the front more than the back part of the book. The front part contained the logarithmic values for numbers beginning with 1 and continued through numbers beginning with 9 at the back of the book.

Benford began to test natural data sets and discovered a consistent number pattern. The frequency of the first digit of a number being a 1 was 30.1%, as shown in the following table. The size of the number is not important. Whether the number is 1.23, 123, or 123,000, each number begins with the number 1.

First Digit	Frequency of First Digit
1	30.1%
2	17.6%
3	12.5%
4	9.7%
5	7.9%
6	6.7%
7	5.8%
8	5.1%
9	4.6%

Named in honor of Frank Benford, Benford's Law only applies to natural data sets that have no artificial biases. For example, the ACT score that is between 1 and 36 is not a natural data set; nor are invoice numbers, weekly hours worked, or codes. Examples of natural data sets would include:

- Sales at a retail store
- Checking account balances at a bank
- Client investment accounts managed by a financial advisor
- Total assets of the S&P 500 companies

Auditors have discovered that they can apply Benford's Law to forensic accounting. Any significant difference between the expected frequency (Benford's Law) and the actual frequency of numbers indicates that some sort of bias exists. Whether the bias is a natural for the business or a result of a fraud requires additional investigation. For example, a grocery store may naturally have a higher proportion of transactions beginning with a 1 or 2; few customers purchase $300.00 or more of groceries at one time. In contrast, a dollar limit that requires management approval of a transaction may result in a fraudster entering a large number of transactions just under that limit.

ACTIVITY

Any time that BoardTown Stores is open, one employee is assigned the responsibility of maintaining the appearance of shelves. This employee returns misplaced merchandise to its proper location and neatly arranges items at the front of the shelves. Any damaged merchandise is removed from the shelves. After the items are scanned into a point-of-sale terminal located in a receiving area, they are packaged to be sold to a salvage business. The system removes the items from BoardTown's perpetual inventory.

Kelly Alford, the store manager, recently learned of Benford's Law and has asked you to analyze the transactions to remove damaged merchandise.

INSTRUCTIONS

Open the spreadsheet FA_CH24 and complete the steps on the Instructions tab.

Source: http://en.wikipedia.org.

End of Lesson Review

Terms Review

exports

imports

contract of sale

letter of credit

bill of lading

commercial invoice

draft

sight draft

time draft

trade acceptance

Audit your understanding

1. What are four of the issues that must be considered before making international sales?

2. What two purposes does a bill of lading serve?

3. How does a sight draft differ from a time draft?

4. Why do many companies dealing in international sales rely upon letters of credit from banks?

5. How does a trade acceptance differ from a draft?

Work together 24-1

Journalizing international sales transactions

The cash receipts and general journals for Nicola Maria Exports, Inc., are given in the *Working Papers*. Your instructor will guide you through the following examples.

1. Using the current year, journalize the following international sales on page 10 of a cash receipts journal and page 5 of a general journal. Sales tax is not charged on these sales. Source documents are abbreviated as follows: memorandum, M; time draft, TD; receipt, R.

Transactions:

July 11. Recorded an international cash sale, $12,000.00. M324.

16. Received a 30-day time draft from Sun Chan for an international sale, $16,000.00. TD31.

23. Received cash for the value of Time Draft No. 10, $22,000.00. R221.

2. Prove and rule the cash receipts journal.

On your own 24-1

Journalizing international sales transactions

The cash receipts and general journals for Courtney's Stone Collections are given in the *Working Papers*. Work this problem independently.

1. Using the current year, journalize the following international sales on page 17 of a cash receipts journal and page 8 of a general journal. Sales tax is not charged on these sales. Source documents are abbreviated as follows: memorandum, M; time draft, TD; receipt, R.

Transactions:

Oct. 8. Recorded an international cash sale, $8,400.00. M256.

17. Received a 45-day time draft from Ashley Patel for an international sale, $6,300.00. TD81.

30. Received cash for the value of Time Draft No. 73, $10,500.00. R205.

2. Prove and rule the cash receipts journal.

24-2 Recording Internet Sales

LO6 Account for an Internet sale.

Internet Sales

More companies are turning to the Internet, also referred to as *electronic commerce* or *e-commerce*, as an additional way of selling goods and services in order to compete globally. An explosive increase in Internet sales is likely due to a boost in global access to the Internet, buyer comfort and confidence in shopping online, and product availability and variety. Internet shopping provides customers the opportunity to browse the products offered by a company, compare competitors' products, and do so at a time and place convenient to the customer.

Selling goods over the Internet, however, also presents some challenges to the seller. The website developed must be easy to navigate and safe to use. Customers must feel that the website uses up-to-date security procedures to protect credit card information as it is being transmitted. The selling company must also be able to accept credit card sales, which means it must contract with a bank to offer this service or with a company that will offer this service to businesses for a fee.

Must-Have Gadgets has prepared a website that will accept credit card orders and transmit the sales information for immediate shipping and billing. An order confirmation is also immediately sent to the buyer, containing information about the order and expected shipping date.

Internet sales at Must-Have Gadgets must be completed with a credit card. At the end of each day, Must-Have Gadgets will be able to print out a terminal summary similar to the terminal summary discussed in Chapter 10. The terminal summary is used as the source document for recording online sales.

Wildlife Management

Agriculture, Food & Natural Resources

In many cities in the United States, the same thing happens each Friday afternoon. City dwellers pack up and vacate the city, choosing instead a quiet country experience. It might take place on a hiking trail, near a lake, or in the forest. If luck is with them, they may even spot some wildlife such as a deer.

Not everyone is excited about the increasing population of wildlife. Each year, deer alone cause millions of dollars of damage to U.S. agricultural crops. This causes a conflict between hunters, environmentalists, conservationists who want increased wildlife, and agricultural producers whose livelihood is threatened by wild animals.

Most states have a department or agency that is in charge of wildlife management. In order to help reach a balance, many states have a program through which producers receive payment for crop and animal losses due to wild animals. However, sometimes the cost of administrating such programs is higher than the amount actually paid out in losses. Administration costs are highest when losses are actually verified by wildlife officials. Without official verification, there is a risk that producers will claim more loss than actually occurred.

CRITICAL THINKING

1. Assume you work in wildlife management. Develop a list of three things you could do to keep administration costs down, but at the same time, have some assurance that the loss claims you receive accurately reflect the loss that occurred.

2. Use the Internet to research crop and animal loss due to wild animals throughout the world. List three wild animals that cause this loss.

Journalizing an Internet Sale LO6

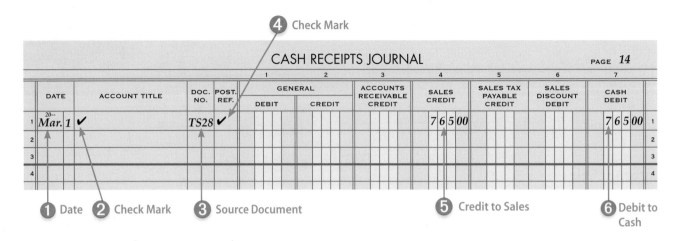

④ Check Mark

CASH RECEIPTS JOURNAL   PAGE 14

					1	2	3	4	5	6	7	
DATE	ACCOUNT TITLE	DOC. NO.	POST. REF.	GENERAL DEBIT	GENERAL CREDIT	ACCOUNTS RECEIVABLE CREDIT	SALES CREDIT	SALES TAX PAYABLE CREDIT	SALES DISCOUNT DEBIT	CASH DEBIT	
¹ Mar. 1 ✔ 20--		TS28	✔				7 6 5 00			7 6 5 00	1
2											2
3											3
4											4

① Date ② Check Mark ③ Source Document ⑤ Credit to Sales ⑥ Debit to Cash

---

March 1. Recorded Internet credit card sales, $765.00. Terminal Summary 28.

Must-Have Gadgets processes its credit card sales at the end of each day. At the same time, the information is electronically transmitted to First Bank, with whom Must-Have Gadgets has contracted to process its credit card sales. This information is transferred to the Federal Reserve Bank and processed in a manner similar to checks. Therefore, Must-Have Gadgets considers these sales to be cash sales.

The asset account **Cash** has a normal debit balance and is debited for the amount of the credit card sales, $765.00. The **Sales** account has a normal credit balance. Therefore, **Sales** is credited for the amount of the sales, $765.00.

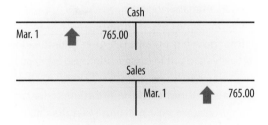

↘ Recording an Entry for an Internet Sale

① Write the date, **20--, Mar. 1**, in the Date column.

② Place a check mark in the Account Title column to indicate that no account title needs to be entered.

③ Write the source document number, **TS28**, in the Doc. No. column.

④ Place a check mark in the Post. Ref. column to indicate that the amounts on this line are not posted individually.

⑤ Write the sale amount, **$765.00**, in the Sales Credit column.

⑥ Write the sale amount, **$765.00**, in the Cash Debit column.

In order to process bank credit cards such as Visa and MasterCard, a business must set up a merchant account with a bank. The business pays a fee to the bank for processing credit card sales.

LO6 Account for an Internet sale.

▶ Audit your understanding

1. What are two reasons why a customer might prefer online shopping?
2. Why is a bank credit card sale treated the same as a cash sale?

▶ Work together 24-2

Journalizing Internet sales transactions

The cash receipts journal for Julia's Organic Bakery is given in the *Working Papers*. Your instructor will guide you through the following examples.

Using the current year, journalize the following Internet sales on page 3 of a cash receipts journal.

Transactions:

Aug. 21. Recorded Internet credit card sales, $1,432.00. Terminal Summary 230.

27. Recorded Internet credit card sales, $2,010.00. Terminal Summary 231.

28. Recorded Internet credit card sales, $1,270.00. Terminal Summary 232.

▶ On your own 24-2

Journalizing Internet sales transactions

The cash receipts journal for Rhonda's Gourmet Gifts is given in the *Working Papers*. Work this problem independently.

Using the current year, journalize the following Internet sales on page 11 of a cash receipts journal.

Transactions:

Feb. 7. Recorded Internet credit card sales, $125.00. Terminal Summary 44.

14. Recorded Internet credit card sales, $289.00. Terminal Summary 45.

28. Recorded Internet credit card sales, $338.00. Terminal Summary 46.

A Look at Accounting Software
Setting Up a New Customer

Merchandising businesses, whether wholesale or retail, have customers. Retail businesses don't typically keep subsidiary ledger accounts for all their customers because there are far too many of them and the sales volume to each customer is small. Merchandise businesses that sell wholesale typically do maintain accounts for each customer because those customers tend to make frequent purchases and

their purchases are large enough to track. As with vendors, there are different types, or classes, of customers. Classes of customers might be based on sales contracts, government regulations, taxes, location, credit terms, product mix, etc. Accounting software systems allow businesses to set up different customer classes to enable recording and reporting accounting information accordingly.

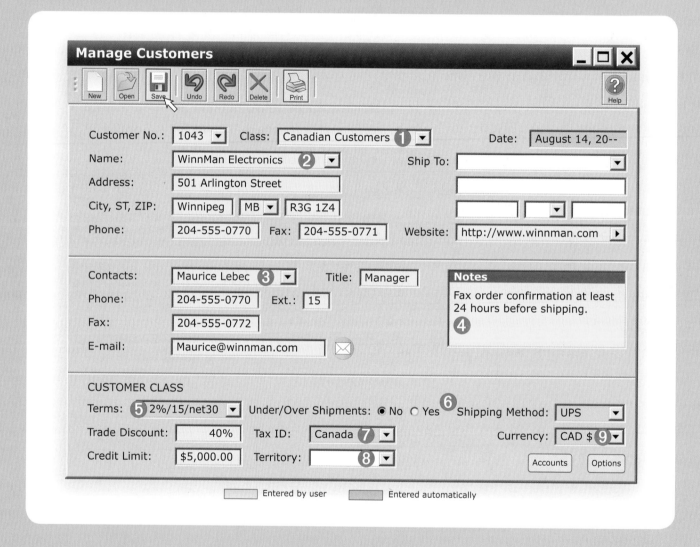

1. To set up a new customer, the user first assigns a customer number. If the business tracks customer sales by class, the user would click on the drop-down list and select the appropriate class for that customer.

2. Next, the user would enter the address, phone number, and web address of the customer. Some customers have multiple addresses—perhaps different branches or stores. The Ship To fields allow the business to track sales to each address while maintaining a total accounting of sales to the central account.

3. In business-to-business dealings, different types of contacts are involved. One person may be responsible for negotiating contracts, while another is responsible for placing orders. Another person may resolve problems with orders. Contact information, then, is very important to users of the accounting system.

4. The Notes field allows the user to record personal or business information about the contact and the business relationship.

5. When the different customer classes were set up, default settings for each class were entered. So, when the Canadian Customers class was selected, those fields with default settings were populated by the system. Alternate settings may be selected by the user as appropriate.

6. Sometimes the inventory of an item may not be sufficient to fill a customer's order. Or, prepackaged bundles of the item may contain quantities that don't match the order. For example, an item might be packaged with 24 items and the customer ordered 20. Many sales agreements allow the business to undership or overship quantities within certain limits. Some customers will not accept quantities other than what they ordered. When that is the case, the system will not allow an order to be filled with a lesser or greater quantity than the order.

7. There are many different tax codes to account for when selling to customers around the United States or around the world. Accounting systems allow businesses to set up different accounts to manage payment of those taxes. Setting a tax profile for each class simplifies this accounting. Canada, for example, has a general services tax which must be paid by the seller.

8. Large companies often manage their sales by geographic territories. Each territory generally has a sales manager and, perhaps, sales representatives. It is necessary in those situations to properly account for sales by territory.

9. For U.S. companies, international business can most often be conducted in U.S. dollars. However, it is sometimes necessary to conduct business in a foreign currency. Selling prices would then be quoted, and invoice payments would be received, in that currency. Currency conversions would generally be handled by the company's bank. However, accountants must enter currency exchange adjustments into the business's accounts.

Chapter Summary

Many companies have entered the export and import market to compete globally and to provide the products and services to meet customer demand.

International sales are more complex than domestic sales. The lack of universal commercial laws in other countries makes it challenging to settle disputes that could arise and affect payment. To process international sales, documentation such as a contract of sale, letter of credit, bill of lading, commercial invoice, and a sight or time draft must be produced for shipment and payment to occur.

Once business relationships have been established and trust is gained, a trade acceptance may be presented instead of a draft. A trade acceptance is an agreement from the buyer to pay directly in the future, unlike a draft for which payment is received from the buyer's bank.

Internet sales (or e-commerce) have exploded due to advances in technology and customers' growing comfort in buying online. Customers are enjoying the luxury of the shopping conveniences afforded by the Internet.

Internet sales are typically completed with a credit card. At the end of each day, the seller prints a terminal summary as a source document for recording online sales.

EXPLORE ACCOUNTING

A Sales Tax Dilemma

With Internet sales reaching over $165 billion and growing almost 15% annually, the issues of whether and how states should tax Internet sales are hot legislative topics.

Currently, sales tax is collected by the seller and paid to the state only on goods sold within the seller's state. Sellers do not collect sales tax on goods shipped outside the state, but buyers are technically required to pay a use tax to the state in which the good is used, consumed, or stored. Since the use tax is difficult to enforce, many states now want to make the sellers collect sales tax on goods purchased out of state on the Internet.

Many state lawmakers feel that online retailers who do not collect sales tax as "brick-and-mortar" retailers do are not doing their share. They argue that states are missing out on critical tax dollars.

Retailers are worried about competition from online sellers since Internet retailers can offer lower costs without collecting sales tax. Retailers say that imposing sales tax with e-commerce will remove the unfair advantage of Internet retailers and level the sales tax playing field.

Internet companies argue that they have to pay shipping. Additionally, they claim they do not use governmental services the way in-state retailers do, such as police/fire protection, and should not be required to charge and collect the sales tax.

A 1992 Supreme Court ruling says businesses must have a physical presence inside a state for the business to be required to collect sales tax. Many think since this decision originated with mail order sales that the definition of physical presence should be updated and broadened to include "a presence in the state" in an effort to address sales tax inequities.

State lawmakers are working hard to make an Internet sales tax a reality. Others are hopeful that Congress will finally step in and establish a federal law.

INSTRUCTIONS

1. Accountants must stay current on tax laws. Search the Internet to see what the current state law is pertaining to an Internet sales tax for your state.

2. Some think that having a "presence in the state" rather than a physical presence should be the requirement to collect sales tax. List three ways that one could have a "presence" and not necessarily a physical presence.

3. Compose a letter taking on the view of the consumer, brick-and-mortar retailer, state lawmaker, or Internet retailer stating your opinion about how Internet sales should or should not be taxed. Be sure to include at least three reasons why you support your decision.

Source: www.forbes.com.

©MAKHNACH_M, ISTOCK

Apply Your Understanding

INSTRUCTIONS: Download problem instructions for Excel, QuickBooks, and Peachtree from the textbook companion website at www.C21accounting.com.

24-1 Application Problem: Journalizing international sales transactions LO 4, 5

The cash receipts and general journals for Jan Hakeem Exports, Ltd. are given in the *Working Papers*.

Instructions:

1. Journalize the following international sales completed by Jan Hakeem Exports, Ltd. during June of the current year. Use page 12 of a cash receipts journal and page 5 of a general journal. Sales tax is not charged on these sales. Source documents are abbreviated as follows: memorandum, M; time draft, TD; receipt, R.

Transactions:

June 1. Recorded an international cash sale, $14,000.00. M79.
       5. Received a 30-day time draft from Bella Lamas for an international sale, $12,000.00. TD27.
       9. Received cash for the value of Time Draft No. 24, $18,000.00. R115.
     12. Received a 60-day time draft from Elias Harmon for an international sale, $7,000.00. TD33.
     19. Received cash for the value of Time Draft No. 21, $22,000.00. R117.
     21. Recorded an international cash sale, $13,500.00. M83.
     25. Received a 30-day time draft from Juan Mendez for an international sale, $26,500.00. TD34.

2. Prove and rule the cash receipts journal.

Peachtree

1. Journalize and post transactions related to international sales transactions to the general journal.
2. Journalize and post transactions related to cash receipts from international sales transactions.
3. Print the cash receipts journal, general journal, and trial balance.

 QuickBooks

1. Journalize and post transactions related to international sales transactions to the journal.
2. Journalize and post transactions related to cash receipts in the Receive Payments window.
3. Print the customer balance detail, journal, and trial balance.

Excel

1. Journalize and post transactions related to international sales transactions to the general journal.
2. Journalize and post transactions related to cash receipts from international sales transactions.
3. Print the cash receipts journal and general journal.

24-2 Application Problem: Journalizing Internet sales transactions LO 6

The cash receipts journal for Jeff's Sports Memorabilia is given in the *Working Papers*.

Instructions:

1. Journalize the following Internet sales completed by Jeff's Sports Memorabilia during August of the current year. Use page 15 of a cash receipts journal. Source documents are abbreviated as follows: terminal summary, TS.

Transactions:

Mar. 5. Recorded Internet credit card sales, $799.00. TS113.
     13. Recorded Internet credit card sales, $1,287.00. TS114.
     20. Recorded Internet credit card sales, $1,109.00. TS115.
     27. Recorded Internet credit card sales, $2,945.00. TS116.

2. Total and rule the cash receipts journal.

Dexter Corporation has both international and Internet sales.

Instructions:

1. Journalize the following transactions affecting sales and cash receipts completed during February of the current year. Use page 3 of both a general journal and a cash receipts journal. Source documents are abbreviated as follows: memorandum, M; receipt, R; time draft, TD; terminal summary, TS.

Transactions:

May 5. Received a 30-day time draft from Cooper Doi for an international sale, $3,000.00. TD10.
8. Recorded Internet credit card sales, $14,500.00. TS23.
12. Recorded an international cash sale, $8,800.00. M8.
14. Received cash for the value of Time Draft No. 4, $22,000.00. R35.
18. Recorded Internet credit card sales, $18,300.00. TS24.
21. Received cash for the value of Time Draft No. 7, $6,000.00. R37.
24. Recorded an international cash sale, $12,400.00. M12.
27. Recorded Internet credit card sales, $7,100.00. TS25.
28. Received a 30-day time draft from Strizi Percheki for international sale of merchandise, $5,000.00. TD11.

2. Prove and rule the cash receipts journal.

Peachtree

1. Journalize and post transactions related to international sales transactions to the general journal.
2. Journalize and post transactions related to cash receipts from international sales transactions.
3. Print the cash receipts journal, general journal, and trial balance.

QuickBooks

1. Journalize and post transactions related to international sales transactions to the journal.
2. Journalize and post transactions related to cash receipts in the Receive Payments window.
3. Print the customer balance detail, journal, and trial balance.

X

1. Journalize and post transactions related to international sales transactions to the general journal.
2. Journalize and post transactions related to cash receipts from international sales transactions.
3. Print the cash receipts journal and general journal.

AAONLINE

1. Go to www.cengage.com/login
2. Click on **AA Online** to access.
3. Go to the online assignment and follow the instructions.

International sales can be stated in terms of U.S. dollars or in the foreign currency. The transaction statements below are stated in terms of the foreign currency of the customer.

Instructions:

1. Journalize the following transactions affecting sales. Use the foreign currency exchange rates given in the table below to translate the amount of the sales into U.S. dollars. Use page 11 of a cash receipts journal. Source documents are abbreviated as follows: memorandum, M. (*Hint:* Review the Global Awareness feature in Chapter 6.)

Transactions:

June 1. Recorded international cash sale, 6,207 Chinese yuan. M48.
8. Recorded international cash sale, 28,731 Mexican pesos. M53.
14. Recorded international cash sale, 4,631 New Zealand dollars. M59.
19. Recorded international cash sale, 453 European euros. M60.
28. Recorded international cash sale, 2,174,060 Indian rupees. M72.

Currency	1 U.S. Dollar Equals…
Chinese yuan	6.3883 yuan
European euro	0.73126 euro
Mexican peso	13.11144 pesos
New Zealand dollar	1.21711 New Zealand dollars
Indian rupee	47.79671 rupees

2. Prove and rule the cash receipts journal.

Crack Down on Identity Theft

Theme: Financial, Economic, Business, and Entrepreneurial Literacy

Skills: Critical Thinking and Problem Solving, Creativity and Innovation, ICT Literacy

PARTNERSHIP FOR
21ST CENTURY SKILLS

Millions have discovered the convenience of shopping on the Internet. Unfortunately, many have not considered the risk of releasing personal information to different websites. What would happen if someone stole personal or credit card information and charged thousands of dollars in someone else's name? This is a form of identity theft and is considered a crime.

Credit card fraud is the most common type of identity theft and is one of the fastest growing crimes in the United States. As many as 9 million Americans have their identities stolen each year. Unfortunately, the victims may be denied loans or job opportunities due to false information on their credit reports.

One way to protect against identity theft is to create strong passwords. A strong password consists of uncommon names and number combinations. Also, be cautious about e-mail scams and suspicious e-mails. Make sure the online business has a secure website and uses a security measure that scrambles your data as it passes through the Internet. This is called **encryption**; a closed padlock image will often appear on a website that uses encryption, or a pop-up window will indicate added security features. In addition, confirm the validity of the online business before conducting business and preferably look for a third-party endorsement such as the Better Business Bureau.

APPLICATION

1. List at least three other types of identity theft besides credit card fraud.
2. Compose a list of five ways in which consumers put themselves at risk for identity theft. For each of these risks, post reminders on a poster, produce a public service announcement, or create a "tweet of the day" on Twitter.

Analyzing Nike's financial statements

A majority of Nike's products are sold outside of the United States. As a result, transactions are conducted in multiple currencies. This exposes Nike to the effects of changes in foreign currency exchange rates, which could have a negative impact on its financial condition.

INSTRUCTIONS

Read the section of Note 1 entitled Foreign Currency Translation and Foreign Currency Transactions on page B-11 of Appendix B. In which financial statement do you find adjustments resulting from translating foreign functional currency financial statements into U.S. dollars?

Accounting Concepts

Since 1973, the Financial Accounting Standards Board (FASB) has assumed responsibility for setting financial accounting standards known as *Generally Accepted Accounting Principles* (GAAP). One of the first tasks of the FASB was to establish a framework that describes the concepts underlying GAAP. That framework continues to guide the FASB's development of new standards.

In the United States, GAAP serves as a guide for reporting and interpreting accounting information. The accounting principles described in this textbook are based on the application of the concepts underlying GAAP. These concepts are described below and referenced throughout the textbook.

In 1973, the international financial community formed an organization with the ambitious goal of creating a universal set of accounting standards. Similar to the FASB, the International Accounting Standards Board (IASB) uses a framework to develop its standards, known as *International Financial Reporting Standards* (IFRS, pronounced ī'-fers).

The FASB and IASB are committed to merging GAAP and IFRS to achieve one universal set of accounting standards. At the time this textbook was written, the FASB and IASB were working to establish a common framework. That framework will provide the foundation for development of accounting standards to be used around the world.

ACCOUNTING PERIOD CYCLE

Changes in financial information are reported for a specific period of time in the form of financial statements.

Financial statements summarize the financial information that a business records. The time period for which financial statements are prepared depends on the needs of the business. An accounting period may be one month, three months, six months, or one year. An accounting period of one year is a fiscal year. Publicly held corporations must prepare fiscal year financial statements. For tax purposes, every business prepares financial statements at the end of each year.

BUSINESS ENTITY

Financial information is recorded and reported separately from the owner's personal financial information.

A business exists separately from its owners. A business's records must not be mixed with an owner's personal records and reports. For example, a business owner may buy insurance to protect the business and insurance to protect the owner's home. Only the insurance obtained for the business is recorded in the business's financial records. Insurance purchased for the owner's personal home is recorded in the owner's personal financial records. One bank account is used for the business and another for the owner.

CONSISTENT REPORTING

The same accounting principles must be followed in the same way in each accounting period.

Business decisions are based on the financial information reported on financial statements. Some decisions require a comparison of current financial statements with previous financial statements. If accounting information is recorded and reported differently each accounting period, comparisons from one accounting period to another may not be possible. If a business were to include $100,000 of supply purchases as a cost of merchandise sold in one period and as an operating expense in the next period, a user of this information could not adequately compare the two accounting periods. Therefore, unless a change is necessary to make information more easily understood, accounting information is reported in a consistent way every accounting period.

FULL DISCLOSURE

Financial statements contain all information necessary to understand a business's financial condition.

Owners, managers, lenders, and investors rely on financial statements to make informed decisions. All relevant financial information must be adequately and completely disclosed on financial statements.

Assume a business only reports total liabilities of $200,000 on its balance sheet. If that total includes $75,000 in current liabilities, then the balance sheet does not adequately disclose the nature of the liabilities. The critical information not disclosed is that $75,000 is due within the current fiscal year. Full disclosure requires an income statement, a balance sheet, a statement of owners' equity, a statement of cash flows, and the notes to the financial statements.

GOING CONCERN

Financial statements are prepared with the expectation that a business will remain in operation indefinitely.

New businesses are started with the expectation that they will be successful. Accounting records and financial statements are designed as though businesses will continue indefinitely. For example, a business buys store equipment for $80,000. After yearly depreciation is recorded and reported based on the expected life of the equipment, the equipment's book value (cost less accumulated depreciation) is $44,000. If the business ended operations and the equipment had to be sold, the amount received might be less, or more, than the $44,000. However, accounting records are maintained with the expectation that the business will remain in operation indefinitely and that the cost will be allocated over the useful life of the equipment. The equipment value, therefore, is $44,000 on the records, regardless of what it may be worth when sold.

HISTORICAL COST

The actual amount paid for merchandise or other items bought is recorded.

The actual amount paid for an item in a business transaction may be different from its market value. For example, assume a business purchases a delivery truck that is advertised for sale at $28,500. The truck has a market value of $30,000. The business negotiated a purchase price of just $27,000. The amount recorded in the accounting records for the delivery truck is the "historical" cost, $27,000—the actual amount paid.

MATCHING EXPENSES WITH REVENUE

The revenue from business activities and the expenses associated with earning that revenue are recorded in the same accounting period.

Business activities for an accounting period are summarized in financial statements. To adequately report how a business performed during an accounting period, all revenue earned as a result of business operations must be reported. Likewise, all expenses incurred in producing the revenue during the same accounting period must be reported. Matching expenses with revenue gives a true picture of business operations for an accounting period. The timing of when cash is exchanged does not impact when a transaction is recorded as either revenue or expense.

For example, in February, assume a business performs $50,000 of services and uses $5,000 of supplies that were purchased in the prior fiscal year. Matching expenses with revenue results in net income of $4,500. Including all required expenses gives readers of the financial statements a more complete picture of the financial condition of the business.

MATERIALITY

Business activities creating dollar amounts large enough to affect business decisions should be recorded and reported as separate items in the accounting records and financial statements.

Business transactions are recorded in accounting records and reported in financial statements in dollar amounts. How the amounts are recorded and reported depends on the amount involved and the relative importance of the item in making business decisions. Dollar amounts that are large will generally be considered in making decisions about future operations. A separate accounting record is kept for items with dollar amounts large enough to be considered in making decisions about future operations. Dollar amounts that are small and not considered important in decision making may be combined with other amounts in the accounting records and financial statements.

NEUTRALITY

The process of making accounting estimates is free from bias.

Many accounting functions require a business to use estimates. These include the estimation of uncollectible accounts receivable and the assignment of a useful life and salvage value for a plant asset. A business must not set or alter these estimates to achieve some other goal, such as reducing net income to avoid income taxes. For example, a business could raise its estimate of uncollectible accounts receivable to reduce its operating income subject to income tax. However, in compliance with the neutrality principle, the book value of accounts receivable in the financial accounts must always be a reasonable and unbiased estimate of the money the business expects to collect in the future.

OBJECTIVE EVIDENCE

A source document is prepared for each transaction.

A source document is an original business paper indicating that a transaction did occur and that the amounts recorded in the accounting records are accurate and true.

For example, a check is the original business paper for cash payments. The original business paper for purchases on account is the purchase invoice. When accounting information reported on the financial statements needs to be verified, an accountant will first check the accounting record. If the details of an entry need further checking, an accountant will then check the business papers as objective evidence that the transaction did occur as recorded.

Many transactions in modern computerized accounting systems are entered directly into the system. Although no paper document is ever prepared, an electronic version of the document is available in the system. The electronic record provides the same objective evidence of the transaction as would a paper record.

REALIZATION OF REVENUE

Revenue is recorded at the time goods or services are sold.

A business may sell goods or services or both. Cash may be received at the time of sale, or the business may agree to receive payment at a later date. Regardless of when cash is actually received, the sale amount is recorded in the accounting records at the time of sale. For example, merchandise is sold for $3,500. The business agrees to an initial payment of $500 with the remaining balance to be divided in four monthly payments of $750 each. The full $3,500 of revenue is recorded at the time of the sale even though $3,000 will be collected later.

UNIT OF MEASUREMENT

Business transactions are reported in numbers that have common values—that is, using a common unit of measurement.

All transactions are recorded in accounting records in terms of money. Useful nonfinancial information may also be recorded to describe the nature of a business transaction. If part of the information in the accounting records is financial and part is nonfinancial, the financial statements will not be clear. For example, if a business states its sales in number of units sold (nonfinancial) and its expenses in dollars (financial), net profit cannot be calculated. Instead, total expenses (financial) are subtracted from the money taken in through sales (financial) to determine net profit.

NIKE INC

FORM 10-K
(Annual Report)

for the Period Ending 05/31/11

FORM 10-K

☑ ANNUAL REPORT PURSUANT TO SECTION 13 OR 15(D) OF THE SECURITIES EXCHANGE ACT OF 1934
FOR THE FISCAL YEAR ENDED MAY 31, 2011

OR

☐ TRANSITION REPORT PURSUANT TO SECTION 13 OR 15(D) OF THE SECURITIES EXCHANGE ACT OF 1934

FOR THE TRANSITION PERIOD FROM _____ TO _____

Commission File No. 1-10635

NIKE, INC.

(Exact name of Registrant as specified in its charter)

OREGON	**93-0584541**
(State or other jurisdiction of incorporation)	*(IRS Employer Identification No.)*
One Bowerman Drive Beaverton, Oregon	**97005-6453**
(Address of principal executive offices)	*(Zip Code)*

(503) 671-6453
(Registrant's Telephone Number, Including Area Code)

SECURITIES REGISTERED PURSUANT TO SECTION 12(B) OF THE ACT:	
Class B Common Stock	**New York Stock Exchange**
(Title of Each Class)	*(Name of Each Exchange on Which Registered)*

SECURITIES REGISTERED PURSUANT TO SECTION 12(G) OF THE ACT:
NONE

Indicate by check mark	YES	NO
• if the registrant is a well-known seasoned issuer, as defined in Rule 405 of the Securities Act.	☑	☐
• if the registrant is not required to file reports pursuant to Section 13 or Section 15(d) of the Act.	☐	☑
• whether the Registrant (1) has filed all reports required to be filed by Section 13 or 15(d) of the Securities Exchange Act of 1934 during the preceding 12 months (or for such shorter period that the Registrant was required to file such reports), and (2) has been subject to such filing requirements for the past 90 days.	☑	☐
• whether the registrant has submitted electronically and posted on its corporate Website, if any, every Interactive Data File required to be submitted and posted pursuant to Rule 405 of Regulation S-T (§229.405 of this chapter) during the preceding 12 months (or for such shorter period that the registrant was required to submit and post such files).	☑	☐
• if disclosure of delinquent filers pursuant to Item 405 of Regulation S-K (§229.405 of this chapter) is not contained herein, and will not be contained, to the best of Registrant's knowledge, in definitive proxy or information statements incorporated by reference in Part III of this Form 10-K or any amendment to this Form 10-K.	☐	☐

• whether the Registrant is a large accelerated filer, an accelerated filer, a non-accelerated filer, or a smaller reporting company. See the definitions of "large accelerated filer," "accelerated filer" and "smaller reporting company" in Rule 12b-2 of the Exchange Act.

Large accelerated filer ☑	Accelerated filer ☐	Non-accelerated filer ☐	Smaller reporting company ☐

	YES	NO
• whether the registrant is a shell company (as defined in Rule 12b-2 of the Act).	☐	☑

As of November 30, 2010, the aggregate market value of the Registrant's Class A Common Stock held by non-affiliates of the Registrant was $2,005,831,959 and the aggregate market value of the Registrant's Class B Common Stock held by non-affiliates of the Registrant was $33,459,424,185.

As of July 18, 2011, the number of shares of the Registrant's Class A Common Stock outstanding was 89,989,447 and the number of shares of the Registrant's Class B Common Stock outstanding was 384,840,843.

DOCUMENTS INCORPORATED BY REFERENCE:

Parts of Registrant's Proxy Statement for the Annual Meeting of Shareholders to be held on September 19, 2011 are incorporated by reference into Part III of this Report.

ITEM 6   Selected Financial Data

	Financial History				
(In millions, except per share data and financial ratios)	2011	2010	2009	2008	2007
Year Ended May 31,					
Revenues	$ 20,862	$ 19,014	$ 19,176	$ 18,627	$ 16,326
Gross margin	9,508	8,800	8,604	8,387	7,161
Gross margin %	45.6%	46.3%	44.9%	45.0%	43.9%
Restructuring charges	—	—	195	—	—
Goodwill impairment	—	—	199	—	—
Intangible and other asset impairment	—	—	202	—	—
Net income	2,133	1,907	1,487	1,883	1,492
Basic earnings per common share	4.48	3.93	3.07	3.80	2.96
Diluted earnings per common share	4.39	3.86	3.03	3.74	2.93
Weighted average common shares outstanding	475.5	485.5	484.9	495.6	503.8
Diluted weighted average common shares outstanding	485.7	493.9	490.7	504.1	509.9
Cash dividends declared per common share	1.20	1.06	0.98	0.875	0.71
Cash flow from operations	1,812	3,164	1,736	1,936	1,879
Price range of common stock					
High	92.30	78.55	70.28	70.60	57.12
Low	67.21	50.16	38.24	51.50	37.76
At May 31,					
Cash and equivalents	$ 1,955	$ 3,079	$ 2,291	$ 2,134	$ 1,857
Short-term investments	2,583	2,067	1,164	642	990
Inventories	2,715	2,041	2,357	2,438	2,122
Working capital	7,339	7,595	6,457	5,518	5,493
Total assets	14,998	14,419	13,250	12,443	10,688
Long-term debt	276	446	437	441	410
Redeemable Preferred Stock	0.3	0.3	0.3	0.3	0.3
Shareholders' equity	9,843	9,754	8,693	7,825	7,025
Year-end stock price	84.45	72.38	57.05	68.37	56.75
Market capitalization	39,523	35,032	27,698	33,577	28,472
Financial Ratios:					
Return on equity	21.8%	20.7%	18.0%	25.4%	22.4%
Return on assets	14.5%	13.8%	11.6%	16.3%	14.5%
Inventory turns	4.8	4.6	4.4	4.5	4.4
Current ratio at May 31	2.9	3.3	3.0	2.7	3.1
Price/Earnings ratio at May 31	19.2	18.8	18.8	18.3	19.4

Selected Quarterly Financial Data

	1st Quarter		2nd Quarter		3rd Quarter		4th Quarter	
(Unaudited) (In millions, except per share data)	2011	2010	2011	2010	2011	2010	2011	2010
Revenues	$ 5,175	$ 4,799	$ 4,842	$ 4,405	$ 5,079	$ 4,733	$ 5,766	$ 5,077
Gross margin	2,434	2,216	2,193	1,960	2,327	2,218	2,554	2,406
Gross margin %	47.0%	46.2%	45.3%	44.5%	45.8%	46.9%	44.3%	47.4%
Net income	559	513	457	375	523	496	594	522
Basic earnings per common share	1.17	1.06	0.96	0.77	1.10	1.02	1.27	1.08
Diluted earnings per common share	1.14	1.04	0.94	0.76	1.08	1.01	1.24	1.06
Weighted average common shares outstanding	479.6	485.8	477.9	487.2	475.3	484.4	469.3	484.4
Diluted weighted average common shares outstanding	488.6	491.6	487.6	494.5	485.5	492.3	478.7	493.9
Cash dividends declared per common share	0.27	0.25	0.31	0.27	0.31	0.27	0.31	0.27
Price range of common stock								
High	74.94	59.95	86.53	66.35	92.30	67.85	89.88	78.55
Low	67.21	50.16	72.13	53.22	81.46	60.89	75.45	66.99

Management's Annual Report on Internal Control Over Financial Reporting

Management is responsible for establishing and maintaining adequate internal control over financial reporting, as such term is defined in Rule 13a-15(f) and Rule 15d-15(f) of the Securities Exchange Act of 1934, as amended. Internal control over financial reporting is a process designed to provide reasonable assurance regarding the reliability of financial reporting and the preparation of the financial statements for external purposes in accordance with generally accepted accounting principles in the United States of America. Internal control over financial reporting includes those policies and procedures that: (i) pertain to the maintenance of records that, in reasonable detail, accurately and fairly reflect the transactions and dispositions of assets of the company; (ii) provide reasonable assurance that transactions are recorded as necessary to permit preparation of financial statements in accordance with generally accepted accounting principles, and that receipts and expenditures of the company are being made only in accordance with authorizations of our management and directors; and (iii) provide reasonable assurance regarding prevention or timely detection of unauthorized acquisition, use or disposition of assets of the company that could have a material effect on the financial statements.

While "reasonable assurance" is a high level of assurance, it does not mean absolute assurance. Because of its inherent limitations, internal control over financial reporting may not prevent or detect every misstatement and instance of fraud. Controls are susceptible to manipulation, especially in instances of fraud caused by the collusion of two or more people, including our senior management. Also, projections of any evaluation of effectiveness to future periods are subject to the risk that controls may become inadequate because of changes in conditions, or that the degree of compliance with the policies or procedures may deteriorate.

Under the supervision and with the participation of our Chief Executive Officer and Chief Financial Officer, our management conducted an evaluation of the effectiveness of our internal control over financial reporting based upon the framework in *Internal Control — Integrated Framework* issued by the Committee of Sponsoring Organizations of the Treadway Commission (COSO). Based on the results of our evaluation, our management concluded that our internal control over financial reporting was effective as of May 31, 2011.

PricewaterhouseCoopers LLP, an independent registered public accounting firm, has audited (1) the consolidated financial statements and (2) the effectiveness of our internal control over financial reporting as of May 31, 2011, as stated in their report herein.

Mark G. Parker
Chief Executive Officer and President

Donald W. Blair
Chief Financial Officer

Report of Independent Registered Public Accounting Firm

To the Board of Directors and Shareholders of NIKE, Inc.:

In our opinion, the consolidated financial statements listed in the index appearing under Item 15(a)(1) present fairly, in all material respects, the financial position of NIKE, Inc. and its subsidiaries at May 31, 2011 and 2010, and the results of their operations and their cash flows for each of the three years in the period ended May 31, 2011 in conformity with accounting principles generally accepted in the United States of America. In addition, in our opinion, the financial statement schedule listed in the appendix appearing under Item 15(a)(2) presents fairly, in all material respects, the information set forth therein when read in conjunction with the related consolidated financial statements. Also in our opinion, the Company maintained, in all material respects, effective internal control over financial reporting as of May 31, 2011, based on criteria established in *Internal Control — Integrated Framework* issued by the Committee of Sponsoring Organizations of the Treadway Commission (COSO). The Company's management is responsible for these financial statements and financial statement schedule, for maintaining effective internal control over financial reporting and for its assessment of the effectiveness of internal control over financial reporting, included in Management's Annual Report on Internal Control Over Financial Reporting appearing under Item 8. Our responsibility is to express opinions on these financial statements, on the financial statement schedule, and on the Company's internal control over financial reporting based on our integrated audits. We conducted our audits in accordance with the standards of the Public Company Accounting Oversight Board (United States). Those standards require that we plan and perform the audits to obtain reasonable assurance about whether the financial statements are free of material misstatement and whether effective internal control over financial reporting was maintained in all material respects. Our audits of the financial statements included examining, on a test basis, evidence supporting the amounts and disclosures in the financial statements, assessing the accounting principles used and significant estimates made by management, and evaluating the overall financial statement presentation. Our audit of internal control over financial reporting included obtaining an understanding of internal control over financial reporting, assessing the risk that a material weakness exists, and testing and evaluating the design and operating effectiveness of internal control based on the assessed risk. Our audits also included performing such other procedures as we considered necessary in the circumstances. We believe that our audits provide a reasonable basis for our opinions.

A company's internal control over financial reporting is a process designed to provide reasonable assurance regarding the reliability of financial reporting and the preparation of financial statements for external purposes in accordance with generally accepted accounting principles. A company's internal control over financial reporting includes those policies and procedures that (i) pertain to the maintenance of records that, in reasonable detail, accurately and fairly reflect the transactions and dispositions of the assets of the company; (ii) provide reasonable assurance that transactions are recorded as necessary to permit preparation of financial statements in accordance with generally accepted accounting principles, and that receipts and expenditures of the company are being made only in accordance with authorizations of management and directors of the company; and (iii) provide reasonable assurance regarding prevention or timely detection of unauthorized acquisition, use, or disposition of the company's assets that could have a material effect on the financial statements.

Because of its inherent limitations, internal control over financial reporting may not prevent or detect misstatements. Also, projections of any evaluation of effectiveness to future periods are subject to the risk that controls may become inadequate because of changes in conditions, or that the degree of compliance with the policies or procedures may deteriorate.

/s/ PRICEWATERHOUSECOOPERS LLP

Portland, Oregon
July 22, 2011

Consolidated Statements of Income

(In millions, except per share data)		Year Ended May 31,				
		2011		2010		2009
Revenues	$	20,862	$	19,014	$	19,176
Cost of sales		11,354		10,214		10,572
Gross margin		9,508		8,800		8,604
Demand creation expense		2,448		2,356		2,352
Operating overhead expense		4,245		3,970		3,798
Total selling and administrative expense		6,693		6,326		6,150
Restructuring charges (Note 16)		—		—		195
Goodwill impairment (Note 4)		—		—		199
Intangible and other asset impairment (Note 4)		—		—		202
Interest expense (income), net (Notes 6, 7 and 8)		4		6		(10)
Other (income), net (Note 17)		(33)		(49)		(89)
Income before income taxes		2,844		2,517		1,957
Income taxes (Note 9)		711		610		470
Net income	$	2,133	$	1,907	$	1,487
Basic earnings per common share (Notes 1 and 12)	$	4.48	$	3.93	$	3.07
Diluted earnings per common share (Notes 1 and 12)	$	4.39	$	3.86	$	3.03
Dividends declared per common share	$	1.20	$	1.06	$	0.98

The accompanying notes to consolidated financial statements are an integral part of this statement.

Consolidated Balance Sheets

		May 31,	
(In millions)		2011	2010
ASSETS			
Current assets:			
Cash and equivalents	$	1,955 $	3,079
Short-term investments (Note 6)		2,583	2,067
Accounts receivable, net (Note 1)		3,138	2,650
Inventories (Notes 1 and 2)		2,715	2,041
Deferred income taxes (Note 9)		312	249
Prepaid expenses and other current assets		594	873
Total current assets		11,297	10,959
Property, plant and equipment, net (Note 3)		2,115	1,932
Identifiable intangible assets, net (Note 4)		487	467
Goodwill (Note 4)		205	188
Deferred income taxes and other assets (Notes 9 and 17)		894	873
TOTAL ASSETS	$	**14,998** $	**14,419**
LIABILITIES AND SHAREHOLDERS' EQUITY			
Current liabilities:			
Current portion of long-term debt (Note 8)	$	200 $	7
Notes payable (Note 7)		187	139
Accounts payable (Note 7)		1,469	1,255
Accrued liabilities (Notes 5 and 17)		1,985	1,904
Income taxes payable (Note 9)		117	59
Total current liabilities		3,958	3,364
Long-term debt (Note 8)		276	446
Deferred income taxes and other liabilities (Notes 9 and 17)		921	855
Commitments and contingencies (Note 15)		—	—
Redeemable Preferred Stock (Note 10)		—	—
Shareholders' equity:			
Common stock at stated value (Note 11):			
Class A convertible — 90 and 90 shares outstanding		—	—
Class B — 378 and 394 shares outstanding		3	3
Capital in excess of stated value		3,944	3,441
Accumulated other comprehensive income (Note 14)		95	215
Retained earnings		5,801	6,095
Total shareholders' equity		9,843	9,754
TOTAL LIABILITIES AND SHAREHOLDERS' EQUITY	$	**14,998** $	**14,419**

The accompanying notes to consolidated financial statements are an integral part of this statement.

Consolidated Statements of Cash Flows

(In millions)	Year Ended May 31,		
	2011	2010	2009
Cash provided by operations:			
Net income	$ 2,133	$ 1,907	$ 1,487
Income charges (credits) not affecting cash:			
Depreciation	335	324	335
Deferred income taxes	(76)	8	(294)
Stock-based compensation (Note 11)	105	159	171
Impairment of goodwill, intangibles and other assets (Note 4)	—	—	401
Amortization and other	23	72	48
Changes in certain working capital components and other assets and liabilities excluding the impact of acquisition and divestitures:			
(Increase) decrease in accounts receivable	(273)	182	(238)
(Increase) decrease in inventories	(551)	285	32
(Increase) decrease in prepaid expenses and other current assets	(35)	(70)	14
Increase (decrease) in accounts payable, accrued liabilities and income taxes payable	151	297	(220)
Cash provided by operations	1,812	3,164	1,736
Cash used by investing activities:			
Purchases of short-term investments	(7,616)	(3,724)	(2,909)
Maturities of short-term investments	4,313	2,334	1,280
Sales of short-term investments	2,766	453	1,110
Additions to property, plant and equipment	(432)	(335)	(456)
Disposals of property, plant and equipment	1	10	33
Increase in other assets, net of other liabilities	(30)	(11)	(47)
Settlement of net investment hedges	(23)	5	191
Cash used by investing activities	(1,021)	(1,268)	(798)
Cash used by financing activities:			
Reductions in long-term debt, including current portion	(8)	(32)	(7)
Increase (decrease) in notes payable	41	(205)	177
Proceeds from exercise of stock options and other stock issuances	345	364	187
Excess tax benefits from share-based payment arrangements	64	58	25
Repurchase of common stock	(1,859)	(741)	(649)
Dividends — common and preferred	(555)	(505)	(467)
Cash used by financing activities	(1,972)	(1,061)	(734)
Effect of exchange rate changes	57	(47)	(47)
Net (decrease) increase in cash and equivalents	(1,124)	788	157
Cash and equivalents, beginning of year	3,079	2,291	2,134
CASH AND EQUIVALENTS, END OF YEAR	$ 1,955	$ 3,079	$ 2,291
Supplemental disclosure of cash flow information:			
Cash paid during the year for:			
Interest, net of capitalized interest	$ 32	$ 48	$ 47
Income taxes	736	537	765
Dividends declared and not paid	145	131	121

The accompanying notes to consolidated financial statements are an integral part of this statement.

Consolidated Statements of Shareholders' Equity

(In millions, except per share data)	Common Stock Class A Shares	Amount	Class B Shares	Amount	Capital in Excess of Stated Value	Accumulated Other Comprehensive Income	Retained Earnings	Total
BALANCE AT MAY 31, 2008	97	$ —	394	$ 3	$ 2,498	$ 251	$ 5,073	$ 7,825
Stock options exercised			4		167			167
Conversion to Class B Common Stock	(2)		2					—
Repurchase of Class B Common Stock			(11)		(6)		(633)	(639)
Dividends on Common stock ($0.98 per share)							(475)	(475)
Issuance of shares to employees			1		45			45
Stock-based compensation (Note 11):					171			171
Forfeiture of shares from employees			—		(4)		(1)	(5)
Comprehensive income:							1,487	1,487
Net income								
Other comprehensive income:								
Foreign currency translation and other (net of tax benefit of $178)						(335)		(335)
Net gain on cash flow hedges (net of tax expense of $168)						454		454
Net gain on net investment hedges (net of tax expense of $55)						106		106
Reclassification to net income of previously deferred net gains related to hedge derivatives (net of tax expense of $40)						(108)		(108)
Total comprehensive income						117	1,487	1,604
BALANCE AT MAY 31, 2009	95	$ —	390	$ 3	$ 2,871	$ 368	$ 5,451	$ 8,693
Stock options exercised			9		380			380
Conversion to Class B Common Stock	(5)		5					—
Repurchase of Class B Common Stock			(11)		(7)		(747)	(754)
Dividends on Common stock ($1.06 per share)							(515)	(515)
Issuance of shares to employees			1		40			40
Stock-based compensation (Note 11):					159			159
Forfeiture of shares from employees			—		(2)		(1)	(3)
Comprehensive income:								
Net income							1,907	1,907
Other comprehensive income (Notes 14 and 17):								
Foreign currency translation and other (net of tax benefit of $72)						(159)		(159)
Net gain on cash flow hedges (net of tax expense of $28)						87		87
Net gain on net investment hedges (net of tax expense of $21)						45		45
Reclassification to net income of previously deferred net gains related to hedge derivatives (net of tax expense of $42)						(122)		(122)
Reclassification of ineffective hedge gains to net income (net of tax expense of $1)						(4)		(4)
Total comprehensive income						(153)	1,907	1,754

| (In millions, except per share data) | Common Stock | | | | Capital in Excess of Stated Value | Accumulated Other Comprehensive Income | Retained Earnings | Total |
| | Class A | | Class B | | | | | |
	Shares	Amount	Shares	Amount				
BALANCE AT MAY 31, 2010	90	$ —	394	$ 3	$ 3,441	$ 215	$ 6,095	$ 9,754
Stock options exercised			7		368			368
Repurchase of Class B Common Stock			(24)		(14)		(1,857)	(1,871)
Dividends on Common stock ($1.20 per share)							(569)	(569)
Issuance of shares to employees			1		49			49
Stock-based compensation (Note 11):					105			105
Forfeiture of shares from employees			—		(5)		(1)	(6)
Comprehensive income:								
Net income							2,133	2,133
Other comprehensive income (Notes 14 and 17):								
Foreign currency translation and other (net of tax expense of $121)						263		263
Net loss on cash flow hedges (net of tax benefit of $66)						(242)		(242)
Net loss on net investment hedges (net of tax benefit of $28)						(57)		(57)
Reclassification to net income of previously deferred net gains related to hedge derivatives (net of tax expense of $24)						(84)		(84)
Total comprehensive income						(120)	2,133	2,013
BALANCE AT MAY 31, 2011	90	$ —	378	$ 3	$ 3,944	$ 95	$ 5,801	$ 9,843

The accompanying notes to consolidated financial statements are an integral part of this statement.

NOTE 1   Summary of Significant Accounting Policies

Description of Business

NIKE, Inc. is a worldwide leader in the design, marketing and distribution of athletic and sports-inspired footwear, apparel, equipment and accessories. Wholly-owned NIKE subsidiaries include Cole Haan, which designs, markets and distributes dress and casual shoes, handbags, accessories and coats; Converse Inc., which designs, markets and distributes athletic and casual footwear, apparel and accessories; Hurley International LLC, which designs, markets and distributes action sports and youth lifestyle footwear, apparel and accessories; and Umbro International Limited, which designs, distributes and licenses athletic and casual footwear, apparel and equipment, primarily for the sport of soccer.

Basis of Consolidation

The consolidated financial statements include the accounts of NIKE, Inc. and its subsidiaries (the "Company"). All significant intercompany transactions and balances have been eliminated.

Recognition of Revenues

Wholesale revenues are recognized when title passes and the risks and rewards of ownership have passed to the customer, based on the terms of sale. This occurs upon shipment or upon receipt by the customer depending on the country of the sale and the agreement with the customer. Retail store revenues are recorded at the time of sale. Provisions for sales discounts, returns and miscellaneous claims from customers are made at the time of sale. As of May 31, 2011 and 2010, the Company's reserve balances for sales discounts, returns and miscellaneous claims were $423 million and $371 million, respectively.

Shipping and Handling Costs

Shipping and handling costs are expensed as incurred and included in cost of sales.

Demand Creation Expense

Demand creation expense consists of advertising and promotion costs, including costs of endorsement contracts, television, digital and print advertising, brand events, and retail brand presentation. Advertising production costs are expensed the first time an advertisement is run. Advertising placement costs are expensed in the month the advertising appears, while costs related to brand events are expensed when the event occurs. Costs related to retail brand presentation are expensed when the presentation is completed and delivered. A significant amount of the Company's promotional expenses result from payments under endorsement contracts. Accounting for endorsement payments is based upon specific contract provisions. Generally, endorsement payments are expensed on a straight-line basis over the term of the contract after giving recognition to periodic performance compliance provisions of the contracts. Prepayments made under contracts are included in prepaid expenses or other assets depending on the period to which the prepayment applies.

Through cooperative advertising programs, the Company reimburses retail customers for certain costs of advertising the Company's products. The Company records these costs in selling and administrative expense at the point in time when it is obligated to its customers for the costs, which is when the related revenues are recognized. This obligation may arise prior to the related advertisement being run.

Total advertising and promotion expenses were $2,448 million, $2,356 million, and $2,352 million for the years ended May 31, 2011, 2010 and 2009, respectively. Prepaid advertising and promotion expenses recorded in prepaid expenses and other assets totaled $291 million and $261 million at May 31, 2011 and 2010, respectively.

Cash and Equivalents

Cash and equivalents represent cash and short-term, highly liquid investments with maturities of three months or less at date of purchase. The carrying amounts reflected in the consolidated balance sheet for cash and equivalents approximate fair value.

Short-Term Investments

Short-term investments consist of highly liquid investments, including commercial paper, U.S. treasury, U.S. agency, and corporate debt securities, with maturities over three months from the date of purchase. Debt securities that the Company has the ability and positive intent to hold to maturity are carried at amortized cost. At May 31, 2011 and 2010, the Company did not hold any short-term investments that were classified as trading or held-to-maturity.

At May 31, 2011 and 2010, short-term investments consisted of available-for-sale securities. Available-for-sale securities are recorded at fair value with unrealized gains and losses reported, net of tax, in other comprehensive income, unless unrealized losses are determined to be other than temporary. The Company considers all available-for-sale securities, including those with maturity dates beyond 12 months, as available to support current operational liquidity needs and therefore classifies all securities with maturity dates beyond three months at the date of purchase as current assets within short-term investments on the consolidated balance sheet.

See Note 6 — Fair Value Measurements for more information on the Company's short term investments.

Allowance for Uncollectible Accounts Receivable

Accounts receivable consists primarily of amounts receivable from customers. We make ongoing estimates relating to the collectability of our accounts receivable and maintain an allowance for estimated losses resulting from the inability of our customers to make required payments. In determining the amount of the allowance, we consider our historical level of credit losses and make judgments about the creditworthiness of significant customers based on ongoing credit evaluations. Accounts receivable with anticipated collection dates greater than 12 months from the balance sheet date and related allowances are considered non-current and recorded in other assets. The allowance for uncollectible accounts receivable was $124 million and $117 million at May 31, 2011 and 2010, respectively, of which $50 million and $43 million was classified as long-term and recorded in other assets.

Inventory Valuation

Inventories are stated at lower of cost or market and valued on a first-in, first-out ("FIFO") or moving average cost basis.

Property, Plant and Equipment and Depreciation

Property, plant and equipment are recorded at cost. Depreciation for financial reporting purposes is determined on a straight-line basis for buildings and leasehold improvements over 2 to 40 years and for machinery and equipment over 2 to 15 years. Computer software (including, in some cases, the cost of internal labor) is depreciated on a straight-line basis over 3 to 10 years.

Impairment of Long-Lived Assets

The Company reviews the carrying value of long-lived assets or asset groups to be used in operations whenever events or changes in circumstances indicate that the carrying amount of the assets might not be recoverable. Factors that would necessitate an impairment assessment include a significant adverse

change in the extent or manner in which an asset is used, a significant adverse change in legal factors or the business climate that could affect the value of the asset, or a significant decline in the observable market value of an asset, among others. If such facts indicate a potential impairment, the Company would assess the recoverability of an asset group by determining if the carrying value of the asset group exceeds the sum of the projected undiscounted cash flows expected to result from the use and eventual disposition of the assets over the remaining economic life of the primary asset in the asset group. If the recoverability test indicates that the carrying value of the asset group is not recoverable, the Company will estimate the fair value of the asset group using appropriate valuation methodologies which would typically include an estimate of discounted cash flows. Any impairment would be measured as the difference between the asset groups carrying amount and its estimated fair value.

Identifiable Intangible Assets and Goodwill

The Company performs annual impairment tests on goodwill and intangible assets with indefinite lives in the fourth quarter of each fiscal year, or when events occur or circumstances change that would, more likely than not, reduce the fair value of a reporting unit or an intangible asset with an indefinite life below its carrying value. Events or changes in circumstances that may trigger interim impairment reviews include significant changes in business climate, operating results, planned investments in the reporting unit, or an expectation that the carrying amount may not be recoverable, among other factors. The impairment test requires the Company to estimate the fair value of its reporting units. If the carrying value of a reporting unit exceeds its fair value, the goodwill of that reporting unit is potentially impaired and the Company proceeds to step two of the impairment analysis. In step two of the analysis, the Company measures and records an impairment loss equal to the excess of the carrying value of the reporting unit's goodwill over its implied fair value should such a circumstance arise.

The Company generally bases its measurement of fair value of a reporting unit on a blended analysis of the present value of future discounted cash flows and the market valuation approach. The discounted cash flows model indicates the fair value of the reporting unit based on the present value of the cash flows that the Company expects the reporting unit to generate in the future. The Company's significant estimates in the discounted cash flows model include: its weighted average cost of capital; long-term rate of growth and profitability of the reporting unit's business; and working capital effects. The market valuation approach indicates the fair value of the business based on a comparison of the reporting unit to comparable publicly traded companies in similar lines of business. Significant estimates in the market valuation approach model include identifying similar companies with comparable business factors such as size, growth, profitability, risk and return on investment, and assessing comparable revenue and operating income multiples in estimating the fair value of the reporting unit.

The Company believes the weighted use of discounted cash flows and the market valuation approach is the best method for determining the fair value of its reporting units because these are the most common valuation methodologies used within its industry; and the blended use of both models compensates for the inherent risks associated with either model if used on a stand-alone basis.

Indefinite-lived intangible assets primarily consist of acquired trade names and trademarks. In measuring the fair value for these intangible assets, the Company utilizes the relief-from-royalty method. This method assumes that trade names and trademarks have value to the extent that their owner is relieved of the obligation to pay royalties for the benefits received from them. This method requires the Company to estimate the future revenue for the related brands, the appropriate royalty rate and the weighted average cost of capital.

Foreign Currency Translation and Foreign Currency Transactions

Adjustments resulting from translating foreign functional currency financial statements into U.S. dollars are included in the foreign currency translation adjustment, a component of accumulated other comprehensive income in shareholders' equity.

The Company's global subsidiaries have various assets and liabilities, primarily receivables and payables, that are denominated in currencies other than their functional currency. These balance sheet items are subject to remeasurement, the impact of which is recorded in other (income), net, within our consolidated statement of income.

Accounting for Derivatives and Hedging Activities

The Company uses derivative financial instruments to limit exposure to changes in foreign currency exchange rates and interest rates. All derivatives are recorded at fair value on the balance sheet and changes in the fair value of derivative financial instruments are either recognized in other comprehensive income (a component of shareholders' equity), debt or net income depending on the nature of the underlying exposure, whether the derivative is formally designated as a hedge, and, if designated, the extent to which the hedge is effective. The Company classifies the cash flows at settlement from derivatives in the same category as the cash flows from the related hedged items. For undesignated hedges and designated cash flow hedges, this is within the cash provided by operations component of the consolidated statements of cash flows. For designated net investment hedges, this is generally within the cash used by investing activities component of the cash flow statement. As our fair value hedges are receive-fixed, pay-variable interest rate swaps, the cash flows associated with these derivative instruments are periodic interest payments while the swaps are outstanding, which are reflected in net income within the cash provided by operations component of the cash flow statement.

See Note 17 — Risk Management and Derivatives for more information on the Company's risk management program and derivatives.

Stock-Based Compensation

The Company estimates the fair value of options and stock appreciation rights granted under the NIKE, Inc. 1990 Stock Incentive Plan (the "1990 Plan") and employees' purchase rights under the Employee Stock Purchase Plans ("ESPPs") using the Black-Scholes option pricing model. The Company recognizes this fair value, net of estimated forfeitures, as selling and administrative expense in the consolidated statements of income over the vesting period using the straight-line method.

See Note 11 — Common Stock and Stock-Based Compensation for more information on the Company's stock programs.

Income Taxes

The Company accounts for income taxes using the asset and liability method. This approach requires the recognition of deferred tax assets and liabilities for the expected future tax consequences of temporary differences between the carrying amounts and the tax basis of assets and liabilities. United States income taxes are provided currently on financial statement earnings of non-U.S. subsidiaries that are expected to be repatriated. The Company determines annually the amount of undistributed non-U.S. earnings to invest indefinitely in its non-U.S. operations. The Company recognizes interest and penalties related to income tax matters in income tax expense.

See Note 9 — Income Taxes for further discussion.

Earnings Per Share

Basic earnings per common share is calculated by dividing net income by the weighted average number of common shares outstanding during the year. Diluted earnings per common share is calculated by adjusting weighted average outstanding shares, assuming conversion of all potentially dilutive stock options and awards.

See Note 12 — Earnings Per Share for further discussion.

Management Estimates

The preparation of financial statements in conformity with generally accepted accounting principles requires management to make estimates, including estimates relating to assumptions that affect the reported amounts of assets and liabilities and disclosure of contingent assets and liabilities at the date of financial statements and the reported amounts of revenues and expenses during the reporting period. Actual results could differ from these estimates.

Recently Adopted Accounting Standards

In January 2010, the Financial Accounting Standards Board ("FASB") issued guidance to amend the disclosure requirements related to recurring and nonrecurring fair value measurements. The guidance requires additional disclosures about the different classes of assets and liabilities measured at fair value, the valuation techniques and inputs used, the activity in Level 3 fair value measurements, and the transfers between Levels 1, 2, and 3 of the fair value measurement hierarchy. This guidance became effective for the Company beginning March 1, 2010, except for disclosures relating to purchases, sales, issuances and settlements of Level 3 assets and liabilities, which will be effective for the Company beginning June 1, 2011. As this guidance only requires expanded disclosures, the adoption did not and will not impact the Company's consolidated financial position or results of operations.

In June 2009, the FASB issued a new accounting standard that revised the guidance for the consolidation of variable interest entities ("VIE"). This new guidance requires a qualitative approach to identifying a controlling financial interest in a VIE, and requires an ongoing assessment of whether an entity is a VIE and whether an interest in a VIE makes the holder the primary beneficiary of the VIE. This guidance became effective for the Company beginning June 1, 2010. The adoption of this guidance did not have an impact on the Company's consolidated financial position or results of operations.

Recently Issued Accounting Standards

In June 2011, the FASB issued new guidance on the presentation of comprehensive income. This new guidance requires the components of net income and other comprehensive income to be either presented in one continuous statement, referred to as the statement of comprehensive income, or in two separate, but consecutive statements. This new guidance eliminates the current option to report other comprehensive income and its components in the statement of shareholders' equity. While the new guidance changes the presentation of comprehensive income, there are no changes to the components that are recognized in net income or other comprehensive income under current accounting guidance. This new guidance is effective for the Company beginning June 1, 2012. As this guidance only amends the presentation of the components of comprehensive income, the adoption will not have an impact on the Company's consolidated financial position or results of operations.

In April 2011, the FASB issued new guidance to achieve common fair value measurement and disclosure requirements between U.S. GAAP and International Financial Reporting Standards. This new guidance, which is effective for the Company beginning June 1, 2012, amends current U.S. GAAP fair value measurement and disclosure guidance to include increased transparency around valuation inputs and investment categorization. The Company does not expect the adoption will have a material impact on its consolidated financial position or results of operations.

In October 2009, the FASB issued new standards that revised the guidance for revenue recognition with multiple deliverables. These new standards impact the determination of when the individual deliverables included in a multiple-element arrangement may be treated as separate units of accounting. Additionally, these new standards modify the manner in which the transaction consideration is allocated across the separately identified deliverables by no longer permitting the residual method of allocating arrangement consideration. These new standards are effective for the Company beginning June 1, 2011. The Company does not expect the adoption will have a material impact on its consolidated financial position or results of operations.

NOTE 2 Inventories

Inventory balances of $2,715 million and $2,041 million at May 31, 2011 and 2010, respectively, were substantially all finished goods.

NOTE 3 Property, Plant and Equipment

Property, plant and equipment included the following:

(In millions)	As of May 31, 2011	2010
Land	$ 237	$ 223
Buildings	1,124	952
Machinery and equipment	2,487	2,217
Leasehold improvements	931	821
Construction in process	127	177
	4,906	4,390
Less accumulated depreciation	2,791	2,458
	$ 2,115	$ 1,932

Capitalized interest was not material for the years ended May 31, 2011, 2010, and 2009.

NOTE 4 Identifiable Intangible Assets, Goodwill and Umbro Impairment

Identified Intangible Assets and Goodwill

The following table summarizes the Company's identifiable intangible asset balances as of May 31, 2011 and 2010:

(In millions)	May 31, 2011			May 31, 2010		
	Gross Carrying Amount	Accumulated Amortization	Net Carrying Amount	Gross Carrying Amount	Accumulated Amortization	Net Carrying Amount
Amortized intangible assets:						
Patents	$ 80	$ (24)	$ 56	$ 69	$ (21)	$ 48
Trademarks	44	(25)	19	40	(18)	22
Other	47	(22)	25	32	(18)	14
TOTAL	$ 171	$ (71)	$ 100	$ 141	$ (57)	$ 84
Unamortized intangible assets — Trademarks			387			383
IDENTIFIABLE INTANGIBLE ASSETS, NET			$ 487			$ 467

The effect of foreign exchange fluctuations for the year ended May 31, 2011 increased unamortized intangible assets by approximately $4 million.

Amortization expense, which is included in selling and administrative expense, was $16 million, $14 million, and $12 million for the years ended May 31, 2011, 2010, and 2009, respectively. The estimated amortization expense for intangible assets subject to amortization for each of the years ending May 31, 2012 through May 31, 2016 are as follows: 2012: $16 million; 2013: $14 million; 2014: $12 million; 2015: $8 million; 2016: $7 million.

All goodwill balances are included in the Company's "Other" category for segment reporting purposes. The following table summarizes the Company's goodwill balance as of May 31, 2011 and 2010:

(In millions)	Goodwill	Accumulated Impairment	Goodwill, net
May 31, 2009	$ 393	$ (199)	$ 194
Other[1]	(6)	—	(6)
May 31, 2010	387	(199)	188
Umbro France[2]	10	—	10
Other[1]	7	—	7
MAY 31, 2011	$ 404	$ (199)	$ 205

(1) Other consists of foreign currency translation adjustments on Umbro goodwill.

(2) In March 2011, Umbro acquired the remaining 51% of the exclusive licensee and distributor of the Umbro brand in France for approximately $15 million.

Umbro Impairment in Fiscal 2009

The Company performs annual impairment tests on goodwill and intangible assets with indefinite lives in the fourth quarter of each fiscal year, or when events occur or circumstances change that would, more likely than not, reduce the fair value of a reporting unit or intangible assets with an indefinite life below its carrying value. As a result of a significant decline in global consumer demand and continued weakness in the macroeconomic environment, as well as decisions by Company management to adjust planned investment in the Umbro brand, the Company concluded sufficient indicators of impairment existed to require the performance of an interim assessment of Umbro's goodwill and indefinite lived intangible assets as of February 1, 2009. Accordingly, the Company performed the first step of the goodwill impairment assessment for Umbro by comparing the estimated fair value of Umbro to its carrying amount, and determined there was a potential impairment of goodwill as the carrying amount exceeded the estimated fair value. Therefore, the Company performed the second step of the assessment which compared the implied fair value of Umbro's goodwill to the book value of goodwill. The implied fair value of goodwill is determined by allocating the estimated fair value of Umbro to all of its assets and liabilities, including both recognized and unrecognized intangibles, in the same manner as goodwill was determined in the original business combination.

The Company measured the fair value of Umbro by using an equal weighting of the fair value implied by a discounted cash flow analysis and by comparisons with the market values of similar publicly traded companies. The Company believes the blended use of both models compensates for the inherent risk associated with either model if used on a stand-alone basis, and this combination is indicative of the factors a market participant would consider when performing a similar valuation. The fair value of Umbro's indefinite-lived trademark was estimated using the relief from royalty method, which assumes that the trademark has value to the extent that Umbro is relieved of the obligation to pay royalties for the benefits received from the trademark. The assessments of the Company resulted in the recognition of impairment charges of $199 million and $181 million related to Umbro's goodwill and trademark, respectively, for the year ended May 31, 2009. A tax benefit of $55 million was recognized as a result of the trademark impairment charge. In addition to the above impairment analysis, the Company determined an equity investment held by Umbro was impaired, and recognized a charge of $21 million related to the impairment of this investment. These charges are included in the Company's "Other" category for segment reporting purposes.

The discounted cash flow analysis calculated the fair value of Umbro using management's business plans and projections as the basis for expected cash flows for the next 12 years and a 3% residual growth rate thereafter. The Company used a weighted average discount rate of 14% in its analysis, which was derived primarily from published sources as well as our adjustment for increased market risk given current market conditions. Other significant estimates used in the discounted cash flow analysis include the rates of projected growth and profitability of Umbro's business and working capital effects. The market valuation approach indicates the fair value of Umbro based on a comparison of Umbro to publicly traded companies in similar lines of business. Significant estimates in the market valuation approach include identifying similar companies with comparable business factors such as size, growth, profitability, mix of revenue generated from licensed and direct distribution, and risk of return on investment.

Holding all other assumptions constant at the test date, a 100 basis point increase in the discount rate would reduce the adjusted carrying value of Umbro's net assets by an additional 12%.

NOTE 5   Accrued Liabilities

Accrued liabilities included the following:

		May 31,	
(In millions)		2011	2010
Compensation and benefits, excluding taxes	$	628 $	599
Endorser compensation		284	267
Taxes other than income taxes		214	158
Fair value of derivatives		186	164
Dividends payable		145	131
Advertising and marketing		139	125
Import and logistics costs		98	80
Other[1]		291	380
	$	1,985 $	1,904

(1) Other consists of various accrued expenses and no individual item accounted for more than 5% of the balance at May 31, 2011 and 2010.

NOTE 6   Fair Value Measurements

The Company measures certain financial assets and liabilities at fair value on a recurring basis, including derivatives and available-for-sale securities. Fair value is a market-based measurement that should be determined based on the assumptions that market participants would use in pricing an asset or liability. As a basis for considering such assumptions, the Company uses a three-level hierarchy established by the FASB that prioritizes fair value measurements based on the types of inputs used for the various valuation techniques (market approach, income approach, and cost approach).

The levels of hierarchy are described below:

• Level 1: Observable inputs such as quoted prices in active markets for identical assets or liabilities.

• Level 2: Inputs other than quoted prices that are observable for the asset or liability, either directly or indirectly; these include quoted prices for similar assets or liabilities in active markets and quoted prices for identical or similar assets or liabilities in markets that are not active.

• Level 3: Unobservable inputs in which there is little or no market data available, which require the reporting entity to develop its own assumptions.

The Company's assessment of the significance of a particular input to the fair value measurement in its entirety requires judgment and considers factors specific to the asset or liability. Financial assets and liabilities are classified in their entirety based on the most stringent level of input that is significant to the fair value measurement.

The following table presents information about the Company's financial assets and liabilities measured at fair value on a recurring basis as of May 31, 2011 and 2010 and indicates the fair value hierarchy of the valuation techniques utilized by the Company to determine such fair value.

	May 31, 2011				
	Fair Value Measurements Using			Assets /Liabilities	
(In millions)	Level 1	Level 2	Level 3	at Fair Value	Balance Sheet Classification
ASSETS					
Derivatives:					
Foreign exchange forwards and options	$ — $	38 $	— $	38	Other current assets and other long-term assets
Interest rate swap contracts	—	15	—	15	Other current assets and other long-term assets
Total derivatives	—	53	—	53	
Available-for-sale securities:					
U.S. Treasury securities	125	—	—	125	Cash equivalents
Commercial paper and bonds	—	157	—	157	Cash equivalents
Money market funds	—	780	—	780	Cash equivalents
U.S. Treasury securities	1,473	—	—	1,473	Short-term investments
U.S. Agency securities	—	308	—	308	Short-term investments
Commercial paper and bonds	—	802	—	802	Short-term investments
Total available-for-sale securities	1,598	2,047	—	3,645	
TOTAL ASSETS	$ 1,598 $	2,100 $	— $	3,698	
LIABILITIES					
Derivatives:					
Foreign exchange forwards and options	$ — $	197 $	— $	197	Accrued liabilities and other long-term liabilities
TOTAL LIABILITIES	$ — $	197 $	— $	197	

Appendix C

Using a Calculator and Computer Keypad

Kinds of Calculators

Many different models of calculators, both desktop and handheld, are available. All calculators have their own features and particular placement of operating keys. Therefore, it is necessary to refer to the operator's manual for specific instructions and locations of the operating keys for the calculator being used. A typical keyboard of a desktop calculator is shown in the illustration.

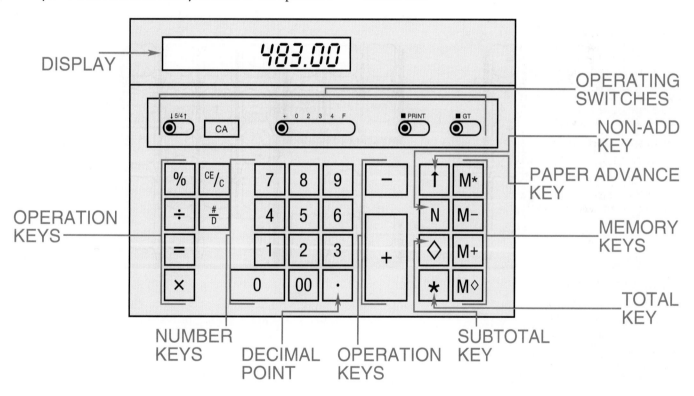

Desktop Calculator Settings

Several operating switches on a desktop calculator must be engaged before the calculator will produce the desired results.

The *decimal selector* sets the appropriate decimal places necessary for the numbers that will be entered. For example, if the decimal selector is set at 2, both the numbers entered and the answer will have two decimal places. If the decimal selector is set at F, the calculator

automatically sets the decimal places. The F setting allows the answer to be unrounded and carried out to the maximum number of decimal places possible.

The *decimal rounding selector* rounds the answers. The down arrow position will drop any digits beyond the last digit desired. The up arrow position will drop any digits beyond the last digit desired and round the last digit up. In the 5/4 position, the calculator rounds the last desired digit up only when the following digit is 5 or greater. If the following digit is less than 5, the last desired digit remains unchanged.

The *GT* or *grand total switch* in the on position accumulates totals.

Kinds of Computer Keyboards

The computer has a keypad on the right side of the keyboard, called the *numeric keypad*. The two basic layouts for the numeric keypad, standard and enhanced, are shown in the illustration. On the standard keyboard, the directional arrow keys are found on the number keys. To use the numbers, press the key called *Num Lock*. (This key is found above the 7 key.) When the Num Lock is turned on, numbers are entered when the keys on the keypad are pressed. When the Num Lock is off, the arrow, Home, Page Up, Page Down, End, Insert, and Delete keys can be used.

The enhanced keyboards have the arrow keys and the other directional keys mentioned above to the left of the numeric keypad. When using the keypad on an enhanced keyboard, Num Lock can remain on.

The asterisk (*) performs a different function on the computer than the calculator. The asterisk on the calculator is used for the total while the computer uses it for multiplication.

Another difference is the division key. The computer key is the forward slash key (/). The calculator key uses the division key (÷).

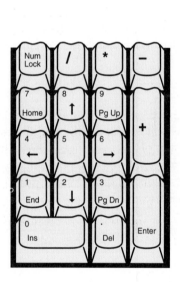

Standard
Keyboard Layout

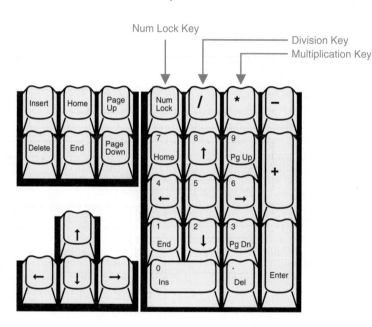

Num Lock Key

Division Key
Multiplication Key

Enhanced
Keyboard Layout

Ten-Key Touch System

Striking the numbers 0 to 9 on a calculator or numeric keypad without looking at the keyboard is called the *touch system*. Using the touch system develops both speed and accuracy.

The 4, 5, and 6 keys are called the *home row*. If the right hand is used for the keyboard, the index finger is placed on the 4 key, the middle finger on the 5 key, and the ring finger on the 6 key. If the left hand is used, the ring finger is placed on the 4 key, the middle finger on the 5 key, and the index finger on the 6 key.

Place the fingers on the home row keys. Curve the fingers and keep the wrist straight. These keys may feel slightly concaved or the 5 key may have a raised dot. The differences in the home row allow the operator to recognize the home row by touch rather than by sight.

Maintain the position of the fingers on the home row. The finger used to strike the 4 key will also strike the 7 key and the 1 key. Stretch the finger up to reach the 7; then stretch the finger down to reach the 1 key. Visualize the position of these keys.

Again, place the fingers on the home row. Stretch the finger that strikes the 5 key up to reach the 8 key, then down to reach the 2 key. Likewise, stretch the finger that strikes the 6 key up to strike the 9 and down to strike the 3 key. This same finger will stretch down again to hit the decimal point.

If the right hand is used, the thumb will be used to strike the 0 and 00 keys and the little finger to strike the addition key. If the left hand is used, the little finger will be used to strike the 0 and 00 keys and the thumb to strike the addition key.

Handheld Calculators

Handheld calculators are slightly different from desktop calculators, not only in their size and features but also in their operation. Refer to the operator's manual for specific instructions for the calculator being used.

On a handheld calculator, the numeric keys are usually very close together. In addition, the keys do not respond to touch as easily as on a desktop calculator. Therefore, the touch system is usually not used on a handheld calculator.

Performing Mathematical Operations on Desktop Calculators

Mathematical operations can be performed on a calculator both quickly and efficiently. The basic operations of addition, subtraction, multiplication, and division are used frequently on a calculator.

ADDITION

Each number to be added is called an *addend*. The answer to an addition problem is called the *sum*.

Addition is performed by entering an addend and striking the addition key (+). All numbers are entered on a calculator in the exact order they are given. To enter the number 4,455.65, strike the 4, 4, 5, 5, decimal, 6, and 5 keys in that order, and then strike the addition key. Commas are not entered. Continue in this manner until all addends have been entered. To obtain the sum, strike the total key on the calculator.

SUBTRACTION

The top number or first number of a subtraction problem is called the *minuend*. The number to be subtracted from the minuend is called the *subtrahend*. The answer to a subtraction problem is called the *difference*.

Subtraction is performed by first entering the minuend and striking the addition key (+). The subtrahend is then entered, followed by the minus key (−), followed by the total key.

MULTIPLICATION

The number to be multiplied is called the *multiplicand*. The number of times the multiplicand will be multiplied

is called the *multiplier*. The answer to a multiplication problem is called the *product*.

Multiplication is performed by entering the multiplicand and striking the multiplication key (×). The multiplier is then entered, followed by the equals key (=). The calculator will automatically multiply and give the product.

DIVISION

The number to be divided is called the *dividend*. The number the dividend will be divided by is called the *divisor*. The answer to a division problem is called the *quotient*.

Division is performed by entering the dividend and striking the division key (÷). The divisor is then entered, followed by the equals key (=). The calculator will automatically divide and give the quotient.

CORRECTING ERRORS

If an error is made while using a calculator, several methods of correction may be used. If an incorrect number has been entered and the addition key or equals key has not yet been struck, strike the clear entry (CE) key one time. This key will clear only the last number that was entered. However, if the clear entry key is depressed more than one time, the entire problem will be cleared on some calculators. If an incorrect number has been entered and the addition key has been struck, strike the minus key one time only. This will automatically subtract the last number added, thus removing it from the total.

Performing Mathematical Operations on Computers and Handheld Calculators

On a computer keypad or a handheld calculator, addition is performed in much the same way as on a desktop calculator. However, after the + key is depressed, the display usually shows the accumulated total. Therefore, the total key is not found. Some computer programs will not calculate the total until Enter is pressed.

Subtraction is performed differently on many computer keypads and handheld calculators. The minuend is usually entered, followed by the minus (–) key. Then the subtrahend is entered. Pressing either the + key or the = key will display the difference. Some computer programs will not calculate the difference until Enter is pressed.

Multiplication and division are performed the same way on a computer keypad and handheld calculator as on a desktop calculator. Keep in mind that computers use the * for multiplication and / for division.

Safety Concerns

Whenever electrical equipment such as a calculator or computer is being operated in a classroom or office, several safety rules apply. These rules protect the operator of the equipment, other persons in the environment, and the equipment itself.

1. Do not unplug equipment by pulling on the electrical cord. Instead, grasp the plug at the outlet and remove it.
2. Do not stretch electrical cords across an aisle where someone might trip over them.
3. Avoid food and beverages near the equipment where a spill might result in an electrical short.
4. Do not attempt to remove the cover of a calculator, computer, or keyboard for any reason while the power is turned on.
5. Do not attempt to repair equipment while it is plugged in.
6. Always turn the power off or unplug equipment when finished using it.

Calculation Drills

INSTRUCTIONS FOR DESKTOP CALCULATORS

Complete each drill using the touch method. Set the decimal selector at the setting indicated in each drill. Compare the answer on the calculator to the answer in the book. If the two are the same, progress to the next problem. It is not necessary to enter 00 in the cents column if the decimal selector is set at 0-F. However, digits other than zeros in the cents column must be entered, preceded by a decimal point.

INSTRUCTIONS FOR COMPUTER KEYPADS

Complete each drill using the touch method. There is no decimal selector on computer keypads. Set the

number of decimal places as directed in the instructions for the computer program. In spreadsheets, for example, use the formatting options to set the number of decimal places. When the drill indicates "F" for floating, leave the computer application in its default format. Compare the answer on the computer monitor to the answer in the book. If the two are the same, progress to the next problem. It is not necessary to enter 00 in the cents column. However, digits other than zeros in the cents column must be entered, preceded by a decimal point.

DRILL C-1 **Performing addition using the home row keys**
Decimal Selector—2

4.00	44.00	444.00	4,444.00	44,444.00
5.00	55.00	555.00	5,555.00	55,555.00
6.00	66.00	666.00	6,666.00	66,666.00
5.00	45.00	455.00	4,455.00	44,556.00
4.00	46.00	466.00	4,466.00	44,565.00
5.00	54.00	544.00	5,544.00	55,446.00
6.00	56.00	566.00	5,566.00	55,664.00
5.00	65.00	655.00	6,655.00	66,554.00
4.00	64.00	644.00	6,644.00	66,555.00
5.00	66.00	654.00	6,545.00	65,465.00
49.00	561.00	5,649.00	56,540.00	565,470.00

DRILL C-2 **Performing addition using the 0, 1, 4, and 7 keys**
Decimal Selector—2

4.00	11.00	444.00	4,440.00	44,000.00
7.00	44.00	777.00	7,770.00	77,000.00
4.00	74.00	111.00	1,110.00	11,000.00
1.00	71.00	741.00	4,400.00	41,000.00
4.00	70.00	740.00	1,100.00	71,000.00
7.00	10.00	101.00	4,007.00	10,000.00
4.00	14.00	140.00	7,001.00	10,100.00
1.00	17.00	701.00	1,007.00	40,100.00
4.00	40.00	700.00	1,004.00	70,100.00
7.00	77.00	407.00	7,700.00	74,100.00
43.00	428.00	4,862.00	39,539.00	448,400.00

DRILL C-3 **Performing addition using the 2, 5, and 8 keys**
Decimal Selector—2

5.00	58.00	588.00	8,888.00	88,855.00
8.00	52.00	522.00	5,555.00	88,822.00
5.00	85.00	888.00	2,222.00	88,852.00
2.00	52.00	222.00	8,525.00	88,222.00
5.00	25.00	258.00	2,585.00	85,258.00
8.00	58.00	852.00	8,258.00	22,255.00
5.00	82.00	225.00	8,585.00	22,288.00
2.00	28.00	885.00	5,258.00	22,258.00
5.00	88.00	882.00	2,852.00	22,888.00
8.00	22.00	228.00	2,288.00	25,852.00
53.00	550.00	5,550.00	55,016.00	555,550.00

DRILL C-4 **Performing addition using the 3, 6, 9, and decimal point keys**
Decimal Selector—2

6.00	66.66	666.66	6,666.99	66,699.33
9.00	99.99	999.99	9,999.66	99,966.66
6.00	33.33	333.33	3,333.99	33,366.33
3.00	33.66	666.99	3,366.99	36,963.36
6.36	33.99	999.66	6,699.33	69,636.36
3.36	99.66	333.66	9,966.33	33,333.66
9.36	99.33	696.36	9,636.69	66,666.99
9.63	33.36	369.63	3,696.36	99,999.33
6.33	33.69	336.69	6,963.99	96,369.63
9.93	69.63	963.36	6,699.33	36,963.36
68.97	603.30	6,366.33	67,029.66	639,965.01

DRILL C-5 **Performing subtraction using all number keys**
Decimal Selector—F

456.73	789.01	741.00	852.55	987.98
−123.21	−456.00	−258.10	−369.88	−102.55
333.52	333.01	482.90	482.67	885.43

DRILL C-6 **Performing multiplication using all number keys**
Decimal Selector—F

654.05	975.01	487.10	123.56	803.75
× 12.66	× 27.19	× 30.21	× 50.09	× 1.45
8,280.273	26,510.5219	14,715.291	6,189.1204	1,165.4375

DRILL C-7 **Performing division using all number keys**
Decimal Selector—F

900.56	÷	450.28	=	2.
500.25	÷	100.05	=	5.
135.66	÷	6.65	=	20.4
269.155	÷	105.55	=	2.550023685*
985.66	÷	22.66	=	43.49779346*

Number of decimal places may vary, due to machine capacity.

Recycling Problems

18-R Recycling Problem: Journalizing transactions related to debt and equity financing
LO2, 4, 5

The journals and loan payment schedule for Best Appliances are given in the *Recycling Problem Working Papers*.

Instructions:

Using the current year, journalize the following transactions on page 9 of a cash receipts journal, page 8 of a cash payments journal, and page 7 of a general journal. Refer to the loan payment schedule when journalizing the December 1 transaction. Source documents are abbreviated as follows: check, C; receipt, R; memorandum, M.

Transactions:

July	1.	Issued twenty 20-year, 8%, $5,000.00 bonds. R465.
	4.	Drew $32,700.00 on its line of credit. R469.
	6.	Sold 200 shares of 6.0%, $50.00 par value preferred stock at par value. R472.
	8.	Issued 3,000 shares of $10.00 par value common stock at par value. R476.
	12.	Signed a 150-day, 10% note to Gaston Company for an extension of time on its account payable, $8,600.00. M49.
	29.	Issued 2,000 shares of $10.00 par value common stock at $10.80 per share. R487.
Aug.	1.	Signed a five-year, 8% note, $50,000.00. R489.
Dec.	1.	Paid cash for the December payment on the August 1 note payable, $1,013.82. C822.
	2.	Paid cash for the monthly payment on its line of credit: principal, $2,000.00, plus interest, $106.68. C823.
	9.	Paid cash for the maturity value of the July 12 note payable to Gaston Company, $8,600.00, plus interest. C834.
	31.	Paid cash for the semiannual interest on bonds. C849.

19-R Recycling Problem: Recording transactions for plant assets
LO1, 2, 3, 4, 5, 6, 7, 8, 9, 10, 11

Innsbruck Accounting records plant assets in two accounts: Equipment, Account No. 1205, and Furniture, Account No. 1215. Equipment is depreciated using the straight-line method. Furniture is depreciated using the double declining-balance method. Forms are given in the *Recycling Problem Working Papers*.

Instructions:

1. Record the following transactions completed during 20X1 on page 1 of a cash payments journal.

Transactions:

Jan.   5.   Bought a computer (equipment) and a work station (furniture): cost, $51,000.00. C310. Computer: estimated value, $17,000.00; estimated salvage value, $1,000.00; estimated useful life, 8 years; plant asset No. 333; serial number, 1455WZM-8. Work station: estimated value, $34,000.00; estimated salvage value, $2,000.00; estimated useful life, 4 years; plant asset No. 334; serial number, 44-5K26YT.

Feb. 26.   Paid property taxes on plant assets assessed at $400,000.00. The tax rate is 0.9%. C335.

Apr.   5.   Bought a copier: cost, $8,600.00; estimated salvage value, $600.00; estimated useful life, 5 years; plant asset No. 335; serial number, LK8GJY. C361.

2. Complete Section 1 of a plant asset record for each new plant asset.

3. Use the form provided in the *Recycling Problem Working Papers* to calculate beginning book value, annual depreciation, accumulated depreciation, and ending book value for each new plant asset.

4. Complete Section 3 of the plant asset records for 20X1–20X4.

5. Record the following transactions completed during 20X5. Use page 2 of a cash receipts journal and page 1 of a general journal.

Transactions:

Jan.   6.   Received cash for sale of a work station, plant asset No. 334, $2,200.00. R278.

July   2.   Received cash for sale of a computer, plant asset No. 333, $7,500.00. M65 and R310.

Dec. 31.   Recorded the adjusting entry for depreciation. Total 20X5 depreciation expense of furniture was $29,500.00. Total 20X5 depreciation expense of equipment was $65,750.00.

6. Complete the plant asset records for each plant asset sold during 20X5.

7. Complete Section 3 of the plant asset record for the copier for 20X5.

20-R Recycling Problem: Determining the cost of inventory using the FIFO, LIFO, and weighted-average inventory costing methods LO2, 3, 4

Dan's Fans began the year with 30 units of its model K45-3SPD ceiling fan in beginning inventory. Each unit sells for $99.95. The following transactions involving model K45-3SPD occurred during the year. Forms are given in the *Recycling Problem Working Papers*. Source documents are abbreviated as follows: purchase invoice, P; sales invoice, S.

Transactions:

Jan.   6.   Purchased 25 units from Westingplace Company for $45.00 per unit, 2/10, n/30. P232.

Apr.   5.   Sold 40 units to Heights Builders, n/30. S315.

      14.   Purchased 25 units from Westingplace Company for $45.60 per unit, 2/10, n/30. P246.

July   5.   Sold 30 units to Cherry Hill Resort, n/30. S346.

Aug.   3.   Purchased 25 units from Westingplace Company for $46.25 per unit, 2/10, n/30. P259.

Dec.   2.   Sold 10 units to Blaine Builders, n/30. S402.

      12.   Purchased 25 units from Westingplace Company for $46.60 per unit, 2/10, n/30. P278.

Instructions:

1. Enter the transactions on the stock record and determine the number of units in ending inventory.

2. Calculate the cost of ending inventory using the FIFO, LIFO, and weighted-average methods.

3. Which of the inventory costing methods resulted in the lowest cost of merchandise sold? Merchandise available for sale is the total cost of beginning inventory plus all purchases during the year.

21-R Recycling Problem: Journalizing entries for accruals and deferrals
LO1, 2, 3, 4, 5, 6, 7, 8

Accounting forms and a partial unadjusted trial balance for Fuenfigger Corporation are given in the *Recycling Problem Working Papers*. Fuenfigger Corporation collected $36,000 on November 1 for six months' rent. On December 31, 20X1, Fuenfigger Corporation has one note receivable outstanding, a 120-day, 6%, $20,000.00 note dated December 1, and one note payable outstanding, a 60-day, 8%, $25,000.00 note dated November 16. After each journal entry, update the T accounts given in the *Recycling Problem Working Papers*.

Instructions:

1. Journalize the adjusting entries for accrued interest income, accrued interest expense, and rent earned on December 31. Use page 14 of a general journal.

2. Journalize the closing entries for all income and expense accounts using page 14 of a general journal. Record the closing entry for both income accounts in one entry.

3. Journalize the January 1, 20X2, reversing entries for accrued interest income and accrued interest expense on page 15 of a general journal.

4. Journalize the payment of cash for the maturity value of the note on January 15, 20X2. Check No. 190. Use page 25 of a cash payments journal.

5. Journalize the receipt of cash for the maturity value of the note on March 31, 20X2. Receipt No. 205. Use page 16 of a cash receipts journal.

6. List the amount of interest income from the note receivable that will be shown on the income statements for 20X1 and 20X2.

7. List the amount of interest expense from the note payable that will be shown on the income statements for 20X1 and 20X2.

8. What is the balance in the Prepaid Rent account on December 31, 20X1? What does it represent?

22-R Recycling Problem: Journalizing adjustments, preparing financial statements, and journalizing end-of-fiscal-period entries for a corporation LO1, 2, 3, 4, 5, 6, 7

Stowe Corporation's unadjusted trial balance and accounting forms are given in the *Recycling Problem Working Papers*.

Instructions:

1. Using the following information, journalize the adjusting entries for the current year ended December 31.

Adjustment Information, December 31

Estimated uncollectible accounts based on aging accounts receivable	$ 3,632.00
Accrued interest income	52.80
Merchandise inventory	191,891.42
Supplies inventory	200.00
Value of prepaid insurance	1,240.00
Annual depreciation expense—office equipment	3,616.00
Annual depreciation expense—store equipment	3,340.00
Accrued interest expense	206.25
Rent income earned	1,980.00

2. Post the adjusting entries to the T accounts.

3. Using the tax table presented in this chapter, calculate the federal income tax expense and journalize the income tax adjustment.

4. Post the federal income tax adjusting entry to the T accounts.

5. Using the unadjusted trial balance and the T accounts, complete the adjusted trial balance.

6. Complete the income statement for the current year. Calculate and record the following component percentages: (a) cost of merchandise sold; (b) gross profit on operations; (c) total operating expenses; (d) income from operations; (e) net addition or deduction from other revenue and expenses; and (f) net income before federal income tax. Round percentage calculations to the nearest 0.1%. Round net addition or deduction from other revenue and expenses *up* to the nearest 0.1%.

7. Analyze the corporation's income statement by determining if component percentages are within acceptable levels. If any component percentage is not within an acceptable level, suggest steps that the company should take. The corporation considers the following component percentages acceptable.

Cost of merchandise sold	Not more than 67.0%
Gross profit on operations	Not less than 33.0%
Total operating expenses	Not more than 27.0%
Income from operations	Not less than 8.0%
Net deduction from other revenue and expenses	Not more than 0.10%
Net income before federal income tax	Not less than 7.90%

8. Complete the statement of stockholders' equity for the current year. As of January 1, Stowe Corporation had issued 16,000 shares of common stock with a par value of $1.00 per share. During the fiscal year, the corporation issued 10,000 additional shares of common stock. The balance in Paid-in Capital in Excess of Par—Common on January 1, 20--, was $40,000.00. As of January 1, Stowe Corporation had issued 2,700 shares of $5.00 par, 5% preferred stock. No additional shares of preferred stock were issued during the year.

9. Complete the balance sheet for Stowe Corporation for the current year.

10. Calculate the corporation's (a) working capital and (b) current ratio. Determine if these items are within acceptable levels. The corporation considers the following levels acceptable.

Working capital	Not less than $200,000.00
Current ratio	Between 4.5 to 1 and 5.0 to 1

11. Using the balance sheet and the following information, prepare a statement of cash flows for the current year.

Cash receipts during the year:

Cash from sales	$1,439,078.18
Cash from interest	447.68
Cash from rent	1,980.00
Cash from sale of store equipment	4,200.00
Cash from issuance of stock	30,000.00

Cash payments during the year:

Cash for inventory	$ 966,504.49
Cash for salaries and wages	283,775.68
Cash for insurance	8,000.00
Cash for interest	2,450.45
Cash for taxes	16,000.00
Cash for rent	29,700.00
Cash for other operating expenses	140,258.66
Cash for purchase of office equipment	5,000.00
Cash for purchase of store equipment	1,500.00
Cash for payment of notes payable	3,500.00
Cash for payment of bonds payable	2,000.00
Cash for payment of dividends	21,120.00
Cash balance at the beginning of the period	$ 22,731.58

12. Journalize the closing entries using page 16 of a general journal.

13. Journalize the reversing entries using page 17 of a general journal.

23-R Recycling Problem: Recording partners' investments and withdrawals, preparing financial statements, and liquidating a partnership LO1, 2, 3, 4, 5, 6, 7

Johannes Kilmeta and Joseph Schwantz are partners in a business called J & J Painters. Journals and forms for completing this problem are given in the *Recycling Problem Working Papers*. J & J Painters completed the following transactions during the current year.

Transactions:

Jan. 15. Received cash of $1,000.00 and equipment valued at $4,000.00 from partner, Johannes Kilmeta, as an investment. Receipt No. 521.

15. Received cash from partner, Joseph Schwantz, as an investment, $5,000.00. Receipt No. 522.

July 31. Joseph Schwantz, partner, withdrew merchandise for personal use, $4,000.00. Memorandum No. 291.

31. Johannes Kilmeta, partner, withdrew cash for personal use, $4,000.00. Check No. 625.

Instructions:

1. Journalize the investments on January 15.

2. Journalize the withdrawals on July 31.

Additional information is given below.

Johannes Kilmeta, Capital, January 1 balance	$11,200.00
Joseph Schwantz, Capital, January 1 balance	11,200.00
Net income for the year ended December 31	14,800.00

3. Prepare a distribution of net income statement for J & J Painters. Net income or loss is to be distributed equally to the partners.

4. Using the balances of the general ledger capital accounts, prepare an owners' equity statement for J & J Painters. The investments made on January 15 are the only additional investments made by the partners this year. The withdrawals made on July 31 are the only withdrawals made by the partners this year.

The partners decided to liquidate J & J Painters on December 31. On that date, after financial statements were prepared and closing entries were posted, the general ledger accounts had the following balances.

Cash	$41,200.00
Merchandise Inventory	3,000.00
Equipment	28,000.00
Accumulated Depreciation—Equipment	25,000.00
Accounts Payable	8,000.00
Johannes Kilmeta, Capital	19,600.00
Joseph Schwantz, Capital	19,600.00

The following transactions occurred on December 31 of the current year.

Transactions:

a. Received cash from the sale of merchandise inventory, $3,300.00. R773.

b. Received cash from the sale of equipment, $2,000.00. R774.

c. Paid cash to all creditors for amounts owed. C718.

d. Distributed gain on realization and loss on realization to the partners on an equal basis. M337 and M338.

e. Distributed remaining cash to partners. C719 and C720.

5. Journalize the transactions. Continue on the next available line of the journals used in instructions 1 and 2.

24-R Recycling Problem: Recording international and Internet sales LO4, 5, 6

Connections Trade, Inc., sells costume jewelry domestically and internationally. The company has Internet sales as well. Journals and forms for completing this problem are given in the *Recycling Problem Working Papers*.

Instructions:

1. Journalize the following transactions affecting sales and cash receipts completed during October of the current year. Use page 24 of a general journal and a cash receipts journal. Source documents are abbreviated as follows: memorandum, M; receipt, R; time draft, TD; and terminal summary, TS.

Transactions:

Oct.   3.   Received a 30-day time draft from Taiwan Importers for an international sale, $5,200.00. TD61.
      6.   Recorded Internet credit card sales, $6,450.00. TS350.
    10.   Recorded international cash sale, $12,600.00. M61.
    13.   Recorded Internet credit card sales, $6,750.00. TS320.
    14.   Received cash for the value of Time Draft No. 68, $2,000.00. R102.
    18.   Received cash for the value of Time Draft No. 71, $6,800.00. R110.
    20.   Recorded Internet cash sale, $18,200. TS321.
    24.   Recorded international cash sale, $9,500.00. M75.
    27.   Recorded Internet cash sale, $3,100.00. TS322.
    30.   Received a 30-day time draft from Swedish Gems for international sale of merchandise, $18,025.00. TD62.

2. Prove and rule the cash receipts journal.

Answers to Audit Your Understanding

Chapter 18, Lesson 18-1, page 557
1. The loan agreement specifies the maximum amount that can be borrowed, the interest rate, term of the agreement, and repayment terms.
2. Prime plus 3%.
3. A non-operating expense.
4. In a section titled Other Expenses.

Chapter 18, Lesson 18-2, page 564
1. To convince the bank that it can repay the loan.
2. The bank can take the collateral and sell it to pay off the debt.
3. Use of funds, business experience, market demand, financial projections, collateral, and capital profile.
4. Investor B.
5. Bonds generally have extended terms such as 5, 10, or 20 years. Also, bonds payable tend to be issued for larger amounts than notes payable.

Chapter 18, Lesson 18-3, page 568
1. No. Dividends do not have to be paid to stockholders unless the earnings are sufficient to warrant such payments.
2. By the dividend rate and par value.
3. Preferred, then common.
4. To earn dividends.

Chapter 18, Lesson 18-4, page 573
1. Lines of credit, notes payable, bonds, common stock, and preferred stock.
2. Interest rates, impact on earnings, repayment terms, ownership control, and debt ratio.
3. The borrowed funds must be invested in the business to earn income higher than the interest charged on the borrowed funds.
4. Highly leveraged or over-leveraged.
5. The debt ratio of the corporation exceeds its debt ratio benchmark.

Chapter 19, Lesson 19-1, page 588
1. Office Equipment is debited; Cash is credited.
2. So that each plant asset can be depreciated individually.
3. Land and anything attached to the land.

Chapter 19, Lesson 19-2, page 593
1. Matching Expenses with Revenue.
2. Original cost, estimated salvage value, and estimated useful life.

Chapter 19, Lesson 19-3, page 597
1. Depreciation is credited to the contra account, Accumulated Depreciation, rather than crediting the asset account.
2. The balance of the asset account is not changed.

Chapter 19, Lesson 19-4, page 602
1. Disposal date, disposal method, and disposal amount.
2. Partial year's depreciation.
3. Cash received less the book value of the asset sold.
4. Other Expenses.

Chapter 19, Lesson 19-5, page 606
1. Depreciation rate.
2. Double declining-balance method.
3. Depreciation expense declines each year.
4. Its estimated salvage value.

Chapter 19, Lesson 19-6, page 609
1. Amortization Expense.
2. Patent.

Chapter 20, Lesson 20-1, page 625
1. (1) Excess inventory requires that a business spend money for expensive store and warehouse space. (2) Excess inventory uses capital that could be invested in other assets to earn a profit for

the business. (3) Excess inventory requires that a business spend money for expenses, such as taxes and insurance premiums, which increase with the cost of the merchandise inventory. (4) Excess inventory may become obsolete and unsalable.

2. At the end of a fiscal year.
3. A business frequently establishes its fiscal year to end when inventory normally is at a minimum because it takes less time to count a smaller inventory.
4. A customary practice is to take a physical inventory at the end of the fiscal year. The physical inventory results are then compared with the perpetual inventory records and the perpetual records are corrected to reflect the actual quantity on hand as determined by the physical inventory.

Chapter 20, Lesson 20-2, page 632
1. The price of merchandise purchased first should be charged against current revenue.
2. Each item in ending inventory is recorded at the earliest prices paid for the merchandise.
3. FIFO.
4. Using the same inventory costing method for all fiscal periods provides financial statements that can be compared with other fiscal period statements. If a business changes inventory cost methods, part of the difference in gross profit and net income may be caused by the change in methods.

Chapter 20, Lesson 20-3, page 635
1. By using the gross profit method of estimating inventory.
2. Actual net sales and net purchases amounts, the beginning inventory amount, and the gross profit percentage.
3. The beginning inventory for the month is the same as the ending inventory from the previous month.

Chapter 21, Lesson 21-1, page 656
1. Realization of Revenue.
2. To avoid the inconvenience of determining how much, if any, of each cash payment is for interest income incurred and accrued during the previous year and how much is incurred in the current year. Companies that choose to use reversing entries do not want to force their accountants to go back and check prior entries when notes are paid in the next period.

Chapter 21, Lesson 21-2, page 663
1. A liability account.
2. An expense account.

Chapter 22, Lesson 22-1, page 684
1. (1) For some accounts, the calculated estimate of the account is also the amount used in the adjusting entry. (2) Other accounts have a current balance when the adjustment is planned. The current balance is typically subtracted from the estimated account balance to determine the amount of the adjustment.
2. Supplies Expense is debited; Supplies is credited.

Chapter 22, Lesson 22-2, page 690
1. Sales, cost of merchandise sold, and operating expenses are used to determine income from operations. Other revenue and other expenses, such as interest income, rent income, interest expense, and gains or losses on plant assets, are not normal business activities. Therefore, they are not included in calculating income from operations and are reported separately.
2. Student answers will vary but could include: bonds payable, long-term notes payable, or mortgage payable.

Chapter 22, Lesson 22-3, page 698
1. Cash basis.
2. (1) Operating activities, (2) investing activities, and (3) financing activities.

Chapter 22, Lesson 22-4, page 706
1. A post-closing trial balance.
2. (1) Closing entry for income statement accounts with credit balances (revenue and cost accounts). (2) Closing entry for income statement accounts with debit balances (cost, contra revenue, and expense accounts). (3) Closing entry to record net income or net loss in the Retained Earnings account and to close the Income Summary account. (4) Closing entry for the Dividends account.
3. Income Summary and Dividends.

Chapter 23, Lesson 23-1, page 727
1. Student answers should include three of the following: the name of the business and the partners, the investments of each partner, the duties and responsibilities of each partner, how profits and losses are to be divided, what happens if a partner dies, how the partnership is to be dissolved, and the duration of the agreement.
2. The partner's drawing account increases by a debit; Supplies decreases by a credit.

Chapter 23, Lesson 23-2, page 734
1. Each partner's share of net income or net loss.
2. Beginning capital amount, any additional investments made during the fiscal period, and each partner's withdrawal of assets during the fiscal period.

3. Compute ending capital as follows: Share of Net Income or Loss *less* Withdrawals *equals* Net Increase/Decrease in Capital. Beginning Capital *plus* Net Increase/Decrease in Capital *equals* Ending Capital.

Chapter 23, Lesson 23-3, page 741

1. As a credit to the Gain on Realization account.
2. As a debit to the Loss on Realization account.
3. Each partner's capital account.

Chapter 24, Lesson 24-1, page 760

1. (1) The lack of uniform commercial laws among countries makes settlement of disputes more difficult. (2) Greater distances and sometimes more complex transportation methods increase the time to complete the transaction. (3) Because it may be difficult to determine a customer's financial condition and to take legal action if a customer does not pay, the risk of uncollected amounts is increased. (4) Unstable political conditions in some countries may affect the ability to receive payments from those countries.
2. The bill of lading serves as a receipt for merchandise received and as a contract for the delivery of the merchandise.
3. A sight draft is payable when the holder presents it for payment. A time draft is payable at a fixed or determinable future time after it is accepted.
4. To assure receipt of payment for those sales.
5. A draft is generally paid by a bank, and a trade acceptance is paid by the buyer. A seller generally has much more assurance of receiving payment from a bank than from a buyer.

Chapter 24, Lesson 24-2, page 763

1. To browse and compare the products offered by companies, and to do so at a convenient time and place for the customer.
2. Credit card sales information is processed in a manner similar to checks. Therefore, these sales are considered cash sales.

Glossary

Accelerated depreciation Any method of depreciation which records greater depreciation expense in the early years and less depreciation expense in the later years. (p. 603)

Accrual An entry recording revenue before the cash is received, or an expense before the cash is paid. (p. 648)

Accrued expenses Expenses incurred in one fiscal period, but not paid until a later fiscal period. (p. 652)

Accrued interest expense Interest incurred but not yet paid. (p. 652)

Activity-based costing (ABC) Allocating factory overhead based on the level of major activities. (p. 638)

Amortization The spreading of the cost of an intangible asset over its useful life. (p. 608)

Assessed value The value of an asset determined by tax authorities for the purpose of calculating taxes. (p. 587)

Bill of exchange *See* draft. (p. 754)

Bill of lading A receipt signed by the authorized agent of a transportation company for merchandise received that also serves as a contract for the delivery of the merchandise. (p. 754)

Bond A long-term promise to pay a specified amount on a specified date and to pay interest at stated intervals. (p. 562)

Bond issue All bonds representing the total amount of a loan. (p. 562)

Capital expenditures Purchases of plant assets used in the operation of a business. (p. 558)

Cash flow The cash receipts and cash payments of a company. (p. 691)

Collateral Assets pledged to a creditor to guarantee repayment of a loan. (p. 559)

Commercial invoice A statement prepared by the seller of merchandise addressed to the buyer showing a detailed listing and description of merchandise sold, including prices and terms. (p. 754)

Contract of sale A document that details all the terms agreed to by seller and buyer for a sales transaction. (p. 753)

Cost accounting The field of accounting that identifies and measures costs. (p. 563)

Cost of capital The ratio of interest and dividend payments to the proceeds from debt and capital financing. (p. 569)

Credit line *See* line of credit. (p. 552)

Debt financing Obtaining capital by borrowing money for a period of time. (p. 552)

Declining-balance method of depreciation A type of accelerated depreciation that multiplies the book value of an asset by a constant depreciation rate to determine annual depreciation. (p. 603)

Defaulting Not making payments on a loan when they are due. (p. 673)

Deferral An entry recording the receipt of cash before the related revenue is earned, or payment of cash before the related expense is incurred. (p. 648)

Deferred expenses Payments for goods or services which have not yet been received. *See also* prepaid expense. (p. 660)

Deferred revenue Cash received for goods or services which have not yet been provided. (p. 658)

Distribution of net income statement A partnership financial statement showing net income or loss distribution to partners. (p. 728)

Double declining-balance method of depreciation A declining-balance rate that is two times the straight-line rate. (p. 603)

Draft A written, signed, and dated order from one party ordering another party, usually a bank, to pay money to a third party. (p. 754)

Equity financing Obtaining capital by issuing stock in a corporation. (p. 565)

Exports Goods or services shipped out of a seller's home country to another country. (p. 752)

Factory overhead All expenses other than direct materials and direct labor that apply to making products. (p. 638)

FIFO *See* first-in, first-out inventory costing method. (p. 626)

Financial leverage The ability of a business to use borrowed funds to increase its earnings. (p. 571)

Financing activities Cash receipts and payments involving debt or equity transactions. (p. 692)

First-in, first-out inventory costing method Using the price of merchandise purchased first to calculate the cost of merchandise sold first. (p. 626)

Foreclosure When the bank or finance company takes possession of mortgaged property. (p. 673)

Gain An increase in equity resulting from activity other than selling goods or services. (p. 600)

Gain on plant assets An increase in equity that results when a plant asset is sold for more than book value. (p. 600)

Gross profit method of estimating inventory Estimating inventory by using the previous year's percentage of gross profit on operations. (p. 633)

Imports Goods or services shipped into the buyer's home country from another country. (p. 752)

Intangible asset An asset that does not have physical substance. (p. 607)

Intellectual property Anything, or any process, that is protected by patent, trademark, or copyright. *See also* intangible asset. (p. 648)

Interest expense Interest accrued on borrowed funds. (p. 555)

Inventory record A form used during a physical inventory to record information about each item of merchandise on hand. (p. 622)

Investing activities Cash receipts and cash payments involving the sale or purchase of assets used to earn revenue over a period of time. (p. 692)

Issue date The date on which a business issues a note, bond, or stock. (p. 565)

Last-in, first-out inventory costing method Using the price of merchandise purchased last to calculate the cost of merchandise sold first. (p. 627)

Letter of credit A letter issued by a bank guaranteeing that a named individual or business will be paid a specified amount provided stated conditions are met. (p. 753)

LIFO *See* last-in, first-out inventory costing method. (p. 627)

Line of credit A bank loan agreement that provides immediate short-term access to cash. (p. 552)

Liquidation of a partnership The process of paying a partnership's liabilities and distributing remaining assets to the partners. (p. 735)

Loss A decrease in equity resulting from activity other than selling goods or services. (p. 601)

Loss on plant assets The decrease in equity that results when a plant asset is sold for less than book value. (p. 601)

Lower of cost or market inventory costing method (LCM) Using the lower of cost or market price to calculate the cost of ending merchandise inventory. (p. 631)

Market value The price that must be paid to replace an asset. (p. 631)

Non-operating expense Expenses that are not related to a business's normal operations. (p. 555)

Number of days' sales in inventory A financial ratio determined by dividing 365 days by the inventory turnover ratio. (p. 642)

Operating activities The cash receipts and payments necessary to operate a business on a day-to-day basis. (p. 692)

Owners' equity statement A financial statement that summarizes the changes in owners' equity during a fiscal period. (p. 730)

Par value A value assigned to a share of stock and printed on the stock certificate. (p. 565)

Partner Each member of a partnership. (p. 722)

Partnership A business in which two or more persons combine their assets and skills. (p. 722)

Partnership agreement A written agreement setting forth the conditions under which a partnership is to operate. (p. 722)

Personal property All property not classified as real property. (p. 587)

Plant asset record An accounting form on which a business records information about each plant asset. (p. 594)

Preferred stock A class of stock that gives preferred shareholders preference over common shareholders in dividends along with other rights. (p. 567)

Prime interest rate The interest rate charged to a bank's most creditworthy customers. (p. 552)

Real estate *See* real property. (p. 587)

Real property Land and anything attached to the land. (p. 587)

Realization Cash received from the sale of assets during liquidation of a partnership. (p. 735)

Return on investment The ratio of the money earned on an investment relative to the amount of the investment. (p. 584)

Revenue expenditure The payment of an operating expense necessary to earn revenue. (p. 552)

Reversing entry An entry made at the beginning of one fiscal period to reverse an adjusting entry made in the previous fiscal period. (p. 649)

ROI *See* return on investment. (p. 584)

Sight draft A draft payable on sight when the holder presents it for payment. (p. 754)

Stated interest rate The interest rate used to calculate periodic interest payments on a bond. (p. 562)

Statement of cash flows A financial statement that summarizes cash receipts and cash payments resulting from business activities during a fiscal period. (p. 691)

Stock ledger A file of stock records for all merchandise on hand. (p. 623)

Stock record A form used to show the kind of merchandise, quantity received, quantity sold, and balance on hand. (p. 623)

Time draft A draft that is payable at a fixed or determinable future time after it is accepted. (p. 757)

Trade acceptance A form signed by a buyer at the time of a sale of merchandise in which the buyer promises to pay the seller a specified sum of money, usually at a stated time in the future. (p. 758)

Underwater mortgage A mortgage that has a balance higher than the value of the mortgaged property. (p. 673)

Unearned revenue *See* deferred revenue. (p. 658)

Weighted-average inventory costing method Using the average cost of beginning inventory plus merchandise purchased during a fiscal period to calculate the cost of merchandise sold. (p. 628)

A

Accelerated depreciation *Depreciación acelerada* Cualquier método de depreciación que registra mayores gastos de depreciación en los primeros años y menos gastos de depreciación en los últimos años. (p. 603)

Accrual *Acumulación* Una entrada registrando ganancia antes de que el efectivo sea recibido, o un gasto antes de que el efectivo sea pagado. (p. 648)

Accrued expenses *Gastos acumulados* Gastos incurridos durante un período fiscal, pero pagados en otro período fiscal posterior. (p. 652)

Accrued interest expense *Gasto del interés acumulado* Interés incurrido, pero aún no pagado. (p. 652)

Activity-based costing (ABC) *Determinación de costo por actividad (costeo ABC)* Asignar los gastos generales de la fábrica basados en el nivel de actividades mayores. (p. 638)

Amortization *Amortización* Distribuir el costo de un activo intangible a lo largo de su utilidad de vida. (p. 608)

Assessed value *Valor asesorado* El valor de un bien determinado por autoridades de impuestos para calcular los impuestos. (p. 587)

B

Bill of exchange *Letra de cambio* (Véase draft *letra de cambio*.) (p. 754)

Bill of lading *Conocimiento de embarque* Un recibo firmado por el agente autorizado de una compañía de transportación para la mercancía recibida, que también sirve como un contrato para la entrega de la misma. (p. 754)

Bond *Bono* Una promesa de largo plazo de pagar una cantidad específica en una fecha específica y de pagar interés a intervalos estipulados. (p. 562)

Bond issue *Emisión de bonos* Todos los bonos que representan la cantidad total de un préstamo. (p. 562)

C

Capital expenditures *Gastos de capital* Compras de activos fijos utilizados en la operación de un negocio. (p. 558)

Cash flow *Flujo de caja* Los recibos y pagos de efectivo de una compañía. (p. 691)

Collateral *Colateral o garantía* Los activos prometidos a un acreedor para garantizar el pago de un préstamo. (p. 559)

Commercial invoice *Factura comercial* Un informe preparado por el vendedor de la mercancía y dirigido al comprador, que muestra un listado detallado y la descripción de la mercancía vendida, incluyendo precios y términos. (p. 754)

Contract of sale *Contrato de venta* Un documento que detalla todos los términos acordados por el vendedor y el comprador para una transacción de venta. (p. 753)

Cost accounting *Contabilidad de costos* La división de contabilidad que identifica las medidas de los costos. (p. 563)

Cost of capital *Costo de capital* El índice de interés y pagos de dividendos a los fondos de deudas y financiamiento de capital. (p. 569)

Credit line *Línea de crédito* (Véase line of credit *línea de crédito*.) (p. 552)

D

Debt financing *Financiamiento de deuda* Obteniendo capital al pedir prestado por un período de tiempo. (p. 552)

Declining-balance method of depreciation *Método de depreciación de saldo decreciente* Un tipo de depreciación acelerada que multiplica el valor contable de un activo por un índice de depreciación constante para determinar su depreciación. (p. 603)

Defaulting *Incumplimiento* No hacer los pagos de un préstamo cuando se vencen. (p. 673)

Deferral *Aplazamiento* Un asiento registrando el recibo de efectivo antes de que los ingresos relacionados son ganados, o pagos de efectivo antes de que los gastos relacionados sean incurridos. (p. 648)

Deferred expenses *Gastos diferidos* Pagos por bienes o servicios que aun no se han recibido. (Véase también prepaid expense *gastos pre pagados*.) (p. 660)

Deferred revenue *Ingresos diferidos* Efectivo recibido por bienes y servicios que aun no han sido proveídos. (p. 658)

Distribution of net income statement *Declaración de distribución de ingreso neto* Un estado financiero de sociedad que muestra la distribución de las ganancias o pérdidas netas a los socios. (p. 728)

Double declining-balance method of depreciation *Método de depreciación de saldo doblemente decreciente* Un índice de depreciación de saldo que es dos veces la del índice sencilla. (p. 603)

Draft *Letra de cambio* Una orden escrita, firmada y fechada por un partido, ordenando a otro partido, generalmente un banco, que pague dinero a un tercer partido. (p. 754)

Equity financing *Financiación de patrimonio* Obtener capital al emitir acciones de una corporación. (p. 565)

Exports *Exportaciones* Bienes o servicios enviados del país de origen del vendedor a otro país. (p. 752)

Factory overhead *Gastos fijos de fábrica* Todos los gastos aparte de los materiales y mano de obra directa que aplican para fabricar productos. (p. 638)

FIFO *PEPS* (Véase first-in, first-out inventory costing method *método de costos de inventario de primero en entrar, primero en salir.*) (p. 626)

Financial leverage *Apalancamiento financiero* La habilidad de un negocio de utilizar fondos prestados para aumentar sus ganancias. (p. 571)

Financing activities *Actividades financieras* Recibos y pagos de dinero que involucran transacciones de deuda o patrimonio neto. (p. 692)

First-in, first-out inventory costing method *Método de costos de inventario de primero en entrar, primero en salir* Utilizando el precio de la mercancía comprada primero para calcular el costo de la mercancía que se vende primero. (p. 626)

Foreclosure *Embargo hipotecario* Cuando el banco o compañía financiera toma posesión de una propiedad hipotecada. (p. 673)

Gain *Beneficio* Un incremento en el patrimonio neto que resulta de actividades aparte de vender bienes y servicios. (p. 600)

Gain on plant assets *Ganancia sobre activos fijos* Un aumento en el patrimonio cuando un activo fijo es vendido por más de su valor contable. (p. 600)

Gross profit method of estimating an inventory *Método de ganancia bruta para estimar un inventario* Un estimado del inventario mediante el uso de los porcentajes de ganancia bruta de años anteriores en operaciones. (p. 633)

Imports *Importaciones* Bienes o servicios enviados al país del comprador desde otro país. (p. 752)

Intangible asset *Activo intangible* Un activo que no tiene forma física. (p. 607)

Intellectual property *Propiedad intelectual* Cualquier cosa o proceso que está protegido por patente, marca registrada, o derechos de autor. (Véase también intangible asset *activo intangible.*) (p. 648)

Interest expense *Gastos de interés* El interés que se acumula en dinero que se ha tomado prestado. (p. 555)

Inventory record *Registro de inventario* Un formulario que se usa durante un inventario físico para registrar información acerca de cada artículo de mercancía a la mano. (p. 622)

Investing activities *Actividades de inversión* Recibos y pagos de dinero que involucran la venta o compra de activos utilizados para generar ingresos sobre un período de tiempo. (p. 692)

Issue date *Fecha de emisión* La fecha en la cual un negocio emite una letra, bono, o acción. (p. 565)

Last-in, first-out inventory costing method *Método de inventario de costos del último en entrar, primero en salir* Se usa el precio de la mercancía que se compra al último para calcular el costo de la mercancía que se vende primero. (p. 627)

Letter of credit *Carta de crédito* Una carta emitida por un banco garantizando que cierto individuo o negocio se le pagará una cantidad específica siempre y cuando las condiciones establecidas se cumpla. (p. 753)

LIFO *LIFO* (Véase last-in, first-out inventory costing method *método de inventario de costos del último en entrar, primero en salir.*) (p. 627)

Line of credit *Línea de crédito* Un acuerdo de préstamo bancario que provee acceso inmediato de corto plazo a efectivo. (p. 552)

Liquidation of a partnership *Disolución de una sociedad* El proceso de pagar las obligaciones de la sociedad y distribuir los activos restantes entre los socios. (p. 735)

Loss *Pérdida* Una reducción en el patrimonio que resulta de actividades aparte de vender bienes y servicios. (p. 601)

Loss on plant assets *Pérdidas en activos fijos* La reducción en el patrimonio que resulta cuando un activo fijo se vende por menos del valor contable. (p. 601)

Lower of cost or market inventory costing method (LCM) *Método de inventario de costo de mercado del menor costo (LCM)* Utilizando el más bajo del costo o del valor de mercado para calcular el costo del inventario final de mercancías. (p. 631)

Market value *Valor de mercado* El precio que se debe pagar para reemplazar un activo. (p. 631)

Non-operating expense *Gastos no operativos* Los gastos que no están relacionados con las operaciones diarias del negocio. (p. 555)

Number of days' sales in inventory *Número de días de inventario para la venta* Un índice financiero que se determina al dividir 365 días por el índice de rotación de inventario. (p. 642)

Operating activities *Actividades operativas* Los recibos de dinero y pagos necesarios para operar un negocio día a día. (p. 692)

Owners' equity statement *Estado de cuenta de capital propio* Un estado financiero que resume los cambios en el capital propio durante un período fiscal. (p. 730)

Par value *Valor nominal* Un valor asignado a una acción e impreso en el certificado de acciones. (p. 565)

Partner *Socio* Cada miembro de una sociedad. (p. 722)

Partnership *Sociedad* Un negocio en el cual dos o más personas combinan sus activos y sus habilidades. (p. 722)

Partnership agreement *Convenio de sociedad* Un acuerdo escrito que establece las condiciones bajo las cuales opera una sociedad. (p. 722)

Personal property *Propiedad personal* Toda la propiedad no clasificada como propiedad inmueble. (p. 587)

Plant asset record *Registro de activo fijo* Un formulario de contabilidad en el cual se registra la información de cada activo fijo de un negocio. (p. 594)

Preferred stock *Acción preferente* Un tipo de acción que le da preferencia a los accionistas privilegiados sobre los accionistas comunes en cuanto a los dividendos y otros derechos. (p. 567)

Prime interest rate *Tase de interés preferencial* La tasa de interés que se le cobra a los clientes más dignos de crédito de un banco. (p. 552)

Real estate *Bienes raíces* (Véase real property *propiedad de inmuebles*.) (p. 587)

Real property *Propiedad de inmuebles* Terreno y cualquier cosa unida al terreno. (p. 587)

Realization *Ganancia* Efectivo recibido de la venta de activos durante la disolución de una sociedad. (p. 735)

Return on investment *Rendimiento de la inversión* La porción de dinero ganado sobre una inversión relativo a la cantidad de la inversión. (p. 584)

Revenue expenditure *Inversión de ingresos* El pago de un gasto operativo para generar ganancias. (p. 552)

Reversing entry *Asiento revertido* Un asiento hecho al principio de un período fiscal para revertir un asiento de ajuste hecho en el período fiscal anterior. (p. 649)

ROI *ROI* (Véase return on investment *rendimiento de la inversión*.) (p. 584)

Sight draft *Letra a la vista* Una letra pagable a la vista cuando el portador la presenta para su pago. (p. 754)

Stated interest rate *Tasa de interés especificada* La tasa de interés que se usa para calcular los pagos de interés periódicos de un bono. (p. 562)

Statement of cash flows *Declaración de flujo de efectivo* Una estado financiero que resume los recibos y pagos de dinero que resultan de las actividades de negocios durante un período fiscal. (p. 691)

Stock ledger *Libro mayor de existencias* Un archivo para el registro de existencias de la mercancía a la mano. (p. 623)

Stock record *Registro de existencias* Un documento que se usa para mostrar la clase de mercancía, la cantidad recibida, la cantidad vendida y el saldo a la mano. (p. 623)

Time draft *Letra de cambio a término* Una letra que será pagada a un plazo o futuro determinado después de que sea aceptada. (p. 757)

Trade acceptance *Acuerdo comercial* Un documento firmado por un comprador en el momento de la venta de mercancía, en la cual el comprador se compromete a pagar al vendedor una suma específica de dinero, generalmente, en un tiempo establecido en el futuro. (p. 758)

Underwater mortgage *Hipoteca sobrevalorada* Una hipoteca que tiene un balance mayor que el valor de la propiedad hipotecada. (p. 673)

Unearned revenue *Ingreso no ganados* (Véase deferred revenue *ingresos diferidos*.) (p. 658)

Weighted-average inventory costing method *Método de inventario de costo promedio* Utilizando el costo promedio del inventario inicial más las mercancías compradas durante un período fiscal para calcular el costo de la mercancía vendida. (p. 628)